HACKING THE TiVo

William von Hagen

Premier

Press

Warning: Doing almost any of the procedures discussed in this book requires opening your TiVo, which instantly *voids* your TiVo warranty *forever*. Also, you can get a serious electrical shock if you're not careful while poking around inside your TiVo, just as you can with any electrical device. Never work on your TiVo while it's plugged in.

The Premier Press logo and related trade dress are trademarks of Premier Press and may not be used without written permission.

Important: Premier Press cannot provide software support. Please contact the appropriate software manufacturer's technical support line or Web site for assistance.

Premier Press and the author have attempted throughout this book to distinguish proprietary trademarks from descriptive terms by following the capitalization style used by the manufacturer.

Information contained in this book has been obtained by Premier Press from sources believed to be reliable. However, because of the possibility of human or mechanical error by our sources, Premier Press, or others, the Publisher does not guarantee the accuracy, adequacy, or completeness of any information and is not responsible for any errors or omissions or the results obtained from use of such information. Readers should be particularly aware of the fact that the Internet is an ever-changing entity. Some facts may have changed since this book went to press.

ISBN: 1-59200-111-4

Library of Congress Catalog Card Number: 2003105364

Printed in the United States of America

03 04 05 06 07 BH 10 9 8 7 6 5 4 3 2 1

Premier Press, a division of Course Technology
25 Thomson Place
Boston, MA 02210

SVP, Retail Strategic Market Group:
Andy Shafran

Publisher:
Stacy L. Hiquet

Senior Marketing Manager:
Sarah O'Donnell

Marketing Manager:
Heather Hurley

Manager of Editorial Services:
Heather Talbot

Senior Acquisitions Editor:
Kevin Harreld

Associate Marketing Manager:
Kristin Eisenzopf

Book Packager:
Justak Literary Services, Inc.

Technical Reviewer:
Mike Baker (aka embeem)

Retail Market Coordinator:
Sarah Dubois

Copy Editor:
Karen Whitehouse

Interior Layout:
Bill Hartman

Cover Designer:
Mike Tanamachi

CD-ROM Producer:
William von Hagen

Indexer:
Sharon Hilgenberg

Proofreader:
Marta Justak

Trademarks

Apple, Macintosh, and Mac OS are registered trademarks of Apple Computer, Inc.

BlessTiVo © 2000 Mike Hill

bootpage.c © 2002 Steve White. All rights reserved.

elseed © Greg Gardner <greg@bah.org>

explore2fs © 2000 John Newbigin

extract-gzip.c © 2002-2003 Steve White. All rights reserved

GAIM2TIVO v0.2 © 2002 by Hermanator <hermanator12002@yahoo.com>

hexedit © 1998 Pixel (Pascal Rigaux)

JpegWriter © 2002 J. Bordens

killinitrd-s2.c © 2003 Steve White. All rights reserved.

Linux is a registered trademark of Linus Torvalds.

MFS Tools © 2000-2002 Steven Lang

Microsoft and Windows are registered trademarks of Microsoft Corporation.

OmniRemote and OmniRemote PRO are trademarks of Pacific Neo-Tek.

OSX CLI Blesser © 2002 Eric C Wagner

SYSLINUX, © 1994-2002 H. Peter Anvin

TiVo is a registered trademark of TiVo Inc.

TiVo Control Station © 2002 G.R Souther

TiVo newtext2osd 1.0 © tivo@wingert.org

TiVo VBI decoder 1.0 © embeem - mbm@linux.com

TiVoWeb © 2001 Josha Foust (tivoweb@lightn.org). The "Tivo Web Project" and TivoWeb" are trademarks of Josha Foust. httpd.tcl © 2000 Stephen Rothwell (sfr@canb.auug.au) SendKeys Tivo Remote Mod © 2000 Jon Squire (jsquire@justice.loyola.edu) TiVo (Web) User Interface © 2001 Josha Foust (tivoweb@lightn.org) CSS Stylesheets © 2001 Mike Baker (mbm@linux.com) All other code copyright of those in the TiVoWeb README.

TiVoNET, TurboNET, and AirNET are trademarks of SiliconDust Engineering Ltd.

TwinBreeze and PowerTrip are trademarks of Weaknees.com.

Two-kernel Monte for MIPS © 2003 MuscleNerd <musclenerd2000@hotmail.com> i386 version of Monte © 2000 Erik Arjan Hendriks <hendriks@scyld.com>

YAC: Yet Another Caller ID Program © 2002 Jensen Harris

zlib compression library © 1995-1998 by Jean-loup Gailly and Mark Adler

All other trademarks are the property of their respective owners.

Acknowledgments

I'd like to thank my wife for putting up with my TiVo obsession and for never carrying out any of her threats. Four TiVos in a two-person house seems just about right to me. And you thought that the Lisp Machines in the dining room were bad!

I'd like to thank embeem (aka Mike Baker) for making this book far better than it would have been without his help. Thanks to embeem and lightn (aka Josha Foust) for substantial contributions to the MFS information in Chapter 9. I'd also like to thank the TiVo hacking community in general, which has freely and selflessly contributed ideas, hacks, and time towards making the TiVo a fun machine. Special thanks to Andrew Tridgell, Dylan, ElectricLegs, embeem, Ingineer, JohnnyDeath, Kazymyr, lightn, MuscleNerd, Otto, Tyger, and countless others. Like everyone, I'd like to thank Linus Torvalds and the Open Source community for Linux. I'd also like to thank the folks at TiVo for making a great product and actively supporting the TiVo hacking community. (What's up with that hashing stuff, guys?)

I would also like to thank the folks at Premier Press for letting me do this book. Special thanks and a big sigh of relief to my agent and book packager, Marta Justak, for not killing me, regardless of how tempting that must have been. Thanks, too, to Karen Whitehouse for the excellent improvements to the text, to Sharon Hilgenberg for her impressive work making it possible to find things in this book, to Kurt Wall for helping and always being a friend, and to Bill Hartman for making this book look great while working within a time warp.

About the Author

William von Hagen is a senior product manager at TimeSys Corporation. He has been a UNIX® devotee for over twenty years and a Linux fanatic since the early 1990s. He has worked as a system administrator, writer, developer, systems programmer, drummer, and content manager. He has written books on such topics as Linux® Filesystems, SGML, Mac OS X, and Red Hat® Linux, and has written for publications including *Linux Magazine*, *Mac Tech*, *Linux Format*, and *Mac Home*. An avid computer collector specializing in workstations, he owns more than 200 computer systems. You can reach Bill at vonhagen@vonhagen.org.

BRIAN:

Hope we get to work together again and, of course, I hope that you like the book! Feedback welcome.

For my wife and best friend—
I love you, Dorothy, and I always will.

Contents at a Glance

Introduction xvi

1 Know Your TiVo 1

2 TiVo Tips and Tricks 21

3 Exploring Your TiVo Hardware 61

4 The Hacker's Tool Chest of TiVo Tools . . . 107

5 Backing Up and Restoring TiVo Data 143

6 Expanding Your TiVo's Storage
Capacity 185

7 Connecting the Universe to Your TiVo . . . 207

8 Working with Your TiVo from Windows
and Macintosh Systems 257

9 Linux and the TiVo 299

10 Getting and Installing New Software
for Your TiVo 343

11 Other TiVo Hacking Resources 363

Index 383

About the CD 403

Contents

Introduction . . . . **xvi**

Chapter 1   **Know Your TiVo** **1**

Why TiVo? 2
What's This TiVo Service I Keep Hearing About? 3
TiVo Service Fees 4
Identifying Your TiVo 4
TiVos and Your Viewing Habits 5
A Short Course in TiVo History 6
TiVo Business Partners and Integrators 9
Partnering with the Networks 9
Showcasing Upcoming Broadcasts 10
Introducing TiVo's Home Media Option 10
TiVo Hardware Models and Features 12
Identifying Your TiVo Software Version 15
TiVo and the Competition 16
ReplayTV 16
UltimateTV 18
Future Trends 18

Chapter 2   **TiVo Tips and Tricks** **21**

Using the TiVo Remote Control 22
TiVo Remote Control Shortcuts 23
Resolving Remote Control Problems 24
Secret TiVo Commands and Modes 25
Activating Backdoor Mode 28
Using Clear-Clear-Enter-Enter Codes 36

Using Clear-Enter-Clear Codes 37

Using Enter-Enter Codes 41

Using Select-Play-Select Codes 43

Using Thumb-Thumb-Thumb Codes 45

The Irritating AutoTest Mode 48

Sorting the Now Playing List in V. 3.0 TiVos 48

Automating Backdoor Mode and Other Codes 50

Legendary TiVo Monitor and Diagnostic Commands 53

TiVo Scheduling Tips and Tricks 56

Using TiVo Wishlists 58

Activating and Using Advanced Wishlists 59

Chapter 3   Exploring Your TiVo Hardware 61

Attaching a Terminal Emulator or Serial Console 62

Opening the TiVo 65

Working with TiVo Disk Drives 66

Removing TiVo Disk Drives 66

Attaching TiVo Disk Drives to Your PC 70

Adding Disk Drives to Your TiVo 73

Power Considerations in TiVo Series 2 TiVos 75

Dealing with Modems 76

Networking Your TiVo 82

Using a PDA as a Remote Control 102

TiVo Hardware Supplies on the Net 103

9thTee.com 103

Hinsdale 103

PTVupgrade.COM 104

TiVo Store 104

Weaknees.com 105

TiVo Sites Outside the United States 105

Other Sources for TiVo Hardware 105

Chapter 4   The Hacker's Tool Chest of TiVo Tools 107

TiVo Tools Overview 109

   TiVoMad Utilities 109

   BlessTiVo 113

   Bootpage 117

   MFS Tools 119

   Useful Linux Tools Outside Most Tools Disks 131

Boot Disks 133

   BATBD—Bill's Accumulated TiVo Boot Disk 136

   Dylan's Boot Floppy 139

   Johnny Death's Boot CD 139

   Kazamyr's Boot CD 140

   Knoppix Linux 141

Chapter 5   Backing Up and Restoring TiVo Data 143

Overview 145

When to Back Up 147

Finding Room for Backups 148

Creating Image Backups Using dd 152

Creating Backups Using MFS Tools 155

   Creating a Simple Backup Using MFS Tools 156

   Creating a Compressed Backup Using MFS Tools 158

   Backing Up an Entire TiVo Disk Using MFS Tools 159

   Backing Up Multiple-Disk TiVo Systems 160

   Advanced Backup Options 161

Backing Up Selected Information from Your TiVo 163

General Information about Restoring TiVo Data 165

Restoring Image Backups Using dd 166

Restoring Backups Created Using MFS Tools 168

   Restoring an MFS Tools Backup Without Adding
   New Space 168

   Restoring an MFS Tools Backup to a Larger Drive 170

Restoring an MFS Tools Backup to a Two-Drive TiVo 171

Advanced MFS Tools Restore Options 173

Verifying TiVo Disks Restored Using MFS Tools 177

Connecting Backup and Restore Commands Using a Pipe 178

Changing TiVo Operating System Versions Using Backups . . . 179

Dumping TiVo Data to Videotape 181

Forbidden Topics Like Video Extraction 182

Chapter 6   Expanding Your TiVo's Storage Capacity. . . . 185

Overview 186

Considerations for Adding Storage 187

What You'll Need for Your TiVo Upgrade 188

Replacing an Existing TiVo Disk with a Larger One 189

Upgrading a Disk Without Using Backup Files 192

Expanding Drives Using Disk Images 194

Expanding a Drive from a Disk Image 195

Using Disk Images Without Intermediate Backup Files 198

Adding a Second Drive to Your TiVo 200

Using the MFS Tools Utilities to Add a Second Drive 201

Using the BlessTiVo Utility to Add a Second Drive 204

Chapter 7   Connecting the Universe to Your TiVo 207

Getting a Command Prompt on Your TiVo 208

Getting a Command Prompt on a TiVo Series 1 209

Getting a Command Prompt on a TiVo Series 2 214

Two Kernel Monte for the TiVo Series 2 221

TiVo Troubleshooting 233

No Picture or Welcome Screen 233

Your TiVo Is Stuck at the Welcome Screen 233

Your TiVo Is Stuck at the Second Welcome Screen 235

Your TiVo Displays a Green Screen 236

Starting FTP and Telnet on Your TiVo 236

Integrating Your TiVo with AOL Instant Messenger 238

Caller ID and Your TiVo 242

News, Sports, Weather, and Your TiVo 243

Using TiVo's Home Media Option 245

    Playing Music or Displaying Photos Using Your TiVo 246

    Scheduling Recordings on Your TiVo over the Internet 248

    Multi-Room Viewing on Your TiVo 253

Chapter 8   **Working with Your TiVo from Windows and Macintosh Systems 257**

Communicating with Your TiVo from Windows 259

    Serial Communications from Windows Systems 259

    Transferring Files over a Serial Connection from Windows 263

    Networked Communications from Windows 265

Creating TiVo Tools Disks Under Windows 272

TiVo Disks and Windows Systems 278

    Exploring ext2 Disk Images Under Windows 278

    Accessing Windows Disks from Your TiVo 280

Integrating Windows Systems with TiVo's Home Media Option 282

    Installing and Using the Windows TiVo Desktop 282

    Playing Windows Audio Formats Other than MP3 287

TiVos and Mac OS X 290

TiVo Disks and Mac OS X Systems 291

    Exploring ext2 Disk Images Under Mac OS X 292

    Blessing a Disk Under Mac OS X 294

Creating TiVo Tools Disks Under Mac OS X 296

Integrating Macintosh Systems with TiVo's Home Media Option 298

Chapter 9   Linux and the TiVo 299

Introduction to Linux and Open Source Software 300
    Overview of the Linux Boot Process 301
    Linux Filesystems and Initial RAM Disks 302
    Obtaining the Source Code for TiVo's Linux 304
Overview of the TiVo Application Environment 305
    The TiVo Startup Process 305
    TCL and iTCL 306
    TiVo's TiVoSH (tivosh) Application 307
TiVo Disk Information 308
    TiVo Disk and Partition Map 309
MFS—TiVo's Media File System 312
    Exploring MFS 312
Using Serial Communications Under Linux 320
    Using minicom for Serial Communications 320
    Transferring Files Using minicom 323
Using a Linux Shell 324
    Job Control in the Bash Shell 325
    Running Commands in the Background 326
    Managing Commands in the Bash Shell 327
Popular Linux Software for the TiVo 329
    Busybox 329
    Emacs 330
    FTP 331
    GCC 333
    NFS 333
    Telnet 335
Burning CDs on Linux Systems 336
Working with TiVo's Home Media Option from Linux 338

**Chapter 10 Getting and Installing New Software for
Your TiVo** **343**

Installing Software on Your TiVo 344
  Identifying Binary File Formats 344
  Uncompressing ZIP and GZ Files 345
  Extracting Files from TAR and TGZ Archives 347
  Safe Locations for Storing Your TiVo Hacks 350
Installing Cross-Compilers for TiVo Development 351
  Selecting and Installing a Cross-Compiler for the
  TiVo Series 1 351
  Selecting and Installing the Cross-Compiler for the
  TiVo Series 2 353
Stand-alone TiVo Tools and Development Projects 354
  An Alternate UI in the TiVo Web Project 354
  The TiVo Enhancement Development Team 361
  The Personal TiVo Home Media Option 361
  Closed Captioning Support Using TiVoVBI 361
  TiVo Utilities Home Page 362

Chapter 11 Other TiVo Hacking Resources **363**

A Byte of Fun—TiVo Advocacy Articles 365
Online Forums for TiVo Information and Discussion 366
  The AVS Forum 368
  The DealDatabase Forums 371
  The TiVo Community Forums 373
TiVo Hardware Web Sites 377
Various TiVo FAQs and Help Sites 378
  Hacking the TiVo FAQ 378
  The Hinsdale FAQs 379
  Seth's TiVo FAQ 379
  TiVo Forum FAQ 380

TiVo Network Hack How-To Guide 380

TiVoHelp.com 380

TiVoStuff.com 381

DirecTiVo Sites and Information 381

TiVo Software Download Sites 381

Index 383

About the CD 403

Introduction

What exactly is TiVo (pronounced tee-vo), and where did it come from? A TiVo system records cable and satellite television instantly on a hard drive rather than on a videotape, thereby enabling you to store and record an endless number of television programs in one place. But that's not all it does. TiVo also offers a host of other features that makes it a truly useful, timesaving device rather than simply a replacement for your aging VCR. In fact, TiVo represents the most exciting revolution in personal entertainment technology since the VCR or the television itself.

Some of the many advantages of TiVo over a VCR include:

- More durable recording capabilities than videotape
- Far easier to use than a VCR
- More storage than a videotape
- Automatically locates and records your favorite programs, regardless of when or where they were broadcast
- Optionally selects programs to record, based on your previous viewing habits

TiVo, Inc. has been in business for a few years now, and they have several TiVo models available. At the time of this book's writing, these models fell into two general classes, known as *TiVo Series 1* and *TiVo Series 2*. (More details about these in Chapter 1, "Know Your TiVo.") Both of these classes can be hacked, er, "upgraded." TiVo, Inc. is continually updating its operating system and its capabilities, while it matures as a company. The former is a win for TiVo customers, while the latter can present impediments to aspiring TiVo hackers. For example, Series 2 models are faster and sexier than Series 1 models, but it is more difficult to get command-line access to Linux on the Series 2 models. Version 4.0, the most recent version of TiVo's software and customized Linux for the Series 2, makes it downright challenging to get command-line access. Luckily, many of the features that "needed" to be added to the Series 1 class and which required command-line access now are provided automatically by Series 2 models. As I'll explain later, however, there are ways around almost everything.

This book does not attempt to replace your TiVo documentation. It doesn't explain how to set up or configure your new TiVo; nor does this book explain all of the features of the TiVo and how to use them. The documentation that comes with your TiVo does a good job of all of that. You will find that I may explain how to use certain features after you've hacked them or extended their capabilities through various TiVo backdoors (think "cheat codes," which are available in different versions of the TiVo software). Think of this book as a companion volume to your TiVo documentation. In this book, I'll explain how you can hack your TiVo—that is, how you can extend its capacity and capabilities beyond those that are provided out of the box. Although you can find some of this information on the Internet, this book is designed to make your life easier by culling the resources and presenting them in one place, and then tailoring the hacking instructions so almost anyone can do it.

This book isn't necessarily a TiVo cheerleading session. Where appropriate, I'll point out the caveats, downsides, and costs of owning and using TiVo. However, like most TiVo owners, I feel that the benefits of owning and using TiVo far outweigh the disadvantages. Your mileage may vary.

How To Use This Book

This book is intended for anyone with some computer experience and curiosity about what's inside their TiVo. The book starts by explaining how to activate secret commands and modes of operation that help you get more out of your TiVo without even opening the box. It then explains how to inexpensively add disk space to your TiVo, increasing the amount and quality of recordings that you can store. I'll also explain how to install and run many freely-available, open source applications on your TiVo, so that you can schedule recordings over the Web, get news, sports, and weather displayed on your TiVo screen, and even check your portfolio while not missing an instant of your favorite television broadcast.

I'll explain how Linux, Macintosh, and Windows users can all work on and get the most out of their TiVos. The software for each platform is organized into system-specific sections, and much of it is provided on the CD that comes with the book. If you've never experimented much with hardware, it isn't "hard," and this book will show you how to do it.

Later chapters of the book explain how to install and run different versions of the TiVo operating system and software on your TiVo, so that you can take advantage of specific, new (or old) features. Your TiVo is a full-fledged computer system— why not make the most of it?

To get started using this book, take a quick tour of TiVo history in Chapter 1 or look at Chapter 2 to see how to get the most out of the TiVo's user interface. Next, read Chapters 5 and 6 to learn how to use the included CD to back up your TiVo and add a bigger disk yourself—for far less than what others might charge. Finally, look at some of the programs described in Chapters 4 and 7, to see what you might find useful to have running on your TiVo—and put it there. Your TiVo is a home entertainment device, a home computer, and this book will help you do almost anything that you want with it. Have a good time!

Let's Have Some Fun

Like any smart appliance (and even most video games), there are plenty of tips and tricks that can help you get more out of your TiVo, even if you decide that you don't ever want to open the box.

To make it easier to find hot tips or usability suggestions, this book identifies this kind of information with a special "TiVo Guide" icon to differentiate it from the standard text of the book. This section look like the following example:

 TIVO GUIDE TITLE

Did you know that your TiVo has many special commands built into its remote control, providing shortcuts to your favorite TiVo commands and even to some hidden menus? To activate these...

Hacking Is a Good Thing

Many people are confused by the word "hacking" (most notably the media), viewing it as an activity done by eccentric geeks with no social skills. This couldn't be further from the truth. That hype sells newspapers, magazines, and gets viewers for the evening news, but it isn't the way that anyone with a frontal lobe uses the word. "Hacking" can be defined as using your ingenuity to explore and improve the capabilities of application software, operating systems, or hardware. You can hack your car by adding a new carburetor, souping up the fuel injection ratio, or adding some high-performance accessory. You can hack your home cable setup by splitting the cable and running it to multiple points in your house. If you don't like your house, you can hack it by adding a new room or moving the doors around. That's what this book is about—expanding the capacity and capabilities of your TiVo and interacting with it in new ways.

This book is *not* about "cracking," which means stealing services or information and doing something illegal, unethical, or immoral with them. Those kinds of activities are the computer equivalent of shoplifting—and, they are just plain wrong.

Installing a new or modified version of your operating system and application software or adding new storage devices to your TiVo are tasks that are as American as apple pie. Roll the "America the Beautiful" soundtrack please....

This Book, Your TiVo Warranty, and a Few Warnings

You do not have to be a Linux hacker or own a single Ministry or KMFDM T-shirt in order to hack your TiVo. This book provides clear, easy-to-follow instructions for a variety of enhancements that almost anyone can perform. Where relevant, each procedure described in this book also lists potential problems that you may encounter and explains how to correct them.

Warning: Doing almost any of the procedures discussed in this book requires opening your TiVo, which instantly voids your TiVo warranty *forever*. Also, you can get a serious electrical shock if you're not careful while poking around inside your TiVo, just as you can with any electrical device. Never work on your TiVo while it's plugged in. Think of this book as the equivalent to a book on home television or automotive repairs, both of which can be dangerous. You can be hurt if you're not careful!

Here are a few other rules to satisfy the lawyers:

Caution: Never work on your TiVo while drinking hot beverages or while driving. Hot beverages may be hot. Don't drink and drive. Look both ways before you cross the street or open your TiVo. A penny saved is a penny earned. Don't run with scissors.

Caveat: Neither the publisher nor I are responsible for any damage to you or your TiVo if you attempt to follow the procedures discussed in this book. Nor are we responsible if a meteor strikes you while reading this book. This book is made of paper, and thus is flammable. We are not responsible for any resulting damage or injuries if you accidentally set this book on fire or drop it on your foot.

This Book and TiVo, Inc.

The folks at TiVo had nothing to do with this book. They are smart people who deserve your support. This book does not explain how to get around the TiVo service or in any way avoid paying TiVo the money that they deserve for their excellent service. The folks at TiVo deserve your support for pioneering an awesome device and a new way of interacting with broadcast media (although it would have been nice if they had left the Series 2 TiVo models as accessible as the Series 1 models). The TiVo folks also deserve cultural kudos for not suppressing the hundreds of bulletin boards and Web sites that have sprung up discussing TiVo hacking and tips and tricks. In many cases, the folks at TiVo go out of their way to contribute to and host community Web sites where TiVo internals are discussed. I can't think of any other company that has been so cool about its products. If you attempt to cheat TiVo, you hurt everyone. Please don't do that.

I do not explain how to extract or edit recorded video from your TiVo's hard drive(s), although this is possible and is discussed at hundreds of Web sites and news posts on the Internet. Nor do I explain how to do anything that the losers in the Recording Industry Association of America (RIAA), the Motion Picture Association of America (MPAA), or the boneheads who voted for the Digital Millennium Copyright Act (DMCA) could construe as a way to avoid weaseling a few more pennies out of their constituencies or making you pay multiple times for something that you already received.

I do not own stock in TiVo, although I've certainly considered it. This book is an attempt to share various experiences with TiVo, Linux, the Mac OS, and even Microsoft Windows. The goal is to help you enhance the capacity and, in most cases, the capabilities of your TiVo. You've paid for your TiVo, and you can do whatever you want to the physical device. If you break it... well, you've already bought it, and you get to keep both pieces. Buy another one. The folks at TiVo shouldn't be too upset about that.

HACKING THE TiVo

Chapter 1

Know Your TiVo

So you've got a TiVo or you're thinking about getting one—now what? If you already have a TiVo, congratulations! This chapter provides some interesting reading about the TiVo, its history, and the features of the TiVo models, including a discussion of the hackability of various TiVo models. If you're still thinking about getting a TiVo, this chapter is definitely for you because it explores the answers to such questions as: which one should you choose, what do different models do, and why would you prefer one particular model to another?

Why TiVo?

TiVo systems are the best example of the most exciting revolution in personal entertainment technology since the VCR or the television itself. Like a VCR, TiVos enable you to record cable and satellite television, but TiVos offer a host of other features that make them a true home recording appliance rather than simply a replacement for your aging VCR.

Like any new terminology, the name for the class of devices that the TiVo belongs to is still adapting. New devices require new terminology, and it usually takes a while for the "right" term to be adopted—think "horseless carriage" as opposed to a "car" or an "automobile." TiVo and TiVo-like devices are referred to as PVRs (Personal Video Recorders), PTVs (Personal Television Receivers), PDRs (Personal Digital Recorders), HDRs (Hard Disk Recorders), DVRs (Digital Video Recorders), or the somewhat arcane IEDs (Intelligent Entertainment Devices). Regardless of what you call them, TiVo devices are the front-runners in the next generation of home video recording. Throughout this book, I'll use the acronym PVR, since that seems to be the most popular term for this class of devices, and has the added benefit of being the term used on the majority of the TiVo Web sites (which should count for something).

PVRs are to VCRs as a refrigerator is to a block of ice. Some of the many advantages of PVRs over a VCR include:

◆ Far easier to use than a VCR

◆ More storage capacity than a videotape

◆ Simultaneous access to a library of recordings

◆ High quality recordings that do not degrade over time

PVRs would be impressive, even if they were simply a replacement for your VCR, but they are much more than that. While PVRs from different manufacturers provide different capabilities, they generally provide some capability that no VCR can touch (nor manufacturer considered), such as automatically locating and recording your favorite programs and those programs it has selected for you based on your viewing habits, regardless of when they are broadcast or on what channel. PVRs can even locate and record programs that feature your favorite actors, directors, or genre.

PVRs are revolutionizing the way that people watch, record, and interact with broadcast and cable television. A TiVo (or similar device) enables you to watch your favorite programs whenever you want—sometimes referred to as *time-shifting* because you can watch what you want when you want, rather than when it was originally broadcast. VCRs can do this to some extent, but they are limited to what fits on a single videotape (unless you happen to have a videotape-changing robot in your living room).

One of the greatest things about the TiVo is that it represents a stellar example of convergence, which is basically the techno-speak term for the tendency of technologies to combine by absorbing and adding related capabilities from each other.

As electronic devices become cheaper and more powerful, each generation of electronic devices tends to be smaller and more capable than previous generations, which is an amazing combination. Think about it, the portable phones of 15 years ago look like field radios from World War II. Today's cell phones fit in your pocket and can be used from almost anywhere in the world; you can browse the Internet, capture and transmit video, and they are available in hundreds of designer colors. In the computer industry, this is humorously referred to as *creeping featurism* (adding more and more features to an existing product), but today's sophisticated electronics and heightened connectivity expectations mean that people expect devices to do more. Why should you need a separate remote control for every electronic device in your house? Why shouldn't your cell phone provide Internet access, tell you the time and date, and let you play games?

The TiVo is all about convergence. Inside each TiVo lurks a fully functional computer system that serves as the brains of your TiVo. The TiVo operating system coordinates among the hard disk where your recordings are stored, the input signal coming from your cable or satellite system, and the commands you issue from your remote control. Your TiVo can record video on its hard drive while displaying an existing recording. A TiVo system that is integrated with Direct TV systems can even record satellite broadcasts while you watch another live broadcast.

Luckily, the TiVo does not have the standard usability or system crash problems that plague many home computer systems. The TiVo is as reliable as a telephone and easier to use than a VCR. A TiVo runs an advanced, popular computer operating system called *Linux*, which you need to know absolutely nothing about in order to use your TiVo. For most people, the relationship between Linux and your TiVo is the same as the relationship between electricity and your telephone. You don't have to know how your telephone works to order a pizza over the phone, and the Linux operating system for TiVo is similarly invisible.

If you've ever worked on your own car or opened up your home PC to fix or add something, the use of Linux will give you some similar opportunities for customizing and enhancing your TiVo experience. I've saved a lot of money and had a lot of fun expanding and experimenting with my TiVo, and you can too. If you have ever added a board, hard drive, or CD-ROM drive to your computer system, chances are that you can easily save yourself some money and feel quite virtuous by following the procedures discussed in this book. If you have any interest or expertise in programming, you can add even more capabilities to your TiVo. No other device provides as much potential for enhancement while improving your lifestyle by its very existence.

What's This TiVo Service I Keep Hearing About?

Like any computer-based device, a TiVo has both hardware and software components. The hardware component is obvious—it's the black or silver box that you got when you purchased your TiVo. As mentioned earlier (and discussed in more detail throughout this book), the TiVo runs Linux, which is probably the world's most powerful and open operating system.

Linux itself is invisible to the TiVo user (but not the TiVo hacker). Beyond building Linux into every box, TiVo, Inc provides an impressively useful and intuitive user interface that is what you see when you hook up your TiVo to your television and wield the TiVo remote control.

In addition to the software that runs on the TiVo itself, TiVo adds one more bit of software, which is a subscription to a service that provides television listings to your TiVo system. The TiVo service provides much more than just a set of television listings—the same listing you can get by reading your *TV Guide* or by looking up local television listings on some Web site. It provides detailed listings for every channel on your local cable or satellite network, including information about the genre of each show, the actors that appear in each show, information about the director (where applicable), and good summary information about the subject of the show itself. Using this enhanced, specially formatted information enables your TiVo to automatically record exactly what you're interested in.

TIP

When watching a program on your TiVo, you can always press the Enter or Display keys on your remote to get detailed information about the show you're watching.

TiVo Service Fees

TiVo, Inc. charges for their listings service in two different ways: as a recurring monthly charge, or as a single charge for the life of a specific TiVo. At the time of this book's writing, the monthly charge was $12.99, which you could hardwire to a credit card to simplify payment. The one-time subscription charge for a single TiVo system is currently $299.00 for a lifetime subscription, where lifetime means the lifetime of a single registered TiVo machine.

NOTE

If you've just bought your first TiVo and it's a Series 2, I'd recommend that you pay for lifetime service and do it now. Series 1 TiVos feature older, slower hardware and have just been around for a while. The Series 2's are the future of TiVo – Series 1's, although easier to hack, have a shorter lifespan.

Identifying Your TiVo

The TiVo can be identified by an internal serial number, known as the TiVo service number, which is stored in a programmable, read-only memory chip in your TiVo, as well as printed on a label on the back of your system. This service number is used by TiVo to track your subscription status, any customer support issues that you may have raised, and to identify any add-on services (such as the TiVo Home Media option) that you may have purchased for that particular TiVo. TiVo also uses this information whenever it needs to download a new version of the TiVo operating system. The first field of a TiVo service number identifies the model of your TiVo, so you don't accidentally get a version of the operating system that is incompatible with your TiVo hardware.

While a TiVo's serial number can be changed, each TiVo also contains a cryptographic chip that stores the public and private encryption keys specific to that unit. This allows TiVo, Inc to transmit content, such as the home media option, that can only be loaded by a specific unit.

TiVos and Your Viewing Habits

Your TiVo automatically downloads program listings and advanced paid programming from the TiVo service weekly, through a local phone call or over the Internet. The TiVo schedules these downloads to occur during off-peak hours because, once downloaded, the information is reformatted and indexed to improve the speed at which you can search for or simply display television programming information. Whenever the TiVo has scheduled a download to occur, it first checks whether it is currently recording something, and reschedules the download for a later time if that's the case. Next, the TiVo displays a screen informing you that it wants to download information and giving you the option of deferring the download until a later time. The latter is useful if you are actively watching a show or planning to record something in the next hour or so.

In addition to this weekly call, the TiVo places daily calls to the TiVo service to check for updated program listings that reflect local programming changes and so on. At the same time, your TiVo uploads two diagnostic files to TiVo central:

◆ A diagnostic log file for the TiVo hardware and software that describes the relative health of your TiVo system.

◆ A viewing information file that contains information about viewer-related events (channel changes, etc) occurring on your TiVo during the lifetime of the log file. This file is anonymous, and does not include information about your TiVo serial number (though, to be honest, that information could be resurrected from Web and FTP logs if anyone really cared).

 NOTE

The viewing information file provides information that TiVo may make available to ratings services, analysts, and so on. Some people may find this odious because TiVo can (in theory) profit from this information by reselling it without your permission, or they are simply invading your privacy by snooping on your viewing habits. I personally could care less. My TiVo has revolutionized my television viewing habits by freeing me from the tyranny of a clock and a calendar. As far as I'm concerned, they're welcome to the few scraps of demographic data that may fall from my plate.

TIVO, PRIVACY CONCERNS, AND ADVERTISING

Many people today are concerned about who has information about them and what is being done with that information. When users discovered that TiVo was sending this information back to TiVo headquarters (regardless of how anonymous it was), the Internet exploded with crankiness. In response, TiVo clarified its privacy policy by enabling users to opt out of the automatic collection of data from their systems. You can do this by calling the TiVo Customer Care telephone number (877-FOR-TIVO) and requesting that they not track or use this information from your TiVo.

TiVo systems can also display pop-up messages, known as Pre-TiVo-Central Messages (PTCMs). These messages display on your TiVo screen whenever you first press the TiVo button on your remote—in other words, before you get to the TiVo Central menus, as the name suggests. After you read them, these messages then are stored in a special section of the TiVo Central menu system, and can be reviewed (and subsequently deleted) by going to the TiVo Messages & Setup menu and selecting TiVo Messages. This screen displays all undeleted marketing/advertising messages on your screen. You can view any message by highlighting the message title, clicking Select to view the message, and then using the arrow wheel to select Delete Message when you've finished reading it. If you want to save the message, simply select Done and click the Select button.

TiVo PTCMs can be service-related messages, such as those that can remind you that your TiVo needs to "phone home" to get updated programming listings, but they also can contain advertising. Many people resent paying for the TiVo service, and then having advertising piped into their homes. Therefore, like the TiVo data collection, you can opt out of receiving advertising PTCMs by calling TiVo Customer Care (877-For-TiVo) and requesting that you no longer receive them. You will still occasionally receive quality-of-service PTCMs, but you won't be subjected to those that are essentially SPAM.

A Short Course in TiVo History

The idea of personal desktop video on a computer system is not unique to TiVo, Inc, although TiVo has made it practical. Personal desktop video systems are the outgrowth of two separate trends of the early 1990s—personal desktop video creation and editing, and the interest of cable/media companies in delivering more than just cable TV to customer's desktops (and charging for it, of course).

In 1989, Avid Technology unveiled the Avid One Media Composer, an advanced video editing system running on Macintosh computers. In October of 1990, a company named NewTek amazed the US video production community by shipping a breakthrough product called the *Video Toaster* for the Commodore Amiga computer. These products enabled users to add text or graphics to an existing video without the need for a separate character generator. Users could modify and create video graphics, and multiplex, combine, and edit existing video sources. Both of these solutions cost exponentially less than any similar video-editing solution, and they worried companies like Chryon, which produced substantially more expensive video-editing hardware and software packages.

High-performance video workstations, such as Silicon Graphics machines, were capable of doing the same sorts of things as the Media Composer and Video Toaster (and more, of course), and already were doing it for expensive, high-budget projects such as the *Jurassic Park* movies. These groundbreaking products put video-editing capabilities in the hands of aspiring video producers (and low-budget cable channels) everywhere.

As companies like Avid and NewTek were pioneering an affordable desktop video-editing device, the companies that were already delivering video to their customers were trying to identify the next big way of making money from their customers. In December of 1993, Time-Warner executive Gerald Levin announced a consuming new initiative for Time-Warner called the *Full Service Network (FSN)*. Combining the power of cable television, cable telephony, on-demand video and film, and home shopping, the Full Service Network was piped into a few thousand test homes and businesses in the Orlando, Florida area.

The Full Service Network was not the first attempt at expanding the horizons of home video service, but it was certainly the most impressive in its scope and the most extensive investment to date from a major consumer firm. Companies like TCI had previously tested video on demand, where customers could request specific videos from their homes and have them piped directly to their televisions. The TCI experiment in this regard was especially humorous, consisting of an armada of employees on roller skates feeding videos into a wall of VCRs whenever a customer requested a specific video. GTE pioneered a short-lived interactive television home shopping service known as *Main Street*, whose name was meant to prophesy how home shopping would eclipse physical shopping malls, just as those malls had once eclipsed downtown streets lined with stores.

The most interesting development that eventually came out of the Full Service Network was the relationship that evolved between two executives from Silicon Graphics, the company that made the set-top boxes that the Full Service Network depended upon. With years of experience in high-bandwidth video delivery and display, Silicon Graphics was a natural choice to provide this technology. TiVo founders Mike Ramsay (former Senior Vice President of the Silicon Desktop Group at SGI and former President of SGI's Silicon Studio, Inc.) and Jim Barton (Vice President of SGI's Systems Software Division and the lead system software architect of the Full Service Network) met in the context of the Full Service Network.

TIP

For more information on the Full Service Network and the big media companies' involvement, including experiments and losses in interactive television and other pre-Internet technologies, John Motavelli's *Bamboozled at the Revolution* (Viking, 2002, ISBN 0-670-89980-1) is an excellent read.

Working against Time Warner's Full Service Network was the sheer fact of how revolutionary its goals were at the time. In late 1993, the Internet boom had barely begun, but the potential for the Internet to eclipse many of the FSN goals was already evident. Also working against FSN was the fact that no special box was required, only a high-speed connection. The number of big media firms and startups that made—and subsequently lost—money trying to broadcast video over the Internet is only superseded by the number of people who have made fortunes delivering porn over the Internet (probably the Internet's most profitable niche to date).

The "eureka moment" that occurred to Ramsay and Barton was that people didn't necessarily need special content piped into their homes—they just needed a better way of interacting with it—namely, by liberating viewers from the constraints of the broadcast schedule. After all, by the mid 1990s, most viewers were getting a hundred or more channels of television delivered to their homes. The TiVo folks put it this way on their Web site:

> "...As the pioneer in digital video recording services, TiVo Inc. was founded on one driving vision: to create and continually enhance a new, easy—and much better—way to watch television. The idea that everyone, no matter how busy life gets, deserves to enjoy the television entertainment of their choice on their time, established the cornerstone of the TiVo philosophy: watch what you want, when you want...."

This basic TiVo concept is an idea that is elegant in its simplicity, giving viewers a way of more easily recording larger amounts of broadcast media and then watching it whenever they want. The keys to this concept are service, software, and affordability. If consumers already were receiving cable broadcasts, what benefits could an auxiliary service provide that would make people willing to pay for it? What benefits could a new piece of hardware for the home provide that would make it attractive to consumers?

In January, 1999, TiVo unveiled its Personal Television Service at the National Consumer Electronics Show in Las Vegas, Nevada. Since then, in partnership with hardware manufacturers such as Philips Consumer Electronics, Thompson, and Sony, and through broadcast alliances with vendors such as AOL, DirecTV, and a variety of broadcast channels, the TiVo has become the leading Personal Video Recorder available today. Originally known as TeleWorld, this term is now used to identify special TiVo broadcasts, and TiVo is the name known throughout the industry. Its combination of affordable hardware, and elegant but easy-to-use way of interacting with TiVo viewers, and partnerships with various cable and broadcast channels have earned TiVo a passionate group of devotees, who would never return to the primitive simplicity of pure cable television and VCRs.

Liberté, egalité, and better TV! Vive le TiVolution!

TiVo Business Partners and Integrators

As anyone who has ever tried to pioneer a new type of computer system or computer-based home appliance has discovered, software and hardware are expensive. Most startup hardware companies who don't want to (or can't) handle the sole expense of hardware production develop a "reference platform," which is basic proof-of-concept hardware required to support their software. If the focus of the company is on software or service (which was the TiVo strategy originally), they then license this hardware design to various manufacturers who specialize in hardware production and partner with them to provide the associated software and services.

TiVo, Inc. writes the software that runs on TiVo machines. They are therefore responsible for software updates, supporting the TiVo service, and general system setup information. As a home appliance, TiVo is very interested in making your initial experience with the TiVo positive, and getting you to connect to the TiVo service as quickly as possible. TiVo makes the majority of its money from subscriptions to the TiVo service, and only recently has begun directly manufacturing TiVo hardware. Until later Series 2 TiVo systems, all of the hardware manufacturing for TiVo was outsourced to other companies. Philips, Sony, Thomson, and Hughes manufacture Series 1 TiVo hardware units, and they make their money selling the hardware. They are responsible for hardware problems and repairs, upgrades to the hard drive, and so forth. Series 2 TiVo models have been manufactured directly under the TiVo brand name, as well as Sony. Hughes and TiVo co-developed the Series 2 DirecTiVo. (The next section explains the differences between various models of TiVo hardware and how to quickly identify the model you have.)

Interestingly enough, TiVo does not generate its own program schedule information. TiVo gets up-to-date programming information from a company called *Tribune,* although it may eventually use other sources of programming information. The core features of the TiVo service are the depth and detail provided by its scheduling information and how the TiVo stores and indexes that information to make it easy to identify programs that you want to record based on a variety of features.

Partnering with the Networks

In addition to hardware and internal software partnerships, TiVo also is actively involved in partnering with existing broadcast networks so they can deliver custom or special interest content to TiVo customers. TiVo is working with networks, such as NBC, Showtime, and Starz, to provide advanced scheduling and interaction mechanisms that simplify recording broadcasts from those networks. These active partnerships and positive relationships with existing broadcast systems are the primary reason that the TiVo does not automatically provide features that enable you to automatically skip commercials, which is available on competing ReplayTV devices. Like any recording mechanism for broadcast media, the TiVo offers a fast-forward (actually, in three impressive speeds) that enables you to fast-forward through advertising. Also, as you'll learn later in this book, various versions of the TiVo operating systems offer ways of easily skipping forward in thirty-second increments, which is (ironically) the lowest common denominator of the time required for most modern TV commercials.

Showcasing Upcoming Broadcasts

The best examples of TiVo's customized programming are its Showcases, which are available on your TiVo by selecting Showcases after pressing the TiVo Central button on your TiVo remote. These showcases are divided into sections dedicated to items identified as features by TiVo headquarters, and a number of sections associated with specific broadcast media such as ShowTime, NBC, Starz, the Discovery Channel(s), HB0, The Movie Channel (TMC), Encore, The Learning Channel (TLC) Cinemax, Flix, Westerns, and the Sundance Channel. These broadcasters use the interactive TiVo platform as a new way to reach a select group of users, freeing themselves from traditional thirty-second TV advertisements. The TiVo Showcases enable broadcast media partners to present highlights of their products and schedules in a new way, targeting people who are obviously interested enough in television viewing to have bought a TiVo. Some of the best known examples of TiVo Showcases have been promotions for new movies such as Austin Powers in *Goldmember*, Adam Sandler in *Mr. Deeds*, and music videos from popular artists such as Sheryl Crow and Counting Crows (no relation ;-)). In these cases, the associated TiVo Showcases included video and audio footage that were available nowhere else. But let's face it—the TiVo Showcases are essentially advertising, although it is advertising that is only available to a relatively select set of people who are obviously interested in television—TiVo owners like us. TiVo's Showcases include its own *TiVolution* Showcase, which discusses items of special interest to TiVo users.

One of the more irritating developments on the TiVo recently has been the continuing emergence of "gold-star" TiVo advertising, which is a set of advertising messages that are downloaded to the TiVo. These appear as items prefaced by a gold star on the initial TiVo central menu. Recent advertisers have included Porsche, which says something about the demographic expectations of TiVo owners (congratulations to all of us!). Unfortunately, this type of advertising is as exciting as the subscription and special offer cards that fall out of magazines you've purchased. This is particularly true in the case of a TiVo, especially if you've bought your TiVo to liberate yourself from putting up with advertising in real time.

Introducing TiVo's Home Media Option

One interesting new potential revenue stream for TiVo is its "Home Media Option," which enables you to easily network TiVo models (even more easily than the procedures explained in Chapter 3, "Exploring Your TiVo Hardware") and to share recordings, music, and photos among networked TiVo models. TiVo provides software that enables Windows and Macintosh users to export their MP3 and digital photograph collections over a home network so that you can play them from your TiVo. This feature is especially attractive if your TiVo is a component of an upscale home theater system but your MP3 collection lives on your PC.

The TiVo Home Media Option is available for a one-time charge (initially $69 for your first TiVo and $49 for any other). It also provides interesting opportunities for TiVo to integrate with online or cable music services, thereby opening some entirely new markets for TiVo integration.

TiVo DON'T DESPAIR, LINUX LOVERS!

Although TiVo itself doesn't offer Linux-side software that works with the Home Media Option, Open Source software comes to the rescue! See the discussion in Chapter 9 entitled "Working with TiVo's Home Media Option from Linux" for software that makes it easy to integrate your Linux-based MP3 and digital photo collections with the Home Media Option. This free software package also enables you to play music stored in the popular Open Source OGG/Vorbis digital music format on your Home Media Option-equipped TiVo.

In even more recent news, TiVo announced that it will begin licensing different levels of the TiVo service and its capabilities to hardware manufacturers. This shouldn't be a surprise, since TiVo receives the majority of its revenues from subscriptions to (and sales of) the TiVo service. The first announced level is a basic version that can be bundled with the next generation of home recording/playback devices, combined DVD/PVRs. As announced, this basic version of the service provides a subset of the current TiVo service and features, providing the standard 30-minute TV buffer to support pausing live television broadcasts, recording television shows by time and date, and so on. We'll have to wait a while to see what comes from TiVo's licensing of different service levels, since devices featuring this service (such as an announced Toshiba SD-H400 DVD/PVR) won't be available until late in 2003.

TiVo's support of other service levels can be a very good thing for TiVo, because each system bundled with the new basic service level will be able to optionally upgrade to the full TiVo service, supporting Wish Lists, Season Passes, and smart searches based on actor, director, and so on. Manufacturers that bundle the basic service with their hardware aren't expected to pass any monthly cost to buyers, which is a great way for TiVo to get its service into homes without the monthly cost requirement that is a stumbling block for many people when purchasing a stand-alone TiVo. I wondered about this before I bought my first TiVo…. At this point, I personally find the TiVo service cost to be just another monthly utility bill (for the one machine on which I haven't paid for lifetime service).

Unfortunately, the availability of the new basic service level is a business-to-business feature that isn't expected to benefit existing TiVo users. At the time of this book's writing, TiVo doesn't plan to offer a less expensive version of this service to owners of existing Series 1 and Series 2 models.

TiVo Hardware Models and Features

Different TiVo models have different capabilities and can be hacked to different extents and in different ways. Let's take a look at the various models of TiVo that have been sold during its history.

Although TiVo has had a number of hardware partners over the past few years, all TiVo units fall into two general classes: TiVo Series 1, which use an IBM PowerPC 403GCX processor running at 50 MHz, and TiVo Series 2, which use a NEC MIPS processor running at 162 MHz. In addition to these fundamental differences, there are two other basic TiVo classes: those made for use with any cable service (often simply referred to as a *Stand-alone TiVo*), and those made for use with DirecTV dish receivers (often referred to as the DirecTiVo).

The connectors on the back of the Series 1 and Series 2 TiVo systems are very similar, as shown in Table 1.1.

Table 1.1 TiVo Connectors

Input/Output	Series 1	Series 2
Audio Right/Left, Video Inputs	2	2
Audio Right/Left, Video Outputs	2	2
InfraRed Control Output	1	1
Serial Control Output	1	1
S-Video Output	1	1
S-Video Input	1	1
RF Output	1	1
RF Input	1	1
USB Ports	0	2
Telephone Connector	1	1

The Audio Right/Left and Video inputs and outputs both use RCA-style connectors. Both controller outputs use 305 MM Minijack Sockets. The S-Video inputs and outputs use the same Mini DIN connectors. The telephone connectors are standard RJ-11 connectors. Stand-alone TiVo units have a standard Channel 3/Channel 4 selector switch next to the RF input.

DirecTiVo units also provide two internal inputs, two coaxial audio outputs, two coaxial video outputs, one standard analog TV input, and a Dolby Digital optical output (using a TosLink connector). DirecTiVo units contain two separate tuners, so that you can watch one show live while you record another, but can only record from non-DTV sources. On all TiVo units you can watch a show that you have already recorded while recording something that is currently being broadcast, but only on the DirecTiVos can you watch one live broadcast while recording another.

Nowadays, all TiVo models sold as new through TiVo or consumer electronics shops such as Best Buy or Circuit City should be TiVo Series 2 machines; however, if you're buying a used TiVo somewhere, you will want to ask whether it is a TiVo Series 1 or Series 2 unit. The easiest way to tell the difference between them is the presence of the USB connectors on all TiVo Series 2 units. Series 1 models do not have these.

The amount of storage that comes with your TiVo (assuming that it has yet to be hacked) is based on the manufacturer and the model number. In most cases, you can identify your machine's manufacturer by looking at the front panel of your PVR, which typically displays the manufacturer's logo. If your front panel only displays a TiVo logo, then you have a Series 2 system made by TiVo. You can also extrapolate the manufacturer of your TiVo from the TiVo service number (which is unique to each unit and is present on the back of each TiVo, on a sticker on the outside of the original shipping materials for the TiVo). Alternatively, you can connect the TiVo to a television, turn on both, look at the onscreen TiVo Central menu (by pressing the TiVo button on the TiVo's remote control, select Messages & Setup, and then select System Information.)

Table 1.2 shows the relationship between the first three digits of a TiVo serial number and the manufacturer and model of each TiVo. In general, the first number represents the hardware generation, the second is the brand of TiVo you're using, and the third digit is the type of TiVo. (For example, all DirecTiVo prefixes end with '1'.)

Table 1.2 TiVo Model Numbers

Digits	Manufacturer	Model
000	Philips	HDR110 or HDR310 Series 1 stand-alone (14 or 30 hours recording capacity, respectively)
001	Philips	DSR6000 Series 1 DirecTV Receiver with TiVo (35 hours recording capacity)
002	Philips	HDR112, HDR212, HDR312, HDR612 Series 1 stand-alone (14, 20, 30, or 60 hours recording capacity, respectively)
010	Sony	SVR-2000 Series 1 Digital Video Recorder stand-alone (30 hours recording capacity)
011	Sony	SAT-T60 Series 1 DirecTV Receiver with TiVo (35 hours recording capacity)

Table 1.2 (Continued)

Digits	Manufacturer	Model
031	Hughes	GXCEBOT Series 1 DirecTV Digital Satellite Receiver
023	Thompson	PVR10UK Series 1 stand-alone, 40 hours, UK only
110	Sony	SVR-3000 Series 2 stand-alone (80 hours)
130	TiVo	TCD130040 Series 2 stand-alone (40 hours)
140	TiVo	TCD140060 Series 2 stand-alone (60 hours)
151	Hughes	Series 2 DirecTV Digital Satellite Recorder (40 hours)
230	TiVo	TCD230040 Series 2 stand-alone (40 hours)
240	TiVo	TCD240040 Series 2 or TCD240080 Series 2 stand-alones (40 or 80 hours, respectively)

The hardware expandability of each TiVo model differs somewhat. The recording capacity of all TiVos can be upgraded in different ways:

◆ By replacing the disk in a single-disk system with a higher-capacity drive

◆ By replacing both disks of a dual-disk system with higher-capacity drives

◆ By replacing the two disks of a dual-disk system with a single, higher-capacity drive

◆ By adding a second disk to an existing single-disk system

Most unhacked TiVo machines have a single disk drive, with the exception of the stand-alone Philips HDR312 and HDR612 TiVo models and some Philips DSR6000 and Sony SAT-T60 DirecTiVo units.

Adding a second drive to any single-disk TiVo Series 1 machine requires that you buy a special mounting bracket for the second drive. Sources for these brackets are listed in the section of Chapter 3 entitled "TiVo Hardware Supplies on the Net."

TiVoSeries 2 machines are somewhat quirkier. The 60-hour TCD140060 Series 2 model, 40-hour TCD130040 AT&T Series 2 model, and the Sony SVR-3000 have internal brackets with space to accommodate a second drive—all you need are a few screws to mount the drives. The TCD230040 and TCD240080 TiVo Series 2 systems and Hughes HDVR2 systems do not have space for a second drive on their existing configuration, but you can buy slightly *Frankensteinian* brackets that will hold two drives for these systems on the Net. Sources for these brackets are also given in the section of Chapter 3 entitiled "TiVo Hardware Supplies on the Net."

CHOOSING THE TIVO THAT'S RIGHT FOR YOU

With such a bewildering assortment of old and new TiVo models, it's difficult to determine which one you should actually buy. While this is a personal choice, here are a few tips that might help you decide.

Choosing between stand-alone and DirecTiVo models is somewhat easy:

◆ If you have DirecTV, you probably want a DirecTiVo system.

◆ If you desperately want to record one live broadcast while watching another, you will need to buy a DirecTiVo, since this is the only type of TiVo with two separate tuners. You will also need to buy a dual-LNB dish with your DirecTV installation.

◆ If you only have cable and never plan to get DirecTV service, you will want to buy a stand-alone TiVo. DirecTiVo units will not work with standard cable service.

Choosing between TiVo Series 1 and Series 2 models is somewhat trickier. Here are a few guidelines:

◆ Both Series 1 and Series 2 machines can be expanded easily to increase their storage capacity.

◆ If you simply want to take advantage of the latest and greatest TiVo features (such as the Home Media Option), you must buy a Series 2 TiVo. Series 1 TiVo models do not support the Home Media Option.

If your goal is hacking a TiVo and having a bit of fun while taking advantage of the world's coolest PVR, I prefer the Series 1 models. TiVo Series 1 models are no longer being produced, their software is no longer being actively upgraded, and they feature slower, less-powerful hardware; however, they were a more open hardware and software platform. Hacking TiVos Series 2 machines is quite possible (as explained in detail later in this book), but it is harder to do—and you also are susceptible to new TiVo software upgrades that may override your carefully hacked system.

Identifying Your TiVo Software Version

TiVo has been constantly improving and upgrading its software since the first TiVo crawled out of the ocean long ago. Different versions of the TiVo software are hackable to different degrees, and you may therefore find that you'd prefer one version to another. Software is, after all, inherently "soft," and can thus be changed in the sense that you can usually install a specific, older version of the TiVo software on a compatible machine if you can locate one.

To identify the version of the software that is currently running on your TiVo system, go to TiVo Central by pressing the TiVo button on your TiVo remote control. Next, highlight Messages & Setup (shown as TiVo Messages and Setup in some versions of the TiVo software), and then press the Select button. Finally, highlight System Information and press Select again.

> **NOTE**
>
> The capabilities and hackability of different versions of the TiVo software are discussed in Chapter 3, "Exploring Your TiVo Hardware."

TiVo and the Competition

PVRs are the wave of the future, and several similar products to TiVo are already available, with more on the way.

That said, this is a book on hacking TiVo machines, not hacking PVRs. I believe the TiVo to be far and away the best of all currently available PVRs, and expect that trend to continue. (It would be nice if TiVo would lighten up a bit regarding the hashing and signature checks in their latest software, but I guess they forgot to ask me.)

For TiVo fans, the core differentiators between TiVo and other PVR systems are the following:

◆ TiVos run Linux, a popular open source operating system. The growing popularity of Linux and its fundamental power as a Unix-like system gives TiVo users access to thousands of open source software projects, many of which you easily can recompile for and install on hacked TiVo systems. The fact that TiVos use Linux for their operating system does not mean that the TiVo software is an open source project.

◆ The TiVo User Interface is consistent, easily navigable, and attractive.

◆ TiVo's Season Passes, WishLists, and general features for locating shows in which users are interested (or might be) are more powerful and usable than those on any other PVR.

Your mileage may vary. A generally good source of comparative information about different PVRs is the PVR Compare site at http://www.pvrcompare.com. This is an excellent site with detailed comparisons among the different PVRs, and it tries to maintain its objectivity (unlike the author of this book).

ReplayTV

ReplayTV systems are the best-known and closest TiVo competitor. Originally designed and manufactured by a company called SONICblue (www.sonicblue.com), the end of dot.com mania and the decline of many hi-tech stocks hit SONICblue hard, and the ReplayTV business was sold to D&M Holdings in April, 2003. D&M Holdings is the parent company of Denon and Marantz, a well-known Japanese company specializing in consumer audio and video electronics, so ReplayTV systems may have found a good home.

ReplayTV systems feature good hardware, good support for many common hardware interfaces (USB, FireWire, and so on), and they are easily expanded and provide good network connection support. ReplayTV systems run an operating system called *Sutter,* which is a custom real-time operating system that makes extensive internal use of XML for data representation and storage. As a custom operating system, Sutter is highly customized to make the most of the underlying ReplayTV hardware. The downside of a custom operating system is, of course, that you can hold a meeting of all of the world's Sutter experts, programmers, and its complete code base in a very small room.

The single ReplayTV feature that gets the most press is its automatic 30-second skip feature. This button makes it easy to skip over commercials without fast-forwarding. (A similar, undocumented feature can be activated on most TiVo models, as explained in Chapter 3.) While users love this feature, broadcast media companies hate it, since they get much of their revenue from selling advertising. SONICblue has been in court for a few years as the result of a lawsuit over this feature by companies whose names you might recognize, such as Paramount Pictures Corporation, Disney Enterprises, Inc., National Broadcasting Company, Inc., NBC Studios, Inc., Showtime Networks Inc., The United Paramount Network, ABC, Inc., Viacom International Inc., CBS Worldwide Inc., CBS Broadcasting Inc., and more. TiVo has gone out of its way to maintain good relationships and even partnerships with many of these companies.

ReplayTV systems offer similar capabilities to TiVo systems in terms of searching for shows by time, title, and even wildcards, although all of these work slightly differently than TiVo. ReplayTV's Zones are roughly equivalent to the TiVo's WishList feature.

ReplayTV systems offer some excellent features that the TiVo does not. For example, ReplayTV's buffer for live television is limited only by the amount of available disk space, rather than being limited to 30 minutes as TiVo is. ReplayTV systems also provide slightly better quality video recording in its highest quality-recording mode, which HDTV owners may find extremely attractive.

Some excellent Internet resources on ReplayTV systems are found at the following:

- ◆ ReplayTV FAQ at http://replayfaq.leavensfamily.com (also available simply as http://www.replaytvfaq.com)
- ◆ ReplayTV Advanced FAQ at http://replayfaq.reidpix.com/faq.asp
- ◆ ReplayTV Revealed at http://www.widemovies.com/replaytv.html
- ◆ ReplayTV vs. TiVo Comparison at http://egotron.com/ptv
- ◆ ReplayTV and TiVo FAQ at http://www.sgsw.com/misc/faq.html
- ◆ AVS Forum at http://www.avsforum.com

UltimateTV

UltimateTV was a Microsoft-backed PVR that is now sold only by DirecTV as an alternative to the DirecTiVo systems (although software updates for older systems are still being released, or were as of April 2003). For the most part, though, it appears that Microsoft largely has shut down UltimateTV. While it's hard to avoid celebrating the failure of any Microsoft-backed enterprise, this section attempts to do so.

UltimateTV systems were a competitor to the DirecTiVo systems, providing integration with WebTV or Dish Network satellite systems. Like DirecTiVo systems, UltimateTV systems can record one live broadcast while you are watching another live broadcast because they provided two physical tuners in each UltimateTV unit. UltimateTV systems did not provide rich programming guide information or a very usable or friendly mechanism for locating and identifying shows of interest. They also lacked features that many PVR owners consider critical, for example, buffering live TV broadcasts while you view a previously recorded program. (UltimateTV systems could do this, but only when the picture-in-picture display was being used.)

UltimateTV systems used a version of Windows CE in their set-top boxes, which provided users with a familiar user interface, but was not easy for users to experiment with and expand. As a Microsoft product, there is much less community spirit and open sharing of information on the Internet regarding UltimateTV. Some useful links are listed below:

- ◆ UltimateTV Hacking Forum at http://www.dealdatabase.com/forum
- ◆ TiVo vs. UltimateTV Comparison at http://www.pvrcompare.com/tivoutvframe.html
- ◆ TiVo, ReplayTV, and UltimateTV Feature Comparison at http://www.pvrcompare.com/featurechart.html.

Future Trends

Because most families today subscribe to some sort of cable or satellite television service, the easiest way to convince people to purchase PVRs is to incorporate them into set-top cable or satellite boxes. Although PVR companies such as TiVo and UltimateTV pioneered this idea, this approach is being used by EchoStar Communications Corporation, the owners of Dish Networks, one of the leading satellite broadcasting systems. EchoStar provides integrated single-tuner PVRs (which it calls PVRs) in its DishPVR 501, 508, and 721 set-top boxes. These systems provide the same sorts of capabilities as the TiVo and the other PVRs discussed above, including pausing, rewinding, and recording broadcast television on internal hard drives. Developed by EchoStar, its PVRs owe no royalties to anyone and are conceptually easier to set up than stand-alone systems such as the TiVo and ReplayTV systems.

Ubiquitous home computing presents a similar problem for stand-alone devices like the TiVo. As hardware and software prices continue to drop and storage and processing capabilities continue to increase, single-board PVR products from a number of companies are beginning to emerge. Many of my friends no longer own stereo systems, instead using their home computers as the basis of their home entertainment centers. Sophisticated video boards bundled with PVR software present the same sort of potential problem to dedicated entertainment devices like the TiVo.

The future provides significant challenges for TiVo. By continuing to aggressively provide sophisticated home audio and video options (such as the Home Media Option), by licensing its software and technologies more aggressively to other vendors (for example, the PVR companies discussed earlier), and by continuing to leverage its expertise by identifying and opening new markets, TiVo should keep going as a stand-alone concern for quite a while. Whether TiVo will be able to maintain its edge is anyone's guess. But you can only take my TiVos when you can pry them from my cold dead fingers.

HACKING THE TiVo

Chapter 2

TiVo Tips and Tricks

Although most of this book is about the physical hacking of your TiVo or installing new commands and software, there are a number of cool things that you can do with your TiVo without opening it.

Some of the items discussed in this chapter are simply informational. The remote control shortcuts discussed in the first section of this chapter provide quick access to portions of TiVo Central that otherwise require a little menu walking, but aren't listed in the TiVo documentation. Similarly, later in this chapter I'll provide suggestions for optimal ways of scheduling programs to guarantee that your TiVo finds your desired programming. The TiVo makes it extremely easy to pick scheduled shows by name within the timeframe of the current programming/guide data that your TiVo currently contains. TiVos also provide some impressively powerful ways of creating wishlists that you can store on your TiVo, and which continue to work, regardless of the programming/guide data that your TiVo currently contains. These lists enable you to use special wildcard characters to match words or sequences of words in upcoming programming titles. For example, have you always wished that you could record every movie with the word "Hacker" in the title? TiVo wishlists are the ticket, but learning to use the special characters that wishlists provide for matching terms can be tricky.

Other TiVo tips and tricks, such as the secret TiVo commands and modes discussed in the next section, change the behavior of your TiVo, what it displays on the screen, or how it responds to various buttons on your remote control. Some of these are dangerous (a warning that will be repeated throughout this chapter). Make sure that you have a disk-copy backup before you attempt any of these tips and tricks. (See Chapter 5, "Backing Up and Restoring TiVo Data," for a discussion of the various ways in which you can back up your TiVo.) Similarly, the section titled "Legendary TiVo Monitor and Diagnostic Commands" in this chapter tells you how to access the TiVo boot monitor, which provides some interesting information about your TiVo and its configuration, but also enables you to trash your TiVo's boot information, rendering it unusable. Be careful—be very, very careful when poking around in the boot monitor.

Using the TiVo Remote Control

The TiVo remote control provides an impressively dense collection of specialized and general-purpose buttons. There are two basic models of TiVo remote controls, as shown in Figure 2.1. The remote control on the left is a TiVo Series 1 remote control (a DirecTiVo, in this case), while the one on the right is for a TiVo Series 2 system. Some of TiVo's hardware partners, such as Sony, have made custom remote controls for their TiVo-based hardware, as shown in the middle of Figure 2.1. The Sony remote is a much heavier, more solid remote than the ones from TiVo and also provides extra features such as a button that lets you jump directly to the "Now Playing" list of recorded programs. It is also a smarter remote, meaning that it can learn the codes required to control your television by scanning through a series of available codes and "watching" for a reaction from your television. The shape of the actual TiVo remotes makes them quite comfortable to hold in your hand during even the longest TiVo marathon.

Comparing the TiVo Series 1 and Series 2 remotes shows that relatively little has changed since day one. The Sony Remote is a different matter—many people prefer it to the standard TiVo remote. The Series 2 remotes are longer, and the buttons are therefore spaced out a bit more on the remote. Some of the buttons that had double functions on the TiVo Series 1 remote now have separate buttons (Live TV and Guide, for example); the Series 2 remotes also fea-

FIGURE 2.1 *TiVo Remote Controls (Series 1 is shown on the left)*

ture a control switch that enables you to hardwire a specific remote to a specific TiVo. This is especially handy if you have two TiVos in the same room since they would otherwise both respond to any remote like some twisted hi-tech synchronized swimming performance. The Series 2 remote control also features a PIP/Window button (presumably for "picture in picture"), which appears to be reserved for future expansion—it currently does nothing.

TiVo Remote Control Shortcuts

In addition to the clearly labeled controls provided on the TiVo remote, TiVo remotes also offer some undocumented shortcut commands. Pressing the TiVo Central button at the top center of the remote followed by pressing any numeric key takes you to a specific portion of the TiVo menu hierarchy. Even though the menus are quite easy to navigate, it's also handy to be able to jump directly to different points that you may want to access quickly. The different number keys on the remote take you to the following locations:

0 - Shows the "TiVo Guy" introductory animation

1 - Season Pass Manager

2 - ToDo List

3 - Search Using Wishlists

4 - Search By Title

5 - Browse By Channel

6 - Browse By Time

7 - Record Time/Channel

8 - TiVo's Suggestions

9 - Showcases

Being undocumented and hence unsupported, these shortcuts could conceivably stop working in some future release of the TiVo software, but the majority of them have remained the same since at least version 2.5 of the TiVo software, so we'll just keep our fingers crossed.

Resolving Remote Control Problems

Getting your first TiVo is typically a great experience, but it does have its irritating aspects. Most TiVos interact with home cable boxes by sending signals through the TiVo's IR Blaster, which is the L-shaped IR device that you position over your cable box's IR input. Your TiVo remote controls the TiVo, so when you tell the TiVo to change channels, it does so by sending the appropriate signal out over the IR Blaster, which feeds the appropriate codes into your cable box, and "the right thing happens." Usually. All cable boxes have different control codes, so your TiVo offers a number of possible controller codes for use when you initially configure your remote. The suggested code list generally offers choices that vary by the sequence of the control codes that they send and the speed at which they send the control codes through the IR Blaster. You may have to experiment a bit with the available choices until you find the optimal set for your cable box. Few things are more irritating than telling the TiVo to change channels and having it change to Channel 16 instead of 162, for example. Just ask my wife, who wanted to take a hatchet to our first TiVo until we found the control codes that best matched our cable box.

The following are some suggestions that should help you set up your TiVo, IR Blaster, and cable box so that they work together optimally. If you are having trouble changing channels on your cable or satellite box using the TiVo, try the following:

◆ If the TiVo appears to try to change the channels but nothing actually happens, make sure that the IR Blaster is plugged into the correct port on the back of your TiVo. It should be plugged into the lower of the two 1/8" jacks under the Cntrl Out label on the back of the TiVo—the top one is for a serial connection, and won't work with the IR Blaster. On some TiVos, the ports on the back are actually labeled IR and Serial.

◆ Make sure that one of the IR Blaster emitters is correctly positioned over the IR receiver on your cable or satellite box. If you aren't sure where the IR receiver is on your cable or satellite box, look for a small square red plastic shape on the front of the box. If you still can't locate it, shine a flashlight or other bright light source onto the front of the cable or satellite box, looking for a transparent section behind which you can see a small, round lens.

◆ Make sure that the IR Blaster emitter you're using is positioned far enough out from the front of your cable or satellite box so that it actually shines into the box's IR receiver. You typically attach the IR Blaster so that its lens can shine into the cable or satellite box's IR receiver by attaching it to the top or bottom of the cable or satellite box using one of the pieces of double-sided adhesive provided in the IR Blaster pack in your TiVo cable kit.

◆ Consider buying a flat IR emitter and using that rather than the IR Blaster provided with your TiVo. These flat IR emitters come with a transparent adhesive strip that enables you to directly attach them over the IR receiver on your cable or satellite box. These are available from a number of vendors, but I recommend the 8160/8170/8170S emitters from SmartHome (http://www.smarthome.com/8170.html). These are single emitters instead of the double-headed IR Blaster that comes with the TiVo. Equivalent double-headed models (8171S/8172) are also available from SmartHome.

◆ If you are using the IR Blaster that came with your TiVo, tuck the second head behind the TiVo to ensure that it isn't accidentally causing distortion.

◆ Consider building a small hood (also known as a *tent* or *fort*) around the cable or satellite box IR receiver so that it can't receive signals from anything other than the IR Blaster or replacement emitter.

◆ Make sure that the front of the TiVo isn't in direct sunlight or a position where it may receive signals from any other IR sources that you may be using, such as audio system remote controls, DVD system remotes, and so on.

◆ Try alternate settings for the remote control codes that your TiVo uses to communicate with your cable or satellite box. These alternate setting are available by navigating through the following TiVo menus: Messages & Setup -> Recorder & Phone Setup -> Cable/Satellite Box -> Cable Box Setup menu. Try slower settings if your TiVo only seems to transmit a subset of the digits of your desired channel.

◆ Configure the TiVo to send three digits rather than just two (in the same TiVo menu as the previous bullet: Messages & Setup -> Recorder & Phone Setup -> Cable/Satellite Box -> Cable Box Setup menu). This causes the TiVo to send leading zeroes in single- or double-digit channel requests.

◆ Configure your TiVo to require that you press Enter after selecting a new channel in order to change to your desired channel. This is useful if your TiVo sends channel change requests to the cable or satellite box prematurely, for example, if you try to change to channel 162 and the TiVo always changes to channel 16 before you've pressed the final digit. If this is happening to you, you should try to locate a slower control code, as suggested earlier in this list.

Secret TiVo Commands and Modes

Let's talk about some of the special remote control codes that activate or modify the behavior of your TiVo, the things that it displays onscreen, and so on. These are not officially supported by TiVo and could therefore vanish or change in any new release of the TiVo software. However, they range from being interesting to being downright useful, and can therefore help enrich your TiVo experience.

The secret commands and modes are simple examples of what are commonly referred to as *Easter eggs*. In the software biz, Easter eggs are undocumented features that are available in a program or operating system that are activated on a date or at a preset time, after a specific or random interval, or in response to an arcane combination of key strokes that most users would never press. Software Easter eggs get their name from the Easter festivities held for children in the United States and other countries, where part of the Easter celebration involves kids getting up and trying to find the Easter candy that the Easter Bunny (or, occasionally, the children's parents) hides for them.

 WARNING

TiVo's secret commands and modes are not accidental—they're in there for a reason. Typically, these sorts of hidden features are there for diagnostic or developmental purposes. As diagnostic tools, they provide access to low-level capabilities that can cause data loss or, in extreme cases, put your TiVo into a state where it must be repaired by TiVo service in order to unscramble it. Be very careful when activating any of the secret commands, codes, or modes discussed in this chapter.

Some of the secret TiVo commands and modes depend on whether other modes already have been activated; while others are available at any time. Some persist even after you have restarted your TiVo and must be disabled by using other codes; while others must be re-enabled each time you reboot the TiVo. (The section later in this chapter, "Automating Backdoor Mode and Other Codes" explains how to automatically re-enable your favorite secret TiVo modes each time you restart your TiVo.)

The various codes available on different versions of the TiVo are typically grouped together, and, accordingly, are named based on the initial key sequence that you must enter using your remote control to activate them. As a quick summary, the next few sections discuss the following:

◆ *AutoTest Mode* These codes cause your TiVo to randomly generate key presses and are presumably used by TiVo QA and System Test personnel. These codes are uninteresting and irritating because you often have to reboot your TiVo in order to stop AutoTest mode. They are listed last in this section because I don't see why anyone would knowingly activate AutoTest Mode twice. This mode is also known as "Bullwinkle" mode.

◆ *Backdoor Mode* This is a special mode on the TiVo that displays additional information about your TiVo, providing additional insights into the state and behavior of the system. Backdoor mode must be enabled before you can access some of the other TiVo modes and commands.

◆ *Clear-Clear-Enter-Enter (CCEE) Codes* These codes primarily activate diagnostic features. Some of these codes require that backdoors be enabled, while others do not.

◆ *Clear-Enter-Clear (CEC) Codes* These codes seem targeted for use by TiVo quality assurance and system test personnel, and require that backdoors be enabled to use them.

◆ *Enter-Enter (EE) Codes* These codes enable you to set variables used by the TiVo, and require that Backdoor mode be enabled in order to use them.

◆ *Select-Play-Select (SPS) Codes* These codes affect the behavior of the TiVo, and include what is probably the most famous and popular TiVo key sequence—the value used to turn the SkipForward button into a 30-second skip button, which is eminently desirable in order to avoid viewing commercials when replaying a stored recording. Don't skip this section! These codes work regardless of whether Backdoor mode is enabled.

◆ *Thumb-Thumb-Thumb (TTT, or Triple Thumb) Codes* These codes reveal hidden screens, expired recordings, and expired showcases on your TiVo. They can be both useful and interesting, and the folks at TiVo would probably be happy if you would re-watch some of the old promotions and commercials that are stored on your TiVo. Backdoors must be enabled in order to use these codes.

Some of these codes can be entered directly from the remote control, while others must be entered from what is known as the Ouija screen. This is the text-entry screen that is used by TiVo when specifying, selecting, or browsing entries from various Pick Programs to Record screens (TiVo Central -> Pick Programs to Record). My favorite is the Ouija screen in the Search By Title section, because it contains a complete set of numbers, the entire alphabet, and a space.

As you'd expect from undocumented features, such as secret codes and Easter eggs, some of the secret control codes are specific to certain versions of the TiVo software. If that's the case, the explanatory text identifies the version of the operating system to which they are specific. This chapter focuses on codes that work on versions 3.0 and later of the TiVo software. Codes that worked on previous versions of the TiVo software are also identified, but are there primarily for historical completeness.

 NOTE

The codes listed in this section were found through the hard work and consistent experimentation of TiVo users all over the world. Special thanks go to Otto, a former senior member of the AVS TiVo Forum, for compiling a centralized list of the codes that was the initial inspiration for this section.

Activating Backdoor Mode

Backdoor mode is one of the more interesting TiVo modes, and must be enabled before you can use some of the other codes discussed in this section. The key sequence required to activate Backdoor Mode is specific to each version of the TiVo software and can be downright tricky to activate in the latest versions. This is because different versions of the TiVo software use different hash values (also known as hash keys) to verify the backdoor code. See the next section, "Hashing 101" if you want more detail about what hashing is and what it does.

Enabling backdoors causes a good deal of new and more detailed information to display throughout the TiVo menu hierarchy. Once backdoors are enabled, the System Information screen not only states that they are enabled, but also displays new information, such as the amount of time that your TiVo has been running without rebooting, the value of many internal variables, pending and past system software updates, whether or not you've opted to disallow receiving PTCMs, and so on. Other portions of the TiVo menu hierarchy also show additional information. More importantly, enabling backdoors makes available to you the use of some of the other special commands and modes that can be activated only when Backdoor mode is enabled.

Most of the hash codes for releases of the TiVo software up to and including V 3.0 are known, and are discussed later in this chapter in "Activating Backdoor Mode on V 3.0 and Earlier TiVos." To activate Backdoor mode on a TiVo model running a more recent version of the TiVo software (and most are), you'll actually have to get your hands dirty in hackerland. For details, see the section later in this chapter on "Activating Backdoor Mode on V3.1 and Later TiVos."

TIP

After activating Backdoor mode as described in the next few sections, try pressing the Channel Down key a number of times to display an in-joke about the game ZeroWing.

Hashing 101

Hashing is a standard computer science term for using an algorithm to transform a sequence of characters into a fixed-length value. The idea behind hashing is that using a sufficiently complex but fast hashing operation will produce unique values, even from similar inputs. These values can then be used to access or verify data quickly. Most databases use a hashing algorithm to generate the index keys used to locate specific database records. For example, without using hashing or an equivalent operation, looking up "von Hagen, Bill" in a database containing entries for both "von Hagen, Bill" and "von Hagen, Connie" would require a laborious set of character comparisons until a unique character was encountered (in this example, "B"). Using hashing to generate a unique value for each of these names and using that hash value in the database where the appropriate record is located is much faster.

The checksums used to verify the integrity of downloaded files are another example of the use of hash values. When a file is uploaded, a checksum is calculated based on the original contents of the file. When someone downloads the file, they can compare it against the checksum to verify that the file is the same as the original—in other words, that it was not modified on the download site and that it was not somehow damaged during the download process. The TiVo uses hashing for both encryption and data verification purposes, but the codes necessary to activate Backdoor mode are an example of hashing for encryption. (See the discussion of the TiVo startup procedure in Chapter 9 for a discussion of hashing used for data verification purposes.) All serious hashing algorithms used in encryption are one-way—meaning, you can't easily decipher the original input from a given hash value, you can only compare the output of the hash algorithm in multiple cases to see if they are the same. TiVos use a well-known hashing algorithm known as SHA1, the Secure Hash Algorithm, Version 1.0. For more information about this algorithm, see http://www.w3.org/PICS/DSig/SHA1_1_0.html for both encryption and verification.

TiVo hash values are impressive. As an example, the following table lists the TiVo resource that contains the hash value for enabling backdoors on systems running Series 3.2 software.

```
ResourceItem 999074/174 {
  Id = 131251
  String = 96F8B204FD99534759A6C11A181EEDDFEB2DF1D4
}
```

The "String" is the output of the SHA1 hashing algorithm from the 3.2 backdoor code. This is not the sequence of characters you have to type when enabling backdoors—this is the sequence of characters that must be generated by the SHA1 algorithm in response to the backdoor code. Therefore, to determine the code, all you have to do is find the random-length string of random characters that generates this output when processed by the SHA1 algorithm. Don't despair. As explained in the next section, the backdoor codes for many TiVo software releases are well known (and listed in this book).

 NOTE

If you're curious about the other aspects of the resource shown above, see the information in Chapter 9 on TiVo's MFS filesystem.

If your TiVo is running a TiVo software release for which the backdoor codes are not known, there are two possible approaches. Brute force attempts to identify the backdoor code are certainly possible, but my supercomputer is down at the moment. For a solution that involves a bit of hacking but is eminently doable, see "Activating Backdoor Mode on V 3.1 and Later TiVo Models" (also known as "If You Can't Find The Key, Change The Lock") later in this chapter.

Activating Backdoor Mode on V 3.0 and Earlier TiVos

If your TiVo is running a version of the software up to and including V 3.0, you're in luck—the hash codes for these versions of the operating system are well known. Known backdoor codes can be entered using the remote, but it must be located on one of the TiVo screens that enable you to enter text, such as the Search by Title or Browse By Name screens. To activate backdoors on a V 3.0 or earlier TiVo system (using Search by Title as an input screen), do the following:

1. Click the TiVo button to display the TiVo Central menu.
2. Navigate down to the Pick Programs To Record menu entry and press Select.
3. Search By Title should be highlighted. Press Select.
4. All Programs should be highlighted. Press Select. The Ouija Screen displays, as shown in Figure 2.2.

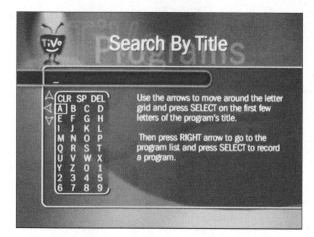

FIGURE 2.2 *Ouija Screen in the Browse By Title Screen*

5. On this screen, enter one of the codes shown in the following table, based on the type of TiVo that you have and the version of the software that you are running. (You can identify your software version by following the instructions in Chapter 1, "Identifying Your TiVo Software Version.)

Enter the strings exactly as shown between the double quotation marks, including any spaces (don't enter the double quotation marks). If you have entered the correct code, the TiVo will bong a few times and display the message "Backdoors enabled!" as shown in Figure 2.3. The TiVo will then return to TiVo Central.

If you're the paranoid sort, the easiest way to verify that the backdoor feature is indeed enabled is to navigate to the System Information screen. If it is enabled, the first entry in this screen will state that it is indeed enabled, as shown in Figure 2.4.

Table 2.1 Known TiVo Backdoor Codes

TiVo Software Release	Code
1.3 (US)	Enter "0V1T" and press Thumbs Up.
1.5.0 or 1.51 (UK)	Enter "0V1T" and press Thumbs Up.
1.5.2 (UK)	Enter "10J0M" and press Thumbs Up.
2.0	Enter "2 0 TCD" and press Thumbs Up.
2.5 (US)	Enter "B D 2 5" and press Thumbs Up.
2.5.5 (UK)	Enter "B D 2 5" and press Thumbs Up.
2.5.2 (DirecTiVo)	Enter "B M U S 1" and press Thumbs Up.
3.0	Enter "3 0 BC" and press Thumbs Up.

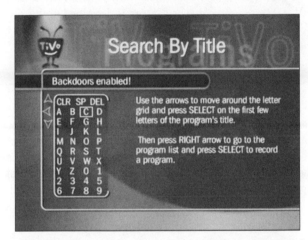

FIGURE 2.3 *Enabling Backdoors in the Browse By Title Screen*

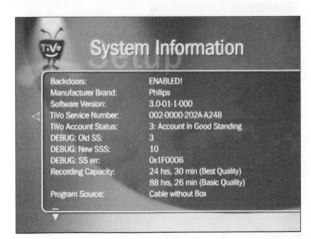

FIGURE 2.4 *System Information Screen indicating that Backdoor Mode is enabled*

Activating Backdoor Mode on V 3.1 and Later TiVo Models

As mentioned previously, the backdoor codes for versions of the TiVo software newer than V. 3.0 are unknown, which is probably a situation that will continue with future TiVo software releases. Fortunately, since we're all hackers here, a relatively simple solution is available for people (like me) who simply must enable backdoors on their TiVo systems.

Prior to Version 4.0 of the TiVo software, backdoors were interesting and occasionally useful; now Version 4.0 of the TiVo software provides an extremely useful screen that can only be seen when backdoors are enabled. This is a Disk Space Usage screen that you can access from the Pick Programs To Record screen off TiVo Central. Until now, guess-timating the amount of remaining free space on your TiVo was truly a black art—depending on the number of recordings you have, the quality level at which they were recorded, the size of your disk drive minus the space TiVo uses for system partitions, and the sacrifice of a chicken. No more! To display this screen (only available on V. 4.0 systems), enable backdoors as described in this section, navigate to the Pick Programs To Record screen, press Zero on your remote control, and then press the Thumbs Up key. The Disk Space Usage screen shown in Figure 2.5 displays!

NOTE

TiVo machines run Linux, which, like all Unix-like systems, reserves some amount of extra space in each filesystem for use during emergencies. (The amount of extra space allocated can be changed ——or eliminated—when you create a new Linux partition.) The calculations shown on the Disk Space Usage screen may therefore not identify the exact amount of free space available down to the last byte, but the values shown are accurate as far as the system's perception of available space is concerned.

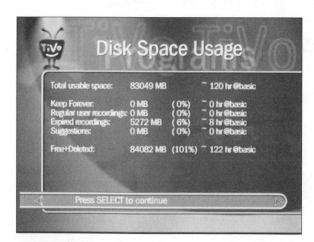

FIGURE 2.5 *Getting Information About Disk Space Use*

The process of enabling backdoors on TiVo V. 3.1 and later systems involves some techniques that are explained later in this book, and which you therefore may not have encountered yet, if you're a front-to-back or random-access reader. Where necessary, each of the following steps provides cross-references to the appropriate sections of the book.

WARNING

The instructions in this section for enabling backdoors require that you use a hexadecimal editor to actively modify data in raw Linux partitions. Making a mistake during this process can render your TiVo disk unusable, turning your TiVo into an expensive electric paperweight. I strongly suggest that you either clone your disk to an identical disk and work on the copy (by using the Linux **dd** utility to save an exact image of your disk to a spare drive with enough free space to hold it); or you use the **mfstool** utility to back up your TiVo disk before performing the following instructions. (See Chapter 6, "Backing Up Your TiVo Data" for a discussion of backup alternatives before proceeding. Some backup methods will cause you to lose any recordings that you may have stored on your TiVo disk.) Do not proceed without backing up your drive unless you are extremely comfortable with working on disks at a very low level or just don't care. Don't make me say "I told you so."

To make it possible to enable backdoors on TiVo systems running versions of the TiVo software newer than V. 3.0, do the following:

1. After backing up your TiVo drive or throwing caution to the winds, remove Your TiVo hard drive and put it in an x86 or IA/32 PC, as described in, "Adding TiVo Hard Drives To Your PC," in Chapter 6, "Expanding Your TiVo's Storage Capacity." Make sure that you've jumpered the drive correctly so that it does not conflict with any other drive on your system! See Chapter 8, "Working with Your TiVo from Windows and Macintosh Systems," for information about trying to do this on a Macintosh. [I apologize in advance for the fact that this section is PC-centric. I love my G4 as much as anyone, but PCs are as ubiquitous as locusts (but locusts don't run Linux).]

2. Obtain and burn one of the TiVo boot disks containing the tools that you need to edit the TiVo partitions. See the section of Chapter 4 entitled "Boot Disks" for a discussion of the various boot disks. If you are not using a boot disk that includes the hexedit utility (in other words, the BATBD disk), make sure that you have access to a Linux partition on the boot disk of your PC where you have downloaded or built a statically-linked copy of the hexedit utility. Chapter 4 also provides more detailed information on the hexedit utility.

3. Boot using the TiVo CD that you created in the previous step, selecting a byteswapped boot configuration from the boot menu. You must boot with the TiVo disk byte-swapped in order to access the partitions used by the TiVo. After booting your

system using the TiVo boot CD, follow any other instructions (such as mounting the CD) that are associated with the specific boot CD that you are using.

4. Use the **pdisk** utility to display the partition map on the TiVo drive; then write down all of the partitions that are identified as MFS Application partitions. These are the partitions that you will have to search through for backdoor hash values.

TIP

If the list of partitions on your disk is too long to fit on a single screen, you can scroll back to previous messages by holding down the Shift key and pressing the Page Up key on your keyboard.

5. If you're not using the BATBD, make sure that you have access to a statically linked version of the hexedit utility (or one that is compiled against the same libraries and library versions as those used on your boot disk).

6. Use the hexedit application to edit each of the partitions identified in Step 4, specifying the name of the partition that you want to edit as a command-line argument. The following example command edits partition 12 on a hard drive attached as a slave drive on the PC's second IDE interface:

```
# hexedit /dev/hdd12
```

NOTE

If you're not sure how to identify the partition you should be editing, see Chapter 3's discussion of Linux disk-drive naming conventions for more information.

7. Once the hexedit application starts, your screen will look something like that shown in Figure 2.6. Use the following commands to locate and replace the appropriate strings from Table 2.2:

   ◆ After starting hexedit, press the Tab key to move the cursor from the hexadecimal section of the display to the ASCII section of the display.

   ◆ Press Ctrl-s (hold down the Ctrl key and press the letter "s") to display the search prompt, press the Caps Lock key to ensure that what you type is completely in uppercase, and then enter one of the strings shown in Table 2.2. The string that you enter depends on the version of the TiVo software that your TiVo disk is running.

◆ Once the hexedit application locates the specified string, it will position the cursor at the beginning of the search string. Enter the following string as the new hash:

5CA5D9DBE5338BAB8690C79C9A9310BCD3A8F23B

Simply typing in the ASCII display will overwrite the existing values there.

◆ After you have entered the new string, press Ctrl-s to search for the specified string again. The hexedit utility will prompt you as to whether you want to save your modifications—double-check that you have entered the string correctly, and answer "Y" to save the modified partition, if that's the case.

◆ Repeat the previous three steps twice, once for each instance of the backdoor hash in the TiVo filesystem.

◆ After you reach the end of the partition, press Ctrl-x (hold down the Ctrl key and press the letter "x") to save all of your modifications to the file and return to the Linux command prompt. If you do not want to save your changes and wish to exit at any time, press Ctrl-c (hold down the Ctrl key and press the letter "c").

Table 2.2 TiVo Software Releases and Hashes

TiVo Software Release	String To Search For
3.1	96F8B204FD99534759A6C11A181EEDDFEB2DF1D4
3.2	96F8B204FD99534759A6C11A181EEDDFEB2DF1D4
4.0	61508C7FC1C2250E1794624D8619B9ED760FFABA

FIGURE 2.6 *Editing a partition using the Linux hexedit utility*

8. After repeating Step 7 for every partition that you identified in Step 4, shut down the Linux system by executing the Shutdown Now command.

 NOTE

The next time you boot your PC, press the CD drive's Eject button to remove the CD to ensure that your PC doesn't accidentally reboot from the CD.

---

9. Remove the hard drive and restore any jumpers on the drive to the pins where they were located when you removed the drive from the TiVo.

10. Put the drive back in your TiVo and plug in the TiVo. It should go through its standard boot sequence.

11. After the TiVo boots, follow the procedure described earlier in "Activating Backdoor Mode on V 3.0 and Earlier TiVo Models," using the backdoor code "3 0 BC". This should enable backdoors on your system!

Congratulations! You are now a bona fide TiVo hacker, and can access the "Free Disk Space" screen.

Using Clear-Clear-Enter-Enter Codes

Like the majority of the other special TiVo codes discussed in this chapter, the name of this class of TiVo codes is based on the sequence of keys that you must press on your remote in order to activate them. These codes are all initiated by pressing the Clear key on your remote, the Clear key again, the Enter key, and the Enter key again. You then enter an additional key to activate a specific feature. Clear-Clear-Enter-Enter (CCEE) codes must be entered from the TiVo System Information screen (TiVo Central -> Messages & Setup -> System Information).

Most of the CCEE codes activate diagnostic features, though few of them actually seem to work in Versions 3.0 and later of the TiVo software, on which this book focuses. Most of the CCEE codes also require that Backdoor Mode be enabled, though some work regardless. The following alphabetical list explains each of the CCEE codes that have been discovered in the various TiVo software releases:

◆ *C-C-E-E 0* In versions of the TiVo software prior to Version 3.0, this option enabled you to enter a specific Dial-in Configuration Code, presumably to send logs and other information back to TiVo support. This option no longer does anything in Versions 3.0 and later of the TiVo software. Pressing this key sequence with backdoors enabled still makes the triple-ding that indicates success, but nothing seems to happen.

◆ *C-C-E-E 2* In versions of the TiVo software prior to Version 3.0, this key sequence toggled a Special Mode: DEBUG option in the System Information screen. After activating this feature, you had to exit and then re-enter the System Information screen in order to see the message. When this option was enabled, debugging output was written to the file **/var/log/tvdebuglog** on the TiVo system. Once set, this option would survive across reboots, but shouldn't be left on for long because it could fill up your TiVo **/var** partition. This option no longer seems to work in V. 3.0 and later TiVo software releases, regardless of whether you have enabled backdoors.

◆ *C-C-E-E 3* In versions of the TiVo software prior to Version 3.0, this key sequence was supposed to initiate a special call to TiVo headquarters. This option required that backdoors be enabled, but it no longer seems to do anything obvious in Versions 3.0 and later of the TiVo software. Pressing this key sequence with backdoors enabled still makes the triple-ding that indicates success, but nothing seems to happen.

◆ *C-C-E-E 7* Still supported in Versions 3.0 and later of the TiVo software, this option causes a timestamp message to be written to the file **/var/log/tverr** log file. It is assumed that this option is used by TiVo customer support to generate timestamp messages in TiVo logs to help identify problems. Messages written to the **tverr** log file have the following format:

```
SetupDebugContext:OnNumber[NNN]: USER PROBLEM LOGSTAMP
```

◆ *C-C-E-E 8* In versions of the TiVo software prior to Version 3.0, this key sequence displayed the Channels You Watch screen with no channels selected, providing a quick and easy way to clear your current list of selected channels. This key sequence doesn't do anything in Versions 3.0 and later of the TiVo software, regardless of whether you have enabled backdoors.

Using Clear-Enter-Clear Codes

The name of this class of TiVo codes is based on the sequence of keys that you must press on your remote control in order to activate them. These codes are all initiated by pressing the Clear key on your remote, the Enter key, and the Clear key again. You then enter an additional key to activate a specific feature. Clear-Enter-Clear (CEC) codes must be entered from the TiVo System Information screen (TiVo Central -> Messages & Setup -> System Information).

Most of the CEC codes affect the behavior of the TiVo, and all of them require that you have enabled backdoors. All of the CEC codes work in Versions 3.0 and later of the TiVo software, although few of them do anything that would interest most people. Like many of the TiVo special modes, the CEC codes seem targeted for use by TiVo quality assurance and system test personnel. The following alphabetical list explains each of the CEC codes that have been discovered:

◆ *C-E-C 0* Turns off listing Schedule Suggestions in the ToDo List screen. Schedule Suggestions are items listed on the TiVo Suggestions screen (TiVo Central -> Pick Programs To Record -> Schedule Suggestions) that the TiVo plans to record. The resulting list only displays scheduled items from your Wish Lists or Season Passes.

- ◆ *C-E-C 1* Performs the same tasks as C-E-C 0.
- ◆ *C-E-C 2* Turns on displaying Schedule Suggestions in the ToDo List screen. Normally, this will only take effect the next time the TiVo updates the ToDo List. See the "ThumbsDown-ThumbsDown-ThumbsUp Instant Replay Code," later in this chapter for information on rebuilding the ToDo List.
- ◆ *C-E-C 3* Performs the same tasks as C-E-C 2.
- ◆ *C-E-C 4* Forces the TiVo Suggestions screen to rebuild.
- ◆ *C-E-C 5* Toggles overshoot correction when fast-forwarding. Overshoot correction is an automatic feature of the TiVo that backs up the current recording a small amount if you press Play while fast-forwarding; it is intended to correct for the amount of time between the point at which you see that commercials are over and your show starts, and the time when you actually hit the Play button. Overshoot correction is very useful, unless you have the reflexes of a cobra or videogame addict.
- ◆ *C-E-C 6* Displays the Node Navigator, which is a hidden mechanism that provides direct access to the TiVo menu internals. The Node Navigator is shown in Figure 2.7. Using the Node Navigator can be extremely dangerous to the health of your TiVo——simply exploring the TiVo menu hierarchy can occasionally break things even if you don't think that you've changed anything. Don't use the Node Navigator without a complete backup of your TiVo disk(s). On the other hand, now that I've satisfied my conscience, you can do a few cool things in the Node Navigator, such as visiting Node 1 in V. 3.0 and later TiVo software releases to specify an exact value for the overshoot correction discussed in the entry for the C-E-C 5 key sequence in this section. For another cool feature doable via the Node Navigator, see the section later in this chapter entitled "Activating and Using Advanced Wishlists."

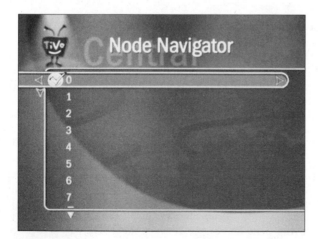

FIGURE 2.7 *The TiVo Node Navigator screen*

◆ *C-E-C FastForward* Reboots the TiVo. This works quite well, and can be equally useful if you have hacked your TiVo and want the new changes to take effect without actually pulling the plug and plugging it back in again. Rebooting the machine using this key sequence is easier on your hardware.

◆ *C-E-C SkipForward* Causes the TiVo to behave as if it has run out of guide data, and, therefore, is often referred to as Boat Anchor Mode. This is probably intended for use by the TiVo QA and System Test folks—it's not something that you and I would want to do.

◆ *C-E-C Slow* Creates a file called **/tmp/mwstate** on your TiVo, which provides a snapshot of the state of the **myworld** application and is used by the TiVoWeb application and some TiVo test code (**/tvlib/tcl/tv/screenTestsFramework.tcl**). The following is an example of an **mwstate** Insert file

```
context {
    id {121}
    pTextM {(null)}
    mode {1}
    currentPos {0}
    duration {0}
    replayStart {0}
    replaySize {0}
    playStatus {0}
    fShowRecordingDotM {false}
    fTrickPlayEnabledM {true}
    beginTime {
        pTextM {0:00}
    }
    middleTime {
        pTextM {(null)}
    }
    endTime {
        pTextM {1:00}
    }
    title {Farscape}
    startTimeM {12152 14400}
    endTimeM {12152 18000}
    recordingDurationM {3600}
}
```

```
recorder {
    nAction {0}
    nCache {1}
    cache0 {
        idRecording {1510079/-1}
        idProxy {2}
    }
}
```

◆ *C-E-C ThumbsUp* Enables you to display and explore the TiVo log files on your TV screen from anywhere in the TiVo menu hierarchy. Figure 2.8 shows an example of a TiVo log file displayed using this key sequence. Once a log file is displayed, the up and down arrows enable you to scroll through the information in each log; the right arrow takes you to the next log file, and the left arrow returns you to the standard TiVo menus. The ThumbsUp and ThumbsDown keys take you to the bottom and top of whatever log file is currently displayed. Viewing the log files can be quite useful if your TiVo seems to be behaving strangely or responding slowly—examining the log files often can help you identify failing hardware or other problems that may require a call to TiVo customer support.

◆ *C-E-C ThumbsDown* Shuts down the **myworld** program on your TiVo, which is the program responsible for almost all of the TiVo functions. If you have a bash shell running on your TiVo, you can re-execute the **myworld** command to restart the TiVo—otherwise, your only alternative is to power-cycle the TiVo (that's geek-speak for turning it off and on again).

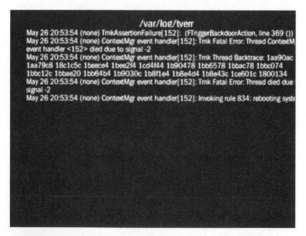

FIGURE 2.8 *Displaying log files on the TiVo screen*

Using Enter-Enter Codes

The name of this class of TiVo codes is based on the sequence of keys that you must press on your remote control to activate them. These codes are all initiated by pressing the Enter key twice on your remote, followed by an additional key to activate a specific feature. Enter-Enter (EE) codes must be entered from the Ouija screen in the TiVo Search by Title screen (TiVo Central -> Pick Programs To Record -> Search By Title -> Category), and they require you to enable backdoors. The specified prompt displays in the text entry area at the top of the screen—after entering a value, you press the same EE code again for the code to be accepted. An example of this screen is shown in Figure 2.9. Since the Enter-Enter codes all take numeric values, you can enter them using the numeric portion of the TiVo remote control keypad, rather than navigating through the Ouija screen.

FIGURE 2.9 *Setting a variable using Enter-Enter codes*

All of the EE codes are used to set internal values used by the TiVo, and still work in Versions 3.0 and later of the TiVo software. Unlike many of the TiVo special modes, the EE settings can be quite useful in tailoring the TiVo's behavior exactly the way you want it. The following alphabetical list explains each of the EE codes that have been discovered:

◆ *E-E 1* Displays the Speed1: prompt and turns on the Record LED on the front of your TiVo until you supply a value. The Speed1 setting enables you to specify a three-digit number that represents the percentage of the TiVo's normal playback speed that the first fast-forward speed consists of. (The TiVo fast-forward button has three speeds, which you step through each time you press the fast-forward button.) For example, specifying a value of "400" would set the first fast-forward speed to 4 times the normal playback speed. Specifying a "1" would set the first fast-forward speed to 1 percent of the TiVo normal speed (which could hardly be considered fast-forward). The default setting for the first fast-forward speed is 300% of normal speed. After entering the new value using the TiVo remote control's numerals (or the Ouija screen, if you insist), press Enter-Enter-1 for the TiVo to accept the new value and turn off the red LED on the front of the machine. These values are reset to their default values whenever your TiVo reboots.

◆ *E-E 2* Displays the Speed2: prompt, which enables you to set the second of the TiVo fast-forward speeds. This is the percentage of the TiVo's default playback speed that the second fast-forward speed consists of. The default setting for the first fast-forward speed is 2000% of normal speed. After entering the new value, press Enter-Enter-2 again for the TiVo to accept the new value.

◆ *E-E 3* Displays the Speed3: prompt, which enables you to set the second of the TiVo fast-forward speeds. This is the percentage of the TiVo's default playback speed that the third (highest) fast-forward speed consists of. The default setting for the first fast-forward speed is 6000% of normal speed. After entering a value, press Enter-Enter-3 again for the TiVo to accept the new value.

◆ *E-E 4* Displays a Rate1: prompt, whose function is unknown.

◆ *E-E 5* Displays a Rate2: prompt, whose function is unknown.

◆ *E-E 6* Displays a Rate1: prompt, whose function is unknown.

◆ *E-E 7* Displays an Inter: prompt,, which enables you to specify the duration of TiVo interstitials. Example of TiVo intersititials were animations featuring the TiVo mascot that displayed between each menu screen in early versions of the TiVo software, but they are no longer used. The only remaining Interstitial is the opening TiVo animation that displays whenever you restart your TiVo, or in response to pressing "0" when the TiVo Central menu displays. This setting is therefore vestigial, and not very useful. If you insist on entering a value, you must press Enter-Enter-7 again for the TiVo to accept the new value.

◆ *E-E 8* Displays an Open: prompt, whose function is unknown.

◆ *E-E 9* Displays an **int.disabled**, or **int.enabled** prompt that toggles interstitials. As explained in the E-E-7 code entry, intersititials were TiVo animations featuring the TiVo mascot that were displayed between each menu screen and are no longer used. Toggling the value of this variable doesn't seem to have an effect in Versions 3.0 and later of the TiVo software, though you must still press Enter-Enter-8 again for the TiVo to accept the new value.

◆ *E-E FastForward* Displays a Delay: prompt that enables you to tweak one of the values used to calculate overshoot correction. The default value for this variable is 957. When overshoot correction is enabled, the delay and offset (set using the E-E-Rewind key sequence, discussed next) values are used in overshoot correction calculations. (See the C-E-C-5 and C-E-C-6 codes discussed earlier in this chapter for other settings related to overshoot correction.) After setting the delay and offset values, you must display any recorded program, play it, pause it, and press FastForward for the new values to take effect. The delay and offset values used in TiVo software Version 1.3 (750 and 1000, respectively) are remembered fondly by many long-time users, and are worth experimenting with.

◆ *E-E Rewind* Displays an Offset: prompt that enables you to tweak one of the values used to calculate overshoot correction. The default value for the offset is 2000. See the explanation of the E-E-FastForward code for additional information about how this value is used.

◆ *E-E TiVo* Enables you to set the TiVo clock, using the same format as that used by the TiVo **settime** command, which is YYYYMMDDhhmm[ss]. Be careful when setting this value, as setting it incorrectly could cause your TiVo to believe that all of its guide data has expired. If you accidentally munge the time using this command, use the Make Test Call command (TiVo Central -> Messages & Setup -> Recorder & Phone Setup -> Phone Connection -> Make Test Call) to automatically set the clock correctly without reloading your guide data.

Using Select-Play-Select Codes

The name of this class of TiVo codes is based on the sequence of keys that you must press on your remote control to activate them. All these codes are initiated by pressing the Select key on your remote, pressing the Play key, and then pressing the Select key again. You then enter an additional key to activate a specific feature, and press the Select key again. All of these codes are best entered while playing back a recording, since the Select key is used to, er, select things in the TiVo menus, and the Play key is irrelevant when you already are playing back a recording.

All of the Select-Play-Select (SPS) codes activate cool features, and can be used regardless of whether you have enabled backdoors. The following alphabetical list explains each of the SPS codes that have been discovered:

◆ *S-P-S 9 S* Toggles between displaying a clock and elapsed time display in the bottom right corner when replaying recordings or watching live TV, as shown in Figure 2.10. After you activate this, repeating the same key sequence will turn off the clock, but you have to pop back to another menu and then return to playing back the recording for the display to actually go away. When using this code on systems running TiVo V. 3.0 and 3.1 software releases, only a clock displays, while TiVo V. 3.2 and later software releases display both a clock and an elapsed time display. The latter is handy when resuming the playback of a recording that you've already started watching because it tells you where you are in the recording.

◆ *S-P-S 30 S* Toggles 30-second Skip mode, and is therefore the TiVo's most famous Easter egg. ReplayTV owners tend to go on and on about this feature, and after activating this key sequence, we rave too. Entering this key sequence turns the Skip-Forward button into a 30-second skip button. This button is therefore very handy in skipping through commercials when playing back a recorded program.

◆ *S-P-S InstantReplay S* Toggles between displaying a cryptic status message in the bottom right corner while playing back a stored program or while watching Live TV, as shown in Figure 2.11. The status message provides information about the routine that the TiVo is currently executing, and gives you the feeling that you're watching television inside a debugger. Like the S-P-S-9-S clock display, you can press this key sequence again to disable the status message, but you must pop back to another menu, and then return to playing back the recording for the display to actually go away.

◆ *S-P-S Pause S* Toggles between whether the Play bar vanishes quickly or within a few seconds. The Play bar provides a graphical representation of where you are in the playback of a stored recording or where you are in the TiVo live TV buffer. You should only activate this feature if you have good peripheral vision or a photographic memory, because when active, this option causes the Play bar to display for something like only a quarter of a second.

FIGURE 2.10 *A clock displayed in a Playback screen*

FIGURE 2.11 *The status messages displayed in a Playback screen*

Using Thumb-Thumb-Thumb Codes

The name of this class of TiVo codes is based on the sequence of keys that you must press on your remote control to activate them. These codes are all initiated by pressing some combination of the ThumbsUp and ThumbsDown keys, followed by an additional key to activate a specific feature. These codes perform different tasks based on the location from where you activate them.

The Thumb-Thumb-Thumb (TTT) codes activate a variety of features, including new screens, expired recordings, expired showcases, and a few general interface changes. The TTT codes require that backdoors be enabled before the codes can be used. The following alphabetical list explains each of the SPS codes that have been discovered:

◆   *ThumbsDown ThumbsDown ThumbsUp InstantReplay* If entered in the ToDo List (TiVo Central -> Pick Programs To Record -> ToDo List), this code activates the display of scheduled suggestions in the list. Scheduled Suggestions are items from the TiVo's Suggestions screen (TiVo Central -> Pick Programs To Record -> TiVo's Suggestions) that the TiVo is planning to record, and which are therefore present in the ToDo List (TiVo Central -> Pick Programs To Record -> ToDo List). If this code is entered in the Now Playing list (TiVo Central -> Now Playing), this code displays hidden recordings. These are advertisements, promotional messages from TiVo, and so on that are stored in reserved space on your TiVo disk. These hidden recordings are normally displayed as star messages on the main TiVo screen or within messages from TiVo for a fixed period of time. You can display any of the hidden recordings by navigating to the recording and pressing the right arrow key on your remote. Figure 2.12 shows a sample screen containing these entries as activated by this code sequence.

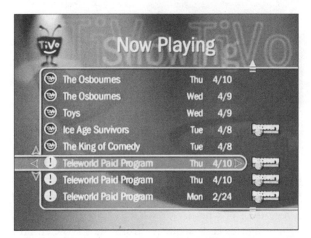

FIGURE 2.12 *A Now Playing list displaying hidden recordings*

NOTE

If you activate this code in the ToDo list you'll see *Teleworld Paid Programming* and Adv*anced Paid Programming* entries. *Teleworld Paid Programming* entries are the video clips that are recorded for showcase items and gold star promotions.

If you activate this code in the Now Showing screen, the Teleworld recordings are added to the end of the Now Playing list. The most interesting aspects of this code is to view expired TeleWorld items or, occasionally, to catch a glimpse of promotional items before they're enabled.

◆ *ThumbsDown ThumbsUp ThumbsDown Instant Replay* Entering this code from the Now Playing screen (TiVo Central -> Now Playing) causes the TiVo to display a new screen, Clips On Disk. This screen contains the same files as shown by the previous code, but organizes them based on the names of the files that contain the clips. You can view any of these clips by navigating to the clip and pressing the right arrow key. Unfortunately, if your system has no hidden clip files, this code sequence reboots your TiVo. Figure 2.13 shows a sample Clips On Disk screen.

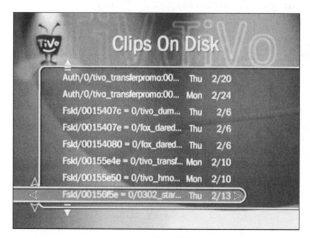

FIGURE 2.13 *The Hidden Clips On Disk screen*

◆ *ThumbsDown ThumbsUp ThumbsDown Record* Entering this code from the Showcases screen (TiVo Central -> Showcases) results in the TiVo displaying all showcases on the machine, regardless of whether they have expired. You can hide these by re-entering the code. Entering this code sequence from the TiVo Central menu causes the TiVo to display a Menu Item backdoor screen, as shown in Figure 2.14. This screen displays the current date in two formats: the number of days since January 1, 1970 (the standard Unix beginning of time) and also in the normal style. If there is a star menu item at the bottom of the TiVo Central screen, this screen also displays information about that item, including its expiration date (the date beyond which it will no longer display on your TiVo screen). To close this screen, simply use the left arrow key.

◆ *ThumbsDown ThumbsUp ThumbsDown Clear* Entering this code from the TiVo Central screen changes all of the screen display fonts to Helvetica Italic, as shown in Figure 2.15. Entering this code again returns them to the standard Helvetica screen font.

◆ *ThumbsDown ThumbsDown ThumbsDown Enter* Writes debug messages to the TiVo log file, **/var/log/tvlog**. I didn't see any direct correlation between the messages in this file and the times I entered this key combination, but your mileage may vary. It's not very interesting, regardless.

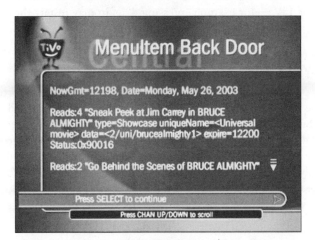

FIGURE 2.14 *The Menu Item Backdoor screen*

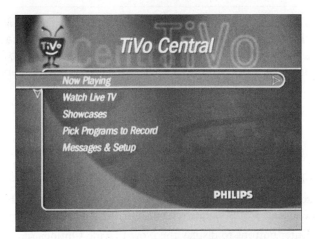

FIGURE 2.15 *TiVo screens using an italic font*

The Irritating AutoTest Mode

AutoTest mode must be entered while viewing a description from the Now Playing screen (TiVo Central -> Now Playing). Once this mode is entered, the TiVo randomly generates key presses to simulate someone using the TiVo. Backdoors must be enabled to start AutoTest mode, which is presumably present for TiVo QA, System Test, or Burn-in use.

To enter AutoTest mode, go to the Now Playing screen, view the description of any stored recording, and press the 1, 2, and 3 keys on your remote, followed by the ChannelDown button. A message is written to the log file, stating "***** Auto_test mode unlocked! *****". You can then press 4 to initiate the automatic key-press generation. Once you are in AutoTest mode, you can press 5 to change the test, press 7 or 8 to change the delay between key presses, or press 4 again to terminate the test. Once you are in AutoTest mode, it is difficult to completely exit it without rebooting your TiVo—for example, pressing 4 again may restart the automatic test.

Sorting the Now Playing List in V. 3.0 TiVos

By default, the items in the Now Playing list (TiVo Central -> Now Playing) are sorted based on the date when they were recorded. This is less than useful, since you're more likely to be looking for a specific show by name than you are to search for something that you recorded on a specific date (unless your memory is lots better than mine). Version 4.0 of the TiVo software builds in the capability to sort the items in the Now Playing list based on recording date, expiration date, or name. Luckily, a special key sequence in all 3.x versions of the TiVo software enables you to do the same thing. This secret key sequence doesn't require backdoors to be enabled—it works anytime, as long as you're running some 3.x version of the TiVo software.

 NOTE

Version 4.0 of the TiVo software now enables you to group entries by name, which reduces the size of your Now Playing list; for example, if you have a season pass to a specific show and thus have multiple episodes of the same show on your TiVo. Versions 3.x of the TIVO software described in this section don't provide the grouping feature.

To enable the sorting feature of the Now Playing list in a TiVo machine running version 3.x of the TiVo software, do the following:

1. Navigate to the Now Playing list from TiVo Central.
2. Enter the following key sequence: Slow 0 Record ThumbsUp. The second character is a Zero. Check out the initials - S0RT! The screen shown in Figure 2.16 displays.
3. Press the Display or Enter buttons to display the Now Playing Options screen, as shown in Figure 2.17.

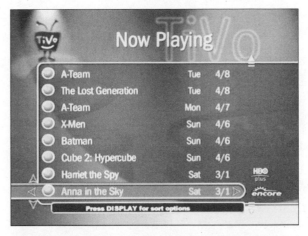

FIGURE 2.16 *The Now Playing list after activating sorting*

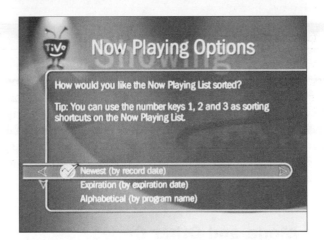

FIGURE 2.17 *Sorting options for the Now Playing list*

4. Select the way in which you'd like items in the Now Playing list to be sorted, and press Select. The Now Playing list redisplays, sorted based on your selection. Figure 2.18 shows a version 3.x Now Playing list sorted alphabetically.

This special sorting mode is not permanent; it goes away if you reboot your TiVo (or if the TiVo reboots itself). You can manually re-enable it at any time; you can also disable it yourself by repeating the same key sequence that you used to activate it. See the next section for information about automatically re-enabling this feature when TiVo reboots.

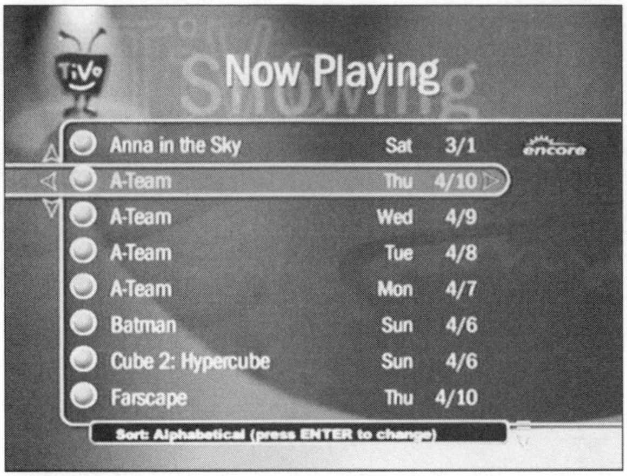

FIGURE 2.18 *An alphabetically sorted Now Playing list*

SORTING TIPS AND TRICKS

Once you've activated sorting on your version 3.x system, you can re-sort the entries in the list from the Now Playing screen without entering the Now Playing Option screen by selecting a number corresponding to the type of sorting in which you're interested. Press 1 on your TiVo remote to re-sort the list based on the time that you recorded the program. Press 2 on the TiVo remote to re-sort the list based on the recording's expiration date (useful if you want to see what the TiVo is most likely to delete if it runs low on space and "needs" to record something). Press 3 on the TiVo remote to re-sort the list alphabetically.

Automating Backdoor Mode and Other Codes

As interesting and useful as the commands are that you can access from the TiVo Backdoor mode, Backdoor mode itself is not permanent. If your TiVo reboots due to a scheduled software upgrade or because the power goes out, you must manually re-enable Backdoor mode. This isn't a huge hassle, but why do something manually if you can configure your TiVo to do it automatically!

One approach to automatically enabling Backdoor mode on a hacked TiVo is to install a modified version of the TiVo's **tivoapp** binary that has been patched to enable backdoors (this is available from posts on the AVS forum discussed in Chapter 11). However, this isn't very flexible, because it only turns on backdoors and doesn't enable you to automatically enable any other settings.

My preferred approach is to install the TiVoWeb application on a hacked TiVo, and then take advantage of its built-in Web server and Web-based remote control to automatically execute the key sequences necessary to turn on enable 30-Second Skip mode, enable backdoors, and so on. (See Chapter 10 for more information about TiVoWeb.) The TiVo system provides an application called **http_get**, which is normally used to retrieve updates from TiVo headquarters. However, you can also use this command in your **/etc/rc.d/rc.sysinit** startup script to send the correct commands to the TiVoWeb Web server and its component applications by using the TiVo loopback Ethernet interface address, 127.0.0.1. All Unix and Unix-like systems provide a loopback address as a convenience for connecting to the local system over an internal interface that is always at the IP address 127.0.0.1. Using **http_get** to send these commands to the Web server's **sendkey** command via the loopback interface enables you to automatically (although somewhat slowly) enable various TiVo modes, as in the following example from my **rc.sysinit** script, which starts 30-Second Skip mode:

```
#
# Activate 30-Second skip mode using TiVoWeb and http_get
#
# Give TiVoWeb time to initialize
#
sleep 120
#
# Get to a well-known location in the menu hierarchy
#
http_get -T 0 -C 0 -D . -U http://127.0.0.1:80/sendkey/livetv
#
# Begin viewing a recorded show
#
http_get -T 0 -C 0 -D . -U http://127.0.0.1:80/sendkey/tivo/tivo/select/select
#
# Give the show time to start
#
sleep 10
#
# Enable 30-second skip
#
http_get -T 0 -C 0 -D . -U http://127.0.0.1:80/sendkey/select/play/select
http_get -T 0 -C 0 -D . -U http://127.0.0.1:80/sendkey/num3/num0/select
#
# Go back to TiVo Central
#
http_get -T 0 -C 0 -D . -U http://127.0.0.1:80/sendkey/tivo
```

 NOTE

The commands in this example are broken up to make them more readable—you can actually send as many commands as you want to TiVoWeb's sendkey module.

The **http_get** command's -T and -C options are mandatory arguments that ordinarily identify the transaction code and the call id, which are irrelevant in this case, so we simply supply a value of 0. Similarly, the -D option identifies the directory relative to which the command should be executed. When retrieving files as part of a daily or weekly call, this directory is typically **/var/packages**, but it is irrelevant in this case, so I simply pass an argument of '.', which means "the current directory" in Unix/Linux-speak. The important argument is the URL that you want to contact, which is specified using the -U command-line argument. The URL for each **http_get** command in this example begins with the string "http://127.0.0.1:80/sendkey", which means "use the HTTP protocol to contact the host at the address 127.0.0.1, using port 80, and tell it to execute the **sendkey** command there." The values after the **sendkey** command on each line represent a sequence of TiVo remote commands that the **sendkey** command should execute.

The previous example automatically turns on 30-Second Skip mode whenever I restart my TiVo. You can enable backdoors by doing the same thing, as in the following example:

```
#
# Enable backdoors on 3.0 box - long
#
# Go to Pick Programs to Record, Search By Title
#
http_get -T 0 -C 0 -D . -U http://127.0.0.1:80/sendkey/down/down/down
http_get -T 0 -C 0 -D . -U http://127.0.0.1:80/sendkey/select/select
#
# Go to Talk Shows -> Don't Specify a Subcategory, or anything
# that never has a show that begins with a 3 in your area.
#
http_get -T 0 -C 0 -D . -U http://127.0.0.1:80/sendkey/down/down/down/down
http_get -T 0 -C 0 -D . -U http://127.0.0.1:80/sendkey/down/down/down/down/down
http_get -T 0 -C 0 -D . -U http://127.0.0.1:80/sendkey/down/down/down/down/down
http_get -T 0 -C 0 -D . -U http://127.0.0.1:80/sendkey/down/down/select/select
#
# Hack and Laboriously crawl through the Ouija screen...
#
#  Enter 3
#
http_get -T 0 -C 0 -D . -U http://127.0.0.1:80/sendkey/num3
#
#  Pick Space
#
http_get -T 0 -C 0 -D . -U http://127.0.0.1:80/sendkey/up/right/select
```

```
#
#  Enter 0
#
http_get -T 0 -C 0 -D . -U http://127.0.0.1:80/sendkey/num0
#
#  Pick Space (Still positioned there in Ouija)
#
http_get -T 0 -C 0 -D . -U http://127.0.0.1:80/sendkey/select
#
#  Enter B
#
http_get -T 0 -C 0 -D . -U http://127.0.0.1:80/sendkey/down/select
#
#  Enter C and Thumbs Up
#
http_get -T 0 -C 0 -D . -U http://127.0.0.1:80/sendkey/right/select/thumbsup
```

If you want to activate your own favorite backdoors by using this mechanism in your
/etc/rc.d/rc.sysinit file, but are unsure what commands to send, see the discussion of the TiVo
Web application in Chapter 10 for more information about starting TiVoWeb and displaying
its Web-based remote control. To see the command that you should send for any key on the
Web-based remote, simply position your cursor over that key on the TiVoWeb Web page and
observe the URL shown in the status bar at the bottom of the screen.

Legendary TiVo Monitor and Diagnostic Commands

Aside from the secret commands and modes discussed earlier, stand-alone TiVo models also
provide some other hidden commands of interest in the TiVo boot (ROM) monitor, which
you can access using the serial connection provided on the back of your TiVo.

 NOTE

To be honest, the commands that you can access through the ROM monitor are fairly
uninteresting with the exception of the **bootparams** command, but they are included
here for completeness. The examples in this section are taken from a Series 1 TiVo –
Series 2 TiVos provide more of a command-line interface to the boot PROM,

To access the TiVo ROM monitor:

1. Connect the serial Channel Change port on the back of your TiVo to a 9-pin serial port on your PC using the cable that came with your TiVo. You will need to get a null-modem adapter on your TiVo, as well as a gender changer to mate the null-modem connector to your PC serial port.

2. Start a terminal emulator on your PC—minicom on Linux systems and HyperTerminal on Windows systems are usually present by default. After starting the terminal emulator, configure it for 9600 baud, 8-bit word length, no parity, and 1 stop bit. Most terminal emulators offer a setting for the latter three settings labeled something like 8N1. You should also disable hardware and software flow control, and verify that the terminal emulator is configured to use the serial port to which you've connected your TiVo. This is usually COM1 on Windows systems or **/dev/ttyS0** on Linux systems.

3. Plug in the TiVo and immediately press the Return or Enter key on your keyboard.

4. The TiVo displays a Verify password: prompt on Series 1 TiVos, and a "what is password?" prompt on Series 2 TiVos. Enter a password of "factory" (without the quotation marks), and press Enter. This should display a message like the following:

```
Console switched to DSS port
------- System Info --------
Processor speed = 50 MHz
Bus speed      = 25 MHz
Amount of DRAM  = 16 MBytes
Video configuration 3, Serial number 0
Enet MAC address= 0:4:ac:e3:0:54
Hostname       = debug-13
Auto disk locking disabled
----------------------------
IDE err = 0x4
IDE drive 0 doesn't challenge security..  Assume insecure device
IDE drive 1 challanges with 0x10001
Respond with 0x6f576955
Check keys a few more times
Respond with 0x6f576955
Respond with 0x6f576955
Respond with 0x6f576955
Drive should be unlocked now.
  --- Device Configuration ---
  Power-On Test Devices:
    000  Enabled   System Memory [RAM]
```

```
    -----------------------------
    Boot Sources:
      002  Enabled   EIDE disk Controller [EIDE]
    gateway: 192.168.1.227
    -----------------------------
      B - Boot from disk
      N - Network (tftp) boot
      X - print extended menu
    ->
```

If the "factory" password doesn't work, you can set the ROM monitor password from a bash prompt on a hacked TiVo by executing a command like the following:

```
crypto -u -srp password
```

where "password" is the password that you want to set for ROM monitor access.

Once the ROM monitor prompt displays, you can display a larger menu of available options by entering the 'x' (for extended) command. The following menu displays:

```
 B - Boot from disk
 N - Network (tftp) boot
 U - Update flash from tftp flash image
 T - Teleworld menu
 V - Print TiVo Prom Version
 W - Word Write
 R - Word Read
 P - Change Boot Parameters
 M - Configure Memory
 C - Configure Video
 E - Configure Ethernet
 K - Set backdoor password
 k - Verify backdoor password
 z - Change Serial Number
 Z - Run memory tests
 1 - Enable/disable tests
 2 - Enable/disable boot devices
 3 - Change IP/MAC addresses
 4 - Ping test
 5 - Toggle auto disk locking
 6 - Toggle automatic menu
```

```
7 - Display configuration
8 - Save changes to configuration
9 - Unlock TiVo Secure Disk
0 - Exit menu and continue
```

 WARNING

Be very careful when poking around in the ROM monitor. If you are not careful, you can accidentally set or change the TiVo boot parameters and configuration to the point it will not boot.

Some of the more interesting of these commands are the following:

p — Enables you to change the TiVo boot partition. Pressing "p" displays the following:

```
->p
Old: root=/dev/hda4
New(- to abort): -
```

This information tells us that my TiVo boots from **/dev/hda4**. To change this to the other boot partition (**/dev/hda7**), enter **root=/dev/hda7** at the New: prompt. To exit from this menu item without changing the boot partition, you *must* enter a dash ("-"). Simply pressing Enter changes the value of the boot partition variable to null, which would be bad—your TiVo wouldn't boot. You can also change the boot partition from a hacked TiVo by using the **boot-param** command.

v — Displays the TiVo PROM version.

8 — Saves any changes that you've made to the configuration.

TiVo Scheduling Tips and Tricks

The capability of TiVo to record programs identified by a number of criteria makes it a powerful tool for customizing your television viewing experience. Its basic ability to time-shift shows, recording them so that you can then watch them at your convenience rather than scheduling your life around the *TV Guide*, lets you watch what you want to watch when you want to watch it.

The TiVo's ability to compile a local database of the kinds of things that you like to watch and automatically record shows that it "thinks" that you would like is a great feature. Once you've had your TiVo for a while (and providing that you have some free space on its disk), you'll find that you are pleasantly surprised by what your TiVo has recorded for you.

The fact that the TiVo continually maintains a 30-minute buffer of broadcast television is a great convenience if you're watching live TV; this feature enables you to pause the television and return to it within 30 minutes without losing anything. You can combine this feature with the TiVo recording capabilities in a variety of interesting ways. For example, I generally like to watch the evening news, but don't always get home in time to see the beginning. My solution to this is to program the TiVo to always record one minute of the evening news on my favorite channel, only keeping one copy of this one-minute recording around. This causes the TiVo to only waste a minute's worth of disk space, but more importantly it forces the TiVo to always tune to my favorite local news channel and begin loading the 30-minute buffer with the news from the right channel. Whenever I get home, I rewind the TiVo to the beginning of the buffer and fast-forward through the 30-minute buffer, only stopping for the news items that interest me. No commercials, no local "cat-up-a-tree," human-interest crapola. I also set this to "Record at Most" one instance of these, so that my disk doesn't accidentally fill up with old news.

The TiVo makes it extremely easy to schedule the recording of shows that you can locate through the commands on its Pick Programs to Record menu. Locating and selecting shows to record is well documented in the *TiVo Viewer's Guide* that comes with your TiVo; however, it's important to understand the basic capabilities of different types of scheduled recordings. Below is a quick reference for the various methods for locating shows that you want your TiVo to record, while highlighting the differences among them.

With your TiVo, you have four basic ways of scheduling programs to record:

◆ Scheduling a recording of specific duration on a specific channel at a specific time. This is accomplished by using the Record by Time or Channel menu (TiVo Central -> Pick programs to Record -> Record by Time or Channel). This menu provides three options:

  ◆ Browse By Time, which enables you to browse through shows that are to broadcast at a specific time on any of the channels that you receive.

  ◆ Browse By Channel, which enables you to browse through shows that are to broadcast on a specific channel that you receive.

  ◆ Manually Record Time/Channel, which enables you to record what is broadcast on a specific channel for a specific period of time.

◆ Explicitly identifying shows by name and scheduling them to be recorded. This recording option enables you to browse through available shows by genre or simply browse through all upcoming shows for shows of interest.

◆ Explicitly identifying shows by name and then getting a Season Pass to a number of broadcasts of that show on a specific channel at a specific time. Season Passes enable you to automatically schedule recording 1, 2, 3, 4, 5, or All episodes of a specific show on a specific channel at a specific time. (The TiVo Version 4.0 software also enables you to schedule recording up to 10 episodes of a selected show.) This is a powerful recording option that makes it easy to automatically record every episode of your favorite prime-time drama or comedy.

◆ Defining a WishList is a powerful, flexible mechanism for recording all instances of a show regardless of when or on what channel they are broadcast. This option makes it easy for you to tell your TiVo to record every instance of any show based on criteria including portions of its title, portions of its description, actors performing in the show, the director of a show, or even the type of show (Movies, Sports, Comedy, and so on).

With the exception of the explicitly scheduled recording of a program at a specific time period, Season Passes, and Wishlists, all of the TiVo's recording options depend on the guide data stored on the system. So the recording options, therefore, enable you to locate shows to record only within a roughly two-week period. TiVo's wishlists are its most flexible and powerful mechanism for finding shows in which you're explicitly interested.

Using TiVo Wishlists

TiVo's wishlists enable you to define sets of keywords, actors, and directors to identify shows that you'd like to record. The guide data provided on the TiVo is more extensive than that used by any other DVR, making it easy for the TiVo to find shows you're interested in recording regardless of when and on what channel they're being broadcast. TiVo wishlists are not tied to specific channels or times, but provide a general way of searching whatever guide data your TiVo contains, at any time.

When creating wishlists, keep in mind the following handy tips:

◆ The "*" (generated by pressing Slow on your TiVo remote control) is a wildcard character that matches any sequence of characters. For example, if you want to create a single WishList that will record both episodes of *King of the Hill* and *King of Queens*, you could enter the title keyword "King." If you wanted to expand this to also catch the movie *Kings of Oblivion*, you could enter "King*" as your title keyword, which would match all three.

◆ You can use double quotation marks (generated by pressing the Pause key on your TiVo remote control) to restrict your WishList to multiple words appearing in a specific order. For example, if you only wanted to record episodes of *Perry Mason* but not the *Mason Perry Summer Special*, entering "Perry Mason" inside double quotes would record only the former.

◆ Special characters such as hyphens, slashes, and periods that may appear in show titles should be replaced by spaces in your WishList entries. Dollar signs in program names should be replaced with a capital "S." With the exception of double quotes and the asterisk, any other characters that are not present on the Ouija screens that you use to create wishlists are simply ignored.

Having the ability to loosely define shows you're interested in recording based on portions of the title, show description, or an actor or director involved in the show, make the TiVo a very flexible mechanism for telling your TiVo what you want to record. The ability to use wildcards and quotation marks to refine the shows that your wishlists will match provides additional power. However, as described below, wishlists have an even more powerful, hidden feature—

the ability to create wishlists that combine any or all of these ways to describe what you want to record.

Activating and Using Advanced Wishlists

Wishlists make it quite easy to locate shows that you want to record based on keyword or specific actor or director names, but TiVo gives you even more power in its wishlists—in an undocumented feature, of course. This feature, known as TiVo Advanced Wishlists, enables you to combine all of these types of searches into complex wishlists. Only interested in recording science fiction movies starring Arnold Schwarzenegger? No problem. Only want to record *Star Trek the Next Generation* shows that feature Wil Wheaton as Wesley Crusher? No problem!

To access the TiVo Advanced WishLists, enable backdoors on your system. Next, begin creating a WishList by going to the TiVo Central -> Programs to Record -> Search Using Wishlists page. Select Create New WishList. When the Create WishList screen displays, press "0" on your remote control, and the screen shown in Figure 2.19 displays.

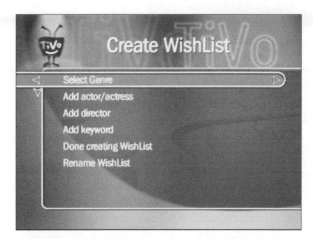

FIGURE 2.19 *The Advanced WishList creation screen*

From this screen, you can create an Advanced WishList using any combination of the items that you use to create standard WishLists. By default, the Advanced WishList uses a logical or to match shows—in other words, selecting the genre science fiction & fantasy and the actor Wil Wheaton would match any shows that contained those items. This is probably not what you want to do. To make any item in the list mandatory, select the Edit List option, and the screen shown in Figure 2.20 displays. Following the instructions at the top of the screen, select any items that you want to make mandatory and press ThumbsUp while they are highlighted.

Figure 2.21 shows the finished wishlist used as an example in this section. The power of Advanced WishLists enables you to create wishlists for very specific combinations of specific items so that you don't record more than you want, but always record the exact broadcasts that you love best.

FIGURE 2.20 *Making items mandatory in an Advanced WishList*

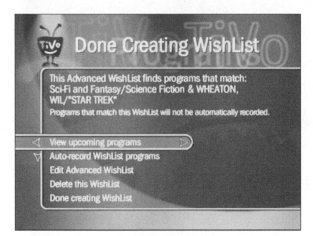

FIGURE 2.21 *A finished Advanced WishList*

PERMANENTLY ENABLING ADVANCED WISHLISTS

To make advanced wishlists permanently available to you, regardless of whether you have enabled backdoors, use the Clear-Enter-Clear 6 code (with backdoors enabled) to display the Node Navigator, and then carefully navigate to node 30. When you select this node, you can then select Expert mode to guarantee that Advanced Wish-Lists are always enabled for you. This mode will then remain active even after rebooting your TiVo, whether you have backdoors enabled or not. TiVo comes through again.

HACKING THE TiVo

Chapter 3

Exploring Your TiVo Hardware

The previous chapters provided a general introduction to TiVo culture, your TiVo hardware and software options, and keys to opening up some of the hidden features of the TiVo software. Now, it's time to actually crack the nut (or the TiVo, in this case). This chapter explains how to access your TiVo in new ways and physically open your TiVo. It also generally paves the way for the hardware and software modifications discussions later in the book.

Before opening TiVo, please refer to this book's Introduction, especially the section entitled "This Book, Your TiVo Warranty, and a Few Warnings." In a nutshell, once you open TiVo, your warranty is null and void—only a pleasant memory.

NOTE

In this chapter, I provide generic descriptions for working with your TiVo, which means that you should be able to use them on TiVo Series 1, Series 2, and Direc-TiVo models. Discussions regarding TiVo software apply through release 4.0. Although things will surely change in future TiVo releases, this chapter focuses mainly on existing hardware (which can't change) and contains relatively few references to the TiVo software, and then only pertaining to standard portions of the TiVo GUI that are probably not prone to change.

Attaching a Terminal Emulator or Serial Console

As you follow the instructions in this book, you may want to set your TiVo to display a serial prompt over its primary serial port. Doing so enables you to access your TiVo from a terminal emulator such as minicom on Linux systems, HyperTerminal on Windows systems, and other similar applications. Of course, if you still have an ancient computer terminal sitting around, as I do, you can attach it to your TiVo.

As I mention in Chapter 2, "TiVo Tips and Tricks," attaching a terminal emulator to your TiVo is easy. After doing so, you will still have to follow one of the procedures described in Chapter 7 to display a command prompt on your TiVo—this section only discusses the hardware side of things.

Most TiVos come with a 10-foot cable that has a $1/8$-inch male jack at one end and a 9-pin male serial connector at the other. If you have such a cable, you'll need two additional components—a null-modem connector and a 9-inch gender changer, usually referred to as a *gender bender*. The null-modem connector is necessary because the TiVo serial port is wired to enable devices to control your TiVo, not to enable passive devices to communicate with it. Null-modem connectors simply swap two of the wires between the two systems, thereby enabling communications. The gender bender is necessary because most PC serial ports also have male connectors—the gender bender converts a male connector to a female connector or vice versa (hence the name) so that you can connect two devices with the same type of pins (in this case, the TiVo serial cable and the null-modem connector that you attached to your PC's serial port).

Connect the ⅛-inch jack on one end of the serial cable to the serial Cntrl Out port on the back of your TiVo, which is the uppermost of the two connectors. Do not connect the jack to the IR port, which you probably will be using to control your TiVo. On the 9-pin end of the cable, connect the gender bender to the cable's 9-pin connector and then connect the null-modem adapter to the end of the gender bender. You can then connect the gender bender to the 9-pin serial port on your PC using the cable that came with your TiVo.

 NOTE

If your gender bender or null modem connector has a screw connector that enables you to firmly connect multiple connectors, you may need to remove the screw connector in order to make a secure connection between the null modem adapter, the gender bender, and your PC's serial port.

Once you've made the connection between your TiVo and your PC, you'll need to start a terminal emulation program on the PC in order to communicate with your TiVo. The most commonly used terminal emulation and serial communications software packages are minicom, which usually comes by default with Linux systems, and HyperTerminal, which comes with Windows systems.

 NOTE

Most Macintosh systems don't have standard serial ports, so they are not covered here. If you're a Macintosh user and want to communicate with your TiVo, your best bet is to put your TiVo on your home network and communicate with it using a Macintosh program like FAT Telnet (on older Macs) or Telnet (on Mac OS X systems).

After starting the terminal emulator on your Windows or Linux system, configure it for 9600 baud, 8-bit word length, no parity, and 1-stop bit. Most terminal emulators offer a setting for the latter three settings, labeled something like 8N1. You should also disable hardware and software flow control and verify that the terminal emulator is configured to use the serial port you've connected to your TiVo, which is usually COM1 on Windows systems or **/dev/ttyS0** on Linux systems.

Unless you just want to examine the output of the TiVo's ROM monitor (as explained in "Legendary TiVo Monitor and Diagnostic Commands," in Chapter 2), you'll also need to have a program running on the TiVo with which you can communicate, such as the Linux command interpreter, as explained in Chapter 7, "Connecting the Universe to Your TiVo."

MAKING YOUR OWN SERIAL CABLE

If your TiVo didn't come with a serial cable, you can buy one from one of the vendors discussed at the end of this chapter or simply make your own by buying the appropriate connectors at your local electronics store. You'll need a male DB9 connector, a 1/8-inch male jack, and a length of cable containing at least three wires. You'll probably have to buy cable with four or more wires and just ignore the extra strands.

To create a serial cable that is analogous to the one that should have come with your TiVo, wire it up as shown in Table 3.1

Table 3.1 Standard TiVo Serial Cable Wiring

1/8-Inch Jack	9-Pin Connector
1/8-inch Tip	DB9 Pin 3
1/8-inch Ring	DB9 Pin 2
1/8-inch Sleeve	DB9 Pin 5

Of course, if you're making your own TiVo serial cable, you might as well make a custom one that eliminates the need to add a null-modem connector at the end. As explained earlier, the null-modem connector just swaps two of the wires between a serial cable and another connector (like your PC's serial port). To create a custom serial cable that connects your TiVo to your PC, wire it up as shown in Table 3.2.

Table 3.2 Null Modem TiVo Serial Cable Wiring

1/8-Inch Jack	9-Pin Connector
1/8-inch Tip	DB9 Pin 2
1/8-inch Ring	DB9 Pin 3
1/8-inch Sleeve	DB9 Pin 5

For general reference, TiVos have three or four serial ports, depending on whether they are Series 1 or Series 2 systems, as shown in the following table. The type of TiVo you are hacking determines the serial port to which you should direct certain applications on the hacked TiVo, such as the TiVo/Linux program that displays a command prompt. Table 3.3. shows the names and uses of the serial ports on different models of the TiVo.

Table 3.3 TiVo Serial Ports

Device	Description
/dev/ttyS0	IR port on the front of your TiVo and the IR Cntrl (IR Blaster) port on the back of your TiVo
/dev/ttyS1	TiVo modem
/dev/ttyS2	Debug port on the TiVo Series 1. DSS Serial port on the back of TiVo Series 2 models
/dev/ttyS3	DSS Serial port on back of TiVos Series 1

Opening the TiVo

Drum roll, please! Now the fun really begins. Experimenting with hidden commands and control codes is certainly interesting, but the key to expanding your disk storage or adding new software to your TiVo is physically getting inside it.

 NOTE

Please refer to this book's Introduction, especially the section "This Book, Your TiVo Warranty, and a Few Warnings," before opening your TiVo. In a nutshell, once you open your TiVo, your warranty is null and void—only a pleasant memory. You will find plenty of places that can repair TiVos (and even do the upgrade for you, if you're truly paranoid) at the end of this chapter, but keep in mind that by opening your TiVo, you're eliminating the folks at TiVo as one of these places.

The only tools that you'll need to open your TiVo and remove the disk drive(s) are a number 10 Torx screwdriver and a number 15 Torx screwdriver. A Torx screwdriver has a six-point, star-shaped head and provides superior gripping power and protection from stripping, which is better than standard slotted or Phillips-head screwdrivers. Sets of Torx screwdrivers are available at most computer shows, Sears, your local Home Depot, and probably most larger auto parts stores. The Torx screws on the TiVo case are number 10 Torx screws; the screws that hold the drive(s) in place and on the drive bracket are a combination of number 10 and number 15 screws.

Both TiVo Series 1 and Series 2 models come apart easily. To remove the cover, use the number 10 Torx screwdriver to detach the three (Series 1) or four (Series 2) screws on the black edge on the back of the machine. After you remove these screws, pull the top straight back an inch or so and lift it off when you can see into the front of the machine. I sometimes use a regular screwdriver to pry between the black trim and the back of the machine. You can also use a screwdriver to carefully separate the top from the machine's plastic front panel, but be careful when doing so—the plastic front panel is lightly attached to the steel frame of the TiVo.

 NOTE

You will find a silver sticker labeled "Warranty void if this seal is broken" spanning the black and silver portions on the back of TiVo Series 1 machines. Given that you're opening the machine, you may as well peel this sticker off or break it. Series 2 models do not have such a sticker, but it's clear that the same idea applies when simply opening the machine.

Working with TiVo Disk Drives

By now, I'm sure that you are eager to find out how to physically remove and replace the disks in your TiVo and how to add another disk to single disk systems. Though some early TiVos came with two disks, single-disk systems are much more common nowadays—and prime for upgrading by adding a second disk!

You will usually remove your TiVo drive to back it up or to replace it with another, larger disk. You should back up your TiVo as soon as possible after buying it (see Chapter 5, "Backing Up and Restoring TiVo Data," for the details). The longer you wait, the greater the amount of data you will have to back up—if you want to preserve shows that you've recorded.

Removing TiVo Disk Drives

The interiors of TiVo systems are very different depending on the model. Figure 3.1 shows the inside of a single-drive TiVo Series 1 (shown from the top). To remove the disk drive, use the number 15 Torx screwdriver to remove the two screws near the front of the TiVo that attach the disk drive bracket to the TiVo frame.

 WARNING

For goodness sake, unplug your TiVo before working on it! Not doing so might give you a serious electric shock and a smoking Van der Graf Generator Afro, as well as cause damage to your TiVo. Similarly, TiVo power supplies are not shielded; in other words, all their components are out in the open, with no enclosing case like those around most PC power supplies. Be careful not to touch any part of the TiVo supply because some of the components store a charge that can be painful or even fatal in rare cases.

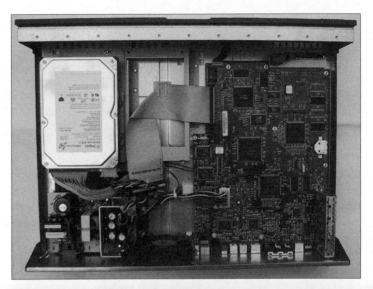

FIGURE 3.1 *The inside of a single-drive TiVo Series 1 machine*

After removing these screws, remove the two cables on the back of the disk drive that attach the TiVo to the motherboard and the power supply. The four-wire connector is the power connector; the other cable is an IDE (Integrated Drive Electronics) cable that transfers data to and from the motherboard. Series 1 machines use a multistrand IDE cable, whereas most PCs and Series 2 machines use a flat cable known as a *ribbon cable*. Don't worry about remembering which way these cables attach to the drive; both of these connectors are shaped so that they attach to the drive in a specific way.

 NOTE

On DirecTiVo and some older Series 2 machines, you will also have to disconnect a fan on the drive bracket that is connected to the motherboard by a small connector. Make sure that you reconnect this when reassembling your TiVo—not doing so will cause the TiVo to overheat and cause glitches in operation.

After you've detached the cables, you can remove the disk drive and bracket by sliding it one-half inch toward the back of the machine and then lifting it straight up. Be careful when handling the disk drive—it contains your TiVo data!

> **NOTE**
>
> All Series 1 machines are designed to have two disk drives, but they provide only a mounting bracket for each drive that is currently in the system. If your Series 1 TiVo has only a single drive and you want to add a second one, you'll need to buy another bracket to mount the second drive. Sources for drive brackets (and more) are listed in the section "TiVo Hardware Supplies on the Net" later in this chapter.

Series 2 models are very different from Series 1 models, and there's lots of variety among the different Series 2 models. Figure 3.2 shows an AT&T Series 2 TiVo (model TCD140060) with the top off. Note that the drive in the system is mounted in a totally different way than those on the Series 1. This bracket comes predrilled with holes that enable you to mount a second drive without any special hardware except for a few screws and washers.

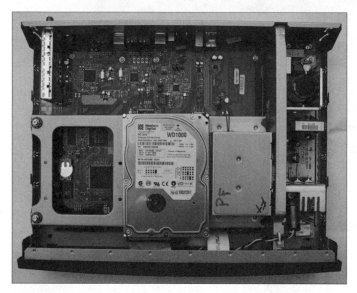

FIGURE 3.2 *A single-drive Series 2 60-MB AT&T TiVo*

To remove the drive from this type of Series 2 machine (after removing the lid, of course), use the number 15 Torx screwdriver to remove the two screws that attach the drive bracket to the machine and detach the wire that connects the fan to the motherboard. The remainder of the bracket is held in place by two pins at the end of the bracket farthest from these screws, which protrude through the vertical bracket between the TiVo motherboard and the power supply.

To remove the bracket and the drive from the TiVo, put the fingers of one hand under the end of the bracket nearest the power supply and lift the opposite end of the bracket (where you removed the screws). You can then wiggle the bracket from side to side, pulling toward the end where you removed the screws until the drive and bracket slip out of the machine.

Figure 3.3 shows a TiVo-branded Series 2 machine with the top off. Note that the drive in the system is mounted in a totally different way than those on the Series 1 or the AT&T Series 2 shown earlier. Also notice that this model of TiVo is designed to hold only one disk drive. Luckily, it can easily hold two when used with custom drive brackets that you can buy over the Internet, as I will describe in the section "TiVo Hardware Supplies on the Net" later in this chapter.

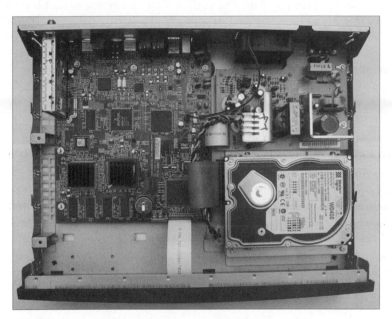

FIGURE 3.3 *A single-drive Series 2 40-MB TiVo from TiVo*

To remove the drive from this type of TiVo Series 2 machine, use the number 10 Torx screwdriver to remove the two screws that attach the drive bracket to the base of the TiVo (near the front of the machine). After disconnecting the IDE and power cables, you can remove the bracket holding the drive by sliding it one-fourth inch toward the power supply and then lifting it straight up and out of the machine.

After removing the drive from whatever model of TiVo you have, disconnect it from the bracket on which it is mounted so that you can put it in your PC for backup purposes. Attaching a TiVo drive to your PC is described in the next section. See Chapter 5 for various methods for backing up your TiVo.

Attaching TiVo Disk Drives to Your PC

PCs are the preferred hardware platform for hacking your TiVo because they are ubiquitous, fast, and cheap. After removing a disk drive from your TiVo, attaching it to your PC is easy to do because TiVos and modern PCs use the same types of IDE drives.

To put a TiVo drive in your PC, shut down the PC and remove the top (for desktop systems) or the side cover that gives you access to the disk drives, motherboards, and cards. Next, locate the IDE cables that are attached to the IDE interfaces on your motherboard (or, in rare cases, to an IDE or EIDE controller card). IDE cables are flat, 40-pin ribbon cables with the same sort of connectors on the ends that you saw in your TiVo when you removed its drive.

In order to add your TiVo drive to your PC, you'll have to connect it so that it does not conflict with drives that are already installed in your PC. Most PCs have two IDE interfaces, known as *primary* (IDE-1) and *secondary* (IDE-2). The cable from each IDE interface can be attached to a maximum of two hard or CD-ROM drives. If two drives are attached to a single cable, they must be configured as master and slave drives by connecting pins known as *jumpers* that are located on the back or bottom of the hard drive or CD-ROM drive. *Master* is the term used for the first drive on an IDE interface; *slave* is the term used for the second drive on the IDE interface.

Although the hard drives used by different operating systems are physically the same, the way in which data is stored on them by each operating system is different. Modern Windows PCs store data using disk formats known as FAT-32 (32-bit File Allocation Table) and NTFS (NT File System). Linux systems store data in a variety of formats, most commonly the EXT2 or EXT3 filesystem formats. If you are attaching your TiVo hard drive to your PC to back it up, you will also need to access a hard drive in the PC once you boot from a TiVo tools disk—so that you will have a place to save the backup file. In order to do so, you must have at least one FAT-32, EXT2, or EXT3 partition in your PC at the same time that you attach the TiVo drive. The FAT-32, EXT2, or EXT3 drive in your system must have sufficient free space for the backups. The space required to save a backup of a TiVo drive ranges from 816MB to the total size of the disk drive you are backing up. For more information on backing up your TiVo, see Chapter 5.

 NOTE

Whether your PC normally runs Microsoft Windows or Linux, all of the bootable tools disks available for hacking the TiVo actually boot your PC into a miniature version of Linux. Don't believe anything you've heard about Linux being cryptic or hard to use—and telling you exactly what to do is the purpose of this book. Just follow the instructions carefully, and you'll be a white-belt TiVo hacker in no time.

ADDING AND REMOVING DRIVES WITH MOBILE RACKS

If you plan on doing much TiVo hacking, you'll be spending a fair amount of time inserting and removing TiVo drives from your PC. To simplify these procedures, I put drive racks in my PC. *Drive racks* are trays that enable you to insert and remove disk drives from the front of your machine, and they look like the hi-tech equivalent of desk drawers. Also known as *mobile racks,* they fit into the kinds of slots in which you insert CD drives in the front of your machine, and they are connected to your motherboard with a standard IDE cable. To add a drive, put it into a tray (provided with the rack) and connect it to the power and IDE cables inside the tray. Then slide the tray into the rack, push down on the handle to lock it in place, and use a circular key (much like an old-style PC key) to turn it on and make it available to your PC. Figure 3.4 shows a sample drive rack with the tray inserted.

Whenever I build a new PC, I attach a rack to each of the secondary IDE interfaces in the PC and configure the boot and CD-ROM drives as masters on each IDE interface. I then jumper whatever drive I want to use as a slave, put it in one of the racks, and access it as the slave on whichever IDE interface the rack is connected. No fuss, no muss.

Drive racks are available at most component-level computer stores, various online component dealers (check http://www.pricewatch.com and search for "Mobile Rack" to do comparison shopping), and online sites like eBay (search for "Mobile Rack") for between $10.00 and $20.00.

FIGURE 3.4 *A removable hard drive rack with tray inserted*

To continue attaching your TiVo drive to your PC, you must set the jumper (or jumpers) on the TiVo drive so that it does not conflict with any existing drive in your PC. To do so, you must know how the current drives are connected. You can determine how the hard drive and the CD-ROM drive are connected in one of two ways: automatically or manually.

The PC automatically tells you how the drives are connected—just look at the information in your PC's BIOS (Basic Input Output System), which is the chip that controls the PC's configuration. To examine the drive configuration using the BIOS, reboot the PC (without attaching the TiVo hard drive yet—you'll do that in a minute or two) and immediately press the appropriate key on your keyboard to enter the PC's BIOS screen—usually either Delete or F1 on your keyboard; the appropriate key should be listed on the screen after you reboot your PC. Once you see the BIOS screen, it should display entries for Primary Master, Primary Slave, Secondary Master, and Secondary Slave. The values beside these entries should explicitly identify the drives that are attached to these interfaces or display the word "Auto," which means that the drives attached to each interface will be automatically detected when you boot your PC. If Auto displays, you can use the arrow keys to navigate to each of these entries and press Enter (aka Return) to force the system to probe that interface to see what's connected.

By tracing cables and examining jumpers, you can manually identify how the drives are connected. To do so, turn off the PC and follow each of the IDE cables from your PC back to the hard drive and the CD-ROM drive. The hard drive that your PC boots from is known as the *boot drive*, and it is usually connected as the master on the first IDE interface on your system. If connected to the same IDE cables as your hard drive, your CD-ROM drive is probably jumpered as the slave on the primary IDE interface (IDE-1). If your CD-ROM drive is connected to your other IDE cable (IDE-2), it is probably jumpered as the master on that interface.

Once you know how your current drives are connected, you can proceed to jumper your TiVo drive so that it does not conflict with existing drives in your PC. A guide to the jumpers on your hard drive that will cause the drive to be recognized as a master or slave drive is usually printed on the top of the hard drive.

 WARNING

Be careful when reading the jumper information; although they are usually written from left to right, just as the jumpers are physically located on the hard drive, some jumper settings are listed relative to a jumper key, which is a single pin on the left or right side of the hard drive jumpers.

TiVo drives should be jumpered as indicated in Table 3.4, depending on how your PC hard drive and CD-ROM drive are currently connected.

After you jumper your TiVo drive and attach it to your PC, you can verify that it is jumpered and attached correctly by rebooting the PC, entering the BIOS, and examining the Primary and Secondary IDE interfaces as described earlier in this section.

 WARNING

If you are adding a TiVo drive to a Windows system, do *not* let the Windows system boot into Windows with the TiVo drive attached. Windows may decide to reformat or damage the TiVo drive, because it cannot identify the format of the TiVo drive. To ensure that this does not occur, put a bootable floppy in the PC's floppy drive or a bootable CD (such as one of the TiVo boot disks discussed in Chapter 4, "The Hacker's Toolchest of TiVo Tools") in the PC's CD-ROM drive before starting the PC.

Table 3.4 Jumper Settings for TiVo Hard Drives in a PC

Hard Drive	CD-ROM Drive	TiVo Drive Setting
Master, IDE-1	Slave, IDE-1	Master, IDE-2
Master, IDE-1	Master, IDE-2	Slave, IDE-1
Master, IDE-1	Slave, IDE-2	Slave, IDE-1
Single Drive, IDE-1	Master, IDE-2	Slave, IDE-1; Rejumper HD as Master, IDE-1
Single Drive, IDE-1	Slave, IDE-2	Slave, IDE-1; Rejumper HD as Master, IDE-1
Cable Select, IDE-1	Master, IDE-2	Slave, IDE-1; Rejumper HD as Master, IDE-1

After following the instructions in this section and verifying that your PC can correctly find all of its drives, follow the instructions in Chapter 5 to back up the drive. Once you complete the backup, you can shut down the PC and return the drive to your TiVo—that is, if you are just doing a backup. If you want to restore the backup to a new, larger disk and make more space for storing recordings available to your TiVo, you can turn off the PC and insert the new, larger drive and follow the procedure described in Chapter 6, "Expanding Your TiVo Storage Capacity."

Adding Disk Drives to Your TiVo

This section explains how to physically add a second disk to your TiVo. See Chapter 6 for information on preparing the disk so that the TiVo can use it to store recorded programs—simply adding a drive to your TiVo won't help unless it's prepared for use by the TiVo as described in Chapter 6. Before continuing, however, here is a list of what you may need to add a second drive:

◆ Number 10 Torx screwdriver

◆ Number 15 Torx screwdriver

◆ Disk drive jumpers

◆ Drive mounting bracket and screws, depending on your TiVo model

◆ Screws for mounting new drives, depending on your TiVo model

◆ Plastic/rubber washers for suppressing drive noise (optional)

◆ Two-connector IDE cable

◆ Y-power cable

Physically adding a second drive to a TiVo is easy. As mentioned earlier, all Series 1 machines come with room for mounting two drives, but they use a special bracket to physically attach each drive to the frame of the TiVo. Series 2 models are somewhat more complex because different models have different requirements. The AT&T TiVos don't require a special bracket and come predrilled so that you can easily add a second drive without special hardware other than four screws. The Series 2 machines manufactured by TiVo are designed to hold only a single drive, but they can be expanded to hold two drives through the use of the special brackets shown in Figure 3.5. All special brackets that you need for the Series 1 and Series 2 machines are readily available from the sources mentioned in the section "TiVo Hardware Supplies on the Net" later in this chapter. The folks at Weaknees.com make the black plastic bracket shown in Figure 3.5, which is the best bracket for adding a second drive to the Series 2 machine from TiVo. The metal ones shown in Figure 3.5 will also do the job, but they're just too clunky for me.

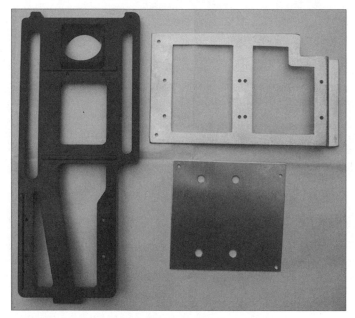

FIGURE 3.5 *Mounting brackets for Series 2 machines*

After you've prepared the second drive as described in Chapter 6, "Expanding Your TiVo's Storage Capacity," and attached it to the appropriate mounting bracket for your TiVo, make sure that you set the jumpers on the drive so that the new drive is identified as a slave drive. The jumper settings necessary to do so depend on the type of drive you are adding, and they are usually printed on the label at the top of the drive. If your drive didn't come with jumpers, you can purchase a pack of them at your local Radio Shack or other electronics store.

If you are adding a second drive to a Series 1 machine, you'll need to liberate the power cable from the TiVo frame. As shipped, the power connector for the second drive is tie-wrapped to the bottom of the TiVo case. Carefully clip the tie-wrap with a pair of diagonal cutters and free the power connector. You will need to remove the IDE cable from the plastic clip that holds it to the bottom of the TiVo case so that you can run it over the second drive in order to connect it. You will also need to flip the connector over so that you can attach it to the IDE connector on the new drive. Don't worry—you can easily connect it only one way, the plastic nub at the top of the connector fits into a similar notch on the IDE connector on the drive.

TiVo Series 2 models are somewhat more complex. The IDE cables shipped with any Series 2 machine have only a single connector and are, therefore, capable of being connected only to a single drive. In order to attach a second drive, you must acquire a new IDE cable with two drive connectors. Luckily, suitable IDE cables are usually provided when you purchase a new disk drive and also with most of the Series 2 drive brackets. If necessary, you can also obtain a two-connector IDE cable at most electronics or computer stores. You can then disconnect the original IDE cable in your TiVo and insert the new one in your TiVo. (Be careful when seating the cable on the motherboard—pushing too hard might crack the motherboard and kill your TiVo.) You can then attach each of the IDE connectors on the new IDE cable to each of the drives. Again, don't worry; they are easily connected only one way because the plastic nub on the top of each connector fits into a similar notch on the IDE connector on each drive.

Similarly, most Series 2 machines don't have a spare power connector for the disk drive. You may need to buy a Y-power cable, often referred to as a *splitter,* in order to run DC power to your second disk drive. These are also readily available at most electronics or computer stores. In order to use a splitter, remove the power connector from your existing disk drive and plug it into the male end of the splitter. You can then run one of the ends of the Y to your original disk drive and the other end to the new drive.

Most Series 2 TiVos will require one of the special brackets shown in Figure 3.5 to mount the new drive and remount your existing one. I prefer the black bracket shown in Figure 3.5 (from Weaknees.com) for adding drives to Series 2 machines from TiVo. This bracket is superior to any other bracket for the Series 2, because it comes with new power and IDE cables and is (optionally) available with fans to increase the cooling inside your TiVo. It also comes with clear, detailed instructions for installing the bracket.

Series 2 60-MB AT&T TiVos don't require a special bracket because there is already room for a second drive on the existing bracket. If you have one of these TiVos, you will need to buy screws to attach the drive to the bracket. You may also want to purchase some plastic or rubber washers to use when attaching the drive, in order to reduce noise from the drive that might otherwise be transmitted through the mounting bracket.

Power Considerations in TiVo Series 2 TiVos

The power supplies in Series 2 machines are less powerful than those in Series 1 machines, which is understandable because all Series 1 models were designed with two drives in mind, whereas all Series 2 machines ship with only one drive and (as explained in the previous section), some don't even provide space for a second drive without a special bracket. Some users who have put a second drive in Series 2 machines have reported power supply failures.

The point at which disk drives require the maximum amount of power is shortly after you turn them on. Much like starting a car requires an initial burst of power to get the engine started, disk drives require initial bursts of power to start the platters inside the drive rotating (known as *spinning up the drive*) and then launch the drive heads so that they can read and write data. If you are putting two disk drives in a Series 2 machine, you want to stagger the point at which the drives spin up so that they draw their initial bursts of power at slightly different times.

There are two easy ways to ensure that both your drives don't spin up and launch their heads at the same time. The first approach is to make sure you use two different disk drives, from different manufacturers, inside your TiVo. Because the drives are physically different, they will spin up and launch at slightly different times, so you shouldn't have a problem.

If you want to be almost totally safe, you can also buy (or make) a device that induces a delay between the times when the two drives spin up. Doing so will enable you to safely use two identical drives and will also protect you from the off chance that two drives from two different manufactures have exactly the same spin up and launch timing. The folks at Weaknees.com make such a device, which they call *PowerTrip*. This device is a small box with power connectors at each end, one male and one female. To connect it, you simply insert it between the power connector and your disk drive by plugging the power connector into the appropriate connector from the PowerTrip and plugging the PowerTrip's other connector into the disk drive. Doing so induces a slight initial delay between the times the PowerTrip receives supply power to the disk drive. Voila! No worries.

 NOTE

I am not an employee of Weaknees.com and am not being paid to promote their products. However, I do know a good thing when I see one.

Dealing with Modems

When you initially install a TiVo, you walk through a series of steps known as *Guided Setup*. The TiVo walks you through this process if it notices that it has no guide or connectivity information. TiVo's Guided Setup helps you configure your remote control and television to work together, collects information about your cable or satellite service, and lets you specify your zip code so that the TiVo can locate local numbers that you can use to obtain regular programming guide information and updates. During Guided Setup, the TiVo connects to TiVo HQ using an 800 number (in the United States) and uses the zip code information that you provided to download a list of local number that the TiVo can call for these updates.

The TiVo always requires a phone line in order to run through the Guided Setup process and, by default, requires continuous access to a phone line in order to make daily and occasional weekly calls for programming and guide updates. This section provides solutions to common problems encountered with modems and phone lines, and also discusses how people with broadband connections at home can add network connectivity to their TiVos and use the Internet to download programming and guide information.

TiVo | UPDATING TIVO CONFIGURATION INFORMATION

If you buy a used TiVo, change cable or satellite providers, or move to a different area, you will need to reconfigure your TiVo. This enables you to identify your new location to TiVo HQ so that the TiVo knows your cable provider in order to download guide information that reflects your cable or satellite provider, and doing so also causes the TiVo to attempt to find new (local) phone numbers to call for programming and guide updates. Getting weekly programming updates via a toll call can be quite expensive. You can redo the TiVo's Guided Setup process at any time by selecting this command from the TiVo's Restart or Reset System menu (select TiVo Central, Messages & Setup, Restart or Reset System, Guided Setup).

Getting a Phone Line for a TiVo Anywhere

Unless your house is more modern than mine, you have a limited number of telephone jacks available. If you're reasonably handy, you can easily run a new phone line from one of your existing phone jacks to somewhere near your TiVo. This may not always be feasible for aesthetic reasons and may not be physically possible if you're renting or own a condo that you don't feel like drilling holes through.

A great solution in these cases is a wireless phone jack. These jacks consist of two parts: a base unit that you plug into an electric outlet anywhere in your house and attach to an existing phone jack and an extension unit that you plug into an electric outlet near your TiVo and connect to the TiVo using the extension unit's phone jack. Voila! Instant phone connection at your TiVo without running any additional wires, tearing up or stapling phone cords to your baseboards, and drilling holes in your floor. Wireless phone jacks work by using your home's electric wiring to transmit and receive specially encoded phone signals, which they encrypt and decrypt between base and extension units.

Wireless phone jacks are available from many different manufacturers, including the General Electric Company, Phonex, and RCA. My favorites are the 920 and 930 units made by RCA, which offer built-in surge suppression. These and similar wireless phone jacks are available from your local electronics store or on eBay, where they typically go for about $25 to $30.

Dealing with a Blown Modem

The TiVo's modem and phone line are potentially weak links in your TiVo enjoyment. If the modem or phone line goes bad, your TiVo will run out of guide information in a week or so, at which point services such as WishLists and Season Passes will no longer work, and the TiVo will become much less fun than usual. Fixing a bad phone line is fairly easy to do, but fixing a blown modem can be a problem if you are not a hardcore electronics geek. You can send the TiVo off to be serviced, but—gasp—you will be without a TiVo for some period of time. If the modem is the problem, you may be tempted to buy a new TiVo. This is good news for TiVo, but expensive for you. It is especially bad news for you if you've purchased lifetime service for your TiVo, since lifetime service is tied to your TiVo's serial number, which is stored in an EPROM (Erasable Programmable Read-Only Memory) on your TiVo's motherboard and cannot be moved easily (or legally, probably) from one TiVo to another.

The modems in TiVo Series 1 machines often go bad, which is not all that surprising since they're a few years old now and are custom-built machines. Modem problems manifest themselves in different ways:

◆ Your TiVo has problems dialing and holding the phone line, but downloads work correctly if you dial for it and connect the phone line when you hear the remote modem answer.

◆ You repeatedly get a no dial tone message when trying to connect over a phone line that you know to be good—that is, the phone line works fine with a telephone connected to it.

If you're handy with a soldering iron, you can generally fix these problems by replacing and resoldering a few parts on your TiVo. You can diagnose the scope of the parts that you need by consulting the TiVo Repair Kit guide at http://www.9thtee.com/images/E-Legstivomodem.jpg. ElectricLegs, a well-known TiVo hacker, developed these tests and the parts kits associated with them. The parts kits are sold through 9thTee.com, an excellent vendor of a variety of TiVo-related parts and services, as I discuss in the section "TiVo Hardware Supplies on the Net" later in this chapter.

Actually repairing the modem in your TiVo when possible requires some ability to use and control a soldering iron. If you aren't a wizard with a soldering iron or simply aren't willing to take the chance that your repair efforts might increase the amount of damage to your TiVo, you can pay to have the repairs done or find an alternative solution.

Getting someone to attempt to repair your modem is usually successful, but there are no guarantees that the problem is actually fixable. Sometimes things just break, and stay that way. You'll also be without your TiVo for some period of time, which can be hard to deal with. As I explain in the next few sections, there are quick and easy alternatives to repairing your modem—use an external modem or use an Internet connection to download programming and guide information.

Using External Modems with the TiVo

Before PCs became the center of most people's computing universe and the price of internal modems dropped to under $10, people commonly bought external modems. Because modems were external to a computer system, they didn't depend on the bus architecture or characteristics of a given computer and could, therefore, be used with any computer system. External modems are largely a thing of the past, but they have special value for TiVo owners whose internal modems have gone bad. Picking up an inexpensive external modem will enable you to get your TiVo up and running within minutes, and usually for less than $15 (search eBay for

External modem). If you already have an old modem in a drawer in your basement, you can fix your TiVo for free. The default speed of the TiVo's built-in modem is 33,600 baud (usually referred to as a "33.6" modem), but you can use any external modem as long as it is 9600 baud or better.

To use an external modem rather than your TiVo's internal modem, your TiVo needs to be running system software Version 3.0 or greater. You'll also need the following:

◆ External modem, preferably 33.6 or better

◆ Power supply for the external modem

◆ 25-pin-male to 9-pin-female serial adapter

◆ ¹/₈-inch DSS to 9-pin male serial cable

Most external modems have old-style, 25-pin-female serial connectors. You will need the 25-pin-male to 9-pin-female adapter to attach the external modem to the ¹/₈-inch serial cable that you should have received with your TiVo. If you don't have this cable, you can buy one from one of the sources listed in the section "TiVo Hardware Supplies on the Net" later in this chapter, or you can make one as described in the section "Attaching a Terminal Emulator or Serial Console" earlier in this chapter. I've used older US Robotics Sportster modems to repair various friends' TiVos with absolutely no problems.

Many external modems provide some external configuration settings through DIP switches, which are a row of numbered up and down switches that should be visible on the back of the modem. Different modems support different settings, but the settings for a 3.6 US Robotics Sportster in Table 3.5 provide a good idea of the configuration settings that your modem may require.

Table 3.5 DIP Switch Settings on an External Modem

DIP Switch	Position	Meaning
1	DOWN	DTR Ready Override
2	UP	Verbal Result Codes
3	DOWN	Display Result Codes
4	UP	Echo Offline Commands
5	DOWN	Auto Answer Off
6	UP	Carrier Detect Normal
7	UP	Load NVRAM Defaults
8	DOWN	Smart Mode

You will also need to configure your modem to disable DTR, RTS, and flow control. On most Hayes-compatible modems, you can do so by sending the following two sequences of characters (strings, in programmer-speak) to the modem from your computer by using a terminal emulator (and null-modem cable) before you attach it to your TiVo:

```
AT&D0&H0&I0&R1&W0
AT&D0&H0&I0&R1&W1
```

These strings disable DTR, RTS, and flow control and write this configuration to two different saved configuration profiles in the nonvolatile random access memory (NVRAM) where your modem stores its default configuration information. The entries in these strings have the following meanings:

- ◆ AT. Get the attention of the modem, telling it that you are going to be sending it commands.
- ◆ &D0 (D zero). Ignore DTR.
- ◆ &H0 (H zero). Disable CTS and Xon/Xoff flow control.
- ◆ &I0 (I zero). Disable RX flow control.
- ◆ &R1 (R one). Ignore RTS.
- ◆ &W*n*. Writes the configuration information to profile *n*. Profile 0 is usually used when your modem initially powers on, but saving it to both profiles can't hurt.

Some modems do not implement the &H and &I commands correctly. If you receive errors when you enter the previous strings in your terminal emulator, try removing the &H0 and &I0 commands from the previous strings and entering the AT&K0 (K zero) command on a separate line, which disables all flow control on many modems. You can then execute the AT&W0 and AT&W1 commands to save the update profile information.

Finally, if your modem's speaker is active, you'll hear the classic modem song as your modem negotiates communication speeds and until it establishes a connection. To keep things quiet on most modems, add the &M0 (M zero) command to the previous strings to turn off the speaker.

TIP

For a complete list of the Hayes modem commands used by most modems, see Web sites such as http://readthetruth.com/modems.htm or http://www.lisa.univ-paris12.fr/Electronik/Hayes.htm. The Hayes command set is named after an early pioneer in reliable, affordable modems that were subsequently cloned by hundreds of other vendors (who also adopted the command set, which, therefore, became a standard).

[TiVo] CORRECT SETTINGS IN AN EXTERNAL MODEM

If your modem is old or you experience frequent power failures, you may find that your modem may forget its settings. If you have a network connection to your TiVo and aren't using the serial line as a console, you can leave the external modem connected to your TiVo and add a command like the following to the end of the **/etc/rc.d/rc.sysinit** file, which is executed each time your TiVo reboots. On a Series 1 machine, add this command:

```
echo "AT&D0&H0&I0&R1&W0" > /dev/ttyS3
```

On a Series 2 machine, add this command:

```
echo "AT&D0&H0&I0&R1&W0" > /dev/ttyS2
```

Both these commands will write the correct profile settings for your modem and cause it to resave them. Your modem should be reset correctly each time your TiVo reboots for one reason or another.

Of course, if you had to modify the strings you used to get your modem to work, make sure you enter the values your modem required—don't just retype these strings and expect it to work!

After you make the specified settings, detach the modem from your PC and null-modem cable. You can then attach the 25-to-9 adapter to the modem's serial connector, attach the TiVo's serial cable to the 9-pin connector, and plug the $1/8$-inch jack into the Serial Cntrl Out connector on the back of your TiVo.

The final step for using an external modem with your TiVo is to set your Dial Prefix so that the TiVo knows to communicate via the serial port and uses the correct speed for the modem you're using. The Dial Prefix command is found in different places in the TiVo menus depending on the version of the TiVo software you are running. For TiVo 3.x and earlier systems, the Dial Prefix is located in the Change Dial Options menu (select TiVo Central, Messages and Setup, Recorder & Phone Setup, Phone Connection, Change Dial Options). For TiVo 4.x systems, an equivalent Set Dial Prefix command is located in the Phone Dialing Options screen (TiVo Central, Messages and Setup, Settings, Phone & Network Settings, Edit Phone or Network Settings, Phone Dialing Options).

Once you've located the Dial Prefix or Set Dial Prefix command, use one of the settings in Table 3.6 to tell the TiVo to use PPP over the serial port at the specified speed to make your daily calls. Make sure you do not try to use a speed setting that is faster than the maximum speed of your modem—that simply won't work.

Table 3.6 Dialing Prefixes for Different Modem Speeds

Modem Speed	Dial Prefix
9600	,#396
19,200	,#319
38,400	,#338
57,600	,#357

TIP

To get the comma, press Pause on your TiVo remote. To get the hash mark, press Enter on your TiVo remote.

At this point, you should be able to execute the Make a Test Call command from the same menu, and the call should succeed! If it does, congratulations! You now have another notch in your TiVo hacking belt! If not, check the call log in **/var/log/Otclient** on the TiVo to see if an error was reported. If the end of the log file does not show an error message, try setting the Dial Prefix to use a slower call speed. On my favorite US Robotics Sportster modems, I typically use the 19,200 communication speed simply because the phone lines in my area have a fair amount of noise.

Networking Your TiVo

You may want to put your TiVo on your home network for a variety of reasons, including the following:

- ◆ Because it's there.
- ◆ To more easily transfer files of one sort or another to and from your TiVo.
- ◆ To more easily connect to the TiVo from any system in your house (not just one with a serial connection to the TiVo).
- ◆ To use TiVoWeb to control your TiVo from a browser on any other machine on your home network.
- ◆ To use the network for obtaining programming and guide data instead of a much slower modem that requires a phone line.

Any and all of these reasons are great for connecting your TiVo to your home network, but the last one is probably the most pragmatic. Modems are reliable but slow and obviously require access to a phone line. If you have your TiVo on your home network and your home network has a constant connection to the Internet (as with cable or DSL broadband connections), you can bypass using the modem all together by configuring your TiVo to make your daily and weekly calls over the network. See the section "Using the Network to Make Daily Calls" later in this chapter for specific information on the settings necessary to use a network rather than a modem for these calls.

As you might expect, because of fundamental hardware differences, different models of TiVos are networked in different ways. Series 1 are networked through a diagnostic port that is located on the Series 1 TiVo motherboard. Series 2 machines are networked by using wired or wireless USB adapters.

Networking 101

Like most modern computer systems, TiVos can communicate with other systems and devices over a type of network called *Ethernet,* using the TCP/IP (Transmission Control Protocol/Internet Protocol) and UDP (Universal Data Packet) protocols. Ethernet was invented by Xerox Corporation at Xerox PARC (Palo Alto Research Center) in the early 1970s. Like most things they've invented—except for the photocopier—Xerox failed to make money from Ethernet, which was actually commercialized by many companies (like 3COM, which was founded by the inventor of Ethernet networking, Bob Metcalf, who knew a good thing when he invented it).

Until a few decades ago, the Internet was a fairly techie term, used only by people whose employers or academic experience offered connectivity to the Internet or its predecessor, the Arpanet. The creation and popular explosion of the World Wide Web and the advent of e-mail as a replacement for phone calls changed all that; suddenly there was a reason for people to want (or perhaps even need) access to the Internet.

Early home Internet connectivity was primarily done through dialup connections that emulated TCP/IP connections over dialup lines using protocols such as SLIP (Serial Line Internet Protocol), CLSIP (Compressed SLIP), or PPP (Point-To-Point Protocol). Unless you were a serious computer geek, developer, or researcher, a home network was somewhat rare, but the advent of broadband access to the Internet through cable and telephone providers changed all that. A few years ago, my home network was connected to the Internet through a Linux system that I'd set up as an on-demand SLIP gateway that also regularly dialed out to my ISP, connected using command scripts, and retrieved my mail to a local mail server. Hardly nerdy at all. Today, like many people, I have always-on connectivity to the Internet through a $100 Linksys gateway that connects all the machines on my home network to the Internet via my cable modem.

The point of this trip down memory lane is that home networks are becoming more common but that many people have never needed to set one up. If you use a single PC, Mac, or workstation as your sole home machine, a straight connection to a cable or DSL modem works just fine. However, the instant you want to enable multiple machines to communicate over a home network, you may encounter unfamiliar terms like hubs, switches, 10-BaseT, RJ45, crossover-cables, uplink ports, packets, gateways, routers, Cat5, and a variety of others that pass for popular nouns among nerdier users. This section provides a quick overview of these terms.

It tells you how to set up a trivial home network and makes you comfortable with the network-related terms that are used throughout this book. For more detailed information, consult any of the hundreds of books available on home networking.

The basic element of a modern network connection is a standard Ethernet cable, which is just a length of multistrand cable with connectors on either end that enable you to connect a network card in your personal computer (or whatever type) to another network device. The most common connectors used today are plastic connectors known as RJ-45 connectors, which are transparent plastic jacks that look like a fatter version of standard telephone cable connectors. Ethernet cables that use these connectors are often known as 10-BaseT, 100-BaseT, or even 1000-BaseT, where the numeric portion of the name indicates the speed of your network—the cables are the same. 1000-BaseT is more commonly known as gigabit Ethernet, and if you actually use gigabit Ethernet in your house, I'm proud to know you. 10/100 (that is, 10 megabit or 100 megabit) Ethernet is the standard nowadays. If you run across the term Cat5 when buying or researching Ethernet cables, that term stands for Category 5 cabling, which has to do with shielding that insulates the cable from outside electromagnetic influence—and also with not giving off poisonous smoke if the plastic exterior of the cable burns off, which isn't a big concern for most home networks; if your house is on fire, you probably have bigger worries than inhaling the smoke from your smoldering Ethernet cables.

 NOTE

As another historical note, you may also encounter the term 10-Base2 when researching network cards. This is an older type of 10-megabit Ethernet cabling that uses shielded BNC (Bayonet Neill-Concelman, or Baby N Connector) cables. Unless you are using some really old Ethernet cards or need to connect older workstations to your home network, you should stay away from these cards unless they also have 10/100 BaseT connectors and, in most cases, even then since these cards typically offer only 10 megabit network communication speeds.

The best way to visualize the Internet or any Ethernet network is as an extremely long piece of cable to which some huge number of computers and network devices are attached. In the simplest case, you must use a device called a *hub, switch,* or *router* to attach multiple machines to an Ethernet. A *hub* is a device with multiple incoming connectors for attaching the Ethernet cables from different machines, with a single output connector that attaches it to another Ethernet device such as a cable modem, another hub, or a switch, router, or gateway. Network communications on any incoming port of the hub are broadcast to all other devices on the hub and are also forwarded through the outgoing connection. *Switches* are much like hubs on steroids because they keep track of how network connections between different machines are made and reserve dedicated internal circuitry for established connections. Switches are, therefore, both typically faster and more expensive than hubs because they do more.

Gateways and *routers* are similar to hubs and switches, but are designed to provide connectivity between different networks. If a machine that you are trying to connect to isn't immediately found on your local network, the request is forwarded through your gateway, which then sends it on. Network communication is done using discrete units of information that are known as *packets*. Packets contain the IP (Internet Protocol) address of the host that they are trying to contact. IP addresses are in the form of NNN.NNN.NNN.NNN, and are the network equivalent of a post office box, uniquely identifying a specific machine. Packets for an unknown local host are sent through your gateway. Routers are expensive, sophisticated pieces of hardware that direct network communication between multiple networks, translate packets between different network communication protocols, and limit network traffic to relevant networks so that your request to retrieve a file from a machine in your son's bedroom isn't broadcast to every machine on the Internet.

The most common way to connect machines on a home network is to use a hub or home gateway that is then connected to your cable or DSL modem. The difference between these is that a hub simply forwards packets through its outgoing connector (known as an *uplink port* because it links the network connections on that device with those on another and is, therefore, wired differently). A home gateway may convert internal network addresses to addresses that are compatible with the outside world before sending the information on through its outgoing or uplink connector. If you're using a hub to connect your home network to your cable or DSL modem, each machine on your home network would require an IP address that is unique on the Internet. This can be expensive, since most ISPs charge money for each unique host that can be connected to the Internet from your home at any given time. Home gateways provide a way around this because they enable your home network to use a special type of IP addresses known as non-routable IP addresses to assign unique internal network addresses. The gateway then internally translates these to appropriate external addresses if you're trying to connect to a machine on the Internet. The most common non-routable IP addresses are in the form of 192.168.*X.Y*, where *X* and *Y* are specific to how you've set up your network.

TIP

If you're really interested, you can get more information about non-routable IP addresses and address translation in the Internet RFCs (Request for Comment) that defined them, 1597 and 1918. Use your favorite Internet search engine to find relevant information, or check out links such as http://www.safety.net/sum1597.html and http://www.howstuffworks.com/nat2.htm.

IP addresses are assigned to computer systems in two basic ways, either statically or dynamically. *Static addresses* are addresses unique to your home network that are always assigned to a particular machine. *Dynamic addresses* are addresses that are automatically assigned to a computer system or network device when you turn it on. Most ISPs use dynamic addresses because only a limited number of IP addresses are available on the Internet. Using dynamic IP addresses enables your ISP to recycle and reassign IP addresses as people turn their machines off and on. Most dynamic IP addresses nowadays are assigned using a protocol called DHCP (Dynamic Host Control Protocol), which fills out the network information for your system when it activates its network interface, including things like the IP address of a gateway system and the IP addresses of DNS (Distributed Name Service) servers that translate between hostnames and the IP addresses that they correspond to.

In order to use static addresses on your home network, you simply assign each machine a unique, non-routable IP address from a given family of non-routable IP addresses. For example, most of my home machines have static addresses in the form of 192.168.6.Y. Since I use a home gateway, I've configured it to do address translation (more specifically known as NAT, or Native Address Translation) to correctly translate between these addresses and the external IP address of my home gateway box.

If you want to use Dynamic IP addresses on a home network, one of the machines on your home network must be running a DHCP server. Most home gateways, such as those from DLink or Linksys, have built-in DHCP servers that you simply configure to hand out IP addresses from a specific range of addresses (192.168.6.2 through 192.168.6.253, in my case). Once you activate address translation on your home gateway, your gateway will route packets appropriately. Remember that your home gateway is probably getting its IP address by contacting your ISP's DHCP server, whereas hosts on your internal network will get their IP addresses from your DHCP server. Don't set up hosts on an internal network to contact your ISP's DHCP server unless you have only a single machine on your home network or want every one of your machines to be visible on the Internet. (An obvious security problem because anyone who knows the address can get to your machine. I'm totally ignoring network security here; that topic deserves its own book or three, which you can get from your local bookstore.)

To return to the subject of this particular book (TiVos, remember?), TiVos are usually configured to obtain IP addresses via DHCP. If you're using a Series 1 machine, you can assign it a static address when you install the network-related software, as I explain in the next section. A bit more work is involved in convincing Series 2 models to use a static IP address, since Series 2 TiVos running versions 3.X and later of the TiVo software provide USB network support out of the box. I tend to use DHCP for systems such as the TiVos because it's simply easier, though figuring out the IP address assigned to your TiVo can be tricky if you haven't hacked it to provide a command prompt. Figuring out your TiVo's dynamic IP address is discussed later in this chapter in the debugging portion of the section "Using the Network to Make Daily and Weekly Calls."

The overview information in this section should have familiarized you with basic home networking terms and concepts. If you have a Series2 machine and have purchased TiVo's Home Media Option (discussed later in this book), TiVo provides a good overview for setting up a small home network on the TiVo HQ Web site at http://www.tivo.com/4.9.8.asp. As you might expect, the Internet is knee-deep in Web sites that provide more general information about home networking. For truly detailed information about setting up and configuring a home network on a specific type of machine and operating system, see any of the hundreds of books on those topics at your local bookstore.

Networking Series 1 TiVos

If you've hacked into a TiVo and examined the **/etc/rc.d/rc.sysinit** startup script, you know that TiVos have been networked at TiVo headquarters from day one. No big surprise—they are Linux boxes, after all. However, this capability was denied the rest of us until a pioneering effort by Andrew Tridgell (Tridge) developed the original network adapter for the TiVos that enabled people to use certain types of older PC-style ISA networking cards to put their TiVos on the network. This effort was especially groundbreaking because TiVos don't have an ISA bus, so the device worked by adding a single ISA bus slot to the TiVo motherboard through the clever use of a diagnostic edge connector that the board provided. You could then put a standard NE2000 or compatible ISA network card in this slot, load a few drivers that Tridge provided, execute standard Linux IP configuration commands, and suddenly your TiVo was wired.

Today, all of the commonly-encountered Ethernet solutions for Series 1 models are from 9thTee.com, which has partnered with Tridge and a company called *SiliconDust.com* to bring you easy-to-install, easy-to-use cards that help you get your Series 1 machines up on your home network. Beyond just the hardware, all of these cards share a common install program called ***nic_install***, which is available from the 9thTee.com site in ISO format and is also provided on the TiVo Series 1 sections of the TiVo boot disk that accompanies this book. More about that later. First, let's discuss the hardware.

 NOTE

Just to be perfectly clear, the networking cards discussed in this section can be used only with Series 1 stand-alone and DirecTiVos. They cannot be used with Series 2 machines, which I discuss in the next section.

Tridge's original adapter design was cleaned up and commercialized thanks to the TiVo fanatics at 9thTee.com, who named their version the TiVoNET board. TiVoNET boards are no longer being manufactured, though they still work fine—if you find one on eBay and also buy a compatible ISA network card. Since the original TiVoNET cards, two other network adapters have been developed and released (developed by the folks at SiliconDust.com and available from 9thTee) that are far easier to configure, install, and use. These are the TurboNet and Air-Net cards.

Figure 3.6 shows a TurboNet network card for the Series 1. Like all Series 1 network adapters, this one also fits onto the diagnostic port of the Series 1 motherboard. TurboNet cards have a built-in RJ-45 Ethernet connector and don't require that you purchase a separate network adapter. TurboNet cards are easy to install and similarly easy to configure and use, but still require that you run a 10-BaseT Ethernet cable to your TiVo from a hub or switch on your home network.

FIGURE 3.6 *A TurboNet network adapter for Series 1 TiVos*

Shown in Figure 3.7, AirNet cards are the height of TiVo Series 1 network evolution. AirNet cards provide a PCMCIA adapter that enables you to use a standard laptop wireless Ethernet card to put your Series 1 machine on your home network as long as the wireless PCMCIA card uses the Intercil Prism2 or Prism2.5 chipset, which includes most of the 802.11b cards on the market. AirNet cards will not work with Cisco 802.11b cards because Cisco cards use their own MAC chipset. It will also not work with 802.11b cards from Dell, because these are actually made by Cisco.

FIGURE 3.7 *An AirNet network adapter for Series 1 machines*

 NOTE

AirNet cards for DirecTiVos are slightly different than AirNet cards for stand-alone Series 1 TiVos. Make sure that you buy the right one. Also, although Figure 1 shows a wireless PCMCIA Ethernet card in the AirNet card, you can also buy them without the PCMCIA card and add your own from the list in Table 3.7.

Table 3.7 shows some inexpensive and common PCMCIA 802.11b cards that use the Prism2 chipset, and should therefore work fine with an AirNet card.

Table 3.7 Common Prism2 PCMCIA Cards Compatible with AirNet

Manufacturer	Model	Antenna
Addtron	AWP-100	No
Addtron	AWP-101	No
AsantÃ©	AL1011	No
Belkin	F5D6020	No
Compaq	WL100	No
CellVisionWLC-100	No	
Demarc	Relia-Wave	No
D-Link	DW-655H	No
D-Link	DWL-650	No
LinkSys	WPC11	No
Proxim	RangeLAN-DS 8434-05	Yes
Proxim	RangeLAN-DS 8433-05	No
SMC	SMC2532W-B	No
SMC	SMC2632W	No
Teletronics	WL-11000	Yes
Zcomax	XI-300	Yes
Zcomax	XI-300B	No
Zcomax	ZFE-300	No
Zcomax	XI-325	Yes
Zcomax	XI-325H	Yes
Zcomax	XI-325H1	Yes
ZoomAir	4105	Yes

Whenever possible, consider buying a PCMCIA card with an antenna, or at least with the capability of attaching one. Although an antenna costs extra, it can enable you to maximize the distance between your TiVo and your wireless access point.

Regardless of which Series 1 network card you buy, installing it in your TiVo is simple. After you've installed it, you can install the necessary software on your TiVo drive by removing it from your TiVo and putting it in your PC, as described in the section "Working with TiVo Disk Drives" earlier in this chapter.

NOTE

The software required for installing a TurboNet Card or AirNet card in your TiVo must be downloaded as an ISO image from 9thTee.com or SiliconDust.com. One URL for this software is http://www.silicondust.com/terms_of_use.html. You must burn a CD of this software in order to boot your PC from it. Burning CDs from ISO images on different types of home computer systems is explained later in this book.

After you've burned a CD of the installation software and installed the TiVo drive in your PC, use the following procedure to install the software for your TiVoNET, TurboNet, or AirNet card:

1. Run the network interface card (NIC) installation command by executing the **/nic_install/nic_install** command, followed by the name of the network card that you want to install, which is either tivonet, turbonet, or airnet. For example, to install the drivers and support software for an airnet card, execute the following command:

```
/nic_install/nic_install
```

2. The installation program then probes your system, locates your TiVo drive, and analyzes its structure, as shown in the following output:

```
TiVo TurboNet/AirNet Installation - 20020907
Copyright 2002 Silicondust Engineering Ltd. All rights reserved.
Detecting TiVo hard drive...
    Trying /dev/hdb...
            Not a tivo drive.
    Trying /dev/hdc...
            Unable to open.
    Trying /dev/hdd...
            kernel=/dev/hdaFigure 3.
            root=/dev/hda4 .
    Found TiVo hard drive - /dev/hdd (Secondary Slave).
Detecting TiVo partitions...
    Active kernel partition = /dev/hddFigure 3.
    Inactive kernel partition = /dev/hdd6.
    Active root partition = /dev/hdd4.
    Inactive root partition = /dev/hdd7.
    Var partition = /dev/hdd9.
Determining software version...
```

```
Partition table:
    0: /dev/hdd start=    933952 length=  1048576
    1: /dev/hdd start=   1982528 length= 56650752
    2: /dev/hdd start=  58895488 length=     8192
    3: /dev/hdd start=  58903680 length= 97397760
Zone table:
    0: inode    size=1
    1: stream   size=18
    2: file     size=66
    3: stream   size=34
            Philips SA running .0-01-1-000
```

3. After the script completes its probe of the system, it checks to see whether the system boots with an initial RAM disk and prompts you to disable it, which must be done in order to correctly install the drivers for your network card. (For more information about initial RAM disks (aka initrds), see the Chapter 9, "The TiVo Startup Process.") The output of this section looks like the following:

```
Scanning for initrd...
    Initrd found to be active
Initrd must be disabled to install the airnet drivers
Ok to disable [y/n]?
```

4. Enter **y** and press Enter (Return) to continue the installation process. At this point, the installation script mounts the partitions that it needs to modify on your TiVo disk, installs the drivers, and prompts you to supply any customizations that you want to make to the card's network configuration. (This example is from an AirNet card installation; your options will differ if you are installing a TurboNet or TiVoNET card.) Output from this section looks like the following:

```
Disabling initrd...
    Complete.
Mounting partitions...
    Root successfully mounted.
    Var successfully mounted.
Checking network script...
    Complete.
Current/New Configuration:
    timing setting = normal
    SSID           = wlan
    encryption     = none
    key            =
```

```
    ip address    = dhcp
    ip subnet mask = dhcp
    ip gateway    = dhcp
    debug level   = off
    daily call    = network
Options
    1: Change timing setting
    2: Change SSID
    3: Change encryption
    4: Change IP address/gateway
    5: Change debug logging option
    6: Change daily call option
    7: Dump log file
    0: Apply and exit
[0..7]?
```

 NOTE

The options displayed in this list are dependent on the type of network card that you are installing. The examples in this section are taken from an AirNet installation. TivoNET and TurboNet installations are very similar—the only difference is the list of options available and the numbers that you have to type to select them.

5. To change the options from this list, enter the number of the option and press Enter (Return). The current setting for the specified variable is displayed, followed by a prompt that enables you to specify a new value, as in the following example:

```
[0..7]? 2
SSID is currently set to "wlan".
New SSID? wvh
```

 NOTE

The SSID value is specific to the AirNet card and identifies the name of the wireless network you want to join. This option applies only when you're using a wireless network and will not be listed if you are installing a TiVoNET or Turbonet card.

TIP

The most common values that you may want to consider changing from this list are number 4, the card's IP address and associate gateway information. As shown in the following example, all TiVoNET, TurboNet, and Airnet cards are initially configured to obtain dynamic IP address information from a Dynamic Host Control Protocol (DHCP) server. Installing the TiVoNET/TurboNet/AirNet server software to use DHCP will automatically start a DHCP client on your TiVo. You will want to change these options if you are not running a DHCP server on your home network or if you simply want to assign a single, well-known address to your TiVo.

6. If you want to manually assign an IP address to your network card, enter **4**, and specify an IP address that is compatible with your network, a subnet mask used to mask bits in that address, and the address of your network's gateway to external IP addresses (required for calling out over the network), as in the following example:

```
[0..7]? 4
IP address is currently set to "dhcp".
Subnet mask is currently set to "dhcp".
Gateway address is currently set to "dhcp".
New IP address [x.x.x.x dhcp]? 192.168.1.30
New Subnet mask [x.x.x.x dhcp]? 255.255.255.0
New Gateway address [x.x.x.x dhcp]? 192.168.1.1
Current/New Configuration:
     timing setting = normal
     SSID           = wvh
     encryption     = none
     key            =
     ip address     = 192.168.1.30
     ip subnet mask = 255.255.255.0
     ip gateway     = 192.168.1.1
     debug level    = off
     daily call     = network
Options
     1: Change timing setting
     2: Change SSID
     3: Change encryption
     4: Change IP address/gateway
     5: Change debug logging option
     6: Change daily call option
     7: Dump log file
     0: Apply and exit
```

7. Consider changing the Daily call option. In most cases, you will want the TiVo's daily call to be made over the network unless you do not have an always-on connection to the Internet. This is the default value when installing a TivoNET, TurboNet, or Air-Net card. If you have a broadband connection to the Internet through a system that is not always on, change the Daily call option to dialup, which will cause your TiVo to continue to use the modem for its daily calls.

8. When you finish changing all the options you want to change, enter **0** and press Return to cause the nic_install program to actually write its changes to your TiVo configuration and startup file, as in the following example:

```
[0..7]? 0
Copying files...
    Complete.
Verifying route executable...
     Complete.
Writing network script...
    Complete.
Updating startup script...
    Complete.
Clear the log file on the tivo [y/n]? n
Unmounting partitions...
    Root successfully unmounted.
    Var successfully unmounted.
Installation Complete.
```

 TIP

If you see the message " after the "`Updating startup scripts`" entry and the nic_install program displays a message similar to "`Error--Unable to find complete string`", this means that your /etc/rc.d/rc.sysinit script probably doesn't contain the following string:

echo **"rc.sysinit is complete"**

The nic_install program looks for this line in order to determine where to insert the network startup commands. If this line is not present, usually you have already modified your `/etc/rc.d/rc.sysint` script. To enable the nic_install program to complete successfully, you must reinsert this command as the last line of your **/etc/rc.d/rc.sysinit** file.

9. Congratulations! You're a few seconds from having your TiVo on the network! Shut down your PC, remove your TiVo hard drive, reset the jumpers (if necessary), and put the drive back in your TiVo. The next time you turn it on, your TiVo should be available on your network. The nic_install program installs both the TiVo FTP daemon and a lite version of the Telnet daemon so that you can, respectively, transfer files to and from the remote machine and log in on the remote machine over the network. Neither the TiVo FTP daemon nor Telnet require authentication, so be careful about who has access to your network and thus your TiVo. A malicious and knowledgeable person on your network could easily delete all or some of the TiVo filesystem, which would probably force you to reinstall the TiVo from backups.

 NOTE

Although the instructions in this section refer to the CD included with this book, you can also download an ISO image of the Series 1 network installation software CD directly from the SilconDust.com Web site and burn it yourself, if you want. The URL for the latest CD is http://www.9thtee.com/nic_cd_20030223.iso.

Networking TiVos Series 2 machines

Thanks to TiVo, its desire to modernize its products, and the march of time in general, Series 2 TiVos are much easier to network than Series 1 machines. Series 2 models provide USB ports that enable you to quickly and easily attach a variety of USB adapters to your TiVo system. Figure 3.8 shows a sample wired USB adapter (left) and wireless USB adapter (right).

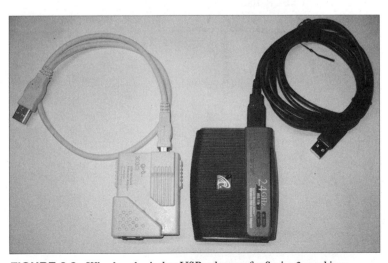

FIGURE 3.8 *Wired and wireless USB adapters for Series 2 machines*

Table 3.8 shows a list of USB Ethernet adapters that are compatible with the Series 2 machines. (A big thanks to the folks on the AVS Forum for compiling the genesis of this list.)

Table 3.8 Wired USB Ethernet Adapters Compatible with Series 2 Machines

Manufacturer	Model
3Com	3C460B
ABOCOM	USB 10/100 Fast Ethernet
ABOCOM	USB HPNA/Ethernet
Accton	USB 10/100 Ethernet Adapter
Accton	SpeedStream USB 10/100 Ethernet
ADMtek	ADM8511 Pegasus II USB Ethernet
ADMtek	AN986 Pegasus USB Ethernet (eval. board)
Allied Telesyn	AT-USB100
Belkin	F5D5050
Billionton	USB-100
Billionton	USBE-100
Billionton	USBEL-100
Billionton	USBLP-100
Compaq	iPAQ Networking 10/100 USB
Corega	FEter USB-TX
D-Link	DSB-650
D-Link	DSB-650TX
D-Link	DUB-E100
Elsa	Micolink USB2Ethernet
Hawking	UF100 10/100 Ethernet
Hawking	UF200 10/100 Ethernet
IO DATA	USB ET/TX

Manufacturer	Model
IO DATA	USB ET/TX-S
Kingston	KNU101TX Ethernet
LANEED	USB Ethernet LD-USB/T
LANEED	USB Ethernet LD-USB/TX
Linksys	USB100M
Linksys	USB200M
Linksys	USB100TX
Linksys	USB10TX
MELCO	BUFFALO LUA2-TX
MELCO	BUFFALO LUA-TX
Microsoft	MN-110
NetGear	FA101
NetGear	FA120
Siemens	SS1001
SmartBridges	SmartNIC 2 PnP Adapter
SMC	202 USB Ethernet
SMC	SMC2208
SOHOware	NUB100 Ethernet

Of course, wireless USB adapters are also available, as shown at the right of Figure 3.8. Table 3.9 shows a list of wireless USB Ethernet adapters that are compatible with Series 2 TiVos. This table also lists the Series 2 models on which each adapter is known to work. Wireless USB adapters are slightly more sensitive to differences in the USB hardware provided on various models of TiVos. If you want to put your TiVo on your network and are explicitly buying a wireless USB adapter for that purpose, I'd strongly suggest that you use a wireless USB adapter that is known to work. If you already have other wireless USB adapters available and want to try them out, do so by all means, and let me know if you discover others that work. I have been able to identify quite a few that do not work, largely the cheap, brand-X wireless adapters that I can't seem to resist trying.

Table 3.9 Wireless USB Ethernet Adapters Compatible with the Series 2

Manufacturer	Model	Known to Work On
Belkin	F5D6050	All Series 2 models
D-Link	DWL-120 V.A	SVR-3000, TCD130040, TCD140060
D-Link	DWL-120 V.D	TCD230040, TCD240040
D-Link	DWL-120 V.E	All Series 2 models
Hawking	WU250	TCD230040, TCD240040
Linksys	WUSB11 V2.6	All Series 2 models
Linksys	WUSB12	TCD230040, TCD240040
Microsoft	MN-510	TCD230040, TCD240040
NetGear	MA101 V.A	SVR-3000, TCD130040, TCD140060
NetGear	MA101 V.B	All Series 2 models
SMC	2662W V.2	All Series 2 models

The version of the TiVo software that your Series 2 is running is critical to whether your TiVo will automatically recognize and configure the network adapter.

Drivers for the USB network adapters listed in the previous two tables are included with TiVo software Versions 3.0 and greater for Series 2 models. If you are only interested in getting programming and guide updates over your home network, putting Series 2 machines running these software versions on your network is trivial. To do so, simply turn off the TiVo and attach your wired or wireless USB Ethernet adapter. If you're using a wired USB Ethernet adapter, make sure that it's correctly connected to your home network and that you're running a DHCP server, as explained earlier in this chapter in the section "Networking 101."

 TIP

Wireless USB adapters are officially supported only under TiVo software version 4.0, though I have not had problems using them with Series 2 TiVos running version 3.x of the TiVo software. If you encounter problems using a wireless USB adapter under earlier versions of the TiVo OS, try using a wired USB adapter or upgrade the version of the TiVo OS that you are running.

Next, power up the TiVo again. The Series 2 should recognize your USB adapter, though it won't say anything about it unless you're running TiVo software version 4.x. If you're running

TiVo software version 4.x, go into the TCP/IP Settings or Wireless Settings menus (available through TiVo Central, Messages and Setup, Settings, Phone & Network Settings, Edit Phone or Network Settings) to verify that your network adapter was detected. You should then try to switch your TiVo to using the network for its daily and weekly calls, as described in the next section. This is the easiest way to test that both the TiVo and your network are configured correctly. If your goal is to be able to use the network to connect and transfer files to your Series 2 model, you'll need to read the first section of Chapter 7, "Connecting the Universe to Your TiVo," which discusses getting a command prompt on Series 2 systems so that you can install network-related software such as Telnet and FTP. Chapter 7 also discusses the specific TiVo software that provides network support in the TiVo's Linux operating system, in case you're working with a version of the TiVo software older than 3.0.

Using the Network to Make Daily Calls

Once you've put your Series 1 or Series 2 machine on your home network, you can easily configure your TiVo to use the network to make its daily and weekly calls over the network. This enables your TiVo to receive programming and guide data updates without requiring access to a phone line. Unless you're using an AirNet card on a Series 1 or a wireless USB adapter on a Series 2, you'll still need access to an Ethernet cable connected to your home network, but, hey, progress is progress. Even a wireless Ethernet connector is far faster than a phone line, and wire connectors are tremendously faster.

TIP

Configuring your TiVo to be able to receive programming and guide updates over the network is not the same thing as putting your TiVo on the network so that you can log into it and transfer files back and forth. If you're using a TurboNet or AirNet card on a Series 1 machine, the program that installs and configures your system also gives you FTP and Telnet access for free—thanks, SiliconDust! However, getting FTP and Telnet access on Series 2 machines is a totally different kettle of fish, "thanks" to PROM and system software updates that have made it much harder to hack into the last few versions of the TiVo software on Series 2 systems (that is, software Versions 3.1 and later). Don't despair, however—it's certainly doable, and this book tells you how in Chapter 7. For now, enable programming and guide updates via the network and enjoy this performance improvement while you read Chapter 7 and begin to flex your hacking muscles.

To enable using the network to receive programming and guide updates, all you have to do is go to the Dial Prefix screen and enter a dialing prefix of **,#401**, which is entered as Pause Enter 4 0 1, and click Select. For Tivo version 3.x and earlier systems, the Dial Prefix is located in the Change Dial Options menu (TiVo Central, Messages and Setup, Recorder & Phone Setup, Phone Connection, Change Dial Options). For TiVo version 4.x systems, an equivalent Set

Dial Prefix command is located in the Phone Dialing Options screen (TiVo Central, Messages and Setup, Settings, Phone & Network Settings, Edit Phone or Network Settings, Phone Dialing Options).

Next, make a test call to test the new dial options—unlike many computer-related tasks, "it should just work." If the call fails, here are a few things to try, in order, before giving in to panic and changing every possible configuration setting:

1. Make sure that your network adapter is firmly connected to your Series 1 or Series 2 machines. It requires a bit of effort to firmly seat TiVoNET, TurboNet, and AirNet adapters on the Series 1 motherboards. This is, of course, by design so that they don't come loose easily. I tend to slide mine on at one end and then rock them back and forth, with my fingers between the front of the TiVo and the back of the card. If you're using an AirNet card, make sure that your PCMCIA card is a Prism 2/2.5 card and that it's firmly seated in the AirNet adapter. Finally, if you're using a USB Ethernet adapter, make sure that the USB connector is firmly seated and pushed in all the way on the back of your TiVo.

2. Verify network connectivity. To do this, check that the Link and Power lights are active on your network adapter, if available. TurboNet cards and most USB network adapters feature a green LED that lights up to indicate Ethernet connectivity. External USB adapters also provide a yellow power LED that lights up when the adapter is receiving power through the USB port.

3. Verify that your TiVo is correctly connected to a hub or switch on your home network and that these are correctly connected to your home network. Not connecting your hub to your DSL or cable modem using the Uplink port is a common mistake. Integrating a hub or switch into your home network was explained in the section "Networking 101" earlier in this chapter.

4. Make sure that a DHCP Server is running on your home network (see "Networking 101" for more information about DHCP servers, the services that they provide, and where to run them).

5. Make sure that you entered the exact string ",#401" for your dial prefix. It would be embarrassing to share how many times I left out the comma when I was first experimenting with this on my original Series 1, so I'll just claim that I've never made that mistake. Oops! If you find that you entered the wrong string, don't tell anybody—simply correct it and try making another test call.

6. If you've jumped ahead in this book and followed the instructions in Chapter 7 to get a command prompt on your TiVo, connect to your TiVo's serial port and make sure that its network configuration is correct using the ifconfig command, as in the following example:

```
bash-2.02# ifconfig -a
lo        Link encap:Local Loopback
          inet addr:127.0.0.1  Bcast:127.255.255.255  Mask:255.0.0.0
          UP BROADCAST LOOPBACK RUNNING  MTU:3584  Metric:1
```

```
          RX packets:1078 errors:0 dropped:0 overruns:0 frame:0
          TX packets:1078 errors:0 dropped:0 overruns:0 carrier:0 coll:0

eth0      Link encap:Ethernet  HWaddr 00:40:36:01:B0:11
          inet addr:192.168.6.248  Bcast:192.168.6.255  Mask:255.255.255.0
          UP BROADCAST RUNNING MULTICAST  MTU:1500  Metric:1
          RX packets:0 errors:0 dropped:0 overruns:0 frame:0
          TX packets:0 errors:0 dropped:0 overruns:0 carrier:0 coll:0
          Interrupt:29
```

This example shows that the Ethernet connection eth0 is working fine on my TiVo, and that the TiVo has the IP address 192.168.6.248. If you don't see an entry for "eth0", this means that your TiVo didn't initialize its Ethernet interface correctly. Use a text editor such as vim or emacs to check the file /var/log/kernel for a message beginning with the string "Configuring network..." to see if there was a problem recognizing your Ethernet card or loading one of the network-related kernel modules. If this is the case on your Series 1, turn off the TiVo and try reseating everything. If this is the case on your Series 2, try another USB Ethernet adapter—yours may simply be bad.

7. If you still suspect a DHCP problem and are running a Linux system, use ethereal, tcpdump, or some similar network packet-sniffing utility to check that your TiVo is actually sending and receiving packets over the network, as well as where they're going. For example, my DHCP server has the IP address 192.168.6.200 on my home network. When I boot a TiVo, I see a packet like the following on my home network (this output is cut from one of the windows displayed by the Linux ethereal utility):

```
192.168.2.200    255.255.255.255    \
     Syslog LOCAL1.INFO: OC8E 400 DHCP SERVER Offered...
```

If you select that packet in ethereal, you'll see output indicating the IP address that the DHCP server offered to your TiVo—for example, something like this:

```
Message: O8CE 400 DHCP SERVER Offered \
     Offering: 192.168.6.248 To: FFFFFFFFFFFF \
                              By: 192.168.6.200
```

This traffic indicates that my DHCP server (which isn't running on my Linux system, but is running on an Apple Airport wireless access point) just handed out the IP address 192.168.6.248.

If you still can't successfully make a daily call, your best bet is to skip ahead to Chapter 7. In order to really diagnose what's happening on your TiVo, you'll need command-line access to it, which is easy on Series 1 systems and reasonably complex on Series 2 models. I'm sure you're up to the challenge.

Using a PDA as a Remote Control

One of the most impressive and interesting things about the TiVo is the tremendous amount of user loyalty and pure creativity that it inspires. You only have to search the Web for TiVo or look at the tremendous number of posts on TiVo sites, such as the AVS Forums (see Chapter 11, "Other TiVo Hacking Resources"), to see the huge number of people who are hacking TiVos, porting Open Source software to them, and developing software that runs on operating systems such as Microsoft Windows and Apple's Mac OS in order to be able to interact with their TiVos. Companies like 9thTee.com, PTVupgrade.net, SiliconDust, and Weaknees.com are churning out TiVo upgrade kits and add-ons, continuing the hardware side of the convergence concept that was discussed in Chapter 1, "Know Your TiVo."

Though not actually TiVo hardware, a truly cool hardware-related TiVo add-on is a piece of software called *OmniRemote Pro,* an optional infrared (IR) amplifier that enables you to use your Palm to control your TiVo. The Web page for this package is at http://www.pacific-neotek.com/omniProfsw.htm. If you're one of the many road warriors who has a Palm or compatible PDA in your holster at all times, this could be just the ticket for unifying all the remotes in your house. The software requires PalmOS 3.0 or better and works on Palms and compatible PDAs, such as the Palm III, IIIx, Palm V, Palm VII, Sony Clie, and Handspring Visor. I use it with an old Palm 3C, and it's great. One of its coolest aspects is that the OmniRemote software actually turns your PDA into a Universal Remote so that you can configure the software and add buttons to create a software remote that controls any and every IR device in your house—you're only limited by the screen real estate on your PDA. The OmniRemote software is also *skinnable,* which means that you can easily change its appearance by creating or importing your own backgrounds using a variety of Macintosh and PC software packages.

Figure 3.9 shows two sample skins for the OmniRemote Pro software, side by side, to give you an idea of just how flexible this software is on PDAs with color and higher screen resolutions. This is a fun piece of software that I highly recommend. It also prevents you from having to panic if your dog eats your remote (speaking from personal experience).

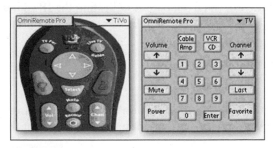

FIGURE 3.9 *Sample OmniRemote Pro screens*

TiVo Hardware Supplies on the Net

As discussed throughout this chapter, there are thousands of TiVo fanatics and TiVo-related Web sites on the Internet. Many of these discuss how to hack various aspects of the TiVo software, but some actually provide the hardware that you'll need to do things like add disk drives to various models of TiVos, and will also do this for you if you're really paranoid about opening up your TiVo or simply don't have the time. This section discusses the best sites that I've found on the Internet for buying TiVo parts, getting your TiVo repaired, and for general TiVo expertise. These are, therefore, my favorite sites—if you have a similar site and it isn't listed here, I apologize in advance, and please let me know about it. More knowledge is always better as far as I'm concerned.

The United States sites in this section are listed alphabetically to avoid any suggestion of prejudice. I've bought things from all of these sites and prefer certain items from each. If you're creating a new TiVo site, maybe you'll want to register it at AAATivo.com for better placement in the next version of this book?

9thTee.com

9thTee is one of the premiere sites for TiVo information, software, repairs, upgrades, and parts and has been in business since 1992, selling networking components, cool stuff, and (apparently) whatever else interests them. As discussed earlier in this chapter, 9thTee was the original commercial vendor for the TivoNET cards (dealing with Tridge directly) and is also the sole distributor for the TurboNet and AirNet cards from SiliconDust.com. If you want to put your Series 1 TiVo on the network, buy a card from these guys—recently, bootleg TurboNet (and probably AirNet) cards have appeared for sale, but buying these is essentially ripping off both 9thTee and Nick at SiliconDust (aka jafa on the TiVo AVS forums). This book is about hacking the TiVo for fun, not about stealing. The people who did the hard work to design the hardware and software and to manufacture and distribute cool TiVo add-ons like these cards deserve your support.

9thTee offers pretty much every TiVo part and add-on you can think of, including modem repair kits for the truly technically inclined who don't want to simply cable up an external modem as described earlier in this chapter. 9thTee has brackets, tools, cables, and whatever else you might need to hack your TiVo yourself, repairs TiVos if you have one that is out of warranty or just want yours repaired *fast*, and will even upgrade your TiVos or sell you an upgrade kit if you want to save some time.

Check out their site at http://www.9thTee.com.

Hinsdale

Hinsdale provides upgrade services and kits for all models of TiVo, provides a speedy repair service for ailing TiVos, and is perhaps best known for its *how-tos*, which describe how to do the upgrade yourself. Not only is this a truly exemplary illustration of most of the good things about the Internet and people in general, it demonstrates their detailed knowledge and expertise. I've heard nothing but good things about Hinsdale in TiVoLand.

Hinsdale accepts all major credit cards, and also accepts PayPal payments. If you're looking for something to do with the profits from an eBay auction, a Hinsdale upgrade might just be what you're looking for.

Check out its site at http://www.newreleasesvideo.com/hinsdale-how-to/upgradeservice.html, or just search for Hinsdale TiVo in your favorite Internet search engine.

PTVupgrade.COM

PTVupgrade.com is a great site for purchasing TiVo kits, getting your TiVo upgraded, and getting a variety of hardware and software-related TiVo information. It is more actively involved in kernel hacking than most of the other TiVo service sites, recently announcing a breakthrough that enables you to use more than 137GB of a given hard drive with your TiVo. (See Chapter 6 for a discussion of hard drive limitations in stock TiVo software distributions). These guys clearly love TiVos and probably know them better at the operating system level than any other site.

PTVupgrade.com specializes in expanding and repairing TiVos and also sells complete upgraded units. The 9thTee site actually resells PTVupgrade.com's upgrade kits and services.

Check out its site at http://www.PTVupgrade.com.

TiVo Store

As you might suspect, TiVo repairs its own hardware and also offers items such as USB network adapters that are guaranteed to work with Series 2 systems, replacement remotes and cables, and cool accessories like TiVo shirts and toys. All of these items are available through the TiVo store at http://store.tivo.com/StoreFront.bok.

If you have a problem with your TiVo hardware, the TiVo site is less than exciting. The primary TiVo customer support site is located at http://customersupport.tivo.com/userWelcome.asp and features a troubleshooting guide for hardware and software problems. Unfortunately, if you're looking for instant help with a dead Series 1 box, you'll wander through a few menus until you finally find out how to contact support from the actual manufacturer of your TiVo. Though I'm somewhat cranky about this, it's not totally surprising—as I discuss in Chapter 1, TiVo makes the majority of its money from selling the TiVo service. Since it doesn't make most of its hardware, we can't really expect them to fix someone else's. They'll be happy to fix Series 2 systems that they manufactured, especially those that are still under warranty. If you have an older Tivo, contact 9thTee or Weaknees for repairs and to talk to certified TiVo fans.

Weaknees.com

Weaknees.com is the other premiere TiVo hardware and software site on the Web. Weaknees is entirely TiVo-related and, thus, is much easier to navigate than any other TiVo supplier's site. It provides an excellent selection of TiVo hardware, software, and information, and it features TiVo repair and upgrade services. In my opinion, the Series 2 expansion brackets from Weaknees are better than anyone else's, and Weaknees' bracket features additional cooling fans to keep your TiVo cool even when recording the longest Farscape or *Rockford Files* marathon. Weaknees is also the creator of the PowerTrip device that helps protect upgraded Series 2 systems from the vagaries and power demands of additional drives when you expand your TiVo's storage capacity.

Weaknees offers pretty much every TiVo part and add-on you can think of, including external modem kits people need to cable up an external modem, as described earlier in this chapter. Weaknees has brackets, tools, cables, and whatever else you might need to hack your TiVo yourself, repairs TiVos if you have one that is out of warranty or just want yours repaired *fast*, and will even upgrade your TiVos or sell you an upgrade kit if you want to save some time.

Check out its site at http://www.weaknees.com.

TiVo Sites Outside the United States

As I mention in Chapter 1, TiVo partnered with Thompson Electronics to provide TiVo hardware in the United Kingdom. If you're a TiVo fan living in the United Kingdom or anywhere outside the United States that uses the same type of power as the UK, you may want to have your TiVo repaired or upgraded by someone in your own neighborhood. PACELink is an excellent firm in the United Kingdom that will be glad to do this for you. Its URL is http://www.pacelink.co.uk. It also offers a variety of services, software, and accessories that enable you to more easily interact with the hardware and services in the United Kingdom, such as the DigiBox.

Other Sources for TiVo Hardware

There are plenty of other sites on the Internet for obtaining TiVo upgrades, service, and general information. The ones listed previously are sites that I've specifically heard good things about, or that I've personally dealt with. (I have never paid for an upgrade, so can't vouch for that aspect of any site I've discussed.) If you have some spare time, google for TiVo Upgrade Kits and surf through the 10 or 20 pages of results. Happy hunting!

One good source of used TiVos and inexpensive, competitive upgrades is eBay.com. I've bought a few used TiVos there and have been happy with the results. As the largest flea market and auction site in the known universe, eBay is a great starting point for getting an upgrade or used TiVo. It's certainly the easiest place to get a Series 1 system for pure hacking pleasure at this point.

TiVo USED TIVOS AND LIFETIME SERVICE

One nice aspect of buying a used TiVo on the Internet is that you can often buy TiVos there with lifetime service already paid for—as mentioned earlier, lifetime TiVo service travels with a specific machine (in most cases), and you can avoid having to pay for the service yourself if you buy such a machine there. You might think that this would make TiVo cranky, but it actually shouldn't. I assume that everyone who's selling their old TiVos with lifetime service on eBay is doing so because they've bought a newer TiVo or DirecTiVo system, and, therefore, TiVo is still getting the appropriate amount of payment for their service.

HACKING THE TiVo

Chapter 4

The Hacker's Tool Chest of TiVo Tools

Thanks to the effort of hundreds of dedicated TiVo hackers and the miracle of the Internet for instant information and file sharing, TiVo hackers today have hundreds of pieces of software from which to choose. Regardless of the model and type of TiVo you're using, you can choose from a tremendous variety of recompiled Linux utilities, TiVo-only software, and personal computer software for operating systems, such as Microsoft Windows, Apple's Mac OS, and Linux that all interacts with your TiVo in interesting and often useful ways.

The corollary of this idea is that the Internet is a tremendous collection of unsorted, essentially random information that isn't verified or kept up-to-date. I could post a page tomorrow explaining how to transmute lead into gold by sacrificing a chicken in a graveyard, and the truly gullible would have no way of knowing whether it was true and useful information unless they actually tried it. The same thing is true about TiVo-related information on the Internet—you have no way of knowing whether the information is up-to-date, complete, or even applies to your machine unless you actually try out the posted instructions and see what happens. This can take a fair amount of time, can be a total waste of that time, and (with instructions explaining how to modify your operating system) can be downright dangerous.

A good example of obsolete information is Frequently Asked Questions, better known as FAQs. In TiVo-Land, one of the best-known FAQs is the "Hacking the TiVo FAQ" (no relation to this book or this author). This FAQ was written a long time ago and hasn't been maintained for years, although it was recently updated to explicitly state that it was out-of-date. It also discusses hacking techniques and software that are largely specific to the Series 1 TiVos. However, because it was written when there essentially was only one type of TiVo and because its authors couldn't see into the future, it doesn't say that it *is* for the Series 1 TiVo. The techniques and environment variables described in that FAQ for getting a command-line prompt on your TiVo 1 won't work on a Series 2 TiVo.

Like most computer system software, software for the TiVo can be divided into two general classes: application software and system software. Application software typically consists of utilities that are run by users and don't require any special privileges in order to execute them. Testing application software is generally fairly safe on systems with reasonable security because normal users can't access or modify resources that they shouldn't.

System software is a whole different ballgame. Not only will software compiled for the Series 1 not run on Series 2 machines, but you can also potentially screw up your Series 2 machine if you overwrite Series 2 software with equivalent Series 1 software on a Series 2 machine. Also, the idea of user-level security is non-existent on a TiVo because all of the TiVo hacks that give you command-line access to TiVos do so as the root user (aka the superuser). On a TiVo, like any other Linux or Unix system, the superuser has privileges to do anything to any file or device on the machine, including bad things.

This chapter is designed to introduce the most popular hacking software for the TiVo, explain what type of TiVo to which it is relevant, and explain any limitations involved in using the software on different types of TiVos.

This chapter also discusses the various bootable TiVo tools disks that you can find on the net, as well as the bootable BATBD disk that accompanies this book. All of the software discussed in this chapter is found on the BATBD disk, and some subsets of it can be found on various other tools disks. The discussion of each tools disk explains which type of TiVo it is intended for use with, what tools and versions of those tools that each disk includes, and provides an overview of using each tools disk. Not surprisingly, since the author assembled the BATBD disk for use with this book, it is the most complete and up-to-date of any of the tools disks, and gets the most extensive discussion.

TiVo Tools Overview

This section discusses software that is designed to run on an x86-based Linux system, and which can be used there to interact with TiVo disks that have been attached to those systems as described in Chapter 3, "Exploring Your TiVo Hardware." These are the tools required to actually do many of the procedures discussed in subsequent chapters, such as backing up and restoring disks, cloning existing disks to larger ones, and examining and otherwise modifying TiVo disk partitions and data.

TiVoMad Utilities

Though largely supplanted by later versions of the MFS Tools utilities, the TiVoMad utilities were an important landmark in TiVo hacking software, and can still be used to upgrade and expand the Series 1 TiVo. For a variety of reasons, explained later in this section, they cannot be used with Series 2 machines. However, since they still work for Series 1 systems and are easily found all over the net (and on the CD that accompanies this book, when mounted in a Series 1 system, byte-swapped mode), they're certainly worth discussing here. In general, you should use the latest versions of the MFS Tools rather than the TiVoMad utilities to add a larger or second disk to your TiVo. The MFS Tools and their command-line options are discussed later in this chapter—their use is explained in Chapter 6, "Expanding Your TiVo's Storage Capacity."

The TiVoMad utilities are a set of scripts, libraries, and executables that enable you to expand the size of the primary drive in your TiVo and to optionally add a second disk at the same time, further expanding your TiVo's storage capacity. TiVoMad (aka Trevor Heartfield) was an early TiVo hacker in the UK, who simplified the process of expanding TiVo disk storage by writing a wrapper script that "did the right thing" using TiVo utilities and libraries that were provided as part of the package.

The basic situation that the TiVoMad utilities are designed for is when you have cloned an existing drive to a larger drive, and want to make the additional space on the larger drive available to your TiVo to store additional recording. You can also add a second drive at the same time, and the TiVoMad utilities will make the space that it contains available to your TiVo.

WITH THIS SOFTWARE, I THEE WED

Although discussed in more detail later, it's important to know that when you add a second drive to your TiVo, the two drives are "married" and must be used together. You cannot subsequently remove the second drive and expect your Series 1 system to work correctly with only the A drive. To "un-marry" two drives, you must back them up using the MFS Tools utilities (discussed later in this chapter), and then restore the backup to a single drive, assuming that the single drive has sufficient space to hold the TiVo data that was contained on the previous two drives. This single drive can be used by itself, and then you can recycle the two drives that are its logical parents.

The TiVoMad wrapper script, **setup.sh**, works by first prompting you for information about whether you're expanding a drive, adding another drive, or a combination of both. It uses that information to create new TiVo-capable partitions on any free space on the original drive and to create TiVo-capable partitions on a second disk, if one is present. Before doing so, it thoughtfully backs up the first disk's partition map so it can be restored if the script encounters a problem. The script then identifies the TiVo's original boot partition and installs an updated version of the standard TiVo **rc.sysinit** script there, along with another command script that remakes the swap space on the expanded primary TiVo drive. It then installs one of two utilities (**mfsadd_a** or **mfsadd_ab**), which it installs as **/tvbin/mfsadd_new**—depending on whether you're simply adding new space to your primary TiVo drive (drive A) or expanding an existing drive while adding a second drive (drives A and B). In addition, the script installs specific versions of some shared libraries required by these utilities and blesses the second drive, if one is present. You then move the drives to the TiVo, as described in Chapter 3, and boot the TiVo. It completes the expansion/upgrade process, removes the libraries, scripts, and utilities that it installed, and then reboots your TiVo. Voila! A larger, better TiVo.

The TiVoMad utilities will only work on Series 1 systems because the utilities and libraries that it installs and attempts to run after rebooting your TiVo are compiled for PPC systems, such as the Series 1 TiVo. They will not run on the MIPS-based Series 2 TiVo, and may actually mess up your machine because some of the libraries that they replace are required for normal functioning of your TiVo.

The TiVoMad utilities are typically found on the net packaged in two different ways—either bundled in a bootable floppy disk image, or in subdirectories of one of the bootable CDs that are available for your TiVo, including the BATBD floppy disk that is provided with this book. Once you have mounted the latter CD (not just booted from it), the TiVoMad utilities are found in the directories **mad31** and **mad32** (for versions 3.1 and 3.2 of the software), with a top-level symbolic link to the **mad32** directory (referred to as ply **mad**) to show that this is the latest and greatest version of the utilities.

Stand-alone versions of the TiVoMad disk are variants of the original TiVo boot and tools' floppy known as "Dylan's Boot Disk" (discussed later in this chapter). It does not contain all of the utilities found on the actual Dylan's Boot Disk, because the disk has been customized to support the expansion and adding of disks. You can create the TiVoMad disk on either a Windows or a Linux system by putting a blank, formatted floppy in the A drive of your PC and executing one of the following system-specific commands:

- ◆ On a Linux system, execute the command **dd if=image-name of=/dev/fd0**, where "image-name" is the name of the file containing the TiVoMad disk image.

- ◆ On a Windows system, execute the **MakeDisk.bat** script by double-clicking it or executing it manually from a command-line prompt.

Like all TiVo tools disks, the disk created by both of these steps is a bootable floppy containing a small, customized Linux implementation that provides the files and commands that you need for the TiVoMad utilities.

TIP

Before shutting down your TiVo to remove its hard drive(s), check the System Information screen (TiVo Central -> Messages & Setup -> System Information) to determine the version of the TiVo software that your TiVo is running. This information is necessary when running the TiVoMad utilities.

Before using the TiVoMad utilities, you should make an image backup of your existing TiVo disk and restore it to a new (usually larger) drive, as explained in Chapter 5, "Backing Up and Restoring TiVo Data." You should do this for several reasons:

- ◆ You can't expand the amount of storage available on a drive that is completely used by your TiVo. This is a book about hacking the TiVo, not about witchcraft, which creating extra space out of nothing would require.

- ◆ You should always make a copy of your TiVo data before doing any of the hacks described in this book. If you encounter problems using utilities, such as the TiVo-Mad utilities, you can always put your original disk back in your TiVo.

WARNING

When you put a TiVo disk in your PC and reboot using a Linux boot disk, such as one containing the TiVoMad utilities, you have direct write access to any of the disks that are attached to your PC. This means that if your PC's original hard drives are still attached and you accidentally specify one of them as a device that you want to format, you could destroy all of the existing data on your PC. Be very careful or, better yet, disconnect your existing PC hard drives when attaching TiVo drives so that you do not accidentally wipe out all of your PC data.

As mentioned earlier, the capabilities of the TiVoMad utilities have been replaced by version 2 of the MFS Tools, which is faster and does not require installing special software on your TiVo. However, if you insist, you can still use the TiVoMad utilities to upgrade or add a disk in a Series 1 machine. After you've created a backup image of your existing disk and restored that to a new (probably larger) disk, you're ready to proceed.

Next, shut down your TiVo and PC and put your TiVo drive in your PC (along with a second drive, if you're adding one), reboot your system from the TiVoMad floppy disk or bootable TiVo tools CD (e.g., the BATBD CD included with this book). If you've booted from the BATBD CD, mount the CD (as explained later in this chapter) and change directory to the /mad directory on the CD.

Next, execute the **setup.sh** script by typing **./setup.sh** and pressing the Return key. Answer each of the requests for information as it prompts you. Much of the information that you enter depends on exactly how you've connected the TiVo drive(s) to your PC. The device names used by the TiVoMad setup script are **hda** for a TiVo drive attached as the master on your primary IDE interface, **hdb** for a TiVo drive attached as a slave on your primary IDE interface, **hdc** for a TiVo drive attached as a master on your secondary IDE interface, and **hdd** for a TiVo drive attached as a slave on your secondary IDE interface.

The questions asked by the TiVoMad setup script are as follows:

1. Enter the device name of your TiVo A Drive:

   Specify the name of the device that corresponds to your main TiVo disk, using the naming conventions explained earlier (hdb, hdc, or hdd).

2. Will your target TiVo have two drives in it?

   Answer "Y" or "N." Your answer to this question determines which version of the TiVoMad upgrade utilities will be installed on your primary TiVo disk. This question is really asking whether you will ever want to add a second disk to your TiVo—not necessarily whether you are adding a second drive now.

3. Is your second drive connected now?

   Answer "Y" or "N." You will only see this question if you answered "Y" to the previous question. Your answer to this question determines whether the TiVoMad utilities will attempt to format a second disk for use with the TiVo at this time.

4. Enter the device name of your TiVo B drive:

   Specify the name of the device that corresponds to your second TiVo disk, following the naming conventions explained earlier. You will only see this question if you answered "Y" to questions 2 and 3.

5. Is your A drive a Quantum Fireball?

   Answer "Y" or "N." This question is only relevant for TiVo systems running Version 2 or earlier of the TiVo software, and then only if the TiVo is using its original disk (which were all 20- or 30-GB Quantum disks). The answer to this question determines if an environment variable (**runideturbo**) will be set to true (Quantum disks) or false (other types of disks). This environment variable will only be set if it is required on your TiVo.

6. Does your TiVo have Version 2.0.1 software (or greater)?

   Answer "Y" or "N." Your response to this question is used to determine whether the **runideturbo** environment variable should be set.

7. Is your target TiVo > 140GB?

   Answer "Y" or "N" based on the largest amount of space that you EVER plan to have in your TiVo, not necessarily the amount of disk space that your TiVo currently contains. The answer to this question determines whether the TiVoMad utilities create a larger swap partition on your primary TiVo drive. By default, Series 1 disks reserve a 64MB portion of the disk for use by the TiVo's Linux operating system. This space is used by the TiVo to move all or some of any running process out of memory so that other tasks can execute (and is also required during the update procedure for larger disks). A larger amount of TiVo storage typically means that your TiVo will need more memory to store its playlists, the list of shows to be recorded, suggestions, and so on. Answering "Y" to this question results in the TiVoMad utilities creating a 128MB swap partition, which is more than enough space to hold the additional information used by a larger TiVo. The TiVoMad utilities create a larger swap partition by creating and specially formatting a new 128MB swap partition, telling the TiVo to use that for its swap space, and then recycling the original 64MB swap partition into a standard EXT2 partition named "Hack" that you can use to store your favorite TiVo hacks without worrying that they'll be deleted. This partition will be located at **/dev/hda14** on larger TiVo systems that have been upgraded using the TiVoMad utilities.

8. Do you want to continue?

   Answer "Y" or "N." This question provides you with a last chance to cancel the upgrading of your TiVo disk(s). If you answer "N," no changes will be made to your TiVo disks, and the TiVoMad setup script will simply exit. If you answer "Y," the upgrade procedure will begin, and changes will be made to the TiVo disk(s) that you identified to the script.

If you answered "Y" to the last question posed by the **setup.sh** script, the upgrade procedure should take less than a minute to complete. Once the script completes successfully, press Ctrl-Alt-Del to shut down your PC, turning it off when you see the message "No more processes left in this runlevel." After removing the TiVo disks and rejumpering them (if necessary), put them back in your TiVo and turn it on. As mentioned earlier, your TiVo will begin to boot, make changes to its internal configuration, and then reboot itself to take advantage of the additional space that has been added.

BlessTiVo

Written by Mike Hill, BlessTiVo is a utility that enables you to quickly and easily prepare a second disk for use with your TiVo. The BlessTiVo utility takes its name from the fact that attaching a second drive to a TiVo requires that the drive be prepartitioned, contain special boot information in the drive's boot sectors, and that the third partition on the drive contains a special TiVo ID string. Among TiVo hackers, the sum of all three of these actions is known as "blessing" the drive for use with your TiVo—hence the name. You typically run the BlessTiVo program from a PC that you have booted from a TiVo tools floppy or a TiVo tools CD, such as the BATBD CD that was included with this book. Versions of the BlessTiVo program are also available for Mac OS X. You can download the Mac OS X version of the BlessTiVo program from the URL http://http://www.weaknees.com/mactivo.php. It is also in the Macintosh directory of the BATBD CD, for your convenience.

 NOTE

As mentioned previously, after booting your TiVo for the first time with a second drive attached, the two drives in that TiVo are permanently associated with each other (well, at least until you reformat them). The software side of this association is accomplished by the main TiVo drive recording the TiVo ID string of its partner.

The most common way to prepare a second drive for use in your TiVo is by using the MFS Tools, discussed later in this chapter. When restoring or expanding a backup to a new, larger drive using MFS Tools, you can automatically prepare and add a second drive at the same time by appending its name to the MFS Tools command line. This is a fine solution if you are using a PC to restore and expand the backups, and that system has two free IDE connectors so that you can mount both of the drives intended for the TiVo at the same time.

If your PC only has a single free IDE connector, you can do the same thing in two steps by using both the MFS Tools and the BlessTiVo program. First, you would attach the new hard drive to a PC and restore and expand your backup image to that drive. Next, you would shut down the PC, remove the newly prepared TiVo disk, and insert the second drive that you want to use with your TiVo. After rebooting, you would use the BlessTiVo program to prepare the second drive by itself. At this point, you can shut down the PC again, remove the second TiVo drive, and insert both drives into your TiVo after setting their jumpers correctly.

Similarly, if you are not a Pentium-class PC user, you can use the BlessTiVo command to prepare a second drive to use with your TiVo with the BlessTiVo program. Unfortunately, the MFS Tools commands are not open source and are not freely available for Macintosh systems, but the Macintosh version of BlessTiVo at least makes it possible to augment your existing TiVo storage from a Macintosh. (See Chapter 8, "Working with Your TiVo from Windows and Macintosh Systems," for more information about TiVo-related applications for the Macintosh and using your Macintosh to work with TiVo storage.)

Using the BlessTiVo command on a PC is quite straightforward—after attaching the drive you want to bless to your PC or Mac OS X system, reboot the system from a TiVo tools disk.

When you see the command prompt ('#'), execute the BlessTiVo command, specifying the name of the drive that you want to format on the command-line after the BlessTiVo command, as in the following example:

```
BlessTiVo /dev/hdx
```

In this example, "**x**" represents the identifier for the disk that you want to format. The device names used by the BlessTiVo command are **/dev/hdb** for a TiVo drive attached as a slave on your primary IDE interface, **/dev/hdc** for a TiVo drive attached as a master on your secondary IDE interface, and **/dev/hdd** for a TiVo drive attached as a slave on your secondary IDE interface. As a safety feature, the BlessTiVo command does not allow you to specify **/dev/hda** as the drive to be formatted, because this drive is typically the boot disk used by your PC or Mac OS system.

For example, if the drive that you want to prepare for use in your TiVo is attached as a slave on your secondary IDE interface, you would execute the following command:

```
BlessTiVo /dev/hdd
```

When you execute the BlessTiVo command, the program first checks to see if the drive exists and can be opened. If you see error messages such as "No device specified," "Too many command line options," or "Unable to connect to /dev/hdx," these usually mean that you accidentally specified the wrong drive on the BlessTiVo command-line, you specified the name of the drive incorrectly (no spaces in device names!), that you set the jumpers on the drive incorrectly when you put it in your PC or Mac, or that you do not have sufficient privileges to write to the drive. Re-check the command-line arguments that you specified, verify that the drive jumpers are set correctly, and, if you are not running from the BATBD disk, make sure that you are executing the BlessTiVo command as a Linux or Mac OS X user with superuser or administrative privileges. Make sure that you have not connected the drive as the master device on your primary IDE interface—as a safety precaution, the BlessTiVo command will not permit you to bless a drive that is attached as **/dev/hda**.

After the BlessTiVo program verifies that it can find the specified drive, it then examines the drive to determine whether the drive already contains DOS or Linux partitioning information. If the drive already contains valid partitions, the BlessTiVo command warns you of this fact and asks if you want to proceed. Although this extra paranoia may be irritating if you're sure that you know what you're doing, this extra verification step is quite handy if you've accidentally specified the wrong disk name and are attempting to overwrite the wrong drive, for example, your primary Windows partition or other data that you may want to use again in the future.

The BlessTiVo command also asks you to verify that you want to proceed even if the specified disk contains no partitioning information. This can be handy if the disk you have specified contains data partitioned in a format that the BlessTiVo command does not understand, such as Mac OS X partitions.

If you reply "Y" to whichever of these confirmation requests you see, the TiVo blesses the specified drive by performing the following operations:

◆ Erases the first few sectors of the drive to eliminate any existing partitioning information.

◆ Writes a valid boot page to the first sector of the drive.

◆ Creates three partitions on the drive.

◆ Writes the TiVo ID string to the third partition.

The BlessTiVo command displays a status message as it completes each of these steps, and displays a final summary message as it exits. This summary message displays the amount of storage available on the newly formatted drive.

WARNING

The summary message displayed at the end of the BlessTiVo process is very important. You should always check this value to make sure that it is within 3 gigabytes of the total size of the disk that you are adding. If the size of the disk that you are blessing is not reported as being within 3 GB of the actual size of the disk, do not add this drive to your TiVo. If you do so, the two drives will be married, and you will not be able to take advantage of the storage that is really available on the second disk without backing up the drives, reformatting them, and so on.

If the BlessTiVo command reports the drive size incorrectly, this is usually due to one of two problems:

◆ The drive is not jumpered to take advantage of Logical Block Addressing (LBA), which is commonly used on newer, larger hard drives. Check the manual that came with your drive, or check the jumper settings. You may accidentally have set the wrong jumper when configuring the drive to add it to your PC or Mac OS X system.

◆ The Linux kernel that you are booting from is not capable of recognizing disks with the storage capacity of the hard drive that you are trying to format. This is not a problem if you have booted from a TiVo tools disk, such as the BATBD disk included with this book, but may be a problem if you are executing the BlessTiVo command from the command-line of an older Linux system.

Assuming that the amount of storage reported as available on the new drive is within 3 GB of the physical size of the drive, you can now shut down the system by pressing the Ctrl-Alt-Delete keys on a PC or by executing the shutdown command on your Mac. Once the system shuts down, you can remove the drive from your desktop system, verify or set the jumpers so that the drive is configured as a slave drive, and insert it into your TiVo. After you power up the TiVo, the startup process may take slightly more time than is normally required while the

TiVo integrates the new storage and updates its internal drive and capacity information. After the TiVo boots, you should be able to go to the System Information screen (TiVo Central -> Messages & Setup -> System Information) and verify that the storage capacity of your TiVo has increased. If it has not, turn off your TiVo and verify that you set the jumpers correctly so that the drive is identified as a slave disk. This is a common oversight in the excitement of TiVo hacking and expanding your TiVo's storage capacity before the next *Star Trek* or *South Park* marathon begins.

For experienced TiVo hackers, the BlessTiVo command provides some additional command-line options that enable you to individually execute each of the stages of the BlessTiVo process. These options can be specified on the command-line after the name of the drive that you want to bless, and consist of the following:

◆ *erase* Erase the first few sectors of the drive to eliminate any existing partitioning information. This stage of the BlessTiVo process does the same thing as the Linux/Unix **dd** command that is often used to wipe the partition map on an existing drive.

◆ *bpage* Write a valid bootpage to the first sector of the drive. This stage of the BlessTiVo process is the equivalent of the **bootpage** command discussed later in this chapter.

◆ *part* Create three partitions on the drive. This stage of the BlessTiVo process is the equivalent of the actions of the **pdisk** program discussed later in this chapter.

◆ *id* Write the TiVo ID string to the third partition. This stage of the BlessTiVo process is the equivalent of the **GenAddDiskTiVoID** program that is found on some TiVos or a subset of the actions of the MFS Tools **mfsadd** command.

Bootpage

The bootpage utility reads and writes TiVo boot information from the first sector of the master disk in your TiVo, which is the disk from which your TiVo boots. The information in the master drive's boot sector is as follows:

◆ The partition where the bootable kernel for your TiVo is located.

◆ An alternate partition from which to load a kernel if booting from the primary bootable kernel fails.

◆ The network hostname of your system

◆ The default IP address of your system

◆ The default MAC address of your system

The boot and alternate boot partition information in your master boot disk's boot sector is critical to the TiVo boot process. The boot partition is not the partition from which the Linux kernel (the actual operating system) is loaded, but instead identifies the partition that the running kernel uses as the root filesystem for your TiVo. Like any Linux or Unix system, the TiVo's boot partition is where startup information and the basic commands necessary for the TiVo boot process are stored. The network-related information stored in your master disk's boot sector is rarely used. Items that can be configured using the TiVo's system software, such as your system's hostname and IP address, are typically overridden by explicit commands in your TiVo's startup files.

As you might expect, any changes made in the boot sector of a TiVo hard disk will only take effect the next time you boot your TiVo using that hard drive as the master/boot drive.

The general syntax of the bootpage command is the following:

```
bootpage [options] <device>
```

As specified on the bootpage command-line, <device> is the base name of a disk, not the name of any specific partition. Valid device names are therefore in the form **/dev/hda**, **/dev/hdb**, and so on

The bootpage command's command-line options are listed below:

- *-A <partition>* Sets the name of the alternate boot partition identified in the boot sector of the specified <device>.
- *-a* Displays the name of the alternate boot partition identified in the boot sector of the specified <device>.
- *-B <partition>* Updates the boot partition information in the boot sector of the specified <device> to <partition>.
- *-b* Displays the name of the current boot partition identified in the boot sector of the specified <device>.
- *-C* Writes the bootpage of the specified <device>.
- *-f* Switches the primary and alternate boot partitions of the specified <device>, making the former boot partition the alternate boot partition, and making the former alternate boot partition the primary boot partition.
- *-H <hostname>* Sets the default hostname of the TiVo to <hostname> in the boot sector of the specified <device>.
- *-h* Displays the default hostname of the TiVo, as identified in the boot sector of the specified <device>.
- *-I <ipaddress>* Sets the default IP address of the TiVo to <ipaddress> in the boot sector of the specified <device>.
- *-i* Displays the default IP address of the TiVo, as identified in the boot sector of the specified <device>.
- *-M* Sets the default MAC address (hardware network address) of the TiVo to <macaddress> in the boot sector of the specified <device>.
- *-m* Displays the default MAC address of the TiVo, as identified in the boot sector of the specified <device>.
- *-P <params>* Sets current boot parameters to the list of parameters specified in <params>. As you'll see later in this book, clever manipulation of the TiVo's boot

parameters is the key to successfully hacking into later versions of the TiVo's Linux operating system.

◆ *-p* Gets a list of the boot parameter information stored in the boot sector of the disk identified by <device>. These boot parameters are typically just a string of command-line arguments that can be passed to the Linux kernel at boot time.

◆ *-W <filename>* Writes the bootpage information from the specified <device> to the file <filename>.

The TiVo's use of duplicate kernel and root filesystem partitions, discussed in more detail in Chapter 9, "Linux and the TiVo," is a clever way of ensuring the dependability and reliability of your TiVo in almost any circumstances except severe hardware failures. Because the TiVo is a consumer appliance designed for regular daily use, TiVo Inc. can't afford to have the system get into a state where you would have to locate and invoke your local Linux wizard in order to correctly configure it. TiVos therefore use primary and alternate boot partitions, both to simplify upgrades and for protection from hardware problems. When TiVo Inc. releases an upgraded version of the TiVo's Linux kernel, that kernel is loaded into your system's alternate boot partition as part of the upgrade process. If this kernel is downloaded and installed successfully, the TiVo uses the **bootpage** command to set the partition containing the updated kernel as your TiVo's new boot partition and sets the partition where the current kernel is located as the new alternate partition. Should a problem occur, the system always can fall back to the previous kernel by loading it from the alternate partition.

MFS Tools

Ah, the near-legendary MFS Tools utilities! The MFS Tools are the Swiss army knife of TiVo utilities, and were written by Steven Lang, aka Tiger. The MFS Tools utilities are a tremendously powerful and eminently useful set of utilities for your TiVo that largely replace all other disk backup, disk restore, disk expansion, and disk addition utilities for the TiVo. They take their name from the Multimedia File System (MFS), which is the partition format and organization used by the TiVo to store and locate your recordings. (For more information about MFS, see Chapter 9.) The MFS Tools are not open source but are freely available in binary format. Here's a fun fragment from the MFS Tools README on that very subject:

Q. Will you be releasing the source to MFS Tools?

No.

Q. Please?

No.

Q. pretty pleez o plzz?!!! i will be ur best friend!!! !!!!

Don't make me turn this car around.

Q. You are a disgrace to the open source movement!

Sorry, ESR, I love open source and free software and all that. I think both concepts have good ideas behind them. However, I also respect TiVo's wish to keep some things out of the public eye, as they have made clear to me in past exchanges.

The combination of great free tools and an excellent sense of humor is what TiVo hacking is all about, as far as the author of this book is concerned. While I'm a big fan of open source, I'm a bigger fan of having fun and getting the job done, regardless of whether the source code is available. The MFS Tools unquestionably get the job done, and for free.

 NOTE

The MFS Tools actually consist of a single utility named **mfstool** that actually pro-vides a suite of commands that perform various, related functions. A *command suite* is the term used to describe a command whose first argument specifies the function that the command is to perform, with subsequent command-line arguments being specific to the way in which the command suite is used. Confusing? Many other peo-ple think so, too, but this simplifies program maintenance in many ways.

Since the **mfstool** utility performs multiple functions and the notion of command suites may be alien to most users, many tools disks (including the one provided with this book) create multiple symbolic links to the **mfstool** executable with names that indicate the specific function that they are intended to perform. Supported symbolic links for the mfstool program are things like backup, restore, and **mfsadd**. To mini-mize or at least change the amount of confusion related to these commands, this chapter (and the rest of this book) specifies the full, generic command-line syntax for each example of the **mfstool** utility.

The mfstool command suite performs the following basic functions, which are also the key-words that you must supply as the first argument on the **mfstool** command-line in order to invoke those functions:

- ◆ *add* Enables you to add partitions to a TiVo disk to take advantage of all space available. Also enables you to add a second TiVo disk to an existing TiVo disk.

- ◆ *backup* Backs up TiVo disks in a special format that minimizes the space required to store the backups or the number and type of files that are actually backed up.

- ◆ *info* Provides information about the status of the MFS volumes on one or more TiVo disks.

- ◆ *restore* Restores TiVo data from backup files in the format created by the **mfstool backup** command.

When specifying the names of TiVo disks on any mfstool command-line, you must use the standard convention **/dev/hda** for a drive attached as a master on your primary IDE interface, **/dev/hdb** for a drive attached as a slave on your primary IDE interface, **/dev/hdc** for a drive attached as a master on your secondary IDE interface, and **/dev/hdd** for a drive attached as a slave on your secondary IDE interface. The **mfstool** commands that accept partition names on the command line use the same naming conventions, except that the numeric identifier(s) for the specific partition(s) must be appended to the basic device name.

Other features common to all of the commands in the mfstool suite are default values for the disk(s) that you are working with, and two environmental variables that can be used to override these default values. If no disk drives are specified on the command-line of any command in the mfstool command suite, the default disk(s) **/dev/hda** and **/dev/hdb** are used. If you want to work with other disks but still don't want to specify them on the command-line for some reason, you can override these default values by setting the values of the **MFS_HDA** and **MFS_HDB** environment variables to the name of the device(s) or file(s) that contain the data with which you are working. This occasionally can be useful when you are working with specific partitions or partitions with nonstandard device names. Setting environment variables in Linux is explained in Chapter 9.

There have been two major releases of the MFS Tools utilities, Versions 1.0 and 2.0. Version 2.0 was created when Series 2 machines first appeared and adds features such as being able to deal with byte-order differences between Series 1 and Series 2 systems. One of the especially cool features of the MFS Tools is that they do not require the use of a special kernel, boot parameters, and so on. Given sufficient privileges on any Linux system, the MFS Tools can make all of the disk modifications that they require to correctly restore backup data (whether byte-swapped or not), create new partitions, and so forth.

The next few sections explain each of the primary **mfstool** commands in more detail, discussing the command-line options specific to each. The information in these sections is provided as reference information for these commands. For information about using these commands to back up and restore data from your TiVo, see Chapter 5. For information about using these commands to expand the storage on an existing TiVo, see Chapter 6.

The mfstool add Command

The mfstool suite's **add** command enables you to expand the set of MFS volumes on one or two TiVo disks. The **mfstool add** command is typically used in one of two ways:

◆ To increase the number of MFS volumes available on a new, larger disk after an existing TiVo disk has been copied to it using the Linux **dd** command (as explained in the section of Chapter 6 entitled "Expanding an Existing TiVo Disk without Losing Anything").

◆ To add a second drive to an existing single-drive TiVo system. When used in this fashion, the **mfstool add** command is a complete replacement for the BlessTiVo command discussed earlier in this section.

Using the **mfstool add** command to perform these functions is explained in Chapter 6.

Command-line options for the **mfstool add** command are as follows:

◆ *-r scale* This option enables you to trade off between the amount of RAM required to track disk usage on your TiVo drives and the efficiency of the storage used on those drives. The TiVo's MFS partitions can store data in 1, 2, 4, 8, or 16 MB allocation units. Choosing a smaller allocation unit size increases the efficiency of your TiVo's storage, because less space will be "wasted" when recordings do not completely fill an allocation unit. However, because more allocation units are required to store a recording if the allocation units themselves are smaller, the TiVo uses more memory when tracking smaller allocation units. For example, assume that the allocation unit was 16 MB and the TiVo was trying to store a recording that required 20 MB of disk space. This would require two allocation units and would completely fill the first one but waste 12 MB of disk space in the second. In order to keep track of the recording, the TiVo would have to keep information about both allocation units in memory. On the other hand, with an allocation unit of 4 MB, the recording would require 5 allocation units but no disk space would be wasted. However, the TiVo would have to keep information about 5 allocation units in memory to keep track of that recording.

Acceptable values for this option are 0 (corresponding to a 1MB allocation unit), 1 (corresponding to a 2MB allocation unit), 2 (corresponding to a 4MB allocation unit), 3 (corresponding to an 8MB allocation unit), and 4 (corresponding to a 16MB allocation unit). In general, the larger the allocation unit value, the less RAM used (making the TiVo more responsive when displaying menus, changing and processing options, and so on), but the greater the amount of storage that may be wasted when storing recordings.

WARNING

The partitions created by TiVo when preparing a system use the allocation unit size of 1 MB (scaling value 0). However, when adding partitions, the **mfstool add** command uses a value of 4MB (scaling value 2) in order to not overload your TiVo's memory when tracking relatively huge amounts of disk storage. To be safe, you should not use allocation unit values lower than 4 MB in most cases (scaling value "2"), so that the system has enough memory to perform maintenance and self-repair procedures whenever the system restarts. This is especially true on Series 1 machines, which have much less memory (16MB) than Series 2 systems (32 MB).

◆ *-x drive1 drive2* Expand the set of MFS volume to use all available space on all drives listed in the **mfstool add** command-line. This option creates extra partitions on each drive in order to use all existing space, and also adds the new partitions to the list of partitions available to the TiVo. If a second drive is specified on the command-line and that drive does not contain existing MFS volumes, the disk's partition table will be erased and re-created with only MFS volumes present. Any existing data on any new drive that is added to the MFS volume set will be lost.

◆ *-X drive* Expand the set of MFS volumes to use all available space on a single drive. This option is much like the -x option, but only creates TiVo partitions on a single drive, adding them to the storage available to hold recordings on that drive. This option can be specified multiple times on the same command-line (as in the sample command, **mfstool add -X /dev/hda -X /dev/hdb**), but that's somewhat silly.

◆ *NewApp NewMedia* These two command-line options enable you to specify the device names of a pair of MFS partitions (one application region, NewApp, and one associated media region, NewMedia) that will then be immediately added to the existing set of MFS volumes. In order for this command to work correctly, both partitions must already exist and the partitions must be of the type "MFS."

The mfstool backup Command

The **mfstool** suite's **backup** command enables you to back up the contents of one or more TiVo disks. If a single disk is specified, it must be the first or only disk from your TiVo; if two disks are specified, they must be specified in the order that they would be encountered on your TiVo (i.e., master first, and slave second).

Backups created using the **mfstool backup** command can be saved as files on various types of storage device (disk, tape, DVD, etc.) and can also be written to standard output so that the output of the **mfstool backup** command can immediately be used as input by a parallel **mfstool restore** command. This can be useful if you simply want to clone one disk to another or collapse two disks to a single disk without requiring the intermediate storage space that would otherwise be required by a backup file.

Given that you have to physically remove the drive(s) from your TiVo to back them up, TiVo backups aren't something that you want to perform as regularly as we all back up the personal data on our personal computers. (We all do back up our personal computers, right?) Using the **mfstool backup** command to back up TiVo disks, and when you should consider doing so, is explained in Chapter 5, "Backing Up and Restoring TiVo Data." Using the **mfstool backup** command to provide input to a **mfstools restore** command in order to clone a disk is explained in Chapter 6.

Command-line options for the **mfstool backup** command are as follows:

◆ *-1 -9* Create a compressed backup, with lower numbers indicating lower compression. While compressing a backup reduces the amount of space required to store the backup, it also increases the time required to perform the backup. The recommended compression value is -6, which seems to provide the best trade-off between space savings and decreased performance.

◆ *-a* Back up all of the data on the original disk(s). This maximizes the space required for the backup, but preserves any recordings that you may have on the original disk(s).

◆ *-f N* When backing up data from the specified disk(s), include all video streams with a filesystem identifier (**fsid**, in MFS terms) below N. The default value for N is 2000, because most of the nonprogrammatic filesystem data required for generic TiVo operation (primarily background animations and graphics files) has identifiers whose IDs are less than this value. These are rarely included in filesystem updates received from TiVo due to their size—TiVo assumes that you already have them on the system that you are updating. They must therefore be included in backups to guarantee standard operation.

◆ *-l N* When backing up data from the specified disk(s), include all video streams whose size is less than N megabytes. Common values are 32 or 64 (MB). Using this option overrides any value specified with the -f option.

◆ *-o file* Specifies the name of the output file to which backup data should write. Most backup files require between 200 and 900 MB of disk space. As with most Linux applications, a dash ('-') can be specified instead of a filename, which indicates that the backup should be written to standard output. In this case, the output of the **mfstool backup** command can be piped to an **mfstool restore** command, enabling you to clone one TiVo disk to another without requiring any intermediate disk space for the backup image.

◆ *-s* Reduces the size of the backup image by shrinking the number and size of the TiVo volumes that you are backing up. This operation condenses all of the volumes recorded in the backup file, usually enabling multidisk backups to subsequently be restored to single disks that are at least the size of the original TiVo A drive. Any MFS filesystems that are not used will not be included in the backup.

◆ *-T* Used with the -l option to specify that the number used for video stream size calculation will be the total amount of space allocated to a given video stream, rather than the amount of space that is actually used by the data that it contains. This option also causes the entire amount of space allocated to each file to be included in the backup, rather than the amount of space that is actually used by the data in the file.

◆ *-t* Used with the -l option to specify that the number used for video stream size calculation will be the total amount of space actually used by that video stream, rather than the amount of space that is allocated to a given file on the disk. This option is especially useful in versions of the TiVo software greater than Version 2.0, where video streams could span multiple files.

◆ *-v* Excludes the **/var** directory from the backup. This directory is normally included because it is used by many system functions, but all of the necessary files and directories that it can contain will be re-created by your TiVo, if the directory is not found when you power on your TiVo. Depending on the size of your **/var** directory, excluding it from backups using this option can reduce the size of your backups by up to 128 MB. Since most TiVo hacks are stored in the **/var** directory, this option can also be used to guarantee that a TiVo backup is as generic as possible, without including the fruits of your hacking experiments.

The mfstool info Command

The mfstool suite's **info** command displays information about the MFS volumes on one or more disks that you identify on the command line. This is the same sort of information displayed by the **pdisk** command's "p" command, but does not display information about the standard Linux or swap volumes present on the specified disk(s).

The mfstool restore Command

The mfstool suite's **restore** command enables you to restore backup files created using the **mfstool backup** command, and also automatically enables you to allocate any free space remaining on the target disk(s) to the TiVo MFS filesystem. This command will automatically create any MFS volume pairs necessary to enable your TiVo to take advantage of any free space available on the target disk(s), minus any fragments that fall outside the allocation boundaries of the MFS filesystem. Such fragments are portions of the free space on your disk that are smaller than the size of the allocation unit used when creating the MFS filesystem(s). You can think of these as the remainder of dividing the amount of free space on your disk by the size of your allocation units.

As you might expect, the **mfstool restore** command is the most complex and powerful of the commands in the mfstool command suite. Creating backup files is one thing, but restoring them, correctly handling any byte-swapping present in the backup file, analyzing any free space remaining on the target disk(s) when the operation completes, and automatically creating new MFS partitions to fill that space is a complex set of operations. However, doing all of these tasks using Version 2.0 or better of the MFS Tools command suite is far easier and less nerve-wracking than performing each of these tasks manually and in the right order.

Command-line options for the **mfstool restore** command are as follows:

- ◆ *-B* Disables automatic detection of byte swapping, forcing the restore to be done with byte-swapping.

- ◆ *-b* Disables auto-detection of byte swapping, forcing the restore to occur without byte-swapping. This option is necessary when you are restoring backups made to the TiVo Series 2 with Version 1 of MFS Tools.

- ◆ *-i file* Identifies the file from which backup data should be read. As with most Linux applications, a dash ('-') can be specified instead of a filename, which indicates that the backup should be read from standard output. In this case, the **mfstool restore** command can read backup information piped to it from an **mfstool backup** command, enabling you to clone one TiVo disk to another without requiring any intermediate disk space for the backup image.

- ◆ *-l* Does not fill up the partition table on the target drive, providing the opportunity to subsequently add another pair of MFS volumes to the target disk(s). Of course, this option cannot guarantee that there will actually be free space available on the target drive(s), and can therefore not guarantee that it will be possible to add additional MFS volumes. This option is implied when the -**x** option is used.

- ◆ *-p* Causes the restore process to attempt to optimize the partition layout to provide optimal performance based on the disk/data access patterns used by TiVo machines. Using this option attempts to minimize disk head movement by positioning frequently-accessed application data in the middle of the disk(s) and storing video data on the outside cylinders of the disk(s).

◆ *-q* Suppresses the progress display that is typically displayed when executing a restore operation. Specifying this option twice suppresses all status information, only displaying error messages if any occur.

◆ *-r scale* This option enables you to trade off between the amount of RAM required to track disk usage on your TiVo drives and the efficiency of the storage used on those drives. The TiVo's MFS partitions can store data in 1, 2, 4, 8, or 16 MB allocation units. Choosing a smaller allocation unit size increases the efficiency of your TiVo's storage, because less space will be "wasted" when recordings do not completely fill an allocation unit. However, because more allocation units are required to store a recording if the allocation units themselves are smaller, the TiVo uses more memory when tracking smaller allocation units. For example, assume that the allocation unit was 16 MB and the TiVo was trying to store a recording that required 20 MB of disk space. This would require two allocation units and would completely fill the first one but waste 12 MB of disk space in the second. In order to keep track of the recording, the TiVo would have to keep information about both allocation units in memory. On the other hand, with an allocation unit of 4 MB, the recording would require 5 allocation units but no disk space would be wasted. However, the TiVo would have to keep information about 5 allocation units in memory to keep track of that recording.

Acceptable values for this option are 0 (corresponding to a 1 MB allocation unit), 1 (corresponding to a 2MB allocation unit), 2 (corresponding to a 4 MB allocation unit), 3 (corresponding to an 8 MB allocation unit), and 4 (corresponding to a 16 MB allocation unit). In general, the larger the allocation unit value, the less RAM will be used (making the TiVo more responsive when displaying menus, changing and processing options, and so on), but the greater the amount of storage that may be wasted when storing recordings.

◆ *-s size* Specifies the size in megabytes of the swap partition to create when restoring from backups. The default size of a TiVo swap partition is 64 MB, but can be increased up to 511 MB by using this option. A swap partition larger than 64 MB is required when your TiVo contains drives that provide more than 120 MB of storage for recordings. Larger swap partitions can also provide substantial performance improvements on TiVo machines with large drives or which run relatively large numbers of programs (e.g., TiVoWeb, FTPD, and telnet come to mind). When upgrading TiVo drives, it is always a good idea to set the swap space to 128 MB (by specifying a numeric value of 127, like any good C program would expect).

◆ *-v size* Specifies the size in megabytes of the **/var** partition that should be created when restoring from backups. The default size of the **/var** partition is 128 MB, which you may want to increase if you are planning to install significant amounts of extra software (such as your favorite hacks).

◆ *-X drive* Extends the MFS volume **setf** to fill the specified drive. This is similar to the -x option but only fills a single drive rather than all available drives. Multiple instances of this command can be specified on the **mfstool restore** command line (**-X /dev/hda -X /dev/hdb**), which is interesting, but rarely useful.

◆ *-x* Extends the MFS volume set to fill all of the drives onto which backup data is restored. Using this option creates extra pairs of FS partitions on the target drive(s) and adds entries for them to the table of usable space available on the TiVo, even if they are not actually required to save the data that you are restoring.

◆ *-z* Zeroes out any partitions that were not backed up, such as the inactive bootstrap, kernel and root partitions, as well as the **/var** partition if it is not in use. Swap space is automatically re-created, and is not zeroed out. Using this option may slightly increase the time required to restore your TiVo data, but ensures that the TiVo cannot attempt to use these partitions.

PDisk

The pdisk (Partition Disk) utility was originally developed for users of early versions of Linux on Macintosh and other systems that used processors in the Motorola 68000 (aka 68K) family. Although Linux already provides similar utilities such as **fdisk**, **cfdisk**, and **sfdisk**, a separate utility was developed for Macintosh systems for at least two of the following reasons:

◆ Summary information about the partitions on Macintosh hard disks (known as the partition map) is stored differently than it is on any other type of system.

◆ Instructions and data are stored and used in a different order on 68000 and related processors, compared to how they are stored on x86 and Pentium-class processors. (More about this later in this section.)

◆ It was an opportunity to write yet another utility program.

◆ The author of **pdisk** didn't like the way any other Linux disk partitioning tool worked.

On computer systems that use Motorola 68000 chips or their successors, the PowerPC (PPC) chips, instructions, and data are byte-swapped, compared to the order of x86 and Pentium-class instructions and data. If you envision a computer instruction as consisting of two side-by-side bytes, 68000 and PPC read these bytes from right to left, while x86 and similar processors read the bytes left to right. This is known as their byte-order—68K and PPC chips are known as Big-Endian (because they read from the "big" or "top" end of a word), while x86 and Pentium-class processors are known as Little-Endian.

Thanks to improvements in higher-end TiVo utilities such as the MFS Tools and BlessTiVo (itself largely outmoded), it is rarely necessary to use the **pdisk** utility to do most common TiVo tasks. Before BlessTiVo and MFS Tools provided features for automatically creating and adding new partitions, **pdisk** was the only utility in town for doing these sorts of things. However, **pdisk** can still be extremely useful to TiVo hackers because it enables you to manually create partitions of different types, including partitions in the standard Linux **ext2** and swap filesystem types. As explained in the section of Chapter 10, "A Safe Location for Storing Your TiVo Files," there are good reasons to consider creating your own partitions to hold software on your TiVo because its software updates can overwrite any of the default partitions on your TiVo, which may cause you to lose your hard-won TiVo hacks.

CHANGING BYTE-ORDERS IN MID-STREAM

As discussed earlier in this book, Series 1 models use a PPC processor, so it was quite natural for Series 1 machines to adopt the Macintosh partitioning and disk/data format conventions. Series 2 systems use MIPS processors, which can be used as either little-endian or big-endian processors. This was an interesting quandary for TiVo, who obviously had a big investment in the software and tools they had developed for the Series 1, especially system-level software such as the MFS filesystem. All TiVo software obviously had to be recompiled for the Series 2 systems, because MIPS processors use different instructions than PowerPC processors, but recompiling something is different than rewriting it. It's a common misconception that the reason that Series 1 and Series 2 TiVos use different byte-ordering is due to the change in processors, and that Series 2 machines therefore use the MIPS processor in little-endian mode. In reality, examining the kernel source and the ideturbo (high-speed IDE) module shows that the change in byte-ordering is actually due to extra calls to the `idetivo_bswap_data` function. Having the kernel source is a great mechanism for a little hi-tech detective work. Series 2 TiVos use the MIPS processor in big-endian mode.

The change in byte-ordering between Series 1 and Series 2 TiVos is a small change, but is something that you have to be aware of when you're hacking your TiVo, especially when restoring backups created with different versions of the MFS Tools utilities. For example, Version 1.0 of the MFS Tools utilities is hardwired to use big-endian, PPC byte ordering because that was the way all TiVo data was organized when Version 1 of these utilities was released. Version 2.0 of the MFS Tools utilities tries to automatically detect the appropriate type of byte ordering to use, but can't easily do this since these utilities are designed to run on a PC, rather than running natively on the TiVo. For this reason, Versions 2.0 and greater of the MFS Tools utilities add extra command-line options (**-b** and **-B**) that enable you to restore backups created with Version 1 of the software, changing the byte order however you'd like.

 NOTE

Like most disk partitioning utilities, **pdisk** focuses on creating and manipulating a disk's partition map (aka partition table). Some types of filesystems, such as the TiVo's MFS filesystem, are automatically initialized when an unformatted partition of a specific type is detected. Other types of partitions, such as the Linux **ext2** and swap partitions cannot be used until they have been specially formatted for use as those types of filesystems, using programs such as **ext2fs** and **mkswap**.

The **pdisk** command can be used in two different ways: with command-line options that simply display information and exit, or in interactive mode, where you can enter additional commands to execute specific **pdisk** functionality until you decide to terminate the **pdisk** command. The remainder of this section begins by providing a summary of popular **pdisk** command-line options, and then it provides an overview of the internal options provided by the **pdisk** command. For complete information about **pdisk** options, download the source code and associated online reference information for **pdisk** from URLs such as http://tivohack.sourceforge.net or http://www.wasteland.org/tivo.

TIP

Most versions of the **pdisk** command ignore the first few sectors of the drive where the bootpage is stored. If you format a new disk using the **pdisk** command, you will either need to subsequently use the bootpage command to write a valid bootpage or use the **dd** command to bring over the first few sectors from an existing drive.

The following example shows the output of the **pdisk** command, displaying a listing of the partition table on a stock TiVo Series 1 with a 20MB Quantum disk:

```
# pdisk -l /dev/hdd
Partition map (with 512 byte blocks) on '/dev/hdd'
 #:              type name             length    base    ( size )
 1: Apple_partition_map Apple                63 @ 1
 2:            Image Bootstrap 1          4096 @ 64      (  2.0M)
 3:            Image Kernel 1             4096 @ 4160    (  2.0M)
 4:             Ext2 Root 1             262144 @ 8256    (128.0M)
 5:            Image Bootstrap 2          4096 @ 270400  (  2.0M)
 6:            Image Kernel 2             4096 @ 274496  (  2.0M)
 7:             Ext2 Root 2             262144 @ 278592  (128.0M)
 8:             Swap Linux-swap         260096 @ 540736  (127.0M)
 9:             Ext2 /var               262144 @ 800832  (128.0M)
10:              MFS MFS application region 1048576 @ 1062976 (512.0M)
11:              MFS MFS media region  24777728 @ 2111552  ( 11.8G)
12:              MFS New MFS Application    1024 @ 26889280
13:              MFS New MFS Media      17104896 @ 26890304 (  8.2G)
14:       Apple_Free Extra               4000 @ 43995200  (  2.0M)
```

Commonly used **pdisk** command-line options are as follows:

- ◆ *-h* Displays a usage message for the **pdisk** command and then exits.
- ◆ *-i <device>* Starts the **pdisk** command in interactive mode, examining the specified <device>. When running pdisk in this mode, you can update any aspect of the specified <device> as long as you have sufficient privileges to do so.
- ◆ *-l <device>* Lists the partitions on the specified <device> and then exits.
- ◆ *-r <device>* Starts the **pdisk** command in read-only mode, examining the specified <device>. When using **pdisk** in this form, you cannot make any changes to any aspects of the data or partition map for the specified <device>.
- ◆ *-v* Displays the version and compilation date of the version of the **pdisk** command that you are using.

You can enter pdisk's interactive mode by using the **-i** command-line option or simply by executing the **pdisk** command followed by the name of the disk you are interested in examining or working with. The most commonly used commands in pdisk's interactive mode are the following:

- ◆ *-C <type>* Creates a new partition of the specified <type>.
- ◆ *-c* Creates a new PPC Linux partition of type **ext2**. The partition is not immediately ready for use—a filesystem must subsequently be created on that partition through the use of the **ext2fs** command.
- ◆ *-d <n>* Deletes partition <n>.
- ◆ *-h* Displays a quick reference list of the **pdisk** commands that are currently available, including a short description of each.
- ◆ *-i* Initializes the partition map, deleting any existing entries.
- ◆ *-n <name>* Assigns the specified <name> to a partition.
- ◆ *-P* Prints the current partition map, ordered by the base address.
- ◆ *-p* Prints the current partition table, ordered by the partition number.
- ◆ *-q* Quits **pdisk** without saving any changes that you have made.
- ◆ *-r <n> <m>* Reorders the entry for partition <n> to entry <m> in the partition map.
- ◆ *-s <n>* Changes the size of the partition map to <n> bytes.
- ◆ *-w* Writes the partition table to disk, saving any changes that you have made.
- ◆ *-x* Enters expert mode. Once in expert mode, the most useful expert-level commands are as follows:
  - ◆ *-?* Displays a quick reference list of the commands available in expert mode, along with short command descriptions.
  - ◆ *-M <n>* Clears the bit identifying partition <n> as an MFS media partition.
  - ◆ *-m <n>* Sets the bit identifying partition <n> as an MFS media partition.

◆ *-Q* Exits expert mode and the **pdisk** command without saving any changes that you may have made.

◆ *-q* Exits expert mode and returns you to the **pdisk** command's standard interactive mode.

Useful Linux Tools Outside Most Tools Disks

TiVos are Linux systems, so it isn't surprising that there is a huge number of standard Linux tools that can be useful when hacking your TiVo. This section provides an overview of the most popular of these, all of which are found on the BATBD that is included with this book.

The commands described in the previous section are TiVo-specific hacking tools; the ones in this section are just generic Linux tools that will be useful when hacking or simply poking around on your TiVo. The commands in this section are all tools that you will want to run on your x86 system, while one or more TiVo disks are attached. These are not commands that you want or need to cross-compile to execute them on your TiVo. Standard Linux commands that are already preinstalled on your TiVo or that you may want to recompile for your TiVo (or install from precompiled versions provided on the BATBD disk) are discussed in Chapter 9 in the section entitled "Popular Linux Software for the TiVo."

GenROMFS

The **genromfs** command generates a ROM (Read-Only Memory) filesystem image from the contents of a specified directory. ROM filesystems are used on your TiVo to trick it into executing a user-defined set of commands when the system boots. Ordinarily, a TiVo running Versions 2.5 and later of the TiVo software checks the contents of the system's startup files to make sure that the system has not been hacked. (For more information about the details of how the TiVo verifies these files, see the section of Chapter 9 entitled "The TiVo Startup Process.") Creating your own ROM filesystem enables you to cause the TiVo to execute commands stored in this filesystem, using the procedure described in the section of Chapter 7 entitled "Getting a Command Prompt on Your TiVo." This section simply explains the syntax of the **genromfs** command—we'll save the fun stuff for Chapter 7.

The **genromfs** command takes the following command-line options:

◆ *-A <alignment>,<pattern>* Aligns all objects matching <pattern> to at least <alignment> bytes, where <alignment> must be at least 16 bytes and must also be a power of two.

◆ *-a <alignment>* Aligns regular file data to <alignment> bytes, where <alignment> must be at least 16 bytes and must also be a power of two.

◆ *-d <directory>* Uses the specified directory as the source of the files that will be written to the ROM filesystem image file. The files and directories in the specified <directory> will appear in the root directory of the ROM filesystem image that you are creating.

◆ *-f <file>* Writes the ROM filesystem image into the specified <file>.

◆ *-h* Displays a usage message listing the command-line options available for use with the **genromfs** command.

◆ *-V <volumename>* Assigns the specified <volumename> to the ROM filesystem that you are creating. This is not the name of the file to which the ROM filesystem image will be written, but the internal volume identifier contained in the ROM filesystem.

◆ *-v* Provides verbose output when executing the **genromfs** command.

◆ *-x <pattern>* Excludes all objects matching <pattern> when creating the ROM filesystem image. Any objects matching <pattern> will not be included in the ROM filesystem image. The specified <pattern> can be any string of characters, and is used as a substring when checking against the names of items that could potentially be written to the ROM filesystem. The specified <pattern> can also use standard Linux/Unix regular expression syntax as long as it is quoted to prevent wildcard characters from being expanded on the **genromfs** command line, rather than internally by the **genromfs** command itself. For example, to match any filename containing the words "foo" and "bar", separated by any number of characters, you could use the regular expression **foo*bar**, but you would have to enclose this string within single quotation marks on the **genromfs** command line to prevent the shell from expanding the asterisk wildcard.

HexEdit

The **hexedit** (hexadecimal editor) command enables you to modify files, disks, and disk partitions directly. On Linux and Unix systems, disk and disk partitions are a series of bytes just like any file in those filesystems, and therefore can be opened, read, and written by any command that can access regular files. As shown in Chapter 2, the **hexedit** command is an interactive, screen-oriented command that makes it easy to search and modify the contents of a disk, disk partition, or file in both ASCII and hexadecimal modes. Figure 4.1 shows a sample hexedit screen.

The **hexedit** command is provided on the BATBD disk that accompanies this book, and is also available as part of the Knoppix Linux distribution. For the truly adventurous, you can read more about the **hexedit** command on its home page at the URL http://www.chez.com/prigaux/hexedit.html. If you find that a newer version is available and you want to download and compile it yourself, the source is available at the URL http://merd.net/pixel/hexedit-<version>.src.tgz, where <version> is the dot-separated version of the hexedit program. At the time that this book was written, the latest version was version 1.2.4, which is the version that is provided on the CD that accompanies this book.

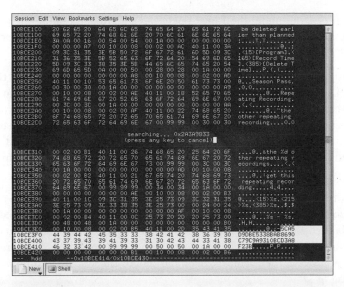

FIGURE 4.1 *Editing a partition using the Linux hexedit utility*

Script

The **script** command is a standard Linux/Unix utility that captures a transcript of all of the input and output from a single shell until you terminate the script command. It is part of the **linux-utils** package that is part of almost every Linux distribution. The default output file to which everything you type, and every response to each of those commands is captured is **type-script**. You can write output to a specific file by supplying its name on the **script** command-line. If the file does not already exist, it will be created. If the file already exists, its existing contents will be overwritten, so be careful.

Although not a useful diagnostic tool in its own right, the **script** command can be quite useful if you are having problems getting specific commands to work or if you are receiving odd error messages. By keeping a transcript of the shell in which you executed a specific command, you can then exchange this information with other knowledgeable TiVo hackers, who may be able to identify the source of the problem once they can see exactly what's happening. For this reason, a copy of the **script** command is included on the BATBD disk for your convenience.

Boot Disks

Previous sections of this chapter discussed various utilities for your TiVo, explaining the function of each and the various options that each provides to customize its behavior. Random collections of software are interesting, but the real key to actually using them successfully is packaging them—making them available for easy use. Packaging system-level software for a system like the TiVo is a more interesting challenge than simply packaging a single application so that you can install it on your current operating system. TiVo systems, and therefore most TiVo-related utilities, run under the Linux operating system and require the power and flexibility of specially-tuned versions of the Linux kernel and core libraries in order to work successfully.

Linux is discussed in greater detail in Chapter 9, but the key fact at this point is that most TiVo utilities require Linux to work correctly. Installing a separate operating system on the personal computer of every potential TiVo hacker is an obvious alternative, but hardly a reasonable solution. Most people use and depend on software that runs under operating systems such as Apple's Mac OS and Microsoft's Windows. While disk space is cheap, installing other operating systems and configuring a home computer to choose between them is impractical.

A practical solution for using tools that run under another operating system is to prepare stand-alone, bootable disks that enable you to run that operating system for as long you need it in order to use those tools. Most modern personal computers can easily be configured to boot from removable media such as floppy disks and CDs without requiring any changes to the existing software and operating system that is installed on the system's hard drive. Boot from these, run the tools that they provide, then remove them and reboot the system—no fuss, no muss, no messy dual-booting.

 NOTE

> This section is in no way a suggestion that people should not run Linux as their primary operating system. It is simply a recognition of the fact that most people could care less what operating system is running on their PCs, and would probably prefer not to know. An operating system exists to enable people to run the software that they need to accomplish whatever they need to accomplish. Since 75 percent of the commercial, home-user software available today is targeted at Windows machines, most people run Windows. Sad but true for a Linux and Mac OS X fan like the author.

Linux is a product of the Open Source movement, which states that the source code for software should (or must) be freely available. Beyond the huge amount of powerful software that this makes available to everyone, a side effect is that it is easy to freely distribute Open Source software in compiled form as long as the source code for that software can also be provided upon request. Since this book isn't a philosophy text, we can ignore the social and productive implications of this openness and look what it buys us directly. In the case of every aspiring TiVo hacker, Linux and open source means that it's relatively easy for TiVo fanatics to create bootable floppy disks and CDs that contain all of the tools that you may need to hack your TiVo and to freely distribute them. Floppy disks are small and therefore have obvious limitations in terms of how much software they can contain, but their contents are easily downloaded for the same reason. Now that almost every personal computer system has a CD drive, CDs are the way to go whenever possible—they can hold around 600 MB, which is sufficient to hold the operating system and a good-sized collection of relevant software.

Distributing free, bootable floppies and CDs presents an interesting problem. It's easy enough to distribute the software that they contain, but producing a bootable disk is slightly more complex than just installing application software. To be bootable, any media must have boot information in a special location on the disk (the boot block), and must provide special files relevant to the operating system that it provides. These files must also have special names, special attributes, and even be located in special locations on the disk. Not an easy thing to expect every home computer user to do—most people want to use the hammer, rather than making one.

To simplify distributing bootable media, most bootable tools disks are distributed as disk images. Floppy disk images usually have the extension IMG to show that they are a floppy image. CD images usually have the extension ISO to show that these are images of disks in the International Standard Organization 9660 format—a common, portable format for CDs that can be read by multiple types of computer systems. These image files come with special programs that write them directly to the floppy or CD. Rather than writing images to the floppy or CD as standard files and directories, these programs literally start writing at the beginning of the floppy or CD and stop at the end. When I fill an ice-cube tray, I generally hold one end under the faucet and let the water run down to fill each of the compartments for each future ice cube. Letting nature worry about which water goes into which ice cube—I only need to use them individually after the tray is full and the ice cubes freeze.

Like any software, the programs used to write floppies and CDs is operating-system specific—meaning, you use different programs to accomplish this, depending on the type of computer that you have and the operating system that it runs. Windows users can use programs such as Nero; Mac OS X users can use iTunes or Roxio's (formerly Adaptec's) Toast program; Linux and Unix users can use programs such as **dd** or **cdrecord**. There are many more such utilities for each of these operating systems and others—these are just my personal favorites. If you want to create (*burn*) your own copies of a TiVo tools disk from an IMG or ISO file, the programs required to do so will be discussed later in this book, along with a general discussion of the TiVo tools that are available for that operating system.

The remainder of this section discusses the various bootable TiVo tools disks that are freely available for Pentium-class x86 systems, including the one provided with this book. IMG and ISO files for all of the systems can be freely downloaded from the Internet if you want to compare and contrast them. See my TiVo Software Index at http://www.vonhagen.org/tivo for a list of up-to-date pointers to all things TiVo.

Earlier sections of this book have stressed the differences between Series 1 and Series 2 machines, but nowhere is this difference more important than when deciding which tools disk you want to use when hacking your machine. Selecting the right tools disk is the hi-tech equivalent of choosing between buying Torx or slotted screwdrivers—you cannot get the job done if you select the wrong type. In the case of some of the system software provided on TiVo tools disks, you can even permanently screw up your TiVo by selecting the wrong disk. The following table shows the mapping between tools disks and TiVo models. Make sure that you select the right one!

Characteristics of Various TiVo Tools Disks

```
Tools Disk        Type       TiVo Types Disk Is Usable on
                             Series 1        Series 2
------------------------------------------------------------

Dylan's           Floppy     Yes             No
TiVoMad           Floppy     Yes             No
Kazamyr           CD         Yes             No
Johnny Death      CD         With Care       Yes
BATBD             CD         Yes             Yes
Knoppix           CD         Somewhat        Somewhat
```

The remainder of this section discusses the most common bootable TiVo tools disks available on the Internet, highlighting the type(s) of TiVos that each is designed to work with, the tools that each contains, and any specifics that you need to know when hacking your TiVo using that specific boot disk.

 NOTE

While you can instantly boot your Pentium-class personal computer using any of the bootable TiVo tools disks discussed in this section, you won't be able to do much unless you have put the disk that you want to work with in your PC. This should either be a new disk that you are preparing for use with your TiVo or an existing TiVo drive. Removing disks from your TiVo and installing new or existing TiVo disks into your PC is explained in the section of Chapter 3 entitled "Working with TiVo Disk Drives."

The discussion of the TiVo tools disks in this section focuses on explaining the contents of the most popular TiVo tools disks. Information on using them is provided in the more task-oriented chapters of this book, such as Chapter 5 ("Backing Up and Restoring Your TiVo data"), Chapter 6 ("Expanding Your TiVo's Storage Capacity"), and Chapter 7 ("Connecting the Universe to Your TiVo").

BATBD—Bill's Accumulated TiVo Boot Disk

I'm obviously a fan of the bootable TiVo tools disk that comes with this book, BATBD, since I put it together. The name stands for "Bill's Accumulated TiVo Boot Disk," which is intended to highlight the fact that most of the tools on this disk have been rolled up from other TiVo boot disks. Although I built and added a few of my favorite utilities (hexedit, script, etc), most of the value that this disk provides is that it is designed to work with both Series 1 and Series 2 systems, that it provides preassembled collections of TiVo software that you can easily install on your TiVo, and that it also contains ready-to-install compilers for desktop systems that will enable you to compile your own software. It also makes a dandy coaster. This tools disk began life as a clone of Johnny Death's boot CD, into which I folded the Series 1 support provided on Kazamyr's boot CD. I then added archives of the cross-compilers I use on my desktop Linux system, archives of my Series 1 and Series 2 **/var/hacks** directories, and some of my favorite utilities.

When you boot your personal computer from the BATBD CD, the boot menu gives you three boot options: working with a Series 2 machine, working with a Series 1 system in byte-swapped mode so that you can mount and access TiVo partitions, and working with a Series 1 model in standard byte-order with Directory Memory Access (DMA) enabled to improve performance when backing up your Series 1. Each of these boot options loads a Linux filesystem that is created in your personal computer's memory. These types of filesystems are generally known as Random-Access Memory (RAM) disks, because they are portions of memory that are configured to look like an actual disk drive to your personal computer. In the case of Linux systems, these are referred to as initial RAM disks, because they are RAM disks that provide the initial filesystem for Linux.

Each of the initial RAM disks provided by the BATBD disk is tailored to the type of TiVo with which you are going to be working. The BATBD initial RAM disks contain all of the tools (MFS Tools, BlessTiVo, BootPage, PDisk, and so on) discussed in this book for both Series 1 and Series 2 machines—in other words, everything that you will need to back up, restore, and hack your TiVo. The initial RAM disk used by the Series 1 boot options also provides two versions of the TiVomad utilities for your convenience—using the latest one (3.2) is generally preferable, but you may want to use the older version if your TiVo is running a software release prior to Version 2.0.1.

Another key difference between the BATBD disk and the other TiVo tools disks is the software that the CD provides beyond the scope of the bootable kernel and associated initial RAM disks. Linux systems that boot from a CD load the Linux kernel and associated initial RAM disk into memory, but the CD itself can still contain files and directories that aren't required by the boot process. These aren't available to you until you actually mount the CD, which is Linux-speak for making it available to users so that you can go to that directory and explore its contents.

Installing the software found on the BATBD disk—once you've booted from it—is explained in Chapter 10, "Getting and Installing New Software for Your TiVo." The following items are found in various directories of the mounted BATBD disk:

- ◆ *connectivity* a directory containing TiVo software for connecting to and communicating with other systems.
- ◆ *floppy* A directory that contains an image of a bootable floppy disk that contains the MFS tools. This directory also contains the RAWRITE.EXE utility used to create a bootable disk from this image file under Microsoft Windows systems.
- ◆ *hack_dirs* A directory that contains archive files of complete directories of utilities that have already been compiled for your TiVo, and which are correctly organized so as to make them easy to install on your TiVo. These archive files are stored in the

Linux **tar** format. Installing these archives on your TiVo is explained in Chapter 10. All of the software that these archives contain is freely available on the Internet, but as single files and utilities that you would have to download one at a time. Since I've been accumulating these programs for years and have already organized them into the directory structure that they require, sharing them with the readers of this book in an easy-to-install, easy-to-use format seemed like "the right thing to do."

◆ *HISTORY* A text file that gives the history of changes made to different versions of the BATBD CD.

◆ *img* A directory that contains the files that can be assembled into a hacker's ROM filesystem for 3.x TiVos by using the **genromfs** utility.

◆ *img_monte* A directory that contains the files that can be assembled into a hacker's ROM filesystem that uses monte to bootstrap a hacked kernel from a standard one.

◆ *isolinux* A directory used by the CD boot process.

◆ *killinitrd* A directory containing versions of a utility used to remove an initial RAM disk (initrd) from various versions of the TiVo kernel.

◆ *macintosh* TiVo-related utilities for use on a Macintosh personal computer running Mac OS X.

◆ *monte-mips* A directory that contains the Two-Kernel Monte software required to successfully boot hacked versions of later Series 2 machines.

◆ *settings-backup* TCL scripts for backing up personalized information on your TiVo.

◆ *src* Source code for many of the TiVo-specific utilities that are built into the BATBD CD.

◆ *text* A directory that contains text files which provide additional information about things like the BlessTiVo program, hacking Series 2 DirecTiVo machines as originally done by TiVo hacker mlar, general information about DMA, the GNU Public License (GPL) under which most of the software on the BATBD disk has been released, using TiVos with network connections and DSL broadband, and the original Series 1 "Hacking the TiVo FAQ," for historical completeness.

◆ *tiVoweb-tcl-1.9.4.tar* An archive file that contains the TiVoWeb application, which is a powerful Web server and control application that runs on your TiVo, which you can access from any Web browser, enabling you to program, explore, and generally interact with your TiVo. This is an amazing program! While TiVo Inc. now offers remote, Web-based programming for Series 2 systems on which the Home Media Option has been purchased and activated, TiVoWeb works on both Series 1 and Series 2 TiVos, for free. TiVoWeb requires some appropriate network configuration to enable you to securely access it from computers outside your home network, but we're all hackers here, right? For detailed information about installing and using the TiVoWeb program, see Chapter 10.

◆ *windows* A directory that contains TiVo-related utilities for Microsoft Windows systems.

- *x86bin* A directory that contains handy TiVo programs precompiled for your Pentium-class desktop system, such as BlessTiVo, bootpage, busybox, and the **hexedit** and **script** utilities.

- *xcompilers* A directory that contains prebuilt compilers that you can install and use on any Linux system to build your own TiVo software. These compilers are what are known as *cross-compilers* because they run on one type of system but produce executable programs that run on another. In this case, they run on desktop personal computers that use Pentium-class x86 processors, but they produce executables that run on either the PPC or MIPS architectures.

The BATBD is full of fun things that I've accumulated or built over time—I hope you find it useful.

Dylan's Boot Floppy

Dylan's Boot Floppy is truly the pioneering boot disk for hacking the Series 1 TiVo, but it is somewhat constrained by both its age and the space limitations of a floppy disk. Designed for use on the Series 1, you still can use the software that it contains with extreme care to back up and restore data from the Series 2 TiVo, but I'd advise against it.

Dylan's boot disk contains all of the Series 1-related tools discussed in this book, such as MFS Tools v1.0, BlessTiVo, BootPage, PDisk, and so on, as well as standard Linux utilities (such as **dd**) that you can use to back up TiVo disks in raw format. You can obtain a copy of the IMG image file for Dylan's Boot Disk from http://www.tivofaq.com/hack.

Johnny Death's Boot CD

Johnny Death's CD was created by AVS TiVo community member johnnydeath primarily for use in hacking Series 2 DirecTiVo machines, although it provides options for booting your TiVo in byte-swapped mode to simplify working with TiVo Series 1 disks.

Like the BATBD disk described earlier, Johnny Death's Boot CD contains files and directories not required by the boot process, but which are only available after you mount the CD. The following are found in various directories of the mounted Johnny Death CD:

- *devbin-s2* A directory that contains a complete set of many of the most common Linux utilities, precompiled for use on a Series 2 TiVo. The name of this directory stands for "Developer's Binary Directory, Series 2."

- *floppy* A directory that contains an image of a bootable floppy disk containing the MFS tools. This directory also contains the RAWRITE.EXE utility used to create a bootable disk from this image file under Microsoft Windows systems.

- *genromfs* The utility used to create a ROM filesystem that is used as part of the process of hacking Series 2 systems running version Version 3.x of the TiVo software.

- *img* A directory that contains the files that can be assembled into a hacker's ROM filesystem by using the **genromfs** utility.

◆ *mfstools.1* A directory containing static and dynamically-linked versions of Version 1 of the MFS Tools utilities with its accompanying documentation. Although Version 2 of the MFS Tools provides additional capabilities, using Version 1 of the MFS Tools utilities can be simpler if you are working only with the TiVo Series 1 disks and existing backups of those disks.

◆ *mfstools.2* A directory that contains static and dynamically-linked versions of Version 2 of the MFS Tools utilities with its accompanying documentation.

◆ *other* A directory that contains text files that provide additional information about the BlessTiVo program, hacking Series 2 systems as originally created by TiVo hacker mlar, general information about DMA, the GNU Public License (GPL) under which most of the software on the BATBD disk has been released, using TiVos with network connections and DSL broadband, and the original Series 1 "Hacking the TiVo FAQ," for historical completeness.

◆ *tivoftpd-0.0.1* A directory that contains executable File Transfer Protocol (FTP) Daemon for the Series 2 TiVo, along with complete source code so that you can recompile it yourself, if desired. A daemon is Linux/Unix-speak for a process that is always running on a system, waiting to service incoming requests of one sort or another. Running an FTP daemon on your TiVo makes it easy to transfer files to and from your TiVo over a network. For more information on FTP and FTP daemons, see Chapter 9.

◆ *tivonet* A directory that contains the scripts and auxiliary software used to install a TiVoNet, TurboNet, or AirNet card on a Series 1 machine.

Johnny Death's CD is a great boot CD if you are primarily concerned about hacking the Series 2 TiVo and DirecTiVos. The BATBD CD included in this book owes a tremendous amount to this CD.

Kazamyr's Boot CD

Kazamyr's Boot CD was created by AVS TiVo community member kazamyr as the ultimate TiVo Series 1 hacking disk, and it still holds that title—if you're only interested in the Series 1. It provides multiple boot options for booting in byte-swapped mode, with and without DMA access for high-speed backups.

Like the BATBD and Johnny Death disks described earlier, Kazamyr's Boot CD contains files and directories not required by the boot process, but which are only available once you mount the CD. The CD primarily contains a number of text files that discuss different aspects of hacking the Series 1 TiVo; the CD also provides a **mfstools.1** directory that contains archives of static and dynamic versions of the MFS Tools utilities, Version 1.

You can obtain a copy of the ISO image of Kazamyr's boot CD from http://www.9thtee.com/tivobootcd.htm.

Knoppix Linux

Knoppix Linux actually has absolutely nothing to do with the TiVo. Rather, Knoppix Linux is a complete Linux distribution that boots and runs from the CD. It is often mentioned on the net in the context of TiVo hacking because it comes with a copy of the **hexedit** utility that is required to defeat the unknown hash code used by Series 2 machines running Version 4 and later of the TiVo software. (Defeating the hash code is explained in Chapter 2, in the section "Activating Back Door Mode on V3.1 and Later TiVos.") The hexedit utility is included on the BATBD CD provided with this book, so Knoppix Linux may no longer be as exciting as it once was—in terms of TiVo hacking.

Regardless of its value to the TiVo hacking community, Knoppix Linux is still an amazing Linux distribution if you are curious about Linux. It is a complete, up-to-date Linux distribution that includes the latest version (4.3) of the Linux XFree86 X Window System implementation, as well as the complete KDE desktop software suite. And, it's free! I even use Knoppix Linux as a portable diagnostic tools disk when troubleshooting general Windows networking problems, because it contains all of the networking tools I typically need, and it enables me to run Linux on systems that run Windows by default. Impressive, if not amazing!

You can obtain a copy of the ISO image of Knoppix Linux from the Knoppix Linux Web site at http://www.knopper.net/knoppix/index-en.html.

 TIP

If you're using Knoppix Linux for diagnostics purposes, you won't be able to use the Linux/Unix **su** command to become the root user because this is disabled on the Knoppix boot CD. However, you can use the **sudo /bin/bash** command to get a root shell, which is probably a more modern approach to su'ing all over the place

HACKING THE TiVo

Chapter 5

Backing Up and Restoring TiVo Data

Your TiVo is both a computer system and a home entertainment appliance, and should therefore be backed up at various times. Like any other computer system, you should back up your TiVo occasionally simply to guarantee that you don't lose critical data. In the case of the TiVo, settings for features like WishLists and Season Passes are personalized aspects of the TiVo system software that you may want to protect against hardware failures or accidental loss during a TiVo software upgrade—while this has never happened to me, others have reported this problem over the years, and it's always better to be safe than sorry.

The fact that your TiVo is a home entertainment appliance that stores recordings that you may treasure is another motivation for backing up your TiVo. You may want to back up your TiVo occasionally to protect recordings that are important to you and that you want to continue to view on your TiVo. Saving such "critical" recordings to long-term media like video tape (explained later in this chapter) or to other computer systems via the network are easy and safe ways of moving or cloning data from your TiVo onto external storage where it is safe from the vagaries of hardware failures and accidental deletion.

 PHYSICIAN, UN-UPGRADE THYSELF

Like all computer systems, your TiVo is ruled by its operating system software, which presents another significant reason for backing up your TiVo, although it might be frowned upon by the head TiVo office—protecting your TiVo against software upgrades, that is. As described earlier, different releases of the TiVo software have different capabilities and different levels of TiVo-induced security measures (for example, hashing). Each software release from TiVo Inc. provides enhancements such as improved recording quality, increased capabilities in WishLists, the user interface in general, and so on. However, if you've hacked your TiVo and are happy with it as it is, you may not want to get any other TiVo software release. The ability for TiVo Inc. to remotely upgrade your system can be a good thing if you just want the latest and greatest software, but it's a bad thing if you don't want your system upgraded. You can't apply the mantra, "don't fix it if it isn't broken" if someone else controls the upgrade process. To protect yourself in this case, it's important to have a backup of your TiVo so that you can roll back to the software version that you liked after being upgraded against your will, and it is also useful to discourage your TiVo from upgrading itself by setting special boot parameters. This process is described later in this chapter in "Changing TiVo Operating System Versions Using Backups."

Video extraction, which is the term used to describe the process of transferring saved video from your TiVo to another system, is an especially touchy subject in DVR circles. Video extraction and depriving TiVo Inc. of revenues from the TiVo service are the two forbidden topics on public TiVo discussion areas such as the AVS forums, but for two totally different reasons.

Depriving TiVo Inc. of service revenue (generally known as "stealing service") is wrong for obvious reasons. First, $12.95 a month or $300 for lifetime service simply isn't worth stealing. The folks at TiVo have worked long and hard to make the TiVo the great entertainment appliance it is. Perhaps I'm old-fashioned, but I think that people deserve to be rewarded for good work. If the TiVo service is available in your area and you don't want to pay for it, that's really too bad. You should. Things are somewhat different if you live outside the US in an area where the TiVo service is unavailable, but you still want to own and use a TiVo. This book can't help you in that circumstance because some greedy fool would use those techniques in areas where the service is available, and that would be wrong. However, if you poke around on the net long enough, you can find posts and pages from people in distant areas like Australia that do not have access to the TiVo service but have worked around the problem.

Extracting video from your TiVo so that you can save it to long-term storage that you can watch using devices other than the TiVo is a totally different matter. It isn't discussed in this book because doing so may encourage the legal locusts from the MPAA and the RIAA to descend on TiVo Inc. (or me) in a frenzy of self-serving avarice, suing TiVo into a stupor. This worked with ReplayTV, and I'd hate to see TiVo get the same sort of legal cancer. Recording broadcast television and movies for resale is wrong. Recording them for your own personal use should be totally legal. They broadcast it, we received it, and we probably sat through the commercials at least once—I think we've paid our dues and fulfilled the contract. However, it's still a touchy subject that is best avoided until a more enlightened future time. Luckily, as described in the last section of this chapter, there are easy and totally legal ways of recording broadcast television that have nothing to do with your TiVo. These aspects of the topic are fair game.

Overview

There are two basic ways to back up any computer system:

◆ Unstructured backups, where your backup is essentially an exact copy of a disk or disk partition. This type of backup requires no information about the organization of the data on disk because you are simply making a raw, image copy of a disk or partition.

◆ Structured backups, where your backup is a copy of the data and relevant data structures on the disk. This type of backup must be done using a program that understands how the data on a disk or disk partition is organized, and then uses that information to traverse the disk or partition in a structured fashion.

Each of these backups techniques has specific advantages. Unstructured backups are easy to do, require no special software, and serve as a complete snapshot of an entire disk or partition at a given moment in time, down to files that the system has marked for deletion but which have not yet been purged from or overwritten on the disk. Unstructured backups of the TiVo use the Linux version of one of the original Unix utilities, an age-old utility called *dd*, which stands for "dump data." The dd program does exactly that by leveraging the fact that all native system data on Unix/Linux systems is stored as a stream of bytes and can be accessed in that way. As explained in more detail later in this chapter, the dd utility has two mandatory arguments, which are the names of its input and output files.

Structured backups take less space than unstructured backups because they are performed by utilities that understand the organization of the files, directories, and relevant data structures on the filesystems they back up. They access the data on the disk or partition that you are backing up through actual filesystem data structures, and therefore only back up the portions of the filesystem that actually contain data. If you only have 1 GB of data on a 10 MB partition, structured backups will only require 1 GB of storage space (at most, and perhaps less, if you are doing compressed backups).

Several structured backup utilities are available for the TiVo, the best being MFS Tools utilities. The **mfstool** backup utility is specially designed to back up all of the types of filesystems that the TiVo uses, and features many different options to customize what you are backing up and how you are backing it up. Doing structured backups of your TiVo using the **mfstool** backup command is discussed later in this chapter, in the section "Creating Backups Using MFS Tools." The structured backups of a TiVo drive that do not include your recordings are usually between 100 and 200 MB in size.

The MFS Tools utilities recognize the format of all of the types of filesystems used by your TiVo, from standard Linux **ext2** filesystems to the MFS filesystems that are specific to the TiVo, and back each up differently. On a hacked TiVo, you could also choose to back up the data in the TiVo's standard Linux **ext2** filesystems (**hda4**, **hda7**, and **hda9**) by using the standard Linux **tar** (tape archiver) and **cpio** (Copy Input to Output) utilities. Each uses its own archive formats, but they are quite common in Linux/Unix circles. The primary difference between the two utilities is that the **tar** utility cannot back up special Linux/Unix files such as the entries in the **/dev** and **/proc** directories, but otherwise is the ubiquitous standard for archiving Linux/Unix directories. The **tar** utility takes the name of one or more directories or files as a command-line argument, and creates an **ar** archive file that contains the specified directories and files. The **cpio** utility is much less widely used, but has more sophisticated capabilities. It can back up any type of Linux/Unix file, but requires that a list of files and directories to back up be supplied as its standard input, and writes an archive of those files and directories to its standard output (which users typically redirect into a file).

 NOTE

While the Linux/Unix structured backup utilities discussed earlier can be useful for backing up selected portions of the Linux filesystems on your TiVo, using the MFS Tools utilities is the only way to do a structured backup of your TiVo that you can subsequently use to restore your TiVo to a completely usable state.

The downside of structured backups is that they are very sensitive to the consistency and condition of the filesystem. If the filesystem is corrupted, the utility that you are using to make structured backups may not be able to follow the organization of files and directories on the disk, and may simply bail out. On TiVo filesystems that store information in a standard Linux filesystem format, such as the root and /var partitions' use of the ext2 filesystem format, you can usually correct this sort of problem by running the e2fsck utility to clean up those filesystems before doing the backup. This won't help if there are problems with any of your MFS filesystems. Similarly, if the underlying hardware on which a filesystem is stored begins to go bad, you may not be able to make structured backups due to read errors on the hard drive.

 IF TIVOS CRASH AND STRUCTURED BACKUPS FAIL...

If one of the drives in your TiVo is going bad and occasionally flakes out (i.e., your TiVo crashes or structured backups fail), creating an unstructured backup of that disk may be the solution to your problem. You can use the **dd** program to create an image backup of the entire disk, and then either replace the disk or reformat it. (The former is preferable, but the latter may work.) After you have replaced or reformatted the disk, you can then restore the backup to the new disk (as explained later in this chapter), and then retry the structured backup. If you are lucky and the reason that the backup failed and your TiVo crashed was repeated read/write errors to the disk, you just might be able to recover all of your TiVo settings and existing recordings.

When to Back Up

To some extent, the differences between the two types of backups dictate when it is appropriate to use one over the other. You can make an image backup at any time, because it always uses the same amount of space as the media that you are backing up. In other words, making an image copy of a 30 GB disk will always require 30 GB of backup storage, regardless of whether the disk contains 1 byte of data or 29 GB of data. If you can afford the disk space, keeping an image backup around is never a bad idea. However, since unstructured backups save an exact snapshot of the entire disk, people rarely do them except when they first get a TiVo, and perhaps later when the TiVo disk is almost full of recordings that they want to save.

TIP

Because unstructured backup images are so large, they are often split into multiple files, which are therefore small enough to fit on removable media (such as CDs or backup tapes for offline storage) until you need them. Use the Linux/Unix **split** command and the Linux/Windows RAR utility for this purpose.

If conserving disk space or minimizing the amount of potentially extraneous information in your backups is a concern, the best time to use the MFS Tools to do a structured backup of your TiVo is the day that you get it, before going through the Guided Setup process. This gives you a completely virginal image of your TiVo's hard drive. You can then restore this to your TiVo at any time to start over from ground zero. A virginal backup image can also come in handy if you or a friend encounters hardware problems and needs to completely restore a TiVo to its original, out-of-the-box state.

For personal reuse, you may find it preferable to use the MFS Tools to do a structured backup of your TiVo immediately after going through the Guided Setup process so that the backup contains the information about your local TiVo dialup connection. Disk space is cheap nowadays. Similarly, it is also a good idea to do a backup after any new TiVo software release in order to eliminate the need to re-upgrade your system if you have to reinstall from backups for one reason or another.

One thing to remember about backing up your TiVo using the MFS Tools utilities is that, unlike many structured backup utilities, the MFS Tools do not perform incremental backups. Every backup of a primary TiVo disk done with the MFS Tools is a complete backup of the subset of the partitions on that TiVo disk (and the data that they contain), which is required to successfully boot your TiVo. This means that MFS Tools backups are always relatively large even if little has changed on your TiVo since the last time you did an MFS Tools backup. This also means that restoring one MFS Tools backup to a disk on which a previous MFS Tools backup has been restored will completely overwrite the previous backup data.

Finding Room for Backups

Whether you're creating structured or unstructured backups, the fact remains that backup files take up a fair amount of space. Unstructured backups of disks and partitions require exactly the same amount of space as each disk or partition that you back up. Structured backups of a TiVo disk, even without saving any of your recordings, generally take between 200 and 800 MB. Where should you put your backups?

Disk space is cheap nowadays, but getting to it may be an issue. The primary hard drives in most people's computer systems are relatively large, usually ranging from 10 GB to well over 100 GB. TiVo tools CDs, such as BATBD, use RAM disks to hold their filesystems and are primarily designed to give you access to the TiVo disks. Luckily, there's an easy solution to this problem, which capitalizes on the flexibility of Linux and its ability to interoperate with the different types of filesystems used on a variety of personal computers.

NOTE

The versions of Linux provided on the BATBD CD can only access storage located on Windows disks that have been formatted with the FAT32 filesystem. If the filesystems on your personal computer are formatted using the NTFS (NT File System) format, you will not be able to access them after booting from the BATBD CD. Chalk up another piece of proprietary crap to Microsoft.

If your primary desktop machine is a Windows system and you don't know what type of filesystem it uses, you can find out from Windows by opening the My Computer folder on your desktop, right-clicking the icon for your system's C drive, and then selecting Properties from the context-sensitive menu that displays. The resulting dialog box displays information about the disk including the type of filesystem that it contains, as shown in Figure 5.1.

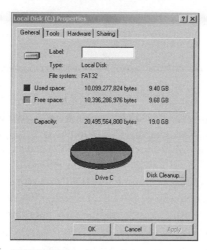

FIGURE 5.1 *Determining the type of filesystem on a Windows drive*

As discussed earlier, even the kernels on TiVo tools CDs that do byte-swapping only activate byte-swapping for the devices attached as the slave device on your primary IDE interface (**/dev/hdb**, in Linux terms), the master drive attached to your secondary IDE interface (**/dev/hdc**, in Linux terms), and the slave drive attached to your secondary IDE interface (**/dev/hdd**, in Linux terms). The master drive on your primary IDE interface is never byte-swapped, and therefore provides access to the native filesystems on your personal computer. All you have to do is make them available to the TiVo tools CD from which you've booted. This can be done with a single Linux command.

TIP

When doing backups, you do not need to boot with the byte-swapped kernel even if you are using a Series 1 system. When you restore the backup, the MFS Tools utilities' **mfstool restore** command provides options that make it easy for you to restore both byte-swapped and "normal" backups—as discussed in Chapter 4, the MFS Tools utilities provide internal support for byte-swapping when necessary, regardless of what the kernel provides. However, if you are using a Series 1 system, you always want to boot using a byte-swapped kernel when you are restoring a backup to a TiVo disk. This will enable you to use the **pdisk** command to verify that the TiVo disk has been restored correctly. Mounting and unmounting disks and moving them from one system to another is tedious enough without doing it multiple times because the restore used the wrong byte order.

When you boot from a TiVo tools CD, such as BATBD, you are running Linux. Linux uses its **mount** command to add existing disks and partitions to the filesystem. The syntax of the **mount** command is as follows:

```
mount -t <type> <partition> <mountpoint>
```

In this example, <type> is the type of partition that you are mounting, which would be one of **vfat** (the Linux name for Windows FAT32 partitions), or **ext2** if your desktop system is a Linux system that uses the default **ext2** partition type. The <partition> argument is the Linux name for the disk partition that you want to mount, probably **/dev/hda1** for a Windows C drive and any of **/dev/hda1** through **/dev/hda8** for a Linux system (depending on how you partitioned your disk when you installed Linux). The <mountpoint> argument is the name of a directory in the Linux filesystem (the RAM disk, if you've booted from BATBD) through which you want to be able to access the partition that you're mounting. Linux traditionally puts directories on whichever external filesystem is to be mounted (known as *mountpoints*) in the directory **/mnt**.

TIP

You can use the Linux **fdisk** command to quickly list the types of filesystems on a Linux disk. For example, the command `fdisk -1 /dev/hda` would produce a list of all of the partitions on the drive /dev/hda and their types.

If your desktop computer is a Windows system where the C drive is a FAT32 partition and you have booted from the BATBD CD, you could mount your Windows disk on the directory **/mnt/windows** using the following command:

```
mount -t vfat /dev/hda1 /mnt/windows
```

After executing this command, you could create TiVo backup files in the directory **/mnt/win-dows,** which you would then find in the C: directory on your Windows system after booting it from its own disk rather than the BATBD CD.

If your desktop computer is a Linux system, use the **df** command to see how its partitions are organized before you reboot your system from the BATBD disk. For example, the output of the **df** on my primary Linux system would look like the following:

```
Filesystem          1K-blocks      Used Available Use% Mounted on
/dev/hda7           10080488    987164   8581256  11% /
/dev/hda1             101089     29810     66060  32% /boot
/dev/hda8           30668576  15242724  13867952  87% /home
none                  515532         0    515532   0% /dev/shm
/dev/hda2            2016044       520   1913112   1% /tmp
/dev/hda5           20161172   4249540  14887492  23% /usr
/dev/hda6           15116836   2799492  11549440  20% /usr/local
/dev/hdb1          196015808  83683884 102374840  45% /opt2
```

In this case, the partition **/dev/hda8** is the partition where home directories are located and the partition also has around 13 GB of free disk space, which is enough for most structured TiVo backups. After booting from the BATBD CD, you could therefore mount this filesystem on the directory **/mnt/home** using the following command:

```
mount -t ext2 /dev/hda3 /mnt/home
```

In this case, the **-t ext2** argument is actually unnecessary, because **ext2** is the default partition type for the **mount** command—it is shown here for the sake of completeness. After executing this command, you could create TiVo backup files in the directory **/mnt/home,** which you could then find in the **/home** directory on your Linux system after booting it from its own kernel rather than the BATBD CD.

If you are using a Windows system and your C drive turns out to be formatted using an NTFS filesystem, all is not lost—you can always add another disk to your Windows system, boot into Windows, and format the new drive using the FAT32 filesystem. You then can shut down the system again, add your TiVo disk to this system, and mount the newly-created FAT32 parti-tion as described earlier, using that disk as storage for your backup files.

If you have absolutely no disk space and want to back up a TiVo disk solely for the purpose of immediately restoring it to another disk, you can take advantage of the ability of Linux to con-nect the output of one program to the input of another. In Linux terms, this is done using a pipe, which is represented on the command-line as the "|" symbol. In this way, you can use the **mfstool backup** command to back up your existing disk, writing the backup file to what is known as *standard output,* which the corresponding **mfstool restore** command will then use as its *standard input.* This process is described in more detail later in this chapter in "Connecting Backup and Restore Commands Using a Pipe."

Creating Image Backups Using dd

As mentioned earlier, the **dd** command is one of the oldest and most primal Unix commands around. The **dd** command reads data from one source and writes it to another, with some control over the size of the chunks in which it is read and written at each end, plus the ability to do various forms of data manipulation in between. You'll only need to know about a few of these bells and whistles to use the **dd** command to make image backups of a disk or disk partition from your TiVo. However, it's always nice to know that there are other knobs to turn if future developments in TiVo-land require them.

The first step in creating an image backup of a TiVo disk or disk partition is to take the disk drive out of your TiVo and put it into your desktop PC, as explained in Chapter 3, "Exploring Your TiVo Hardware," in the section "Working with TiVo Disk Drives." As discussed in that section, make sure that you jumper the disk correctly so that it does not conflict with any existing disk in your desktop PC. Also note the IDE interface to which you attached the disk, so that you can be sure that you are backing up the right disk. Few things would be as embarrassing or irritating as trying to use a backup image to restore or expand your TiVo, only to find out that the backup image contained data from the wrong disk or partition.

 NOTE

As explained in the section of Chapter 4 that discusses bootable TiVo tools disks, any of the byte-swapped kernels on these disks (necessary for mounting TiVo Series 1 disk partitions) only byte-swap the secondary disk on your primary IDE interface (**/dev/hdb**), and the primary and secondary disks on your secondary IDE interfaces (/**dev/hdc and /dev/hdd**, respectively. If you want to access the partitions on a TiVo Series 1 disk, that disk must not be attached to your PC as the master drive on your primary IDE interface.

Once the disk is successfully mounted in your PC, you can use the **dd** command to make a backup image of an entire disk at any time, regardless of which of the TiVo kernels on the BATBD disk you have booted from. Reading raw data from an entire disk does not require that you can directly access the specific partitions on the disk, only that you can access the disk itself. (Once you've booted from the BATBD disk, follow the naming conventions given in Chapter 3 for accessing TiVo disks mounted in your PC.) However, if you want to make image backups of specific partitions from a TiVo disk, you will need to boot using a kernel that understands the TiVo's partition table format, and which has the appropriate byte-order for the type of TiVo from which the disk you are copying was taken. If you are working with a TiVo Series 1 disk, you will need to use the BATBD boot option that specifies that it is designed to access TiVo partitions. Since the disks from Series 2 machines do not require byte-swapping to access their partition table, you could boot using either of the other boot options from the BATBD CD to access partitions on a TiVo Series 2 disk. These are the

Series 2 or non-swapped Series 1 boot options, though the former certainly seems to make more sense.

TIP

If you are using a desktop Linux system for your TiVo hacking purposes and want to mount TiVo Series 1 or Series 2 disks without using the BATBD disk, you will need to recompile your kernel. To do so, simply enable the Macintosh Partition Support in the filesystems section of the kernel Configuration menu. Once you've rebuilt the kernel, you can mount the **ext2** partitions from a TiVo Series 2 disk directly. You can also mount the **ext2** partitions from a TiVo Series 1 disk by passing the **hdX=swap boot** option on the kernel command line, where **X** is the letter corresponding to the TiVo disk in your system. You can also create an entry for byte-swapped booting in the configuration files used by the Linux boot loaders, GRUB or LILO, to simplify support for Series 1 disks in the future.

After you've booted your system with the appropriate kernel options, you can use the **dd** command to create an unstructured backup of a TiVo disk by using a command like the following:

```
dd if=<disk> of=<backup-file> bs=32k
```

This tells the **dd** command to read from the disk specified as <disk> (probably one of **/dev/hda**, **/dev/hdb**, **/dev/hdc**, or **/dev/hdd**) and write to the output file <backup-file>. The **bs** option tells the **dd** command to use 32K as both the input and output block sizes, which reflects the block size used on TiVo filesystems.

You can use the **dd** command to create an unstructured backup of a specific partition on your TiVo disk by using a command like the following:

```
dd if=<partition> of=<backup-file> bs=32k
```

This tells the **dd** command to read from the disk specified as <disk> (probably one of **/dev/hdXY**, where **X** is the identifier for the disk and **Y** is the partition number) and write to the output file <backup-file>. As in the previous example, the **bs** option tells the **dd** command to use 32K as both the input and output block sizes, which reflects the block size used on TiVo filesystems.

The **dd** command takes a while to run, given that it is transferring a fairly large amount of data. Unfortunately, the standard versions of the **dd** command provide no visual feedback while they execute. For people who absolutely must have a progress indicator, a specially hacked version of the **dd** command with a progress indicator is available on the net at http://tivohack.source-forge.net/files/fileutils-4.1.bonehead.tar.gz. (I have nothing to do with the naming convention for this file, which is intended to reflect the fact that displaying the progress indicator slows down the overall performance of this version of the **dd** command by approximately 10%.) To display the progress indicator, pass the progress=1 option on the **dd** command line.

EXPLORING TIVO THROUGH VIRTUAL FILESYSTEMS

If you are using a desktop Linux system for your TiVo hacking, making image back-ups of partitions provides interesting hacking opportunities. Once you use **dd** to clone a disk partition to a file, you can then use Linux's loopback filesystem to mount that file as though it were a physical partition on your Linux system. This only works for partitions that are in a format that your desktop system understands, such as the **ext2** partitions in partitions 4, 7, and 9 of any primary TiVo disk.

If you want to mount partition images from a Series 1 system (which is big-endian) on a standard desktop PC (which is little-endian), you will need to convert the byte-order of the filesystem image using the **dd** command's **conv=swab** conversion option, as in the following example:

```
dd if=series1_hda9.img of=series1_hda9_pc_style.img conv=swab
```

You can then mount the "un-byteswapped" image (**series1_hda9_pc_style.img**, from the preceding example) using the **mount** commands described later in this section. For more information about "endian-ness," see the section of Chapter 4 on the **pdisk** command.

Mounting filesystem images enables you to explore the contents of the parent partition without requiring the disk that contains the filesystem still is physically attached in your desktop system. This can be handy if, for example, you would like to actually use your TiVo at the same time that you are learning more about its internals.

To mount a partition image as a file, use a command like the following:

```
mount -o loop <filename> <mountpoint>
```

In this example, <filename> is the name of the file to which you wrote the partition image (using a command like **dd**, as explained later in this chapter), and <mount-point> is the name of the directory on which you want to mount the partition image. For example, the following command would mount the partition image in the file "hda_part4.img" on the directory **/mnt/tivo/part4**:

```
mount -o loop hda_part4.img /mnt/tivo/part4
```

After you have mounted a partition image, you can redirect the directory to it, move around in its files and directories; you can create, edit, and delete files, and generally do anything that you could do if it were an actual disk partition. This also includes running scripts on any Linux system, as well as programs—if you happen to be running a compatible version of Linux on a PPC or MIPS box. (Not much chance of that these days, but you never know...)

If you mount an image file, you must unmount it before shutting down your system or, like any other filesystem, you should use the **fsck** command to verify its integrity before reusing it.

TIP

If, for some reason, you have problems using the specified **dd** command due to errors, try executing the following **dd** command, which uses some of the **dd** command's "forgiveness" options:

```
dd if=<partition> of=<backup-file> bs=32k conv=noerror,sync
```

These options cause the **dd** command to proceed past simple errors that you may encounter if your source drive is having problems. The **sync** option synchronizes, reads, and writes—even after a read error—by padding incomplete reads with the appropriate number of NULL bytes.

Again, whether you are backing up a partition or an entire disk, the **dd** command takes a long time. Creating an image backup of a TiVo partition is a great opportunity to walk your dog around the block or to have a cigarette. Creating an image backup of an entire TiVo disk is a great opportunity to make dinner or go shopping.

Creating Backups Using MFS Tools

The unstructured backups discussed in the previous section are typically huge because they are the same size as the disk or partition that you are backing up. The MFS Tools utilities, discussed in detail in Chapter 4, create structured backups of TiVo disks by walking through the disk's partition table and the actual data structures contained in MFS filesystems. The MFS Tools utilities also conserve some space by automatically skipping certain partitions during the backup process, such as the duplicate kernel and root filesystem partitions on a bootable TiVo disk. As explained in Chapter 4, you can further reduce (or increase) the size of the backups produced by the **mfstool backup** utility by passing various command-line options.

This section explains how to perform a variety of different types of backups using the **mfstool backup** command from MFS Tools utilities. As with the previous section, you will need to have mounted the TiVo disk(s) that you want to back up in your PC before preceding; however, you do not have to boot with any special command-line options if you are using Version 2 of the MFS Tools utilities. Knowledge of the partition table and byte-swapping requirements of TiVo disks was built into Versions 2 and later of these utilities—all of which you need to know to execute the appropriate command. You may need to do a bit more when restoring the data to verify that it was written with the appropriate byte-order. (More about that later in this chapter, in the section entitled "Restoring Backups Using MFS Tools.")

NOTE

If you are unclear on how to attach a TiVo drive to your personal computer or aren't sure of the naming conventions used to access such drives after doing so, please review the section in Chapter 3, entitled "Working with TiVo Disks."

The following information explains how to use the basic capabilities of the MFS Tools utilities, beginning with simple structured backups that use the default settings compiled into the MFS Tools utilities, then moving on to more advanced types of backups. All of these backup commands use the **mfstool backup** command from MFS Tools utilities, showing how different options to the command can affect the size and contents of the backup files that you create.

Creating a Simple Backup Using MFS Tools

The simplest type of structured backup that you can do using the **mfstool backup** command requires only one command-line option, which is the name of the backup file that you want the utility to create. After booting from the BATBD disk, to back up a TiVo disk that is attached to your personal computer as the slave drive on your secondary IDE interface, you would execute a command like the following:

```
mfstool backup -o <output-file> /dev/hdd
```

In this example, <backup-file> is the name of the file to which you want to write the backup data. If you followed the conventions discussed earlier in this chapter for mounting a partition from your primary Windows or Linux disk so that you can access it from the BATBD disk, this file should be the full path of a file on the appropriate disk. For example, if your Windows C drive is mounted as **/mnt/**windows, you could specify a filename such as **/mnt/windows/my_tivo.bak**. If the home partition of a desktop Linux system is mounted as /mnt/linux, you could specify a filename such as **/mnt/home/my_tivo.bak**. Using the Windows disk as an example, you would execute a command like the following:

```
mfstool backup -o /mnt/windows/my_tivo.bak /dev/hdd
```

The **mfstool backup** command displays output like the following during the backup process:

```
Scanning source drive.  Please wait a moment.
Source drive size is 15 hours
Uncompressed backup size: 1309 megabytes
Backing up NNN of 1309 megabytes (M.MM%)
Backup done!
```

The line beginning with "Source Drive" shows the **mfstool backup** command's idea of the capacity of the drive you're backing up, which in this example is a 15MB Quantum disk from a TiVo Series 1 machine. While the **mfstool backup** command is running, the line reading

"Backing up NNN of 1309 megabytes (M.MM%)" is continually updated to show the progress of the backup command. After the command completes its task, congratulations! You've backed up your TiVo!

You can determine the actual size of the backup file produced by the **mfstool backup** command by using the Linux **ls** command, as in the following example:

```
ls /mnt/windows/my_tivo.bak

-rwxr-xr-x   1 root     root     1374030336 Jun 26 12:19 /mnt/windows/my_tivo.bak
```

In this case, the file is 1,374,030,336 bytes in size, which is close to what was predicted.

 NOTE

The actual size of your backups depends on the size of your original drive, the version of the TiVo software that is installed on the disk, any additional information that you may have put in your drive's **/var** partition, and the backup options that you specify. The sizes shown in the examples throughout this chapter will almost certainly not match the size of your backups.

Since this backup command used the defaults provided by the **mfstool backup** command, it's useful to know what they are and what the backup file contains. With no options other than the **-o** option to specify the name of the output file, a backup file produced by the **mfstool backup** command contains the following:

- ◆ A copy of the partition map from the specified disk
- ◆ A copy of the bootpage from the specified disk
- ◆ A compressed copy of the active kernel partition from the specified disk
- ◆ A compressed copy of the active root filesystem partition from the specified disk
- ◆ A compressed copy of the /var partition from the specified disk
- ◆ A backup of the entries in the MFS partitions on the specified disk whose filesystem identifier (fsid) is less than 2000. These are all of the files in the MFS Application and Media regions on the disk that are required for normal operation of your TiVo.

When you restore a backup file created by the **mfstool backup** command, the **mfstool restore** command uses the copy of the original drive's partition map to create the necessary filesystems before restoring their contents. In the case of the Linux swap partition on the TiVo disk, the **mfstool restore** command simply creates an empty partition of the appropriate size (or larger, depending on **mfstool restore** options) and correctly initializes it for use as a swap partition. Backing up a swap partition would be a total waste of time because it is used only by the operating system as a temporary location to provide virtual memory support.

For more details about the restore process and the contents of a backup file created using the **mfstool backup** command, see the section "Restoring Backups Created Using MFS Tools," later in this chapter.

Creating a Compressed Backup Using MFS Tools

The previous section explained how to create a simple structured TiVo backup using the **mfstool backup** command. While still much smaller than the physical capacity of the TiVo disk that you were backing up, these backups are still fairly large—816 MB or so is nothing to sneeze at. A decade or two ago, this was beyond the maximum storage capacity of a good-sized mainframe. Even though disk space is cheap now (I paid $160 or so for my last 200 GB drive), saving disk space whenever possible is never a bad idea. A classic computer maxim goes like this: "The amount of disk space required by users always expands to fill all available storage." This certainly is even truer when programs create 816 MB files with a single command.

The **mfstool backup** command provides built-in options for compressing backup files as they are created. For the hard-core nerds among us, this is done through the used of the Linux **zlib** library, which implements a standard Lempel-Zev compression scheme to reduce disk consumption in output files. For the rest of us, "the files are smaller."

The **mfstool backup** command provides 10 levels of compression (levels 0 through 9), which reflect the tradeoff between compression and execution time. Obviously, compressing data takes some time, which means that creating a compressed backup takes longer than creating a standard, uncompressed backup file. Higher levels of compression do substantial amounts of extra processing to reduce the size of your backup files, but may not have as radical an impact on the size of your backup files as the middle compression levels do. At some point, the savings provided by higher levels of compression isn't worth the time it takes to completely minimize the size of your backup files—saving two or five megabytes of a file that is still a few hundred megabytes in size just may not be worth it.

When using the **mfstool backup** command, compression options are specified using a command-line option that identifies the compression level for which you're looking. These options are therefore -1 through -9, with -9 being the maximum compression level possible. The compression value recommended in the documentation for the **mfstool backup** command itself is -6, which is the one that I typically use. As noted in the MFS Tools documentation, this compression option seems to provide the best tradeoff between savings in backup file size and slower performance of the **mfstool backup command.**

Using a mounted Windows disk as an example of the destination for the backup file that you are creating, the command you would type to perform a compressed backup at compression level 6 is the following:

```
mfstool backup -6 -o /mnt/windows/my_tivo.bak /dev/hdd
```

The **mfstool backup** command displays output like the following during the backup process:

```
Scanning source drive.  Please wait a moment.
Source drive size is 15 hours
Uncompressed backup size: 1309 megabytes
Backing up NNN of 1309 megabytes (M.MM%)
Backup done!
```

This command displays the same output as the **mfstool backup** command without the compressed backup option. The real difference is in the final size of the output file, which you can only determine by actually examining the file by using the Linux **ls** command, as in the following example:

```
ls /mnt/windows/my_tivo.bak
-rwxr-xr-x   1 root     root      601924044 Jun 26 12:38 /mnt/windows/my_tivo.bak
```

In this case, the file is 601,924,044 bytes in size, which essentially is half of the predicted size of the uncompressed backup.

Backing Up an Entire TiVo Disk Using MFS Tools

As mentioned earlier, the default action of the **mfstool backup** command is to back up files only within the MFS partitions of a disk whose filesystem identifier is less than 2000. This seemingly arbitrary number is actually a carefully chosen value that guarantees that the backup file will contain all of the portions of the MFS filesystem(s) that are required for normal operation of your TiVo, without backing up the files that truly take up the majority of the space in any MFS filesystem—your recordings. However, there are a few cases in which you would want to back up everything, namely:

◆ When backing up a failing TiVo disk so that you can restore it to an identical disk in order to replace the failing disk.

◆ When backing up a TiVo disk so that you can subsequently restore it to a larger disk and use the additional space provided by the larger disk to increase the storage capacity of your TiVo.

◆ When backing up your existing TiVo disk simply to protect treasured recordings against accidental deletion or loss due to hardware failure (if the disk itself goes bad).

In any of these cases, you can use additional **mfstool backup** options to increase the amount of information that is being backed up, customize the specific types of items being backed up based on the amount of disk space they consume, or simply back up everything.

Backing up the entire contents of a TiVo is easy enough to do, requiring that you add a single command-line option. The **mfstool backup** option for backing up the entire contents of one or more TiVo drives is the **-a** (all) option. The following example shows the sample command

and resulting output of backing up the entire contents of a TiVo disk that is connected to your personal computer as **/dev/hdd** (the slave drive on your secondary IDE interface):

```
mfstool backup -6 -a -o /mnt/windows/my_tivo.bak /dev/hdd
```

The **mfstool backup** command displays output like the following during the backup process:

```
Scanning source drive.  Please wait a moment.
Source drive size is 15 hours
Uncompressed backup size: 1309 megabytes
Backing up NNN of 1309 megabytes (M.MM%)
Backup done!
```

Although in this case, the size of the backup is the same as our previous backup; full-disk backups are typically much larger. This is not surprising because you are backing up everything contained in the entire disk. As long as you can afford the backup space required to save a backup file of this size, it is nice to have the ability to back up all of your favorite recording at one time.

TIP

Before doing a complete backup that you plan to keep around for a while, take the time to purge any non-essential recordings from the TiVo. You should also use the **backdoor** commands discussed in Chapter 2, "TiVo Tips and Tricks," in the section "Using Thumb-Thumb-Thumb Codes" to display the listings for any Teleworld or other promotional recordings that may still be stored on your disk and delete them. No point in backing up anything that you don't really want to save!

Backing Up Multiple-Disk TiVo Systems

As mentioned when discussing the BlessTiVo command in Chapter 4, "The Hacker's Tool Chest of TiVo Tools," (and discussed in more detail in Chapter 6, "Expanding Your TiVo's Storage Capacity"), adding a second drive to your TiVo effectively marries the two disks so that they "always" must be used together. What this really means is that you cannot remove the second drive and continue to use the TiVo with just its primary disk. Since the TiVo expects to access and use storage on the second drive, it won't take long for the TiVo to attempt to access the second drive and (of course) fail. In the computer biz, this is known as "a bad thing." Fortunately, you can effectively divorce two drives by backing them up together, and then restoring the combined backup to a larger, single drive. The **mfstool backup** command stores a copy of the partition map for both the TiVo drives, but it does not require that the restore be performed on two drives—when restoring a dual-drive backup to a single TiVo drive with sufficient space, the **mfstool restore** command simply re-creates a sufficient number of partitions to hold the restored data on the new, larger drive.

Backing up a dual-drive TiVo is done exactly like backing up a single-drive TiVo, with two exceptions:

◆ You must supply the **-s** (shrink) command-line option to shrink the set of volumes being backed up as much as possible. This causes the **mfstool backup** command to focus on the data contained in any MFS partitions, rather than trying to preserve the actual structure of the volumes and partitions on your disks.

◆ You must supply the names of both TiVo drives on the TiVo command-line and in the correct order, of course.

A sample command-line for backing up a dual-drive TiVo, whose disks are found at **/dev/hdb** and **/dev/hdd** (in other words, as slave drives on both of your IDE interfaces) with output from the **mfs backup** command, would look something like the following:

```
mfstool backup -6 -s -o /mnt/windows/my_tivo.bak /dev/hdb /dev/hdd
```

The **mfstool backup** command displays output like the following during the backup process:

```
Scanning source drive.  Please wait a moment.
Source drive size is 15 hours
    - Upgraded to 57 hours
Uncompressed backup size: 1309 megabytes
Backing up NNN of 1309 megabytes (M.MM%)
Backup done!
```

This command displays the same output as any other **mfstool backup** command, with the exception of the information provided about the size of both of the TiVo drives. As with the previous example, the relationship between the estimated, uncompressed size of the backup and the actual size of the backup file is only a guess—you'll need to use the **ls** command to see the actual resulting size of the output file.

After you've created a single backup file that combines information about both drives of a dual-drive TiVo system, you can restore it to a single drive with sufficient available storage, or to a larger set of drives if you want to maximize your storage at the same time. Restoring backups is explained later in this chapter; restoring a single backup file to a pair of disks is explained in Chapter 6, "Expanding Your TiVo's Storage Capacity," as part of the general discussion of how to add a second drive to your system.

Advanced Backup Options

As discussed in Chapter 3, the options available to the **mfstool backup** command provide a few options that enable you to modify the contents of a structured backup file in general and specific ways. This section highlights these options to help you think about ways of customizing your backups. For the most part, I tend to stick with "standard" backups, rarely taking advantage of the more advanced **mfstool backup** options with the exception of the **-v** option (to exclude **/var** from the backups). With other advanced options, it's tricky to know exactly what a specific backup contains (or does not contain) without actually restoring it and seeing what you get. However, your mileage may vary, so here we go.

The discussion of the TiVo's Media File System (MFS) in Chapter 9 presents ways of identifying the MFS entities associated with specific recordings. If you want to want to create a TiVo backup that is guaranteed to include a specific recording, you can use the **mfstool backup** command's -**f** <fsid> option to ensure that the backup includes the specified recording. This option actually tells the **mfstool backup** command to include all videos with **fsids** less than or equal to the specified <fsid>, which probably means that you'll get other recordings than the one in which you're specifically interested. However, this also means that you won't get other recordings <fsid>s that are greater than the one that in which you're interested.

The -**f** <fsid> option provides a good compromise between minimizing the size of your backup while ensuring that your backup includes a specific recording, without creating a backup of every recording on your TiVo. Continuing with the examples used in the previous sections, the following command would create a compressed backup file containing all video streams with <fsid>s that are less than 2877, which we'll assume is one greater than the <fsid> of the recording we're interested in preserving:

```
mfstool backup -6 -f 2877 -o /mnt/windows/my_tivo.bak /dev/hdb
Scanning source drive.  Please wait a moment.
Source drive size is 15 hours
Uncompressed backup size: XXXX megabytes
Backing up NNN of XXXX megabytes (M.MM%)
Backup done!
```

An alternative to just backing up streams with <fsid>s that are less than a specified number (or the default value of 2000) is to use the **mfstool backup** command's -**l** <size> option to limit the backup to only streams that are under a certain size. This size is based on the actual amount of data that the files contain, rather than the amount of space allocated to each file (which would differ based on the allocation units used for that TiVo filesystem). The assumption behind this option is that files larger than the specified limit will be recordings (which you would not want to save) because the native animations used by the TiVo are all relatively small. Safe values for this <size> cutoff are 32 or 64 MB. This option cannot be used with the -**f** option, because there may be files with <fsids> that are less than the specified value, but which are larger than the specified <size> cutoff.

Continuing with the examples used in the previous sections, the following command would create a compressed backup file containing all video streams with <size> less that 32 MB:

```
mfstool backup -6 -l 32 -o /mnt/windows/my_tivo.bak /dev/hdb
```

The **mfstool backup** command displays output like the following during the backup process:

```
Scanning source drive.  Please wait a moment.
Source drive size is 15 hours
```

```
Uncompressed backup size: XXXX megabytes
Backing up NNN of XXXX megabytes (M.MM%)
Backup done!
```

If you would rather base the size cutoff on the actual amount of space that is actually allocated for a file, rather than the amount of space that is actually used, you can use the **-t** <size> option instead of the **-l** <size> option. In a final permutation between allocated and actual size, you can use the **-T** <size> option to back up all of the space allocated to files that actually use <size> or less of that space.

Backing Up Selected Information from Your TiVo

The previous sections discussed how to do backups of your TiVo, which then can be restored to create a new bootable TiVo disk or disk set. While the **mfstool backup** command provides options for reducing (or simply controlling) the items that are included in the backup files that it produces, it does not support incremental backups. *Incremental backups* is the term used for backups that only contain things that have changed since the previous backup was done. The combination of these two facts has the following implications for backups created using the **mfstool backup** command:

◆ They are always large.

◆ Each backup contains mostly the same files as the previous backup.

◆ Each backup contains identical copies of system files that probably have not changed since the previous backup.

If you aren't interested in backing up your recordings and already have a backup of your TiVo system software in a safe location, there are still several things that you have probably spent a fair amount of time crafting, and therefore would be distressed to lose. These are features like Season Passes and WishLists that you've built up over time. Luckily, a thoughtful TiVo hacker named "angra" was kind enough to create backup and restore commands. If you run these commands on your TiVo, it will save and restore these items to and from text files that you can easily preserve for safekeeping by copying them to another machine. These scripts are located in the BATBD CD's settings-backup directory.

 NOTE

The settings **backup** and **restore** commands must be executed on your TiVo, unlike the **dd** and MFS Tool utilities. Backing up and restoring your TiVo settings therefore requires that you already have configured your TiVo to display a command-prompt, as explained in Chapter 7, "Connecting the Universe to Your TiVo," in the section "Getting a Command Prompt on Your TiVo."

The easiest way to install the settings-backup software on your TiVo is to recursively copy that directory from the BATBD CD to a partition on your TiVo disk while you have it in your desktop PC. For now, let's assume that we simply want to put the software in its own directory in the TiVo's **/var** partition. To do so, perform the following steps:

1. Put the TiVo disk in your PC as described in Chapter 3 in the section "Working with TiVo Disks."

2. If your disk is from a Series 1 machine, boot from the BATBD disk using the **s1swap** option so that you can mount and access your TiVo partitions. If your disk is from a Series 2 machine, boot from the BATBD disk using the default boot option by pressing the Enter key at the boot screen.

3. Mount the partition of your TiVo disk that corresponds to its **/var** partition. This will be the partition **/dev/hdX9**, where **X** is the letter corresponding to where you've attached your TiVo drive to your PC. It could therefore be any of the following **/dev/hdb9**, **/dev/hdc9**, or **/dev/hdd9**—or even **/dev/hda9** if you are working with a disk from a Series 2 system. To mount this partition, use a command like the following:

   ```
   mount /dev/hdX9 /mnt/var
   ```

4. Mount the BATBD CD using a command like the following:

   ```
   mount /dev/hdX /mnt/cdrom
   ```

   As in previous examples, replace **X** with the letter corresponding to your CDROM drive. This will be **b** if your CD ROM drive is attached as the slave on your primary IDE interface; **c** if your CD ROM drive is attached as the master on your secondary IDE interface; or **d** if your CD ROM drive is attached as the slave on your secondary IDE interface. If you specified the correct device, you will see a warning message stating that the CD ROM drive is mounted as read-only, which is true and can be safely ignored.

5. Recursively copy the settings-backup directory from the BATBD CD to the **/mnt/var** partition using a command like the following:

   ```
   cp -r /mnt/cdrom/settings-backup /mnt/var
   ```

6. Unmount the BATBD CD and TiVo **/var** partitions by executing the following two commands;

   ```
   umount /mnt/cdrom
   umount /mnt/var
   ```

   After you have finished this process, put the TiVo disk back in your TiVo and reboot it. If you are using a serial connection to your TiVo, attach the cable at this point and start the terminal emulation program on your PC; if you have put your TiVo on the network, wait until it has booted successfully, and then connect to it by using a utility such as telnet.

When the command prompt displays, change directory to the **/var/settings-backup** directory by using the **cd /var/settings-backup** command. You can then create a backup file of your Season Passes and WishLists by executing the following command:

```
./backup > settings.out
```

This command writes a copy of your Season Passes and WishLists to the file settings output, which you should then copy back to your personal computer and put in a safe place. To restore the settings from this file in the future, transfer it back to the TiVo, copy it to the **/var/settings-backup** directory, make that your working directory by using the **cd** command, and then execute the following command:

```
./restore settings.out
```

 NOTE

Restoring Season Pass and WishList settings using the **restore** command provided in the **settings-backup** directory does not overwrite any existing Season Passes or WishLists, even if they are identical. Before restoring Season Passes or WishLists, you should first clean up your existing Season Passes or WishLists, perhaps deleting or at least renaming any that may have the same names or that might otherwise conflict with the settings that you are restoring. You can then go through the list and delete any duplicates that you do not want to preserve for some reason.

General Information about Restoring TiVo Data

The next few sections discuss how to restore different types of TiVo backups, whether as part of a system upgrade or simply as part of the repair process for a formerly ailing TiVo. Before attempting a restore for whatever reason, it's important to understand what TiVo data you can restore, and where.

As discussed earlier, image backups of an entire primary TiVo disk always include the entire contents of that disk. Restoring an image backup from one primary TiVo disk to another, therefore, always produces a bootable disk, complete with all of the files required for daily operation. Similarly, structured backups of primary TiVo disks created using the MFS Tools utilities always contain at least the minimum information required to create a bootable disk. However, all TiVos and bootable TiVo disks are not created equal.

One common mistake made by people, who own multiple TiVos or who are restoring backups to a TiVo for some other reason, is to restore a backup of one type of TiVo to another and expect it to work. Series 1 and Series 2 systems use different processors, and therefore run completely incompatible kernels, libraries, and executables. This is the equivalent of trying to directly execute a Macintosh program on a Windows machine—it simply won't work, ever. There is absolutely no way to restore a Series 2 image to a Series 1 TiVo machine and expect it to work.

Similarly, there are fundamental differences between many of the Series 1 machines, such as the Sony and Phillips/Hughes models. Backups of these systems are therefore also incompatible, even though they may initially appear to work on both types of systems—the TiVo software upgrade process will certainly become confused in the future if, for example, it knows that you have a Phillips TiVo but encounters Sony data when trying to upgrade the system. You can, however, restore backup images to other models of the same series of TiVo from the same manufacturer, as long as sufficient disk space is available to hold the restored data. For example, you can restore a Series 1 Phillips HDR112 image to a Phillips HDR312, and everything will work fine. Similarly, you can restore a backup image from a Series 2 40 MB TiVo to a Series 2 80 MB TiVo with no problems.

TIP

If the first three digits of your TiVo are the same as the first three digits of the TiVo on which a backup was created, the backups are compatible.

NOTE

When restoring backups made on a system with a smaller disk to a system with a larger disk, you will almost certainly want to use the MFS Tools utilities to reclaim the additional space for storing recordings, as discussed later in this chapter in the section entitled "Restoring an MFS Tools Backup to a Larger Drive".

Restoring Image Backups Using dd

Having created an image backup of one of your disks using the **dd** command as explained earlier in this chapter, you can quickly and easily restore this to another disk by essentially reversing the order of the arguments that you supplied to the **dd** command to create the backup. Be extremely careful when supplying arguments to the **dd** command—specifying the wrong disk drive as the target of a restore operation will destroy any data that it previously contained, which would be bad if you accidentally specified the drive containing the Windows or Linux boot information for your personal computer.

TIP

It doesn't technically matter which of the kernels on the BATBD CD you boot with to restore an image created with **dd**, but it should be the same one that you booted from when you created the backup using the **dd** command. (This guarantees that no byte-order conflicts arise.) Since it is useful to mount partitions from the restored disk to verify that the restore completed successfully, I suggest that you use the byte swapped kernel (i.e., the **s1swap boot** option) when creating or restoring a TiVo Series 1 backup image.

Attach the drive that has the image backup you want to restore to your PC (as explained in Chapter 3 in the section "Working with TiVo Disk Drives") and ensure that you also have access to the partition where the backup is stored (as discussed earlier in this chapter in "Finding Room for Backups"). You then can restore the backup image to the new drive using a command like the following:

```
dd if=<filename> of=/dev/hdX bs=32k
```

The <filename> argument should be the full pathname of the file containing the backup image that you are trying to restore. As always, the **X** in **/dev/hdX** reflects the drive letter associated with where you have mounted the target hard drive in your PC.

This command will take a long time. After it completes, try mounting partitions from the restored disk. You should be able to mount **/dev/hdX4**, **/dev/hdX7**, and **/dev/hdX9**. You can try mounting these in turn, using a command like the following:

```
mount /dev/hdXN /mnt/test
```

Mounting a Linux filesystem verifies that the core data structures of the filesystem are valid. You can then immediately unmount them (before trying to mount another) using the command **umount /mnt/test**.

Once you have restored a backup image and have verified that you can successfully access its partitions, what you do next with the disk depends on why you restored the backup image:

◆ If you were restoring an existing disk image to an identical disk (or even overwriting the original disk) to protect against hardware failures, you could simply put the new disk in your TiVo and begin using it.

◆ If you were restoring an existing disk image to a larger disk to increase the amount of storage available on your TiVo, you could use the MFS Tools utilities to enable the extra space for use by the TiVo (as explained in Chapter 6, in the section "Replacing an Existing TiVo Disk with a Larger One".

TIP

If you cannot mount any of the partitions from the restored disk image after the restore finishes, try the following:

◆ Verify that you booted from a kernel that supports access to the TiVo partition tables. On the BATBD disk, these are the **s1swap** boot option for Series 1 machines and the '**s2** boot option for Series 2 machines (also available at the BATBD CD's boot prompt).

◆ Verify that you are trying to mount the correct partitions. The **ext2** partitions on a TiVo disk are partitions 4, 7, and 9, which you would specify as **/dev/hdXN**, where **X** is the letter for the drive and **N** is the partition number.

◆ Verify that you did not accidentally create the backup image using a non-byte-swapped kernel, if you are restoring it using a byte-swapped kernel. You can reverse byte-swapping when restoring data using the **dd** command by specifying the **conv=swab** option on the **dd** command-line, as in the following example:

```
dd if=<filename> of=<disk-or-partition> bs=32k conv=swab
```

Restoring Backups Created Using MFS Tools

As discussed earlier, backups of primary TiVo disks created using the MFS Tools utilities are complete backups of all of the portions of a TiVo disk that are critical for successful operation of your TiVo. They also can be complete backups of your TiVo in general, if performed as instructed earlier in this chapter in "Backing Up an Entire TiVo Disk Using MFS Tools."

The next few sections discuss different ways of restoring backups created using the MFS Tools utilities. These largely differ in terms of the command-line options used by the mfstool restore command, but are organized into separate sections in order to make them easier to find and use.

Restoring an MFS Tools Backup Without Adding New Space

In most cases, you will be restoring MFS Tools backups to one or more drives that are larger than the drive that you backed up, and then automatically devoting any additional space on the drive(s) for use when storing recordings on your TiVo. If that's your goal, skip this section and go to either of the next two sections. However, there are cases where you may want to do a simple restore, either to the same disk that you backed up, another disk of the same size as the original disk, or to a larger disk on which you do not want to automatically allocate additional space for use with your TiVo. Some cases where these circumstances may be useful are the following:

◆ You suspect that your drive is failing and you can't afford another one at the moment. In this case, after backing up the original drive, you can use the manufacturer's utilities to low-level format the disk so that it marks any failing sectors as bad, then restores a backup of that drive to the drive to try to continue using it.

◆ You want to preserve your original drive as an on-the-shelf backup and happen to have another drive of the same capacity. In this case, you can put the old disk on the shelf, restore the backup to the duplicate disk, and use the duplicate disk in your TiVo.

◆ You want to restore your original disk to a larger disk on which you plan to use the additional space for some other purposes—in other words, without automatically allocating the additional space for use by the TiVo. In this case, you can restore the backup, and then use a command such as **pdisk** (discussed in Chapter 4) to manually create new partitions of types such as **ext2** or MFS. You may want to do this as your TiVo hacking skills evolve and you need additional **ext2** partitions to store new software that you've put on your TiVo.

Restoring an MFS Tools backup to a disk without doing anything else is the simplest case of restoring data to a TiVo disk. To do this, first put the disk that you want to restore to in your PC, and boot from the BATBD disk. Next, execute a command like the following:

```
mfstool restore -i <backup-file> /dev/hdX
```

The **mfstool restore** command's **-i** option specifies the full pathname of the file that contains your backup (<backup-file>). The **mfstool restore** command displays the following output during the restore process:

```
Starting restore
Uncompressed backup size: XXXX megabytes
Restoring NNN of XXXX megabytes (M.MM%)
Cleaning up restore.  Please wait a moment.
Restore done!
```

While the **mfstool restore** command is running, the line reading "Restoring NNN of XXXX megabytes (M.MM%)" is continually updated to show the progress of the restore command. Once the command completes, congratulations! You've just created a new TiVo drive from an existing backup file! You can shut down the PC, return the drive to your TiVo, and boot from it successfully.

NOTE

After restoring a backup to a TiVo disk and booting from that TiVo, the TiVo will still contain directory entries for recordings that were present on the TiVo disk when it was backed up, even though the recordings themselves were not preserved in the backup. You should go to the Now Playing screen (TiVo Central -> Now Playing) and delete the entries for these shows, to minimize confusion as to what recordings are actually residing on your TiVo.

Restoring an MFS Tools Backup to a Larger Drive

By restoring an existing backup to a drive that is larger than the one from which it was made, you can easily add new storage capacity to your TiVo. The **mfstool restore** command provides the **-x** (expand) option so you can restore a backup to a larger drive, and then automatically allocate any additional space on the drive for storage.

To do this, first put the disk that you want to restore to in your PC and boot from the BATBD disk. Next, execute a command like the following:

```
mfstool restore -i <backup-file> -x /dev/hdX
```

The **mfstool restore** command's **-i** option specifies the full pathname of the file that contains your backup (<backup-file>). The **-x** option tells the **mfstool restore** command to expand the set of volumes on the existing disk to allocate any addition storage available on the drive to MFS partitions that the TiVo can use to store recordings.

TIP

If you are expanding the storage capacity of your TiVo beyond 100 MB or so, you should consider increasing the amount of swap space on the drive during the restore process. As explained later in this chapter, this will improve the performance and responsiveness of your TiVo. For more information about increasing swap space, see "Increasing Swap Space on a TiVo Disk," later in this chapter.

The **mfstool restore** command displays the following output during the restore process:

```
Starting restore
Uncompressed backup size: 1309 megabytes
Restoring 14 of 1309 megabytes (1.77%)
```

```
Cleaning up restore.  Please wait a moment.
Restore done!
Adding pair /dev/hdX12-/dev/hdX13
New estimated standalone size: 79 hours (64 more)
```

While the **mfstool restore** command is running, the line reading "Restoring NNN of 1309 megabytes (M.MM%)" is continually updated to show the progress of the **restore** command. As the example output shows, once the restore itself completes, the **mfstool restore** command creates a new pair of MFS partitions (one application region and one media region) to use the additional space that is available on the drive. It then estimates the amount of storage available on the new disk for recordings made at the Basic quality level. The numbers in the example will differ from what you see on your screen because they depend on the size of the drive on which the original backup was made and the size of the drive to which you are restoring the backup.

After the **mfstool restore** command completes, congratulations! You've just created additional storage for your TiVo recordings and created a new drive for use in your TiVo. You can shut down the PC, put the new drive in your TiVo, and boot from it successfully. When your TiVo has booted, you can verify the amount of storage available on the expanded TiVo from the System Information screen (TiVo Central -> Messages & Setup -> System Information).

Restoring an MFS Tools Backup to a Two-Drive TiVo

The **mfstool restore** command also enables you to restore a single backup to a pair of drives. This actually restores the TiVo system information to the first drive, allocates any free space on the first drive for use by your TiVo, and then allocates the space on the second drive for use by your TiVo. This is accomplished by using the same **-x** (expand) option discussed in the previous section—you simply have to specify both of the drives that you want to restore to on the **mfstool restore** command-line.

To do this, first put the disk that you want to restore to in your PC and boot from the BATBD disk. Next, execute a command like the following:

```
mfstool restore -i <backup-file> -x /dev/hdX /dev/hdY
```

The **mfstool restore** command's **-i** option specifies the full pathname of the file that contains your backup (<backup-file>). The **-x** option tells the **mfstool restore** command to expand the set of volumes on the target disks to allocate any additional storage available to MFS partitions that the TiVo can use to store recordings. The drives specified on the command-line must be specified in the order that you will put them in your TiVo: **/dev/hdX** would be the TiVo boot drive, and **/dev/hdY** would be the TiVo slave drive.

TIP

If you are expanding the storage capacity of your TiVo beyond 100 MB or so, you should always increase the amount of swap space on the drive to at least 128 MB during the restore process. You must increase the amount of swap space available, if your new TiVo will contain more than 120 MB of total disk space. As explained later in this chapter, this will improve the performance and responsiveness of your TiVo. You can increase the amount of swap space allocated during a restore by specifying the **-s** <size> option on the **mfstool restore** command line, where <size> is the new amount of swap space that you want to allocate. The default amount of swap space allocated is 64 (MB). A better value for larger drives is 128 (MB). You may even want to increase this to 256 MB, if you will be running additional processes, such as an FTP server, telnet daemon, and TiVoWeb on your expanded TiVo. The **-s** <size> option is discussed in more detail in the "Advanced Restore Options" section later in this chapter.

The **mfstool restore** command displays the following output during the restore process:

```
Starting restore
Uncompressed backup size: 1309 megabytes
Restoring NNN of 1309 megabytes (M.MM%)
Cleaning up restore.  Please wait a moment.
Restore done!
Adding pair /dev/hdb12-/dev/hdb13
New estimated standalone size: 79 hours (64 more)
Adding pair /dev/hdd2-/dev/hdd3
New estimated standalone size: 103 hours (24 more)
```

While the **mfstool restore** command is running, the line reading "Restoring NNN of 816 megabytes (M.MM%)" is continually updated to show the progress of the **restore** command. As the example output shows, once the restore itself completes, the **mfstool restore** command creates a new pair of MFS partitions (one application region and one media region) to use the additional space that is available on the first drive, it creates one or more pairs of MFS partitions on the second drive, and then estimates the amount of storage available on the new disks for recordings made at the Basic quality level. The numbers in the example will differ from what you see on your screen because they depend on the size of the drive on which the original backup was made and the size of the drive to which you are restoring the backup.

After the **mfstool restore** command completes, congratulations! You've just substantially increased the amount of space available on your TiVo for storing recordings. You can now shut down the PC, put the new drives in your TiVo, and boot from them successfully. When your

TiVo has booted, you can verify the amount of storage available on the expanded TiVo from the System Information screen (TiVo Central -> Messages & Setup -> System Information).

Advanced MFS Tools Restore Options

The **mfstool restore** command provides a variety of options that you can use to customize different aspects of your disk layout when restoring a backup created using the MFS Tools utilities. Each of these advanced capabilities is activated by specifying an additional option and any associated values on the **mfstool restore** command line. The following sections discuss these advanced options and the situations in which you might want to use them.

Increasing Swap Space on a TiVo Disk

Like most modern computer systems, your TiVo uses swap space to increase the apparent amount of memory available to the system. Swap space is a specially formatted portion of the disk that the version of Linux running on your TiVo can use as temporary space for processes that are active on your TiVo, but which are waiting for some event to occur in order to continue. Moving paused or lower-priority processes out of main memory and temporarily storing them in the swap space enables the processes that are actively running to use the memory that the paused or lower-priority processes would otherwise have used.

Swap space is also used during certain parts of the boot process. The most important of these is the step where the TiVo verifies that the partitions on your hard drive are usable. Known as a *disk consistency check*, this requires that the process that is doing the check build a table in memory that contains detailed information about your disk drives. The size of this table varies depending upon the size of your disk drives. If your TiVo contains more than 120 MB of total disk space, this process will need more than the default 64 MB of swap space provided on TiVo disk drives.

To increase the amount of swap space that is allocated on your hard drive during a restore, you can use the **-s** <size> command-line option to the **mfstool restore** command. The <size> value is an integer value up to 511, and indicates the number of megabytes of swap space that will be created during the restore process. If you ever plan to have 120 MB or more disk space in your TiVo, you should allocate a minimum of 128 MB of swap space. A better value is 256 MB, especially if you may run processes such as a telnet daemon or the TiVoWeb server on your TiVo. You cannot easily change the amount of swap space that is allocated on an existing disk, so selecting an appropriate value during the restore process is a good idea.

Increasing the Size of the /var Partition on a TiVo Disk

Like all Linux and Unix systems, the TiVo uses a hierarchical set of files and directories to store system information. On Linux and Unix systems, disk partitions used by the system for storing files are mounted on directories in the filesystem, which are known as mountpoints, which are just standard Linux directories that can be recycled as entry points to additional storage. After a partition has mounted on a directory, the storage in that partition then is used by any files and directories created in that directory or any of its subdirectories. By default,

TiVos only have two Linux partitions: the root partition, which is mounted at the directory named / (the "root" of the Linux filesystem), and the **/var** partition, which is used to store applications and variable data such as system logs, temporary space for creating non-critical files, upgrades and advertisements that you have received from TiVo headquarters, and so on.

The default size of the **/var** partition on a TiVo is 128 MB, which is suitable for "normal" use. However, if you decide to install additional applications on your TiVo, you may find that 128 MB is somewhat constraining. The **mfstool restore** command provides the -v <size> option to specify the size of the **/var** partition created when restoring a TiVo from backups. The <size> value that you specify should be an integer value that is interpreted as the number of megabytes that you want to have allocated to the **/var** partition. If you are planning to do some serious hacking on your TiVo or simply want to prepare for doing so in the future without reformatting your disk, you should specify a higher value when using the **mfstool restore** command. A value of 256 MB should be sufficient for most purposes, though you can certainly use higher values if desired. You can always use the **pdisk** command (discussed in Chapter 4) to manually create additional partitions in the future and mount them wherever you want, as long as your disk contains available space.

WARNING

Most TiVo systems running TiVo software releases newer than Version 3.0 use hashing to verify the contents of many of the default files used during system startup. You may not be able to mount additional partitions unless you use some of the techniques explained in Chapter 7, in "Getting a Command Prompt on Your TiVo," to modify the boot sequence and environment on your TiVo. This is probably OK, since you will only be adding and mounting new partitions if you're doing some serious TiVo hacking, but "forewarned is four armed," as they say ;-).

Optimizing the Partition Layout on a TiVo Disk

One of the governing factors in the performance of any computer system is the amount of time that it takes your disk drive to read and write information to and from your disk. Regardless of how fast your computer system is electronically, it is still gated by these physical operations, which require moving the heads of the disk to the location where the data is (or is to be) stored. In computer terms, the head movement necessary to locate data is known as *seeking*; the amount of time required to locate a unit of data on the disk is generally referred to as the *seek time*. Minimizing seeking and seek time when using a computer system is an important, but easily overlooked aspect of system performance and optimization.

Newer TiVos, such as the DirecTiVo and newer Series 2 models, use a slightly different partition layout than original Series 1 systems, in an attempt to minimize the movement of your disk's read/write heads and reduce the average seek time. MFS partitions are located on the outside of the disk to minimize the amount of head movement necessary to access them, while the Linux partitions containing application data are put in the center of the disk, since applications are started/stopped less frequently than video data is read and written.

The **mfstool restore** command's **-p** option restores data to the new disk as described in the previous paragraph. Although today's disks are substantially faster than the drives in, for example, original Series 1 machines, using this option can provide a general performance improvement, and may also reduce the amount of noise generated by your disk as a consequence of having to seek less.

Changing the Block Size When Restoring a TiVo Disk

Different types of computer filesystems use different block sizes when allocating disk space and storing data. The block size of a filesystem is the smallest unit of space that the filesystem can allocate. If a filesystem's block size is 4 MB and you need to store 1 byte of data, the filesystem must still allocate one 4 MB block to store that data. At first, it seems silly to use larger block sizes. Why not simply use a tiny block size and allocate as many blocks as necessary to store a given amount of data?

The reason for larger block sizes is attributed to the system overhead related to allocating and managing blocks in the filesystem. Using a smaller block size means that the system must allocate a greater number of blocks to store files, as well as manage a much higher number of blocks within the filesystem, tracking whether each is used or free (i.e., can be allocated). The data structures within a filesystem that track which blocks are associated with that file, and in what order, must also be correspondingly larger. Selecting an appropriate block size is especially important in systems that routinely create and delete large files, as your TiVo does when recording and deleting videos. Larger block sizes tend to "waste" more disk space because the final block of any file is rarely completely filled with data, but significantly less effort is involved in allocating and using the larger blocks of data required for classically larger video files.

As a more detailed example, assume that a filesytem's block size was 16 MB and the TiVo was trying to store a recording that required 20 MB of disk space. This would require two blocks and would completely fill the first one but waste 12 MB of disk space in the second. In order to keep track of the recording, the TiVo would keep only information about the two blocks in memory. On the other hand, with a block size of 4 MB, the recording would require 5 blocks but no disk space would be wasted. However, the TiVo would have to keep information about 5 blocks in memory to keep track of that recording.

The **mfstool restore** command's **-r** <value> option enables you to specify the block size used within the MFS partitions, created when restoring a backup file created using the **mfstool backup** command. Acceptable values for this option are 0 (corresponding to a 1 MB allocation unit), 1 (corresponding to a 2 MB allocation unit), 2 (corresponding to a 4 MB allocation unit), 3 (corresponding to an 8 MB allocation unit), and 4 (corresponding to a 16 MB allocation unit). In general, the larger the allocation unit value, the less RAM will be used (making the TiVo more responsive when displaying menus, changing and processing options, and so on), but the greater the amount of storage that may be wasted when storing recordings.

The default block size used in partitions created by your TiVo is 1 MB. This was a good value to use with the relatively small drives and small amount of memory used on early TiVos.

However, today's larger, faster drives make using a larger block size an attractive option for improving performance.

Changing Byte Order When Restoring a TiVo Disk

As mentioned over and over throughout this book, the Series 1 models use a big-endian PowerPC processor. The byte order in Series 1 filesystems is therefore different from the byte order used in Series 2 systems (and in desktop Linux systems). The initial version of the MFS Tools utilities didn't concern itself with byte-order because there was only one at the time. However, with the introduction of Series 2 systems, Version 2 of the MFS Tools utilities introduced two options for manipulating the byte-order in a backup file created using the **mfstool backup** command.

You may wonder why this is important. After all, you can still use Version 1 of the MFS Tools utilities to restore backups that it created, and everything will "just work." Unfortunately, this is only true if the kernel that you've booted from uses the same byte order as the one that you were running when you created the backup. A further wrinkle is that Version 2 of the MFS Tools utilities added many other features that increased the power and scope of these utilities. As with so many things, "newer is better."

Tiger, the TiVo hacker who wrote the MFS Tools utilities, took this into account when creating Version 2 of the MFS Tools utilities, adding options that let you permute your backups any way you'd like during the restore process. Ordinarily, the **mfstools restore** command attempts to automatically determine whether byte-swapping should be accomplished by examining the byte order on disks such as **hdb**, **hdc**, and **hdd**. The -b option disables this auto-detection and forces a restore to be performed without byte-swapping. This option is mandatory when restoring a backup of a Series 2 machine that was created with Version 1 of the **mfstool backup** utility. The parallel -B option disables auto-detection and forces a restore to be accomplished with byte-swapping. This option is mandatory when restoring a backup of a Series 1 machine, if you are running a non-byte-swapped kernel, such as the BATBD kernel for Series 2 systems.

TIP

Byte-swapping differences can be a pain in the posterior. When restoring a TiVo backup using **mfstool restore**, you should always boot with a kernel that provides access to the TiVo partition table so that you can query a restored disk's partition table to determine if it was restored correctly. If you are restoring a Series 2 backup, the BATBD disk provides a single boot option because the Series 2 systems don't use byte-swapping. If you are restoring a Series 1 backup, boot with the BATBD's **s1swap** option. If you've gotten the byte-order wrong during your first restore, you may need to restore the backup again with the correct byte-swapping options enabled. However, you can be sure that the restored disk will be readable—and hopefully bootable——on your TiVo.

Verifying TiVo Disks Restored Using MFS Tools

After restoring a backup to a new disk that you want to use in your TiVo, you should always verify that the backup looks reasonably correct by examining the partition table of the new disk using the **pdisk** command, and also by mounting one or two partitions from the restored disk. Moving drives from your PC to your TiVo and back again is something of a pain, and the TiVo is light on feedback if you try to boot from a non-bootable drive. If there's something wrong with your restore, in the best case your TiVo boots to the gray "Just a few more seconds..." screen, and sits there until the end of the universe. In the worst case, you hear lots of disk noise and the red light displays on the front of the TiVo. What the heck does all that mean? In a nutshell (Sorry, O'Reilly guys!), it means that your restore was unsuccessful for one reason or another.

You can verify that the disk you restored your data to has a valid partition table by executing the command **pdisk -p /dev/hdX**, where **X** is the drive letter corresponding to the restored disk. If this command displays a partition table, the restored disk is at least valid and there's a good chance that your TiVo will boot from it. If you don't see a valid partition table and instead see a message that the drive does not have one, make sure that you've booted with a kernel that provides access to the TiVo partition table. If you have restored a Series 2 backup, boot from the BATBD disk's **s2** kernel by pressing Return at the BATBD boot screen. If you have restored a Series 1 backup, boot from the BATBD disk's **s1swap** kernel by entering this value at the BATBD boot screen. If you still cannot see the partition table and are backing up or restoring a Series 1 TiVo disk, try experimenting with the byte-swapping options discussed in this chapter in "Changing Byte Order When Restoring a TiVo Disk."

Once you can see the partition table, you should be able to mount one of **/dev/hdX4** or **/dev/hdX7**, and you also should be able to mount **/dev/hdX9**. As mentioned earlier, the **mfstool backup** command only backs up the currently active root partition from your original TiVo disk to reduce the size of your backup file when doing backups. For this reason, when trying to mount **/dev/hdX4** and **/dev/hdX7**, one of these will fail because it was the inactive root partition.

 TIP

You can use the **bootpage** command to identify the default root partition on a drive. For example, the command `bootpage /dev/hdb` displays the default root partition on the drive **/dev/hdb**.

You can try mounting each of these in turn by using a command like the following:

```
mount /dev/hdXN /mnt/test
```

Mounting a Linux filesystem verifies that the core data structures of the filesystem are valid. You can then immediately unmount them (before trying to mount another) by using the command **umount /mnt/test**.

TiVo CLONING THE ROOT PARTITION ON A RESTORED TIVO

I always prefer to have two root partitions available on any restored TiVo disk. In theory, you will only need the second root partition after a software upgrade has populated it with a new kernel fresh from TiVo HQ. However, in reality, a disk problem could corrupt your existing root partition, leaving you with an unbootable TiVo disk. The truly wizardly among us would just clone the root partition from another TiVo disk using **dd**, but why use your powers if you don't have to?

After restoring a TiVo disk, try mounting both **/dev/hdX4** and **/dev/hdX7** to determine which of them actually contains a valid root filesystem (or use the **bootpage** command to query the disk to identify the active root filesystem). After you know which one is valid, you can clone it to the other using the **dd** command. For example, if **/dev/hdd4** is the valid root partition on a restored TiVo disk and **/dev/hdd7** is just an unmountable hunk of ones and zeroes, you can clone **/dev/hdd4** to **/dev/hdd7** by using the following command:

```
dd if=/dev/hdd4 of=/dev/hdd7 bs=32k
```

You then should be able to mount **/dev/hdd7**. Try it. You'll like it! It's like a free insurance policy. The TiVo won't always be able to switch boot partitions by itself (you may have to do so using the **bootpage** command), but at least the data will be there.

Connecting Backup and Restore Commands Using a Pipe

If the disks on your personal computer do not have the space to create a complete or partial backup of an existing TiVo disk, you can clone an existing disk to another disk by using the **mfstool backup** and **mfstool restore** commands together. You can even use this process to add another disk at the same time. As touched upon earlier, you can do this by taking advantage of the ability of Linux to connect the output of one program to the input of another. In Linux terms, this is done using a pipe, which is represented on the command-line as the "|" symbol. In this way, you can use the **mfstool backup** command to back up your existing disk, writing the backup file to standard output, which the corresponding **mfstool restore** command will then use as its standard input.

All of the command-line options for the **mfstool** backup and **mfstool restore** commands work in exactly the same way when writing to a pipe, with the exception of the options that specify input and output files. When writing to a pipe on a Linux or Unix system, the input and output files are specified as a single dash (-). An example of a command that would back up the contents of the drive attached to your PC as **/dev/hdb** and simultaneously restore that backup to a larger drive attached as **/dev/hdc** would be the following:

```
mfstool backup -o - /dev/hdb | mfstool restore -i - -x /dev/hdc
```

You can use this same approach to do more sophisticated backups and restores, such as when you want to clone your existing drive to a larger one but preserve all of your existing recordings, as in the following example:

```
mfstool backup -o - -a /dev/hdb | mfstool restore -i - -x /dev/hdc
```

As a final example, here is a sample set of backup and restore commands that do a compressed backup of two TiVo drives, and then restore them to a set of two (presumably larger) TiVo drives, thereby increasing the amount of swap space to 256 MB and increasing the size of the **/var** partition to 512 MB. This command is split across two lines for readability in this book (you would ordinarily enter it on a single line, removing the backslash that separates the two commands):

```
mfstool backup -o - -a -s /dev/hda /dev/hdb | \
   mfstool restore -i - -x -s 256 -v 512 /dev/hdc /dev/hdd
```

 NOTE

This command would not work correctly if you were using the BATBD disk's byte-swapped kernel because the **/dev/hda** drive is not byte-swapped, while the others are. In this case, a better approach would be to attach the two original TiVo drives so that they show up on your Linux systems as **/dev/hdb** and **/dev/hdc**, and then attach one of the new drives so that it shows up as **/dev/hdd**. If the new drive is large enough, you could back up both drives to the new larger drive, shut down the system, remove the old drives, and attach the new drive as **/dev/hdb** or **/dev/hdc**. Then use the procedures discussed in Chapter 6 to add the second drive to the new drive that you restored to in the first step. Clear as mud?

Changing TiVo Operating System Versions Using Backups

The version of the TiVo operating system contained on a bootable TiVo disk is inherently backed up as part of any unstructured backup of an entire TiVo disk, or as part of any structured backup created using the MFS Tools utilities. Therefore, restoring that backup image also restores that version of the operating system to the disk on which you are restoring the data.

As mentioned at the beginning of this chapter, the TiVo's ability to be remotely upgraded is both an advantage and a potential problem. If you are simply interested in running the latest and greatest version of the TiVo software and aren't necessarily interested in getting a command prompt on your TiVo, logging in over the network, or running TiVoWeb, automatic upgrading of the software is a great feature. One morning you wake up, and your TiVo has an enhanced user interface, improved audio or video recording capabilities, or perhaps additional commands and options. It's like Christmas!

On the other hand, if you have carefully hacked your TiVo to provide network access, automatically start the TiVoWeb application for remote access to your TiVo, or if you simply want to take advantage of things like backdoors and related special commands and modes, you would be dismayed to find that your TiVo has been enhanced behind your back, and typically in a

TiVo SOFTWARE PROTECTION AGAINST UPGRADES

There is no fool-proof way to protect against software upgrades with the exception of disconnecting your TiVo from the phone line or network connection through which it obtains both programming and updated guide data. However, certain versions of the TiVo operating system support boot parameters that prevent software upgrades in most cases. Passed to the TiVo as boot parameters that are stored in the TiVo's boot-page, these options will protect against all but the most aggressive upgrades.

Your TiVo's boot parameters are set using the **bootpage** command discussed in Chapter 4. Before updating the boot parameters, you'll want to check what they currently are, using a command like the following:

```
bootpage -p /dev/hdX
```

Replace the **X** with the letter corresponding to where the TiVo disk is located in your PC. This will display something like the following:

```
root=/dev/hda4
```

Once you know your current boot parameters, protecting your TiVo against most software updates is done using the following command:

```
bootpage -P "root=/dev/hdYY upgradesoftware=false" -C /dev/hdX
```

Replace the YY with the appropriate letter and number given in the output of the previous **bootpage** command, and replace the **X** with the letter corresponding to where the TiVo disk is located in your PC. After completing this command, only major version TiVo software updates should get through, if anything.

The potential downside of this approach is that the TiVo will continually notice that your TiVo is not upgraded, and may continue to download the upgrades even if you're not installing them. The folks at TiVo may get cranky about this and could disable your account until you talk to them. The best protection against upgrades is to back up your hacks so that you can easily restore them if your TiVo is forcibly upgraded.

way that stops your careful hacks from working. (In some cases, they will even be deleted!). For this reason, it is important to always have a backup available that contains a snapshot of your TiVo when it was customized just the way you wanted it. If your TiVo has been upgraded and you find that you prefer the hacked version with an older TiVo software release to the new, unhacked TiVo software release, you can always restore your old system from backups, returning your system to the state that you desire.

Dumping TiVo Data to Videotape

For computer systems, backups typically refer to external media that contains copies of critical system programs, system configuration data, and user data. In this last sense, your TiVo provides a built-in mechanism for backing up its equivalent of user data, which consists of the programs that you've recorded. Earlier sections of this chapter explained how to back up these recordings as a part of an entire system backup, which is fine if you also want to restore your entire system. However, since most of us still have an old dusty VCR sitting around somewhere from our pre-TiVo days or for the occasional video rental, it's also useful to back up some of your more precious recordings onto videotape, or for sharing them with friends who may have missed a specific episode of your favorite show. Though videotapes are somewhat retro in the age of the DVR, they're still a useful exchange medium—something like what floppy disks are to today's personal computers.

Your TiVo provides built-in support for backing up recordings onto videotape through the Save to VCR command, which is available on the Now Playing screen for any recording. After connecting your VCR to your TiVo (explained in great detail in the TiVo Installation Guide that came with your TiVo), make sure that your VCR is set to record from the input source to which you attached your TiVo. Now put a videotape in the VCR.

 NOTE

If you don't have your TiVo Installation Guide handy and never bothered to connect your VCR after getting your TiVo, you can download PDF versions of the "TiVo Installation and Viewer's Guide" for your TiVo from http://www.tivo.com/4.2.2.asp. (A link to this page is found on the Customer Support portion of the TiVo Web site if the TiVo Web site changes.) Viewing PDF files requires that you have installed Adobe Acrobat Reader on your system, which you can freely download from http://www.adobe.com/products/acrobat/readermain.html.

After selecting the recording that you want to save to videotape from the Now Playing screen, highlight the Save To VCR screen option, and press Select. This displays an auxiliary screen from which you should then select "Start saving from the beginning." This means your TiVo will begin to play the video from the beginning—regardless of whether you've been watching it and are therefore positioned in the middle of the recording. At this point, your TiVo gives you about 10 seconds to press the Record button on your VCR before actually starting to play the recording on your TiVo.

TIP

Although the TiVo displays the recording in real-time so that any VCR can record it successfully, any of the TiVo **backdoor** commands that you already may have activated are available while the recording is playing. If you have activate the 30-second-skip backdoor (described in the section of Chapter 2 entitled "Using Select-Play-Select Codes"), you can use this command (or even the standard fast-forward commands) to skip or fast-forward through any sections of the recording that you may not want to preserve on videotape.

Forbidden Topics Like Video Extraction

As mentioned in the introduction to this chapter, video extraction is one of the touchier subjects in TiVo-land. This is not surprising, because the entertainment industry has one of the highest profit margins in the known universe. One has only to look at the industry's reaction to MP3s and other forms of online audio to see a comic-tragedy of greed unfold. (I'm lumping audio and video entertainment together because they are essentially the same thing, digitally.) If the recording industry had invested the resources spent in trying to stomp out online music, in retailing it fairly and easily, they could have been making money rather than enemies.

You can find a good deal of software and related Web sites on the Internet that describes how to back up personal recordings from your TiVo to other computer systems. Software packages such as ExtractStream (http://www.9thtee.com/extractstream.html) and TyStudio (http://dvd-create.sourceforge.net/tystudio/index.shtml) are rumored to be some of the best, although they are currently oriented towards the 1 TiVos models. The heightened security that is built into the Series 2 makes it more challenging to back up videos from these systems. Although you could apply the same techniques to your Series 2 system after hacking it to get a command prompt as described in Chapter 7. Using the Linux **netcat** utility to send a stream of video data to another computer system is fairly straightforward, and yet another example of the power of Linux. Mapping TiVo MFS filesystem identifiers (fsids) to the specific recordings that you want to back up is easily done through a variety of scripts that are also available on the Internet. If you have sufficient free space on your TiVo, you can even dump specific fsids to files using the **mfs_stream** utility and then create separate audio and video streams using a utility such as **vsplit**. However, I am not going to discuss any of these.

One sure-fire mechanism for backing up videos from your TiVo is to purchase a TV tuner card that will work with your personal computer system. These work with Windows, Linux, and Macintosh systems, and typically come with software tailored to the card that enables you to display incoming video signals in a window on your PC screen. You can put the card in your PC, use the PC as a display device for the TiVo by connecting the TiVo's Cable Out or S-Video connectors to it, and then use the software provided with the card to capture the video and audio that is being displayed on your PC. TV Tuner cards are available online or on eBay at prices ranging from $20 to hundreds of dollars, depending upon quality, sophistication, and the software packages that are included with them.

Not surprisingly, the Open Source movement has produced an excellent video display and recording package in video display software such as xawtv. Many TV tuner cards use Brook-Tree chips, which are well supported in the BTTV drivers, which are included with most Linux distributions. They are also available from http://bytesex.org/bttv.html. The xawtv software for displaying video input from a tuner card under Linux (my personal favorite) is available from http://bytesex.org/xawtv/index.html. xawtv also is easy to set up and use, and works with a large number of available TV Tuner and related video input cards. A list of supported cards is included in the source code, though many more have probably been used successfully. If you are using xawtv with a BrookTree-based TV tuner card, you will probably want to get the specific set of fonts that it uses, which are available at http://bytesex.org/xawtv/tv-fonts-1.1.tar.bz2.

HACKING THE TiVo

Chapter 6

Expanding Your TiVo's Storage Capacity

The core aspects of expanding your TiVo's storage capacity have been discussed previously, but only in terms of the mechanics of each single step. This chapter provides a central resource for simple processes that you can follow to increase the storage capacity of your TiVo, either by replacing an existing drive with a larger one, by adding a second disk drive to your TiVo, or a combination of both.

Since detailed information on the various steps involved in the upgrade processes is provided elsewhere in the book, this chapter contains a large number of references to other sections, so it may seem to duplicate information. The goal of this chapter is usability, perhaps occasionally at the cost of redundancy or duplication.

Overview

Increasing the amount of space available for storing your recorded programming on your TiVo by doing one of the following:

- ◆ Replacing an existing TiVo disk drive with a larger one
- ◆ Adding a second disk drive to your TiVo

You can perform a number of permutations of these two operations. For example, if you are using a TiVo Series 1 that originally came with two disk drives, both of these drives are relatively small. You can replace both of these drives with a single drive that can store substantially more recordings and is fairly inexpensive. You can add a new (larger) second drive at the same time or add it later. If your TiVo only contains a single drive, you can replace that drive with a larger one. You can add a second drive now or later. If you're happy with the capacity of your current TiVo drive, you can continue using that drive and add a second one.

The following table gives the approximate ratio between disk storage and TiVo recording capacity at each of the TiVo quality settings. This information will help you calculate how much additional recording time you should get by using a larger drive in your TiVo or adding a second drive. These values are approximations—the actual correlation between different levels of recording quality and the storage that they require are stored in TiVo's MFS filesystem, and may therefore change between different versions of the TiVo software.

Table 6.1 Comparing Recording Quality and Storage Requirements

Recording Quality Level	Hours Per GigaByte
Basic	1.2
Medium	0.7
High	0.55
Best	0.35

The core tasks of the disk upgrade process are as follows. Since single-drive TiVos are much more common than dual-drive TiVos, these instructions refer to single drives, but the procedure for dual-drive TiVos is the same (except plural):

1. Remove the drive from your TiVo and put it in your PC along with the new drive that you want to use in your TiVo. (Chapter 3)

2. Boot from the BATBD disk, and back up the drive from your TiVo. (Chapter 5)

3. Restore the backup to the new drive, using the **mfstool restore** options necessary to allocate any additional space for use by your TiVo. (This chapter)

4. Put the new drive in your TiVo, and turn it on. (any time)

As you can see, the process is actually fairly simple. The details of each of the steps in this process have been outlined earlier in this book; however, at this point, the primary challenge is threading them together correctly, as explained in this chapter.

Determining how you want to upgrade your TiVo is up to you, but here are some suggestions:

◆ If you have an existing dual-drive TiVo, back up both drives to a single backup and restore that to a larger single drive. The drives used in a stock dual-drive TiVo are small by today's standards and are old by anyone's standards. Since the drives in a TiVo run 24 hours a day, every day, they will eventually go bad. Also, single drives with more storage capacity than the combination of the drives in a dual-drive TiVo can easily be purchased for less than $100.

◆ If you have an existing single drive TiVo Series 1 system, back up that drive and replace it with a larger drive. Eighty or 100 GB drives can easily be purchased for less than $100, and will at least double the storage capacity of your TiVo. More modern drives are usually quieter and more reliable than older drives. Don't wait for a catastrophe to occur before you expand your storage.

◆ If you have a TiVo Series 2, back up its existing drive and restore it to a larger one. You can then keep the original drive as a spare, and add a second drive later.

In general, I prefer to deal with as few variables as possible when upgrading a TiVo. I typically replace the existing drive(s) in an existing TiVo with a single larger drive, making sure that it works (and hack it as needed ;-), and then add a second drive once I'm sure that the first drive is working and configured correctly. Everyone has his or her own approach——some prefer to do everything at once, but I'd rather take my TiVo apart one more time after verifying that the first part of the upgrade worked correctly.

Considerations for Adding Storage

As discussed in detail in Chapter 9, "Linux and TiVo," the heart of the Linux operating system is known as a *kernel*. The kernel is the portion of the operating system that loads into memory as the first step of the boot process, and which ultimately manages access to all of the hardware and software on your TiVo. The Linux kernel communicates with specific types of hardware, such as your disk drives, using a combination of built-in information and hardware-specific sets of instructions called *device drivers*. Linux device drivers can be built into the kernel or can load automatically when the hardware that they are associated with is detected during the system's boot process.

As of the time this book was written, the device drivers for the disk drives in the TiVo Linux kernel can only use approximately 120 GB of disk drive space from each disk drive. This does not mean that the TiVo can't use larger disk drives—it just means that any space above 120 GB will be inaccessible to the TiVo. Subsequent kernel and device driver upgrades will certainly eliminate this limitation, but it's a reality at the moment.

TiVo ALL HAIL THE TIVO KING!

Among the TiVo hackers who hang out on the AVS Forums and similar locations, the title "TiVo King" is given to the person who can add the most storage to their TiVo. At the time of this book's writing, this title was held by the folks at PVRUpgrade.com—and it looks as though they will hold that title for a while. They have just announced software that enables the TiVo to break the 120 MB barrier. Details of how this works have not yet been released, but it will obviously involve a kernel or device driver upgrade. The ability to use larger drives has been present in standard Linux for a long time, but it's great to see this capability migrate to the TiVo. It will also be interesting to see exactly how this is done, given the heightened paranoia—I mean, security—used on the newer TiVo Series 2 models and TiVo software releases.

The downside of this upgrade is, naturally, that you may never have time to watch all of the recordings that can fit on your TiVo. On the other hand, you could go away for a year or so and your TiVo would still capture every *Will & Grace* episode ever released.

What You'll Need for Your TiVo Upgrade

The items that you will need in order to replace the existing drive in your system with a larger one, or to add a second drive to your TiVo, are the following:

◆ #10 and #15 Torx screwdrivers

◆ An IDE disk drive, up to 120 MB in size

◆ This book and the BATBD CD that comes with it

◆ An hour or so of free time

If you are adding a second drive to your TiVo rather than replacing an existing TiVo drive with a larger one, you should buy a bracket to mount the new drive in your TiVo. (For sources for these brackets, see the sections of Chapter 3 on 9thTee.com, Weaknees.com, or PVRUpgrade.com, or search the Web yourself for something like "TiVo Drive Bracket.") You can add a second drive to any TiVo Series 1 machine without a bracket, but the drive won't be attached to anything, and could easily be damaged when moving your TiVo. All TiVo Series 2 machines with the exception of the TCD130040 and TCD130060 Series 2 stand-alone TiVo machines require a mounting bracket because there is nowhere to put the drive without one.

Once you have these items, you're ready to go!

TIP

A variety of TiVo upgrade kits are available from the vendors of TiVo supplies discussed at the end of Chapter 3 in the section entitled "TiVo Hardware Resources on the Web," or from online sites such as eBay. These kits can be useful if you want to quickly and easily get all of the parts necessary to upgrade a TiVo without getting them individually by yourself. These kits fall into two classes: upgrade kits that provide a larger drive for use in your TiVo as a replacement for the drive(s) that came with your TiVo, and those that are designed to add a second disk to your TiVo. If you decide to buy an upgrade kit for adding a second drive to your TiVo, make sure that it includes a bracket for mounting the second drive in your machine. Again, some of the replacement brackets that are available are discussed and shown in Chapter 3.

Replacing an Existing TiVo Disk with a Larger One

For most people, the first step in TiVo hacking is to increase the amount of storage available to your TiVo. This is not only practical, but also a good baptismal experience in TiVo hacking. Adding a new drive requires opening your TiVo and your PC, shuffling disk drives between the two, and then using TiVo backup and restore commands. Once you've completed this task, you'll be more comfortable with your TiVo and its software—and ready to move on to see what else you can do to take full advantage of your TiVo hardware and the software that is available for it.

After you assemble the items listed in the previous section, "What You'll Need for Your TiVo Upgrade," do the following to increase the storage capacity of your TiVo:

1. Follow the instructions in Chapter 3 to open your TiVo, remove its current disk drive, and put it in your PC along with the new drive that you want to use as a replacement.

2. Insert the BATBD disk in your PC's CDROM drive, and reboot your PC, selecting the appropriate boot option for the type of TiVo that you are upgrading. For TiVo Series 2 models, you can simply press Return when the BATBD's boot options are displayed. For TiVo Series 1 models, select the **s1swap** boot option.

TIP

If your PC is not configured to boot from the CD before booting from the hard drive, you will need to update your BIOS Setup options. To do this, press the appropriate key (usually Delete or F2) immediately after booting your PC. Search the basic and advanced boot options menus for an entry like Boot Sequence, and modify this entry so that your computer tries to boot from the CDROM before booting from the hard drive. Exactly where this BIOS option menu is located depends on which BIOS your PC uses, but they're all fairly similar. Exit from the BIOS Setup menus, saving your new settings, and reboot your PC (it will usually reboot automatically at this point).

3. Create a backup of the drive from your TiVo. Because you are upgrading an existing system and will therefore still have your original TiVo drive, it's easiest to use the MFS Tools **mfstool backup** command for your initial backup. This command would look like the following:

```
mfstool backup -o <backup-file> /dev/hdX
```

The value of **<backup-file>** should be the full pathname of a location where you want to store the backup file. You should replace the letter **X** in **/dev/hdX** with the Linux name of the device corresponding to your TiVo disk drive. The device name would therefore be **/dev/hdb** if you installed the TiVo drive as the slave drive on your primary IDE interface; it would be **/dev/hdc** if you installed the TiVo drive as the master drive on your secondary IDE interface; or it would be **/dev/hdd** if you installed the TiVo drive as the slave drive on your secondary IDE interface.

This command only backs up the mandatory sections of your TiVo disk. If you want to back up everything, including any recordings that your TiVo disk currently contains, you must add the **-a** option to the backup command, as in the following example:

```
mfstool backup -o <backup-file> -a /dev/hdX
```

Using the **-a** option creates substantially larger backup files, and will therefore require substantially more disk space than a minimum backup.

NOTE

If anything about this step is confusing, don't worry. Perhaps you haven't read this book from cover to cover? For more information about installing TiVo and other disk drives in your PC, see the section of Chapter 3, "Working with TiVo Disk Drives." For additional information about this backup command, see the section of Chapter 5, "Creating a Simple Backup Using MFS Tools." For suggestions and additional information about your options for where to store the backup file, see the section of

Chapter 5 entitled "Finding Room for Backups." If your PC doesn't have 800 MB of free disk space or if you're simply in a hurry, you can follow the instructions later in this chapter in the section "Replacing a Disk Without Using Backup Files," but I'd strongly suggest that you make a backup at this point if at all possible.

4. Restore the backup to the new drive, using the **mfstool restore** options necessary to allocate the additional space for use by your TiVo. This command would look like the following:

```
mfstool restore -i <backup-file> -x /dev/hdX
```

The value of **<backup-file>** should be the full pathname of the backup file that you created in the previous step. You should replace the letter **X** in **/dev/hdX** with the Linux name of the device corresponding to the new drive that you want to use in your TiVo. The device name would therefore be **/dev/hdb** if you installed the new drive as the slave drive on your primary IDE interface; it would be **/dev/hdc** if you installed the new drive as the master drive on your secondary IDE interface; or it would be **/dev/hdd** if you installed the new drive as the slave drive on your secondary IDE interface. (For more detailed information about this restore command, see the following section of Chapter 5, "Restoring an MFS Tool Backup to a Larger Drive.")

WARNING

Be very careful when entering the name of the new disk drive that you want to use in your TiVo. You can easily overwrite your personal computer's boot drive if you specify the wrong disk drive at this point. The **mfstool restore** command will not warn you if you accidentally specify a disk drive that contains Windows or Linux data.

5. Shut down your PC and remove the TiVo drive and the new drive that you want to use in your TiVo. Put the TiVo drive somewhere safe, and set the jumpers on the replacement disk correctly to ensure that the drive is identified as a Master disk. For more information about setting drive jumpers, see the section of Chapter 3 entitled "Working with TiVo Disk Drives."

6. After putting the new drive in your TiVo, turn it on. You should see the two gray startup screens as the TiVo boots.

Congratulations! You've upgraded your TiVo. You can go to the System Information screen (TiVo Central -> Messages & Setup -> System Information) to see the new amount of storage available on your TiVo. The amount of storage that displays depends on the size of the new disk drive, but it will certainly be more. And more is better.

You will want to do some housekeeping on the new TiVo drive before using it. For example, the backup command used in this section does not back up the recordings on your TiVo, so you will need to go to the Now Playing menu (TiVo Central -> Now Playing) to delete the empty entries for any recordings that were located on the TiVo disk drive that you backed up. If you want to replace an existing TiVo drive with a new one and preserve your recordings, see the next section. The instructions in that section are largely identical to those in this section, except that they use **mfstool backup** options that preserve the entire contents of your original TiVo disk as part of the backup process.

Upgrading a Disk Without Using Backup Files

If you do not have sufficient disk space to make a backup of your TiVo, never fear—you can still replace the drive in your TiVo with a larger one by taking advantage of some of the powerful features provided by Linux.

Assemble the items listed in the above section, "What You'll Need for Your TiVo Upgrade," and do the following to increase the storage capacity of your TiVo without creating any intermediate backup files:

1. Follow the instructions in Chapter 3 to open your TiVo, remove its current disk drive, and put it in your PC along with the new drive that you want to use as a replacement.

2. Insert the BATBD disk in your PC's CDROM drive, and reboot your PC, selecting the appropriate boot option for the type of TiVo that you are upgrading. For TiVo Series 2 models, you can simply press Return when the BATBD's boot options are displayed. For TiVo Series 1 models, select the **s1swap** boot option.

 TIP

If your PC is not configured to boot from the CD before booting from the hard drive, you will need to update your BIOS Setup options. To do this, press the appropriate key (usually Delete or F2) immediately after booting your PC. Search the basic and advanced boot options menus for an entry like Boot Sequence, and modify this entry so that your computer tries to boot from the CDROM before booting from the hard drive. Exactly where this BIOS option menu is located depends on which BIOS your PC uses, but they're all fairly similar. Exit from the BIOS Setup menus, save your new settings, and reboot your PC (it will usually reboot automatically at this point).

3. Back up your TiVo and pipe the output of the backup command to a restore command. This command would look like the following:

```
mfstool backup -o - /dev/hdX | mfstool restore -i - -x /dev/hdY
```

Using dashes as the name of the output file for the backup command and as the name of the input file for the restore command tell these commands not to write to files, but to write to what are known as *standard input* and *standard output*. (This is explained in more detail in Chapter 5, in the section "Connecting Backup and Restore Commands Using a Pipe.") You should replace the letter **X** in **/dev/hdX** with the Linux name of the device corresponding to your TiVo disk drive, and replace the letter **Y** in **/dev/hdY** with the Linux name of the device corresponding to the new drive. The device name would therefore be **/dev/hdb** for a drive attached as the slave drive on your primary IDE interface; it would be **/dev/hdc** for a drive attached as the master drive on your secondary IDE interface; or it would be **/dev/hdd** for a drive attached as the slave drive on your secondary IDE interface.

This command only backs up the mandatory sections of your TiVo disk. If you want to back up everything, including any recordings that your TiVo disk currently contains, you must add the **-a** option to the backup portion of the command-line, as in the following example:

```
mfstool backup -o - -a /dev/hdX | mfstool restore -i - -x /dev/hdY
```

 NOTE

If anything about this step is confusing, don't worry. For more information about installing TiVo and other disk drives in your PC, see the section of Chapter 3 entitled "Working with TiVo Disk Drives." For additional information about the **mfstool backup** and **mfstool restore** commands, see the appropriate sections of Chapter 5. For information about pipes and connecting commands on a Linux system, see the section of Chapter 5 entitled "Connecting Backup and Restore Commands Using a Pipe."

 WARNING

Be very careful when entering the name of the new disk drive that you want to use in your TiVo. You can easily overwrite your personal computer's boot drive if you specify the name of the wrong disk drive at this point. The **mfstool restore** command will not warn you if you accidentally specify a disk drive that contains Windows or Linux data.

4. Shut down your PC and remove the TiVo drive and the new drive that you want to use in your TiVo. Put the TiVo drive somewhere safe, and set the jumpers on the replacement disk correctly to ensure that the drive is identified as a Master disk. For more information about setting drive jumpers, see the section "Working With TiVo Disk Drives," in Chapter 3.

5. After putting the new drive in your TiVo, turn it on. You should see the two grey startup screens as the TiVo boots.

Congratulations! You've upgraded your TiVo, and have even taken advantage of a relatively whizzy Linux and Unix feature. You can go to the System Information screen (TiVo Central -> Messages & Setup -> System Information) to see the new amount of storage available on your TiVo. The amount of storage shown depends on the size of the new disk drive.

Expanding Drives Using Disk Images

You probably remember from Chapter 5, there are ways of backing up your TiVo: unstructured and structured backups. The MFS Tools utilities produce structured backups, which only contain the information required to restore a TiVo disk. Unstructured backups are complete images of TiVo drives, and are therefore the same size as the original drive.

The following sections explain how to back up and restore TiVo disks using unstructured backups. In most cases, the MFS Tools are the preferred mechanism for backing up and restoring TiVo disks because the backups that they produce are smaller. However, you never know—you may need to use disk images to restore a drive if you encounter a bug in the MFS Tools utilities, or if changes in the structure of the MFS filesystem prevent the version of the MFS Tools utilities that you are using from working with a newer TiVo software release. Although disk images are huge, they are nice in that they automatically preserve all of your settings, recorded videos, and so on, as they are complete images of your original disk drive.

Another reason for using the **dd** program is when you encounter read errors on the drive and therefore suspect that your disk drive is failing. You can use the **dd** program to create an image backup of the entire disk, and then either replace the disk or reformat it. (The former is preferable, but the latter may work.) Once you have replaced or reformatted the disk, you can then restore the backup to the new disk (as explained in this section and in more detail in Chapter 5). If you are lucky, you might just be able to recover all of your TiVo settings and existing recordings.

 TIP

After using an image backup to attempt to work around a failing hard drive, you should immediately do a structured backup of that disk so that you have a smaller, consistent backup of the drive available.

Expanding a Drive from a Disk Image

This section explains how to restore an image of an existing TiVo drive to a larger disk, and then how to expand the restored image so that the additional space on the new disk is available for use by your TiVo.

NOTE

This section is designed to provide a quick reference for restoring a disk from an image backup and expanding it. For detailed information about various steps of this process, see the appropriate sections of Chapter 5. For detailed information about creating disk images using the Linux **dd** program, see the section of Chapter 5 entitled "Creating Image Backups Using **dd**." For detailed information about restoring disk images using **dd**, see the section of Chapter 5 entitled "Restoring Image Backups Using **dd**."

Assemble the items listed in the section entitled "What You'll Need for Your TiVo Upgrade," and then do the following to increase the storage capacity of your TiVo using an image backup file:

1. Follow the instructions in Chapter 3 to open your TiVo, remove its current disk drive, and put it in your PC along with the new drive.

2. Insert the BATBD disk in your PC's CDROM drive, and reboot your PC, selecting the appropriate boot option for the type of TiVo that you are upgrading. For TiVo Series 2 models, you can simply press Return when the BATBD's boot options are displayed. For TiVo Series 1 models, select the **s1swap** boot option.

TIP

If your PC is not configured to boot from the CD before booting from the hard drive, you will need to update your BIOS Setup options. To do this, press the appropriate key (usually Delete or F2) immediately after booting your PC. Search the basic and advanced boot options menus for an entry like Boot Sequence, and modify this entry so that your computer tries to boot from the CDROM before booting from the hard drive. Exactly where this BIOS option menu is located depends on which BIOS your PC uses, but they're all fairly similar. Exit from the BIOS Setup menus, saving your new settings, and reboot your PC (it will usually reboot automatically at this point).

3. Create a backup of the drive from your TiVo using the Linux **dd** command. This command would look like the following:

```
dd if=/dev/hdX  of=<backup-file> bs=32k conv=noerror,sync
```

You should replace the letter **X** in **/dev/hdX** with the Linux name of the device corresponding to your TiVo disk drive. The device name would therefore be **/dev/hdb** if you installed the TiVo drive as the slave drive on your primary IDE interface; it would be **/dev/hdc** if you installed the TiVo drive as the master drive on your secondary IDE interface; or it would be **/dev/hdd** if you installed the TiVo drive as the slave drive on your secondary IDE interface. The value of **<backup-file>** should be the full pathname of the backup file that you want to create. The **bs** option specifies the block size that the **dd** program should use when reading and writing data. The **conv=noerror,sync** options are usually unnecessary, but are handy if you encounter any problems reading from the original TiVo disk. These are conversion options that tell the **dd** program how to react to specific conditions, if encountered. The **noerror** option tells the **dd** program not to abort if an error is encountered. The **sync** option tells the **dd** program to pad incomplete reads with NULL bytes if the program encounters a problem reading from the input drive.

 NOTE

For more information about installing TiVo and other disk drives in your PC, see the section in Chapter 3, "Working with TiVo Disk Drives." For suggestions and additional information about your options for where to store backup files, see the section in Chapter 5, "Finding Room for Backups." If your PC doesn't have the gigabytes of free disk space required to create a complete image of your existing TiVo drive, you can follow the instructions in the next section, "Using Disk Images without Intermediate Backup Files."

4. Restore the backup to the new drive, using the **dd** command. This command would look like the following:

```
dd if=<backup-file> of=/dev/hdX bs=32k
```

The value of **<backup-file>** should be the full pathname of the backup file that you created in the previous step. You should replace the letter **X** in **/dev/hdX** with the Linux name of the device corresponding to the new drive that you want to use in your TiVo. The device name would therefore be **/dev/hdb** if you installed the new drive as the slave drive on your primary IDE interface; it would be **/dev/hdc** if you installed the new drive as the master drive on your secondary IDE interface; or it would be **/dev/hdd** if you installed the new drive as the slave drive on your secondary IDE interface. The conversion options used when creating the disk image are not necessary because you are working from a backup file that was correctly written in the previous step.

(For more detailed information about this restore command, see the section of Chapter 5, "Restoring Image Backups Using **dd**.".

WARNING

Be very careful when entering the name of the new disk drive that you want to use in your TiVo. You can easily overwrite your personal computer's boot drive if you specify the name of the wrong disk drive at this point. The **dd** command will not warn you if you accidentally specify a disk drive that contains Windows or Linux data.

5. At this point, you can use either the MFS Tools utilities or the BlessTiVo program to make the extra space on the new drive available to your TiVo. This extra space is the difference between the size of your original TiVo disk and the size of the drive to which you restored the image backup. To use the MFS Tools **mfstool mfsadd** command to add this extra space to the drive to which you restored your image backup, use the following command:

```
mfstool mfsadd -x /dev/hdX
```

You should replace the letter **X** in **/dev/hdX** with the Linux name of the device corresponding to the drive to which you restored your image backup. The device name would therefore be **/dev/hdb** if you installed the new drive as the slave drive on your primary IDE interface; it would **be /dev/hdc** if you installed the new drive as the master drive on your secondary IDE interface; or it would be **/dev/hdd** if you installed the new drive as the slave drive on your secondary IDE interface.

6. Shut down your PC and remove the TiVo drive and the new drive that you want to use in your TiVo. Put the TiVo drive somewhere safe, and set the jumpers on the replacement disk correctly to ensure that the drive is identified as a Master disk. For more information about setting drive jumpers, see Chapter 3, the section entitled "Working with TiVo Disk Drives."

7. After putting the new drive in your TiVo, turn it on. You should see the two gray startup screens as the TiVo boots.

Congratulations! You've upgraded your TiVo. You can go to the System Information screen (TiVo Central -> Messages & Setup -> System Information) to see the new amount of storage available on your TiVo. The amount of storage shown depends on the size of the new disk drive, but it will certainly be more. As is always true for good things, more is better.

Using Disk Images Without Intermediate Backup Files

How can you use image backups to back up and restore a drive without creating any intermediate files? As discussed earlier, the backup files created using **dd** are unstructured backup files that are the exact size of the disk drive that you backed up. If you don't happen to have 20-60 GB of disk space sitting around, but need to do an image backup, such as when you suspect that your existing TiVo disk drive is going bad, no worry. This section explains how to take advantage of some of the powerful features provided by Linux to create and restore an image backup without requiring intermediate disk space. This section concludes by explaining how to expand the cloned disk image on the new drive to use additional space to store TiVo recordings.

 NOTE

This section is designed to provide a quick reference for backing up and restoring a disk using image backup and subsequently expanding the cloned drive. For detailed information about various steps of this process, see the appropriate sections of Chapter 5. For detailed information about creating disk images using the Linux **dd** program, see the section of Chapter 5 entitled "Creating Image Backups Using **dd**." For detailed information about restoring disk images using **dd**, see the section "Restoring Image Backups Using **dd**," in Chapter 5. For detailed information about creating and restoring backups without using intermediate files, see the section of Chapter 5, "Connecting Backup and Restore Commands Using a Pipe." If you are unsure about how to attach or jumper disk drives, see the information about installing TiVo and other disk drives in the Chapter 3, the section entitled "Working with TiVo Disk Drives."

Once you have the items listed in the section entitled "What You'll Need for Your TiVo Upgrade," take the following steps to increase the storage capacity of your TiVo using an image backup file:

1. Following the instructions in Chapter 3, "Working With TiVo Disk Drives," open your TiVo, remove its current disk drive, and put it in your PC along with the new drive that you want to replace it with.

2. Insert the BATBD disk in your PC's CDROM drive, and reboot your PC, selecting the appropriate boot option for the type of TiVo that you are upgrading. For TiVo Series 2 models, you can simply press Return when the BATBD's boot options display. For TiVo Series 1 models, select the **s1swap** boot option.

TIP

If your PC is not configured to boot from the CD before booting from the hard drive, you will need to update your BIOS Setup options. To do this, press the appropriate key (usually Delete or F2) immediately after booting your PC. Search the basic and advanced boot options menus for an entry like Boot Sequence, and modify this entry so that your computer tries to boot from the CDROM before booting from the hard drive. Exactly where this BIOS option menu is located depends on which BIOS your PC uses, but they're all fairly similar. Exit from the BIOS Setup menus, saving your new settings, and reboot your PC (it will usually reboot automatically at this point).

3. Create a backup of the drive from your TiVo using the Linux **dd** command, writing to standard output, and pipe the output of this command into another **dd** command that reads from standard input and writes to the new drive. This command would look like the following:

```
dd if=/dev/hdX  bs=32k conv=noerror,sync | dd of=/dev/hdY bs=32k
```

You should replace the letter **X** in **/dev/hdX** with the Linux name of the device corresponding to your TiVo disk drive, and replace the letter **Y** in **/dev/hdY** with the Linux name of the device corresponding to the new drive. The device name would therefore be **/dev/hdb** for a drive attached as the slave drive on your primary IDE interface; it would be **/dev/hdc** for a drive attached as the master drive on your secondary IDE interface; or it would be **/dev/hdd** for a drive attached as the slave drive on your secondary IDE interface. The **bs** options specify the block size that the **dd** program should use when reading and writing data. The **conv=noerror,sync** options are usually unnecessary, but are handy if you encounter any problems reading from the original TiVo disk. These are conversion options that tell the **dd** program how to react to specific conditions, if encountered. The **noerror** option tells the **dd** program not to abort if an error is encountered. The **sync** option tells the **dd** program to pad incomplete reads with NULL bytes if the program encounters a problem reading from the input drive.

WARNING

Be very careful when entering the name of the new disk drive that you want to use in your TiVo. You can easily overwrite your personal computer's boot drive if you specify the name of the wrong disk drive at this point. The **dd** command will not warn you if you accidentally specify a disk drive that contains Windows or Linux data.

4. At this point, you can use either the MFS Tools utilities or the BlessTiVo program to make the extra space on the new drive available to your TiVo. This extra space is the difference between the size of your original TiVo disk and the size of the drive to which you restored the image backup. To use the MFS Tools **mfstool mfsadd** command to add this extra space to the drive to which you restored your image backup, use the following command:

```
mfstool mfsadd -x /dev/hdY
```

You should replace the letter **Y** in **/dev/hdX** with the Linux name of the device corresponding to the drive to which you restored your image backup. The device name would therefore be **/dev/hdb** if you installed the new drive as the slave drive on your primary IDE interface; it would be **/dev/hdc** if you installed the new drive as the master drive on your secondary IDE interface; or it would be **/dev/hdd** if you installed the new drive as the slave drive on your secondary IDE interface.

5. Shut down your PC and remove the TiVo drive and the new drive that you want to use in your TiVo. Put the TiVo drive somewhere safe, and set the jumpers on the replacement disk correctly to ensure that the drive is identified as a Master disk. For more information about setting drive jumpers, see the section, "Working With TiVo Disk Drives," in Chapter 3.

6. After putting the new drive in your TiVo, turn it on. You should see the two gray startup screens as the TiVo boots.

Congratulations! You've upgraded your TiVo. You can go to the System Information screen (TiVo Central -> Messages & Setup -> System Information) to see the new amount of storage available on your TiVo. The amount of storage shown depends on the size of the new disk drive, but it will certainly be more.

Adding a Second Drive to Your TiVo

As discussed in the beginning of this chapter, there are two ways to upgrade the storage capacity of your TiVo: by replacing an existing drive with a larger one or by adding a second drive. You can always do both, which is my preferred solution——but I prefer not to do both at the same time. Upgrading an existing disk and verifying that it works correctly is easy enough to do, but has its own set of potential problems. Rather than combining those problems with any of the potential problems that can arise when adding a second disk, I prefer to first upgrade an existing disk and verify that everything is working correctly. Then one can easily add a second disk as explained in the following sections.

The following sections explain how to use the MFS Tools and BlessTiVo utilities to add a second drive to your TiVo. Each of these utilities has advantages. The MFS Tools utilities enable you to add an entire disk or specific partitions to the storage capacity of your TiVo. The BlessTiVo utility only enables you to add an entire drive to your TiVo, but is Open Source and is therefore available for both Linux and the Mac OS X.

WARNING

As discussed in more detail in Chapter 4, when you add a second drive to your TiVo, the two drives are "married" and must be used together. You cannot subsequently remove the second drive and expect your Series 1 model to work correctly with just the A drive. To "un-marry" two drives, you must back them up using the MFS Tools utilities (also discussed in Chapter 4), and then restore the backup to a single drive, assuming that the single drive has sufficient space to hold the TiVo data that was contained on the previous two drives. This single drive can be used by itself, and you then can recycle the two drives that are its logical parents.

Using the MFS Tools Utilities to Add a Second Drive

The MFS Tools utilities **mfstool** command provides a command-line option that makes it easy to add a second drive to your TiVo, substantially increasing the amount of space available for recordings. The **mfstool mfsadd** command enables you to quickly add the entire contents of a second drive, and it also enables you to add specific MFS partitions to the storage capacity of your TiVo. The latter can be quite useful for advanced TiVo hackers who want to create their own standard Linux (**ext2**) partitions on a second drive, but still want to use the majority of that drive to provide increased storage capacity for TiVo recordings.

Adding an Entire Drive Using MFS Tools

WARNING

Do not use the procedure described in this section to add a second drive to your TiVo unless that drive is blank or is a copy of an existing TiVo drive. Any drive that is not currently used by MFS—that is, does not contain a valid TiVo partition map—is initialized by the **mfstool mfsadd** command. To add specific portions of an existing drive to your TiVo, use the procedure described in the section entitled "Adding Specific Partitions of a Second Drive Using MFS Tools," later in this chapter.

Adding all of the storage space available on a new disk is easy using the MFS Tools utilities. Once you have the items listed in the section, "What You'll Need for Your TiVo Upgrade," do the following to prepare a second drive for use in your TiVo using the **mfstool mfsadd** command:

1. Insert the drive that you want to use in your TiVo into your PC as described in Chapter 3.

2. Insert the BATBD disk in your PC's CDROM drive, and reboot your PC, selecting the appropriate boot option for the type of TiVo that you are upgrading. For TiVo Series 2 models, you can simply press Return when the BATBD's boot options are displayed. For TiVo Series 1 models, select the **s1swap** boot option.

TIP

If your PC is not configured to boot from the CD before booting from the hard drive, you will need to update your BIOS Setup options. To do this, press the appropriate key (usually Delete or F2) immediately after booting your PC. Search the basic and advanced boot options menus for an entry like Boot Sequence, and modify this entry so that your computer tries to boot from the CDROM before booting from the hard drive. Exactly where this BIOS option menu is located depends on which BIOS your PC uses, but they're all fairly similar. Exit from the BIOS Setup menus, saving your new settings, and reboot your PC (it will usually reboot automatically at this point).

3. To format and partition the entire contents of the newly attached disk so that it can be used by your TiVo for storing recordings, execute the following command:

```
mfstool mfsadd -x /dev/hdX
```

Replace the letter **X** in **/dev/hdX** with the Linux name of the device corresponding to the new disk drive. The device name would therefore be **/dev/hdb** if you installed the new drive as the slave drive on your primary IDE interface; the name would be **/dev/hdc** if you installed the new drive as the master drive on your secondary IDE interface; or the name would be **/dev/hdd** if you installed the new drive as the slave drive on your secondary IDE interface.

WARNING

Be very careful when entering the name of the new disk drive that you want to use in your TiVo. You can easily overwrite your personal computer's boot drive if you specify the name of the wrong disk drive at this point. The **mfstool mfsadd** command will not warn you if you accidentally specify a disk drive that contains Windows or Linux data, and will silently initialize that disk for you.

4. Shut down your TiVo and follow the instructions in Chapter 3 to open your TiVo and add the second drive, jumpering it correctly so that it does not conflict with the existing drive in your TiVo.

5. Turn on your TiVo. You should see the standard two gray startup screens as the TiVo boots.

That's all there is to it! When you put the new drive in your TiVo and boot the TiVo, the TiVo detects the second drive and adds its disk identifier to the primary drive, thereby making the additional storage that it contains available to your TiVo. After your TiVo displays the startup animation, you can go to the System Information screen (TiVo Central -> Messages & Setup -> System Information) to see the new amount of storage available on your TiVo. The amount of storage shown depends on the size of the new disk drive, but it will certainly be more.

Adding Specific Partitions of a Second Drive Using MFS Tools

Adding specific partitions on a second disk to the pool of storage available to your TiVo is easy using the MFS Tools utilities. Once you have the items listed in the section entitled "What You'll Need For Your TiVo Upgrade," do the following to prepare specific partitions of a second drive for use by your TiVo, using the **mfstool mfsadd** command:

1. Insert the new drive that you want to use in your TiVo into your PC as described in Chapter 3.

2. Insert the BATBD disk in your PC's CDROM drive, and reboot your PC, selecting the appropriate boot option for the type of TiVo that you are upgrading. For TiVo Series 2 models, you can simply press Return when the BATBD's boot options are displayed. For TiVo Series 1 models, select the **s1swap** boot option.

 TIP

If your PC is not configured to boot from the CD before booting from the hard drive, you will need to update your BIOS Setup options. To do this, press the appropriate key (usually Delete or F2) immediately after booting your PC. Search the basic and advanced boot options menus for an entry like Boot Sequence, and modify this entry so that your computer tries to boot from the CDROM before booting from the hard drive. Exactly where this BIOS option menu is located depends on which BIOS your PC uses, but they're all fairly similar. Exit from the BIOS Setup menus, saving your new settings, and reboot your PC (it will usually reboot automatically at this point).

3. Use the **pdisk -1 /dev/hdX** command to display the partition map on your TiVo to verify the names of the partitions that you want to add. Replace the letter **X** in **/dev/hdX** with the Linux name of the device corresponding to the new disk drive. The device name would therefore be **/dev/hdb** if you installed the new drive as the slave drive on your primary IDE interface; it would be **/dev/hdc** if you installed the new drive as the master drive on your secondary IDE interface; or it would be **/dev/hdd** if you installed the new drive as the slave drive on your secondary IDE interface.

TIP

TiVo disks can be initialized and partitions created manually using the **pdisk** command, as explained in Chapter 4, "PDisk."

4. Once you know the names of the MFS partitions that you want to add, execute the following command:

```
mfstool mfsadd /dev/hdXN /dev/hdXM
```

Replace the letter **X** with the identifier for the disk drive, as described previously, and replace the letters **N** and **M** with the numbers corresponding to the partitions containing the MFS application and MFS media regions that you want to add.

5. Shut down your TiVo and follow the instructions in Chapter 3 to open your TiVo and add the second drive, jumpering it correctly so that it does not conflict with your existing TiVo drive.

6. Turn on your TiVo. You should see the standard two gray startup screens as the TiVo boots.

That's all there is to it! The TiVo automatically detects the second drive at boot time and adds its disk identifier to the primary drive, making the additional storage that it contains available to your TiVo. After your TiVo displays the startup animation, you can go to the System Information screen (TiVo Central -> Messages & Setup -> System Information) to see the new amount of storage available on your TiVo. The amount of storage shown depends on the size of the new disk drive.

Using the BlessTiVo Utility to Add a Second Drive

Unlike the MFS Tools utilities, the BlessTiVo utility is an open source utility that makes it easy to add an entire drive to your TiVo for use in storing recordings. The BlessTiVo utility is available for systems such as Linux (on the BATBD disk) and Mac OS X (downloadable from http://FOOBAR). For more information about using the BlessTiVo utility on a Mac OS X system, see Chapter 8, "Working with Your TiVo from Windows and Macintosh Systems."

As with the other procedures provided in this chapter, this section provides a procedural guide to using BlessTiVo to add a second drive to your TiVo. For detailed information on the BlessTiVo command, its operation, and any status or error messages that it displays, see the section in Chapter 4, "BlessTiVo." This section is designed to get you up and running with a minimum of fuss and background information. To use the BlessTiVo command to prepare a second drive for use by your TiVo, do the following:

1. Insert the new drive that you want to use in your TiVo into your PC as described in Chapter 3.

2. Insert the BATBD disk in your PC's CDROM drive, and reboot your PC, selecting the appropriate boot option for the type of TiVo that you are upgrading. For TiVo Series 2 models, you can simply press Return when the BATBD's boot options are displayed. For TiVo Series 1 models, select the **s1swap** boot option.

TIP

If your PC is not configured to boot from the CD before booting from the hard drive, you will need to update your BIOS Setup options. To do this, press the appropriate key (usually Delete or F2) immediately after booting your PC. Search the basic and advanced boot options menus for an entry like Boot Sequence, and modify this entry so that your computer tries to boot from the CDROM before booting from the hard drive. Exactly where this BIOS option menu is located depends on which BIOS your PC uses, but they're all fairly similar. Exit from the BIOS Setup menus, saving your new settings, and reboot your PC (it will usually reboot automatically at this point).

3. To format and partition the entire contents of the newly attached disk so that your TiVo can use it for storing recordings, execute the following command:

```
BlessTiVo /dev/hdX
```

Replace the letter **X** with the appropriate identifier for the disk that you want to format. The device names used by the BlessTiVo command are **/dev/hdb** for a drive attached as a slave on your primary IDE interface; it would be **/dev/hdc** for a drive attached as a master on your secondary IDE interface; and it would be **/dev/hdd** for a drive attached as a slave on your secondary IDE interface. As a safety feature, the BlessTiVo command does not allow you to specify **/dev/hda** as the drive to be formatted, because this drive is typically the boot disk used by your PC or a Mac OS system.

TIP

When you execute the BlessTiVo command, the program first checks to see if the drive exists and can be opened. If you see error messages such as "No device specified," "Too many command line options," or "Unable to connect to **/dev/hdx**," see the section of Chapter 4 on the BlessTiVo program for suggestions and solutions.

4. If the drive you are blessing already contains DOS or Linux partitioning information, the BlessTiVo command warns you of this fact and asks if you want to proceed. Answer "Y" if you do, or thank your lucky stars and answer "N" if you do not.

5. The BlessTiVo command asks you to verify that you want to proceed even if the specified disk contains no partitioning information. Answer "Y" to continue. The BlessTiVo command formats and partitions the drive as described in Chapter 4, displaying status messages as it proceeds. When it completes, it displays a final summary message listing the amount of storage available on the newly formatted drive.

WARNING

The summary message displayed at the end of the BlessTiVo process is very important—you should always check this value to make sure that it is within 3 gigabytes of the total size of the disk that you are adding. If the size of the disk that you are blessing is not reported as being within 3 GB of the actual size of the disk, do not add this drive to your TiVo. If you do add it, the two drives will be married and you will not be able to take advantage of the storage that is actually available on the second disk.

6. Shut down your TiVo and follow the instructions in Chapter 3 to open your TiVo and add the second drive, jumpering it correctly so that it does not conflict with your existing TiVo drive.

7. Turn on your TiVo. You should see the standard two gray startup screens as the TiVo boots.

That's all there is to it! The TiVo automatically detects the second drive at boot time and adds its disk identifier to the primary drive, thereby making the additional storage that it contains available to your TiVo. After your TiVo displays the startup animation, you can go to the System Information screen (TiVo Central -> Messages & Setup -> System Information) to see the new amount of storage available on your TiVo.

HACKING THE TiVo

Chapter 7

Connecting the Universe to Your TiVo

Previous chapters of this book have explained how to expand the physical capacity, capabilities, and usability of your TiVo. You've learned how to connect your TiVo to your home network and use an always-on broadband connection as the means for downloading programming and guide updates. This chapter takes your networked TiVo one step further, explaining how to expand the software usability and connectivity of your TiVo by installing software on your TiVo that connects it to the rest of your networked environment.

The key to expanding the software capabilities of your TiVo is getting access to its filesystems. Earlier chapters explained how to attach TiVo disks to other systems and manipulate their contents there, which is all well and good, but that really isn't the sort of interactive computer experience that we've all come to expect. Made a mistake? Shut down the TiVo, remove the disk drive, shut down your PC, install the drive, and reboot from the BATBD CD. That is all fine once or twice, but not suitable for those of us who have come to expect fairly instant gratification. It's as retro as batch mode!

This chapter explains how to start working on your TiVo by starting a command prompt on your TiVo's serial port. When you have your prompt, you can transfer files and software to your TiVo, install and start that software, and generally expand the horizons of your TiVo.

Today's networked universe is all about connectivity—so much of this chapter discusses various system and application software packages that can help make your TiVo a better network and connectivity citizen.

Getting a Command Prompt on Your TiVo

Almost all of the truly fun TiVo software hacks require accessing and updating the TiVo's filesystems and boot sequence. While you can do much of this after putting your TiVo disk in your PC and booting from the BATBD CD, hacking different models of TiVos requires different levels of willingness and commitment to hacking your machine. In a Series 1 machine, the key to getting a shell prompt and installing some basic utilities is as simple as making sure that you're running specific versions of the TiVo software. The Series 2 machines have introduced some new wrinkles into getting a shell prompt. If you're willing to run an older version of the TiVo software, you can restore it to your TiVo Series 2 and follow a marginally convoluted procedure to get a shell prompt—with the added bonus of knowing that you are truly the master of your TiVo, because there's a fair amount of work involved. If you (like me) "need" to be running the latest and greatest TiVo software release on your Series 2 machine, things get even more complex, but they still are eminently doable.

Subsequent sections of this book refer to TiVos on which you have a command prompt (and hopefully network access, as well) as "hacked" TiVos. I'm assuming that once you get a shell prompt on your TiVo, you won't be content to stop there, and will explore networking your TiVo so that you can take advantage of the other software packages described in this chapter. And you should. You're not hurting anyone and you're refining and enhancing the usability of a home entertainment appliance that you've paid for. This seems to me like a good idea.

The next few sections will explain how to get a shell prompt on various models of TiVos, running under various software releases. A shell prompt on your TiVo is essentially a Welcome mat, letting you know that you are indeed the master of your domain and your TiVo—and you can do it easily.

TIP

After following any of the procedures in this chapter to get a command prompt on your TiVo, you may occasionally encounter problems with how the bash shell prompts, displays, or processes input. If this is the case, you can use the Linux command **stty sane** (followed by the Return or Enter keys) to make bash work correctly in whatever terminal emulator or other serial connection application you're using. In some truly weird cases, you may need to type **Control-J stty sane Control-J**, where Control-J is typed by holding down the Ctrl key and pressing the letter "j."

NOTE

As always, I want to give credit where credit is due. The folks on the various TiVo forums discussed later in Chapter 11, "Other TiVo Hacking Resources," are the source of much of this information. (I've largely only tweaked processes to make them easier to follow and understand.) The ability to hack your TiVo as discussed in this section is a testimonial to the power and flexibility of TiVos in general, but even more so to the commitment and continuing curiosity of the members of the TiVo hacking community. The folks credited in the dedication of this book (and many more) are the real heroes here. Especially in the Monte section, TiVo hackers like MuscleNerd, embeem, and d7o did the pioneering work, porting and documenting the monte program on the TiVo, based on the original monte program for Linux (http://www.scyld.com/products/beowulf/software/monte.html) written by Erik Hendriks. In this section, I am largely playing Boswell to their Samuel Johnsons.

Getting a Command Prompt on a TiVo Series 1

As the Homo Erectus of the TiVo hardware family, Series 1 models are great machines that are a pleasure to own and tinker with. As computer systems, they're slower than the Series 2 machines and are essentially end-of-life, in terms of operating system and TiVo software upgrades. For example, TiVo's Home Media Option (HMO) is not available for the Series 1 and probably never will be. The HMO software depends on kernel and software functionality that TiVo Inc. has not ported to the Series 1—and (let's face it) why should they? (Actually, the core problem in TiVo's offering things like the Home Media Option on Series 1 machines is that these systems didn't support networking by default—and TiVo certainly can't officially endorse anyone opening up their Series 1 TiVo to add a networking card.)

NOTE

If you installed a network card in your Series 1 machine, as described in Chapter 3 in the section "Networking Series 1 TiVos," you do not have to follow the procedure described in this section. The **nic_install** script provided with today's TurboNet and Airnet cards for the Series 1 automatically configure your system to start a command prompt on the serial port, and also starts the FTP and telnet daemons discussed later in this chapter in "Starting FTP and Telnet on Your TiVo."

One aspect of the power of Linux is its ability to run on almost any piece of hardware that is smarter than a toaster; the demands of more powerful software are often outside the capabilities of older hardware. TiVo's core mission is video recording—in good conscience, they can't guarantee that their older hardware can perform its basic, guaranteed functions and also import and play audio files and display digital photographs. You can only squeeze so much juice out of an orange. TiVo doesn't even sell the Series 1 anymore, so any investment in upgrading its software is just gravy for the TiVo community. That said, the TiVo Series 1 is a hacker's paradise. Since it is essentially end-of-life in terms of software upgrades, why should TiVo care about what version of the OS you run on it, what software you subsequently install, and so on? Some of the more anal aspects of the more recent releases of the TiVo software have reared their ugly heads in the last revs of the TiVo Series 1 software, but these are easiest enough to undo ;-).

In order to get a command prompt on your TiVo Series 1, you must be running a version of the TiVo software and operating system that is no newer than version 3.1. This is the latest "non-anal" version of the TiVo OS in which the BASH_ENV environment variable can be added to the boot parameters.

 GETTING A SPECIFIC VERSION OF THE TIVO OS

I don't see why TiVo cares what version of the TiVo OS you're running, except in the case where you're running a version that's old enough that their servers want to upgrade it. In which case, your TiVo may suck bandwidth each night downloading upgraded versions of the OS.

If TiVo Inc. would explain how to guarantee that no upgrades would be performed, life for TiVo hackers everywhere would be much better. And hopefully, all TiVo hackers would still be cool enough to pay the monthly or lifetime subscription costs. I know that I do—and I'm happy to do so, because my TiVo is almost as integral to my lifestyle as any other utility.

If you are absolutely desperate for a specific version, you can always ask another TiVo fanatic for a copy of one of their backups—but the best solution for having backups available is to make them yourself from your own machine each time that its software version is upgraded.

To get a command prompt on a TiVo Series 1 running Version 3.1 or earlier of the TiVo OS, do the following:

1. Shut down your TiVo, remove the drive, and put it in your PC as explained in Chapter 3, "Exploring Your TiVo Hardware."

2. Boot your PC using the BATBD CD and selecting the **s1swap boot** option so that you can mount and access TiVo partitions.

3. Use the **bootpage** command to determine which of the possible root filesystems is the active one on your TiVo. This will be either **/dev/hda4** or **/dev/hda7**. For example, if the hard drive from your TiVo is available in your PC as **/dev/hdd** (the slave on your secondary IDE interface), you would execute the following bootpage command:

```
bootpage -p /dev/hdd
```

The **bootpage** command returns a string like **root=/dev/hda7**, which indicates that your TiVo's active root partition is partition **7** of the drive you're looking at.

NOTE

The **bootpage** command returns values relative to where the drive would appear in your TiVo, not where it appears in your PC. The **bootpage** command therefore always will return a value on the drive **/dev/hda**, regardless of where the drive is available in your PC.

4. Mount the specified partition from the drive in your PC so that you can access the files and directories that it contains. For example, if the **bootpage** command returned **root=/dev/hda7** and the TiVo drive is available in your PC as **/dev/hdd**, you would mount the partition using the following command:

```
mount /dev/hdd7 /mnt
```

The files and directories in your TiVo's root partition would then be available under the directory **/mnt**.

5. Change directory to the **/etc/rc.d** directory in the partition that you mounted from the TiVo drive. This directory contains default command files that are executed when your TiVo boots. (The directory name rc.d stands for "run command default.") For example, if you mounted the TiVo partition on the directory **/mnt** (as shown in the previous example), you would execute the following command to change to the right directory on the TiVo drive:

```
cd /mnt/etc/rc.d
```

6. To verify that you're in the right directory, list its contents by typing the **ls** command and pressing the Return or Enter key on your keyboard. You should see a display like the following:

```
finishInstall.tcl  rc.arch          rc.net           rc.sysinit
```

The files with names that begin with **rc** (run command) are specific command files that your TiVo executes when it boots. The file rc.sysinit contains the basic TiVo system initialization commands. The file rc.arch contains architecture-specific startup commands, and is executed by the **rc.sysinit** command file. The file rc.net contains network-related configuration commands, and is also executed by the **rc.sysinit** command file. The **rc.sysinit** command file is the big kahuna in this directory—it is the file that we will be modifying in the remainder of this procedure.

7. Make a backup copy of the file rc.sysinit by copying it to the file rc.sysinit.save. If you accidentally make any mistakes when editing the "real" rc.sysinit file and your TiVo won't boot for some reason, you can always return to its original state by copying the backup file over the one you've modified. To make a copy of the rc.sysinit file with the name rc.sysinit.save, type the following command and press the Return or Enter key on your keyboard:

```
cp rc.sysinit rc.sysinit.save
```

8. Now comes the moment of truth! Type the following command EXACTLY AS SHOWN to append the command that starts the bash shell to the end of the rc.sysinit file:

```
echo "/bin/bash </dev/ttyS3 >& /dev/ttyS3 &" >> rc.sysinit
```

Make absolutely sure that this command is exactly as shown before pressing the Return or Enter key on your keyboard. This command uses a feature of the Linux command interpreter to append the series of characters **/bin/bash </dev/ttyS3 >&** **/dev/ttyS3 &** to the end of the rc.sysinit file. When you next boot your TiVo with this command at the end of your rc.sysinit, it tells your TiVo to start the command **/bin/bash** (the Linux command interpreter). The **<** character tells the TiVo that any input to this command will come from the device **/dev/ttyS3**, which is your TiVo Series 1 serial port. The **>&** characters tell the TiVo that any output (**>**) or error messages (**&**) should also be sent to the device **/dev/ttyS3** (again, your TiVo's serial port). The final ampersand after the second instance of **/dev/ttyS3** in this command tells your TiVo to start the command interpreter in the background, which means that your TiVo can execute other commands while the command interpreter runs.

9. Verify that you've typed this command correctly by using the Linux **tail** command to display the last 10 lines of the file rc.sysinit on your screen, as in the following example:

```
tail rc.sysinit
```

You should see the following output on your screen:

```
if [ ! "$vmstat" = "" ]; then
echo "Starting memory statistic gathering"
vmstat 10 &
fi
[ ! -f /etc/rc.d/rc.sysinit.author ] || /etc/rc.d/rc.sysinit.author
echo "rc.sysinit is complete"
/bin/bash </dev/ttyS3 >& /dev/ttyS3 &
```

Before proceeding, compare the last line on your screen with the last line of the output displayed on your screen. If they are not identical, copy the file rc.sysinit.save over the file rc.sysinit using the Linux **copy** command (cp rc.sysinit.save rc.sysinit), and begin again at step 8 of this procedure.

10. If you are absolutely sure that the last line of the rc.sysinit file looks exactly as shown in the previous example, use the Linux **change directory** command to change your working directory to the root of your Linux filesystem and umount the TiVo partition using the following commands:

```
cd /
umount /mnt
```

Note that there is no **n** in the command used to unmount drives under Linux. Why type an extra character if you don't have to?

You can now remove the BATBD CD from your PC and turn off the PC, so that you can move the drive back to your TiVo. Make sure that the jumpers on the drive are reset to the way that they were when you first removed the drive from your TiVo. Put the drive back in your TiVo and close it up.

Next, connect a serial cable to the TiVo as explained in Chapter 3, in the section entitled "Attaching a Terminal Emulator or Serial Console," and then reboot your PC. If you're running Windows, start HyperTerminal as explained in Chapter 8 in the "Serial Communications from Windows Systems," and turn on your TiVo. If you're running Linux on your PC (congratulations), start the minicom as explained in Chapter 9 in the section "Using minicom for Serial Communications."

Now, the moment of truth! Plug in your TiVo and wait a few minutes while the normal TiVo boot sequence completes. Watch the terminal emulation program that you're running on your screen. After the TiVo boots successfully, you will see the following message in your terminal emulator:

```
bash: no job control in this shell
bash-2.02#
```

The second line is the prompt from bash, the Linux command interpreter, and you've hacked your TiVo! If you're curious about the "bash: no job control in this shell" message (which is harmless), see "Job Control in Bash" in Chapter 9, "Linux and the TiVo." That section includes a TiVo tip for getting a command prompt with job control on your TiVo, but there are some tradeoffs to consider when doing so.

After you have a command-prompt running on your TiVo, you can transfer files to your TiVo over a serial connection. If you're using a Windows system, doing this is explained in Chapter 8, "Working with Your TiVo from Windows and Macintosh Systems," in the section "Transferring Files over a Serial Connection from Windows." If you're using a Linux system, doing this task is explained in Chapter 9, "Linux and TiVo," in the section "Transferring Files Using minicom." Installing software on your TiVo after you've transferred files there is explained in the Chapter 10, "Getting and Installing New Software for Your TiVo," in the section "Installing Software on Your TiVo."

Getting a Command Prompt on a TiVo Series 2

As mentioned earlier, getting a command prompt on a TiVo Series 2 is much more complex than on a TiVo Series 1. This is because later versions of the TiVo software have become progressively restrained about checking various files on the TiVo filesystem that have not been modified. All versions of the TiVo software for Series 2 machines will discard modified files, over-writing them with pristine versions from the TiVo's secret stash of unmodified files. Version 3.2 of the TiVo software even removed the much-beloved BASH_ENV hack described in this chapter.

Luckily, getting a command prompt on a TiVo Series 2 is not impossible, just more complex. You can think of this as being "more of a pain," but I like to think of it as "more of a challenge." This section explains how to get a command prompt on a TiVo Series 2 running Version 3.1or earlier of the TiVo OS. If you are running a newer version of the TiVo software than this version, see the next section, "Two Kernel Monte for the TiVo Series 2," which explains a truly cool way to run any new version of the TiVo software that you want on your TiVo. More pain, but (of course) more gain.

GETTING OLDER VERSIONS OF THE TIVO SOFTWARE

Unless you're interested in features that are specific to a certain version of the TiVo OS (such as the Home Media Option, which wasn't available until Version 4 of the TiVo software, you probably don't care which version of the TiVo OS your TiVo is running. If you don't really care what version of the TiVo software your system is running and you just want to hack around with it, you can get a backup of an older version of the OS as described earlier in this chapter in a tip in the section entitled "Getting a Command Prompt on a TiVo Series 1. " TiVo software release 3.1 is universally accepted as the best version for easy hacking on a TiVo Series 2.

Getting a command prompt on a TiVo Series 2 involves one major step that takes a fair amount of time and therefore requires a bit of forethought. As part of the process of getting a command-prompt on a TiVo Series 2, as described in this section, you will need to back up and restore your TiVo's current drive. This is necessary because you will need to have at least one new partition available on your Series 2 machine to hack into it. Since you need to do a restore to easily get a new partition, I strongly suggest that you install a larger drive (i.e., do a drive upgrade) while you are following the procedure to get a command prompt on your Series 2 system. You can, of course, immediately restore the backup to the drive that you created it from to create the new partition (unless the drive was completely full of recordings). However, it is much safer to keep your old disk handy as a backup, just in case something goes wrong when you follow the procedure described in this section.

There are three possible hard-drive scenarios for the process of getting a command prompt on your Series 2 machine, as follows;

◆ Upgrade to a larger drive during the procedure. In this case, you can keep your old TiVo disk(s) as backups and, therefore, do not need to save a physical backup of the original drive(s).

◆ Upgrade to a larger drive during the procedure, keep a backup of your original drive(s) on disk, and keep your old TiVo disk(s) as backups. Backups are always good. You can sleep more soundly knowing that you have one, just in case.

◆ Re-use your existing disk drive(s) during the procedure by first backing up, and then restoring the backup to the same drive. This is the least palatable of the hard drive options because you don't get any additional space to store recordings, and run the risk of hosing the TiVo if the drive goes bad. Disk drives are relatively cheap so please buy a larger one and use it during the command-prompt procedure if you can.

Both of the last two scenarios require that your PC have sufficient space available to store the backup of your original TiVo disk drive. If your personal computer runs Linux or Windows and has sufficient space available to store a backup, see the section "Finding Room for Backups," in Chapter 5, "Backing Up and Restoring TiVo Data" for tips on mounting existing partitions after booting from the BATBD CD, so you can store your backups there. If your personal computer does not have sufficient space available to store the backup and you are planning to reuse your existing drive, you'll have to add another hard drive to your system to store the backup. If you do this and are running Windows on your personal computer, make sure that you format this disk as a FAT-32 disk so that you can access it from Linux.

To get a command prompt on a TiVo Series 2 running Version 3.1or earlier of the TiVo OS, make a pot of coffee (this is a long procedure), and do the following:

1. Open your TiVo as described in Chapter 3 in the section "Opening Your TiVo," and remove your TiVo's hard drive(s) as described in Chapter 3 in "Removing TiVo Disk Drives."

2. Put your TiVo's disk drive(s) in your PC as described in Chapter 3 in "Attaching TiVo Disk Drives to Your PC." If possible, attach the new drive that you want to use in your TiVo to another IDE interface in your machine at the same time, to minimize

the number of times you have to reboot. Boot your personal computer from the BATBD CD, using the boot option for the TiVo Series 2 machiness.

3. If you are creating a backup file of your original TiVO drive(s) (and I suggest you do, for the reasons outlined before the beginning of this procedure), mount the partition on the hard disk where you are going to store the backup, as explained in Chapter 5, in the section "Finding Room for Backups." For example, if you are storing your backups on a Windows FAT-32 disk partition that is the first partition on the master drive of your primary IDE interface, you can mount it using the command:

```
mount -t vfat /dev/hda1 /mnt/backup
```

If you are mounting an **ext2** or **ext3** partition from a Linux machine, you do not have to specify the filesystem type. For example, if you were mounting the Linux partition **/dev/hda8**, you could simply mount it using the command:

```
mount /dev/hda8 /mnt/backup
```

See the section of Chapter 5 entitled "Finding Room for Backups" if you need more information about identifying the type and location of the partitions on your Windows system, or for locating various partitions on a Linux system.

4. Back up your TiVo drive using one of the following commands. The following examples all assume that your TiVo drive is mounted as the slave drive on your secondary IDE interface (**/dev/hdd**). If your TiVo drive is attached to your PC as a master or on your other IDE interface, substitute the appropriate drive name. For information about mounting and identifying the names of TiVo drives from the BATBD CD, see Chapter 3, the section "Attaching TiVo Disk Drives to Your PC."

 NOTE

If your TiVo had two drives, the drives are married and you must back them up together regardless of whether you are restoring them to one or two new drives. In this case, simply append the name of the second TiVo disk drive—in Linux terms— to the sample command lines shown below.

◆ If you are backing up a single drive and have sufficient space to back up everything (in the worst case, this will require the same amount of space as that available on your original disk), use the following command:

```
mfstool backup -a6so /mnt/backup/tivo-s2.bak /dev/hdd
```

◆ If you are backing up a single drive and don't want to preserve the recordings on your TiVo disk in the backup, use the following command to produce a much smaller backup:

```
mfstool backup -f 4138 6so /mnt/backup/tivo-s2.bak /dev/hdd
```

◆ If you are backing up a single drive to upgrade to a larger drive, and insist on not creating a backup file, use the following command to create the backup and restore it to another drive (**/dev/hdc**, in this example) without requiring any intermediate disk space:

```
mfstool backup -a6so - /dev/hdd | mfstool restore -s 127 -xzpi - /dev/hdc
```

This last command will take a really long time! In this case, you can skip the next step and move ahead to Step 6.

5. When the **backup** command completes, execute the Linux **sync** command to be totally positive that your backup file is consistent, and then restore the backup file to the new drive. Skip this step if you used the "all-in-one" backup and restore command in the previous step.

NOTE

If you did not have sufficient free IDE interfaces to put the old TiVo drive and the new drive in your personal computer at the same time, you may have to shut down your personal computer, remove the old TiVo drive, put in the new drive, and reboot from the BATBD CD. Before proceeding, make sure that you remount the partition where your backup is stored, as explained in Step 3 of this procedure.

The following example uses **/dev/hdc** as the name of the drive to which you are restoring the backup—make sure that you specify the drive name that is appropriate for your system before restoring your backup to it.

WARNING

Be *very* careful when specifying the name of the disk to which you want to restore the backup. The MFS Tools utilities do not warn you if the disk contains data. DO NOT accidentally overwrite a Windows or Linux disk that contains data that you want to see again.

Restore your backup to the new disk using a command like the following:

```
mfstool restore -s 127 -xzpi /mnt/backup/tivo-s2.bak /dev/hdc
```

6. Once the restore process completes successfully, use the **pdisk** command to display the partitions on your newly restored disk, as in the following example:

```
pdisk -p /dev/hdc
```

Write down the name of the last partition on this drive—it will have a blank line after its name and will be identified as being of the type "Apple_Free." We will be using this partition in subsequent steps. This is usually partition 16, but your mileage may vary.

7. Next, identify the name of the default root filesystem on the restored TiVo disk. You will need this information later on, when setting the boot parameters for your system.

   Use the **bootpage** command to identify the active root filesystem on your restored drive, as in the following example:

   ```
   bootpage -1 /dev/hdc
   ```

   The name of the drive that you provide must be the name of your new TiVo drive, and is not necessarily **/dev/hdc**. The **bootpage** command should return either the string **root=/dev/hda4** or the string **root=/dev/hd7**. This is the active root partition on your drive.

8. Next, mount the BATBD CD by typing a command like the following:

   ```
   mount /dev/hdb /mnt/cdrom
   ```

   The device associated with your CD ROM drive may differ from this. If your CD ROM drive is an IDE drive, its device name will be the same as though it were a disk drive. (Mine is attached as a slave on my primary IDE interface, and is therefore **/dev/hdb**. For more information about IDE drive names, see Chapter 3, the section entitled "Attaching TiVo Disk Drives to Your PC."

9. Next, we will create a small ROM (Read-Only Memory) filesystem image that the TiVo can mount and use during the boot process. The BATBD CD contains a template for this filesystem. To create the filesystem image in the file **/romfs.img**, execute the following commands:

   ```
   cd /mnt/cdrom genromfs -f /romfs.img -d img
   ```

 NOTE

If you're curious about exactly what this ROM filesystem contains, use the **cd** to change your working directory to the **/mnt/cdrom/img** directory and examine the file "hacks" in that directory. This file simply waits for the TiVo's **/var/partition** to be mounted, and then it executes a command file called **/var/hack/hackinit** on the TiVo. This file is included in the archives of TiVo applications that you will extract in Step 11 of this procedure. The **/var/hack/hackinit** file simply contains the commands that we want to execute when the TiVo boots.

10. Next, write the ROM filesystem image to the empty partition identified in Step 6, using the **dd** command, which copies data from one file or device to another in raw form. To do this, execute the following command, replacing the **Y** in **YXX** with the letter corresponding to the device name of your new TiVo drive, and replacing **XX** with the partition identifier you obtained in Step 6:

    ```
    dd if=/romfs.img  of=/dev/hdYXX bs=1024 count=1
    ```

    For example, if the new drive for your TiVo was available as **/dev/hdc** and the partition identified in Step 6 was partition 16, you would execute the following command:

    ```
    dd if=/romfs.img  of=/dev/hdc16 bs=1024 count=1
    ```

11. Next, mount partition 9 of the new TiVo disk so that you can create the command file mentioned in Step 9. Partition 9 of any standard TiVo boot disk is the partition that will be mounted as **/var** when the TiVo boots. To mount this directory, execute a command like the following:

    ```
    mount /dev/hdc9 /mnt/tivo
    ```

    If your TiVo disk has a device name other than **/dev/hdc**, change the name in this command to match your configuration.

12. Next, create what will be the TiVo's **/var/hack** directory and populate it with some files. Execute the following commands:

    ```
    cd /mnt/tivo tar xpvf /mnt/cdrom/hack_dirs/hack2.tar
    ```

    The first command makes your working directory the partition that your TiVo will mount as **/var**. The second command extracts the contents of a preprepared archive file on the BATBD CD that contains executable programs that you will want to use on your new-hacked TiVo Series 2 machine, as well as the **hackinit** script mentioned in Step 9.

13. The last step is to set the TiVo's boot parameters to mount the ROM filesystem and start the hacks script that it contains, which in turns invokes the **/var/hack/hackinit** script that you installed in the previous step. Type the following command on one line (not two as shown below) exactly as shown, replacing "XX" with the partition number that you identified in Step 6 and wrote in Step 10. Also, the drive that you specify at the end of the command must be the drive where your new TiVo is located:

    ```
    bootpage -P "root=ROOTDRIVE BASH_ENV=\`mount\$IFS-n\$IFS/dev/hdaXX\$IFS/mnt;echo\
    $IFS/mnt/hacks\`" -C /dev/hdc
    ```

    You should replace root drive with the value of your default root filesystem, as identified in Step 7 of this procedure. This would be either **/dev/hda4** or **/dev/hda7**.

The value set by the **bootpage** command is relative to the drive names that your TiVo will see when it boots. So **/dev/hda** is correct everywhere but the end of the line, where you specify the drive in your PC where the TiVo drive is currently located. The backslash characters are very important here, because they are used to protect commands that would otherwise be misinterpreted by the TiVo's command interpreter. Make sure that the "backquotes" before the "mount" command and after the filename **/mnt/hacks** are indeed backward single quotes (found on the same key as the tilde on a U.S. keyboard. They must not be the standard single quotation marks that share a key with the double quotation mark.)

 NOTE

In case you're wondering, $IFS is an environment variable representing the Linux Internal Field Separator, a value used to separate different elements within a single line. In practice, each instance of the $IFS environment variable is replaced by a space when it is analyzed, enabling us to pass a complex string as a single token using the BASH_ENV environment variable.

After typing this command, execute the following command to make sure that you typed the previous command correctly:

```
bootpage -p /dev/hdc
```

Where the drive name you specify is the name of the new TiVo disk. This command should return a string that looks exactly like the one that you entered, except that all of the backslash characters (\) will be gone. If the value displayed does not match the string you entered (minus the backquotes), retype the command shown at the beginning of this step—perhaps a bit more carefully this time.

14. All that's left now is the cleanup. Execute the following commands to **umount** the CD ROM and your TiVo partition cleanly:

```
cd /
umount /mnt/cdrom
umount /mnt/tivo
```

After these commands complete, shut down your PC, and put the new TiVo drive back in your TiVo, verifying that the jumpers are set correctly.

You can remove the BATBD CD from your PC and turn it off. Now you can move the drive back to your TiVo. Make sure that the jumpers on the drive are reset to the way that they were when you first removed the drive from your TiVo. Put the drive back in your TiVo and close it up.

Next, connect a serial cable to the TiVo (as explained in Chapter 3, in the section "Attaching a Terminal Emulator or Serial Console," and reboot your PC. If you're running Windows, start HyperTerminal as explained in Chapter 8, in the section "Serial Communications from Windows Systems," and turn on your TiVo. If you're running Linux on your PC (congratulations), start minicom as explained in Chapter 9, in the section "Using minicom for Serial Communications."

Now, the moment of truth! Plug in your TiVo and wait a few minutes while the normal TiVo boot sequence completes. Watch the terminal emulation program that you're running on your screen. When the TiVo boots successfully, you will see the following message in your terminal emulator:

```
bash: no job control in this shell
bash-2.02#
```

The second line is the prompt from bash, the Linux command interpreter—now you are a TiVo hacker! If you're curious about the "bash: no job control in this shell" message (which is harmless), see Chapter 9, the section "Job Control in Bash." That section also includes a TiVo tip for getting a command prompt with job control on your TiVo, but there are some tradeoffs to consider when doing so.

After you have a command prompt running on your TiVo, you can transfer files over a serial connection to the TiVo. If you're using a Windows system, performing this task is explained in Chapter 8, in the section "Transferring Files over a Serial Connection from Windows." If you're using a Linux system, refer to Chapter 9, the section entitled "Transferring Files Using minicom." Installing software on your TiVo after you've transferred files there is explained in Chapter 10, in the section "Installing Software on Your TiVo."

Two Kernel Monte for the TiVo Series 2

 WARNING

This section is only for the TiVo Series 2. Do not try this on a TiVo Series 1 machine!

In the procedure described previously, your TiVo booted from a signed kernel, which included an initial RAM disk (**initrd**) that verified the filesystem through hash codes (as discussed elsewhere in this book). This procedure effectively makes it impossible to directly modify any of the files that are verified in the TiVo's root filesystem. Some of these files include favorite text-based targets for modification such as **/etc/rc.d/rc.sysinit**, **/etc/rc.d/rc.arch**, **/etc/inittab**, or system binaries such as **/bin/bash**, **/sbin/init**, and others that you can replace with personalized versions that do "extra things."

By taking advantage of the BASH_ENV environment variable provided in most versions of the TiVo Series 2 kernels prior to software release 3.2, you can convince your TiVo to run your own processes from another partition (**/var**, in our case) by creating a ROMFS filesystem image that you can stash in a spare partition on your TiVo. A file in the ROMFS is executed via the BASH_ENV hack, and itself executes a file containing your special hacks (**/var/hack/hack-init**). This procedure is fine if you're willing to run an older version of the TiVo software forever, but what if you absolutely must have new features like TiVo's Home Media Option? The BASH_ENV hack doesn't work there anymore. Out of luck? Hardly. You just have to be a bit more clever, as explained herein.

This section explains how to use a program called *monte* to boot one kernel as part of the boot process of another kernel. If the second kernel doesn't happen to do signature checks (for example, if its **initrd** has been neutered), it can use a filesystem that contains any modified or new

TiVo EXTRACTING AND LOOKING AT AN INITIAL RAM DISK

If you're curious about the complete list of files on which newer versions of the TiVo software perform signature checks, you'll have to look in the initial RAM (**initrd**) disk used by the TiVo kernel that you're booting. The contents of an **initrd** aren't readily visible ordinarily, but luckily Linux is your friend in this case. Initial RAM disks are just **gzipped ext2** filesystem images, and you can therefore find where they are located in a compiled kernel image. Since you can find them, you can extract them. The **extract_gzip** program provided on the BATBD CD does just this. You can extract the **initrd** from the partition on which your kernel is located or from an image of that partition created using **dd**. To do this, put your TiVo disk in your PC and boot from the BATBD CD. After you've booted, mount the BATBD CD at **/mnt/cdrom** and execute the **extract_gzip** program using the following command-line:

```
/mnt/cdrom/x86bin/extract_gzip <kernel>
```

Where <kernel> is either the partition where the TiVo kernel is located, or the name of a kernel image file that you extracted from your disk using the **dd** command. The **extract_gzip** command will display a message like the following:

```
gzip magic (0x1f8b0800) detected at 0x0014a160 - saving to file 0x0014a160.gz
```

In this case, the file "0x0014a160.gz" is your **initrd**. You then **un-gzip** this file ("gunzip 0x0014a160.gz"), and save the resulting file "0x0014a160" somewhere on your personal computer, and boot to Windows (see Chapter 5, "Backing Up and Restoring Your TiVo," in the section, "Finding Room for Backups." You can then explore like you would any other filesystem image by mounting it under Linux or Mac OS X, or by using a Windows tool (e.g., **explore2fs** on Windows, explained elsewhere in this book). The file containing the signatures and filenames used by the newer TiVo software releases is located at the root of the **initrd**, and is called "signatures."

files that you want. The monte program, named after the old "three-card Monte" card game, is included in the monte-mips directory on the BATBD CD. Using **monte** is only necessary when hacking into Series 2 systems, so only the MIPS version of this utility and associated files are provided on the CD. Series 1 machines can't run the latest versions of the TiVo OS, and I don't see much difference between 3.0, 3.1, 3.2, and so forth on the TiVo Series 1 systems.

The following procedure explains how to use **monte** to boot a hacked version of the 4.0 version of the TiVo software from a system that starts by booting a hacked version of release 3.x of the TiVo software. You can use this same trick to boot un-hackable 3.x versions of TiVo software, but I don't see much point in that. Why not go for the Version 4.0 brass ring? If you thought that the previous section was fun, wait until you finish reading this one!

To follow the instructions in this section, you will need the following:

◆ The BATBD CD that came with this book.

◆ A Series 2 machine running Version 4.0 of the TiVo software.

◆ A backup of a hackable version of the 3.x TiVo software—that is, a version that supports the BASH_ENV hack, release 3.1 or earlier).

◆ Approximately 150 MB of free disk space to store images of the 3.x system's kernel and root filesystem.

◆ You also will need one of the following:

　　◆ A larger disk, which is optional. As in the previous section, it was strongly recommended that you do this as part of a disk upgrade so that you have your original TiVo disk to fall back on if something goes wrong.

　　◆ Sufficient disk space to store a backup of your TiVo Series 2 running Version 4.0.

　　　The procedure in this section requires that you restore 3.x to a TiVo disk drive as an intermediate step. You *must* either have a backup of Version 4.0 to subsequently restore it, or you must be upgrading to a larger drive as part of the process. Also, something could go wrong, and backups are a good thing.

◆ An hour or so of your time.

 NOTE

These instructions assume that you're starting with a system that runs Version 4.0 of the TiVo software. If you're using a stand-alone TiVo Series 2, your TiVo should have been automatically upgraded to this software release in April, 2003. If you're still running an older version of the TiVo OS on your Series 2, you can always upgrade your system manually by backing it up and then restoring a 4.0 backup to it.

To use **monte** to get a command prompt on a hacked version of release 4.0 of the TiVo software, do the following:

1. Open your TiVo (described in Chapter 3 in "Opening Your TiVo") and remove your TiVo's hard drive(s) (described in Chapter 3 in "Removing TiVo Disk Drives").

2. Put your TiVo's disk drive(s) in your PC (described in Chapter 3 in "Attaching TiVo Disk Drives to Your PC"). If possible, attach the new drive that you want to use in your TiVo to another IDE interface in your machine at the same time—this minimizes the number of times you have to reboot. Boot your personal computer from the BATBD CD, using the Series 2 boot option.

3. If you are creating a backup file of your original TiVo drive(s), (and I suggest you do, for the reasons outlined in the previous section), mount the partition on the hard disk where you are going to store the backup, as explained in Chapter 5 in "Finding Room for Backups." For example, if you are storing your backups on a Windows FAT-32 disk partition that is the first partition on the master drive of your primary IDE interface, you can mount it using the command:

```
mount -t vfat /dev/hda1 /mnt/backup
```

If you are mounting an **ext2** or **ext3** partition from a Linux machine, you do not have to specify the filesystem type. For example, if you were mounting the Linux partition **/dev/hda8**, you could simply mount it using the command:

```
mount /dev/hda8 /mnt/backup
```

(See Chapter 5, the section "Finding Room for Backups," if you need more information about identifying the type and location of the partitions on your Windows system, or for locating various partitions on a Linux system.)

 NOTE

If you are following this procedure as part of a disk upgrade and insist on not creating a backup file of your 4.0 system, skip Step 4, but don't send me cranky mail or make me say "I told you so," if something goes wrong.

4. Back up your TiVo drive using one of the following commands. If possible, put the backup on the same partition where the 3.1 or earlier image required by this process is located. You will need access to both the backup image of your TiVo and the 3.x image during this process, and putting them in the same place makes sense.

   The following examples all assume that your TiVo drive is mounted as the slave drive on your secondary IDE interface (**/dev/hdd**). If your TiVo drive is attached to your

PC as a master or on your other IDE interface, substitute the appropriate drive name. For information about mounting and identifying the names of TiVo drives from the BATBD CD, see Chapter 3, the section entitled "Attaching TiVo Disk Drives to Your PC."

NOTE

If your Series 2 machines had two drives, the drives are married and you must back them up together regardless of whether you are restoring them to one or two new drives. In this case, simply append the name of the second TiVo disk drive—in Linux terms—to the sample command lines shown below.

◆ If you are backing up a single drive and have sufficient space to back up everything (in the worst case, this will require the same amount of space as that available on your original disk), use the following command:

```
mfstool backup -a6so /mnt/backup/tivo-s2.bak /dev/hdd
```

◆ If you are backing up a single drive and don't want to preserve the recordings on your TiVo disk in the backup, use the following command to produce a much smaller backup:

```
mfstool backup -f 4138 6so /mnt/backup/tivo-s2.bak /dev/hdd
```

Once the backup command completes, execute the Linux **sync** command to be totally positive that your backup file is consistent.

5. Next, you will restore the 3.0 backed up file to your new drive (or to your existing TiVo drive if you don't have another and made a backup of 4.0). You need to restore a version of 3.X that supports the BASH_ENV hack to extract its kernel and root filesystem.

WARNING

Do *not* perform this step if you didn't create a backup of your Version 4.0 system or you are upgrading to a new drive—re-read the list of requirements earlier in this section instead.

NOTE

If you did not have sufficient free IDE interfaces to put in the old TiVo drive and the new drive that you will be using in your personal computer at the same time, you may need to shut down your personal computer, remove the old TiVo drive, put in the new drive, and reboot from the BATBD CD. Before proceeding, make sure that you remount the partition where the backup of your TiVo and the 3.x backup that this process requires are stored, as explained in Step 3 of this procedure.

The following example uses **/dev/hdc** as the name of the drive to which you are restoring the backup. Make sure that you specify the drive name that is appropriate for your system before restoring your backup to it.

WARNING

Be *very* careful when specifying the name of the disk that you want to restore the backup to. The MFS Tools utilities will not warn you if the disk contains data. DO NOT accidentally overwrite a Windows or Linux disk that contains data—if you ever want to see it again.

Restore your 3.0 backup to the new disk using a command like the following:

```
mfstool restore -s 127 -xzpi /mnt/backup/tivo-s2.bak /dev/hdc
```

6. Once the restore process completes successfully, use the **pdisk** command to display the partitions on your newly restored disk, as in the following example:

```
pdisk -p /dev/hdc
```

If these partitions are not visible, the restore failed. Do not proceed.

7. If the partitions on the restored 3.x disk are visible, use the **bootpage** command to determine the active root partition on the restored drive, as in the following example:

```
bootpage -l /dev/hdc
```

This should return either the string **root=/dev/hda4** or **root=/dev/hd7**. This is the root partition on the restored 3.0 drive. The kernel image for this drive will be located in the partition numbered one less than the root filesystem. For example, the default kernel for a drive whose root partition is **/dev/hda4** will be located in partition 3 of the same drive.

8. Use the Linux **dd** command to extract the kernel and root filesystem from the 3.x disk and save them to files. The name of the drive in these examples will be the name of

the drive where your 3.x TiVo disk is found in your PC, not the drive name returned by the **bootpage** command.

To extract a copy of the active root filesystem from the 3.x TiVo disk, execute a command like the following:

```
dd if=/dev/hdcX of=30_rootfs.img bs=32k
```

Replace the letter **X** in this command with the number at the end of the drive name returned by the **bootpage** command.

To extract a copy of the active kernel from the 3.x disk, execute a command like the following:

```
dd if=/dev/hdcX of=30_kernel.img
```

Replace the letter **X** in this command with the value that is one less than the number at the end of the drive name returned by the **bootpage** command.

That's all you need to use the 3.x disk for—now you can restore the 4.0 image to the new drive (or to your only drive if you created a backup of your 4.0 disk and don't have a new disk).

9. Restore your 4.0 backup image to the drive that you will be using in your TiVo, either a new, larger drive if you are upgrading during this process, or your original drive.

The following example uses **/dev/hdc** as the name of the drive to which you are restoring the backup. Make sure that you specify the drive name that is appropriate for your system before restoring your backup to it.

 WARNING

Be *very* careful when specifying the name of the disk that you want to restore the backup to. The MFS Tools utilities will not warn you if the disk contains data. Do *not* accidentally overwrite a Windows or Linux disk that contains data—if you ever want to see it again.

Restore your backup to the new disk using a command like the following:

```
mfstool restore -s 127 -xzpi /mnt/backup/tivo-s2.bak /dev/hdc
```

10. Once the restore process completes successfully, use the **pdisk** command to display the partitions on your newly restored disk, as in the following example:

```
pdisk -p /dev/hdc
```

Write down the name of the last partition on this drive—it will have a blank line after its name and will be identified as being of type "Apple_Free." We will be using this partition in subsequent steps. This is usually partition 16, but your mileage may vary.

11. Use the **bootpage** command to identify the active root filesystem on your restored 4.0 drive, as in the following example:

```
bootpage -1 /dev/hdc
```

This should return either the string **root=/dev/hda4** or the string **root=/dev/hd7**. This is the active root partition on the 4.0 drive. The kernel image for this drive will be located in the partition numbered one less than the root filesystem. For example, the default kernel for a drive whose root partition is **/dev/hda4** will be located in partition 3 of the same drive.

12. Use the **dd** command to clone the root filesystem and bootable kernel on your 4.0 disk to the backed up versions of those same partitions:

   ◆ If the **bootpage** command in the previous step returned **root=/dev/hda4**, you will be cloning partition 4 of your 4.0 drive to partition 7 of your 4.0 drive, and you will be cloning partition 3 of your 4.0 drive to partition 6 of your 4.0 drive.

   ◆ If the **bootpage** command in the previous step returned **root=/dev/hda7**, you will be cloning partition 7 of your 4.0 drive to partition 4 of your 4.0 drive, and you will be cloning partition 6 of your 4.0 drive to partition 3 of your 4.0 drive.

   To clone the root filesystem partition, execute a command like the following:

```
dd if=/dev/hdcX of=/dev/hdcY bs=32k
```

   Where the name of the drive is the name of your new TiVo drive in your personal computer, and **X** is the number at the end of the string returned by the **bootpage** command in the previous step.

   To clone the kernel partition, execute a command like the following;

```
dd if=/dev/hdcX of=/dev/hdY
```

   Where the name of the drive is the name of your new TiVo drive in your personal computer, and **X** is the number one less than the number at the end of the string returned by the **bootpage** command in the previous step.

 NOTE

You may get an error message when cloning the kernel. This is because some TiVo disks have different-sized partitions for the primary and alternate kernels. TiVo kernels, at the time of this book's writing) are always less than 2 MB, which is the size of the smaller of these two partitions. Again, at the time of this book's writing, you could safely ignore this message. You *do* have a backup image or your original 4.0 disk, right?

13. Next, mount the BATBD CD by typing a command like the following:

```
mount /dev/hdb /mnt/cdrom
```

The device associated with your CD ROM drive may differ from this. If your CD ROM drive is an IDE drive, its device name will be the same as though it were a disk drive. (Mine is attached as a slave on my primary IDE interface, and is therefore **/dev/hdb**. For more information about IDE drive names, see Chapter 3, the section entitled "Attaching TiVo Disk Drives to Your PC."

14. Next, you will create a small ROM (Read-Only Memory) filesystem image that the TiVo can mount and use during the boot process. The BATBD CD contains a template for this ROM filesystem. To create the filesystem image in the file **/romfs.img**, execute the following commands:

```
cd /mnt/cdrom
genromfs -f /romfs.img -d img_monte
```

 NOTE

If you're curious about exactly what this ROM filesystem contains, **cd** to the **/mnt/cdrom/img_monte** directory and examine the file "runmonte" in that directory. This file loads a kernel module used by **monte** and then executes the **monte** command, passing the kernel partition that contains the root filesystem that holds the hacked 4.0 image and several other command-line arguments to the kernel that **monte** will run for you.

15. Next, write the ROM filesystem image to the empty partition identified in Step 10, using the **dd** command discussed in Chapter 5, which copies data from one file or device to another in raw form. To do this, execute the following command, replacing the **Y** in **YXX** with the letter corresponding to the device name of your new TiVo drive, and replacing **XX** with the partition identifier you obtained in Step 10:

```
dd if=/romfs.img  of=/dev/hdYXX
```

For example, if the new drive for your TiVo was available as **/dev/hdc** and the partition identified in Step 10 was partition 16, you would execute the following command:

```
dd if=/romfs.img  of=/dev/hdc16
```

16. Next, write the backups of your 3.x kernel and root filesystem to partitions 3 and 4 of your new TiVo disk, respectively.

To write the backup of your 3.x kernel to partition 3 from the backup image you created in Step 8, execute the following command:

```
dd if=30_kernel.img of=/dev/hdc3
```

Where the name of the drive is the name of your new TiVo drive in your personal computer.

To write the backup of your 3.x root filesystem to partition 4 from the backup image you created in Step 8, execute the following command:

```
dd if=30_rootfs.img of=/dev/hdc4
```

Where the name of the drive is the name of your new TiVo drive in your personal computer.

17. Next, mount partition 9 of the new TiVo disk so that you can install your favorite TiVo hacks. Partition 9 of any standard TiVo boot disk is the partition that will mount as **/var** when the TiVo boots. To mount this directory, execute a command like the following:

```
mount /dev/hdc9 /mnt/tivo
```

If your new TiVo disk has a device name other than **/dev/hdc**, change the name in this command to match your configuration.

18. Next, create what will be the TiVo's **/var/hack** directory and populate it with some files. Execute the following commands:

```
cd /mnt/tivo
tar xpvf /mnt/cdrom/hack_dirs/hack2.tar
```

The first command makes your working directory the partition that your TiVo will mount as **/var**. The second command extracts the contents of a preprepared archive file on the BATBD CD, which also contains executable programs that you will want to use on your newly hacked TiVo Series 2.

20. Now, remove the initial RAM disk in the v4.0 kernel on your system. To do this, execute the following command:

```
/mnt/cdrom/killinitrd/killinitrd-s2-v4.0 /dev/hdX6
```

Where X is the drive letter of the drive we've been working with, your new TiVo drive. Using the same naming conventions, this command displays the following output:

```
Successfully patched /dev/hdX6!
```

21. Add the commands to get a shell prompt for the startup file on the 4.0 root filesystem. You can do this by executing the following commands:

```
cd /
sync
umount /mnt/tivo
mount /dev/hdX7 /mnt/tivo
cp /mnt/tivo/etc/rc.d/rc.sysinit /mnt/tivo/etc/rc.d/rc.sysinit.old
echo "/bin/bash < /dev/ttyS2 >& /dev/ttyS2 &" >> /mnt/tivo/etc/rc.d/rc.sysinit
```

Substitute the drive letter of your new TiVo drive for X in line 4, and type the last command exactly as shown. Be very careful that you specify two right angle brackets (>), not just one. If you accidentally specify only 1, you have just truncated the contents of your new TiVo disk's startup file. Oops! Copy the file **/mnt/tivo/etc/rc.d/rc.sysinit.old** back to the file **/mnt/tivo/etc/rc.d/rc.sysinit**, and type more carefully this time.

22. The last step is to set the TiVo's boot parameters to mount the ROM filesystem and run monte, handling all of the kernel switching, and so on. Type the following command on one line (not two as shown below) exactly as shown, replacing **XX** with the partition number that we identified in Step 10, and wrote in Step 15. Also, the drive that you specify at the end of the command must be the drive where your new TiVo is currently located:

```
bootpage -P "root=/dev/hda4 dsscon=true BASH_ENV=\`mount\$IFS-
n\$IFS/dev/hdaXX\$IFS/mnt;echo\$IFS/mnt/runmonte\`" -C /dev/hdc
```

This command is relative to the drive names that your TiVo will see when it boots, so **/dev/hda** is correct everywhere but at the end of the line, where you specify the drive in your PC where the TiVo drive is currently located. The backslash characters are very important here, because they are used to protect commands that would otherwise be misinterpreted by the TiVo's command interpreter. Make sure that the back quotes before the "mount" command and after the filename /mnt/hacks are indeed backwards single quotes (found on the same key as the tilde on a US keyboard. They must not be the standard single quotation marks that share a key with the double quotation mark.)

After typing this command, execute the following command to make sure that you typed the previous command correctly:

```
bootpage -p /dev/hdc
```

Where the drive name you specify is the name of the new TiVo disk. This command should return a string that looks exactly like the one that you entered, except that all of the backslash characters (\) will be gone. If the value displayed does not match the string you entered (less the back quotes), retype the command shown at the beginning of this step—perhaps a bit more carefully this time.

 NOTE

In case you're wondering, $IFS is an environment variable representing the Linux Internal Field Separator, a value used to separate different elements within a single line. In practice, each instance of the $IFS environment variable is replaced by a space when it is analyzed, enabling us to pass a complex string as a single token using the BASH_ENV environment variable.

23. All that's left now is the cleanup. Execute the following commands to umount the CD ROM and your TiVo partition cleanly:

```
cd /
umount /mnt/cdrom
umount /mnt/tivo
```

After these commands complete, shut down your PC, and put the new TiVo drive back in your TiVo, verifying that the jumpers are set correctly.

You can now remove the BATBD CD from your PC and turn off the PC, and you can move the drive back to your TiVo. Make sure that the jumpers on the drive are reset to the way that they were when you first removed the drive from your TiVo. Put the drive back in your TiVo and close it up.

Next, connect a serial cable to the TiVo as explained in Chapter 2, in the section "Attaching a Terminal Emulator or Serial Console," and reboot your PC. If you're running Windows, start HyperTerminal as explained in Chapter 8, in the section "Serial Communications from Windows Systems," and turn on your TiVo. If you're running Linux on your PC (congratulations), start minicom as explained in Chapter 9 in "Using minicom for Serial Communications." Set your communication speed to 115,200—the speed of the TiVo Series 2 serial port.

Now, the moment of truth! Plug in your TiVo and wait a few minutes while the normal TiVo boot sequence completes. Unlike when booting previous kernels, you will see all of the boot messages for both the 3.x and 4.0 kernels, and will see the complete TiVo startup process. The instructions in this section set the system console to the serial port using the command **dss-con=true** so that you can easily see if something goes wrong during the boot process. Watch the terminal emulation program that you're running on your screen. When the TiVo boots successfully, you will see the following message in your terminal emulator:

```
bash: no job control in this shell
bash-2.02#
```

The second line is the prompt from bash, the Linux command interpreter, which means you are a certified TiVo hacker! The procedure described in this section is not for the weak, and you should be proud if everything works correctly the first time.

If you're curious about the "bash: no job control in this shell" message (which is harmless), see the section "Job Control in Bash" in Chapter 9. The section also includes a TiVo tip for getting a command prompt with job control on your TiVo, but there are some tradeoffs to consider when doing so.

Once you have a command-prompt running on your TiVo, you can transfer files to it over a serial connection. If you're using a Windows system, doing so is explained in Chapter 8 in "Transferring Files over a Serial Connection from Windows." If you're using a Linux system, this part of the process is explained in Chapter 9 "Transferring Files Using minicom." Installing software on your TiVo after you've transferred files there is explained in the Chapter 10 in "Installing Software on Your TiVo."

TiVo Troubleshooting

If you're reading this section, chances are that something went wrong in one of the upgrade procedures discussed earlier in this chapter. No need to panic—everyone hoses his or her TiVo once or twice in the course of hacking it. It's a baptismal experience.

Aside from drastic hardware failures, there are relatively few potential problems when upgrading or hacking your TiVo. The next few sections discuss each of these problems and the most common causes.

No Picture or Welcome Screen

When you first turn on your TiVo, it displays a welcome graphic as it initializes and validates the TiVo software. On a TiVo Series 1, this is a screen that features the TiVo character that displays the message "Your recorder is starting up, Please wait a moment..." at the bottom of the screen. On a TiVo Series 2, this is a gray screen that displays the message "Welcome, Powering up" in the center of the screen. Seeing either of these screens is relatively good news, because it means that the TiVo was able to find its disk and begin loading software. If you do not see a picture or either of these screens on your TiVo, you will want to do the following:

◆ If you have a Series 1 stand-alone TiVo, check the fuse in the power supply, located near the external power connector. It is rare for this to fail, unless there are actual problems with the power supply, but it can happen.

◆ If you have a TiVo Series 2, verify that the stiff white cable that connects the power supply to the motherboard is seated correctly at both ends.

If you still cannot get the TiVo to power on, you may simply have a bad power supply. Companies such as 9thTee.com, PTVUpgrade.com, and Weaknees.com will all assess and repair TiVo problems. Trying to get a TiVo Series 1 through TiVo Inc. is especially frustrating because Phillips and Hughes handles hardware support, and they can be hard to track down.

Your TiVo Is Stuck at the Welcome Screen

If your TiVo displays either of these graphical screens: "Your recorder is starting up, Please wait a moment..." or "Welcome, Powering up," your power supply is obviously fine, so at least you can cross one thing off your list.

If your system seems stuck at the Welcome screen or constantly reboots to this screen, your TiVo is not booting successfully. Some common reasons for this are as follows:

◆ You are trying to boot your system with a kernel or root filesystem intended for another model of TiVo.

◆ Your **/etc/rc.d/rc.sysinit** file doesn't execute correctly. The most common problem with this file is that it has been edited elsewhere and then moved back to the TiVo. This file must *not* be edited on a Windows system without using a Linux-safe editor. Windows systems end each line in a file with a carriage return and linefeed characters (aka CRLF). Linux systems only end each line with a linefeed character. In general, the best idea is never to edit Linux files on a Windows system.

TIP

If you must edit TiVo or Linux text files on a Windows system, you must use an editor like UltraEdit (http://www.ultraedit.com) or GNU Emacs (the world's greatest text editor: http://www.gnu.org/software/emacs/), which is smart enough to end lines "the right way." You can download a demonstration copy of UltraEdit from http://www.ultraedit.com/downloads/index.html. You can get a copy of Emacs for Windows from http://ftp.gnu.org/gnu/windows/emacs/latest. Emacs will sense the end of line characters in any file that it edits and will preserve them in that same fashion.

◆ You are trying to boot a signed kernel on a Series 1 or 2 system and have modified the kernel so that it no longer passes the boot PROM's signature check (perhaps by deactivating the initial RAM disk). Unfortunately, you can do that only on TiVo software releases prior to Version 3.1 of the TiVo software. You will have to fall back to an older version of the TiVo software if you want to keep your modifications, or follow a procedure like the Two-Kernel Monte to chain-boot a hacked kernel, described earlier in this chapter.

◆ You have modified entries in the root filesystem and want to boot a 3.2 or later version of the TiVo software that is still comparing the entries in the root filesystem against the hash signatures. Ordinarily, the TiVo will simply replace modified files such as **/etc/rc.d/rc.sysinit** with virgin copies, but if you've been clever and tried to make this process immutable using the **chattr** command, your TiVo will try to delete them, fail, reboot, try to delete them again, fail.... I think that you get the idea. As in the previous point, you'll either have to fall back to an older version of the TiVo software if you want to keep your modifications, or follow a procedure like the Two-Kernel Monte procedure to chain-boot a hacked kernel.

◆ You have hacked a Series 2 machine, as described in previous sections, but there is a syntax error in the boot parameters that you set using the **bootpage** command. It is extremely important that you escape both of the back quotes (`) in this entry by preceding them with a backslash (\). Make sure that they are indeed back quotes and not standard single-quotes, and that you have also escaped all of the dollar signs ($) in this entry by preceding them with a backslash (\). The back quote character is located in the upper-left corner of most standard, non-Dvorak US keyboards. You can use the **bootpage -p <drive>** command to examine your current settings after the TiVo drive is back in your PC.

◆ You have hacked a Series 2 machine, as described in previous sections, but there is a syntax error in the startup script that is being executed through the BASH_ENV entry in the boot parameters that you set using the **bootpage** command. Check this carefully. This script and any applications that it runs must be marked as executable (**chmod 755 <filename>**) in the directory from which you built your ROMFS image.

◆ Last and least, your disk drive may be corrupted to the point where it is temporarily unbootable or a permanent paperweight. This is truly rare because you can rarely restore a backup or mount partitions (as you probably did when you were hacking it) from a bad drive. However, it is possible. Try restoring a backup to another drive and booting from that one. If the replacement drive boots successfully, try restoring a backup to the drive that you suspect is bad and see what happens. Sorry to say it, but disk problems are usually pilot error—unless the disk is actually on fire, no longer spins, or is making clicking problems (indicating a problem with the disk surface or heads).

Those are all the ways in which I've shot myself in the foot—er, I mean, that I've ever heard about going wrong. If your TiVo is continually rebooting and you're sick of messing with it for the time being, restore the disk from a backup, use it for a while, and try hacking it again. Better yet, buy another one just for hacking, so that you're never inconvenienced by a typo or a versioning problem.

Your TiVo Is Stuck at the Second Welcome Screen

When your TiVo successfully loads a kernel and begins the boot process, it displays a second screen with the message "Almost there, a few more seconds." Seeing this screen is even more exciting than the previous one, because it means that your disk is good, your kernel passed any signature check, and your boot parameters haven't invalidated the boot process. However, if the system hangs at this point or reboots shortly after displaying this screen, the most common sources of problems are as follows:

◆ You are trying to boot a signed kernel on a Series 1 or 2 system and have modified the kernel so that it no longer passes the boot PROM's signature check (perhaps by deactivating the initial RAM disk). Unfortunately, you can do that only on TiVo software releases prior to Version 3.2 of the TiVo software. You will have to fall back to an older version of the TiVo software if you want to keep your modifications, or follow a procedure like the Two-Kernel Monte described earlier in this chapter to use **monte** to chain-boot a hacked kernel.

◆ You have passed the **noinitrd** command as one of your boot parameters. This trick only worked on the 2.03 kernel distributed with original Series 2 machines. If you are using **monte**, you must disable the **initrd** in the kernel that you are attempting to monte using the **killinitrd** command.

◆ You are trying to use **monte** to boot a kernel in which the **initrd** has been disabled, and the program **/sbin/init** isn't found in your root filesystem. See the section in this chapter on "Two-Kernel Monte" for information about getting around this.

◆ You are trying to use **monte** to boot a kernel and root filesystem whose MFS software versions do not match. This could be the case if you are trying to monte a 4.0 OS from a 3.0 kernel, and have simply overlaid the 4.0 filesystems on top of a restored 3.0 disk. You should do this in reverse, overlaying a 3.0 kernel and root filesystem over a restored 4.0 disk, as explained in the "Two-Kernel Monte" section of this chapter.

◆ If you have two drives in your TiVo, verify that you correctly set the jumpers on the disk drives when you put them back in the TiVo. The TiVo is unable to mount and access the second drive if its jumpers are not set correctly.

If you are hacking a Series 2 machine, one good way to see what's actually going wrong is to connect a serial cable to the TiVo's serial port, and then watch the diagnostic and kernel messages that display. Add the entry **dsscon=true** to the boot parameters that you set using the **bootpage** command, and connect a terminal emulator to your serial cable, running at a connection speed of 115,200. You then will see all of the boot messages from the kernel's signature check to the actual kernel boot messages—hopefully, one of these messages will help you identify the problem you're experiencing.

Your TiVo Displays a Green Screen

After your TiVo begins executing the /etc/rc.d/rc.sysinit startup file, MFS problems or inconsistencies can cause your TiVo to display a green screen, almost as though it was a Microsoft Windows system. If you find your TiVo displaying a green screen, ***do not unplug it!*** The green screen indicates that an error has been detected in the TiVo's MFS filesystem, and that the TiVo is running diagnostic and repair routines to try to correct the problem. Be patient, and the problem will usually resolve itself. The amount of time required to repair MFS filesystem inconsistencies depends on the amount of storage in your TiVo. Larger-capacity systems take longer.

Unplugging your TiVo at this point would cause the filesystem repair routines to fail, potentially corrupting the MFS filesystem even further. Get a cup of coffee. Have a cigarette. Walk the dog. Do not unplug the TiVo.

Starting FTP and Telnet on Your TiVo

Admittedly fairly simple, this section explains how to start the telnet and FTP daemons on your TiVo. Telnet is a network-based terminal emulation program that enables you to log in on remote systems over a network. In order to connect to a remote system, a telnet daemon must be running, waiting for incoming connections. (A *daemon* is the Unix/Linux term for a program that is always running when a system is active, and constantly waits to service appropriate requests.) FTP is a file transfer protocol client that you can use to send files to your TiVo and retrieve them from the TiVo, as long as an FTP daemon is running on the TiVo.

If you are hacking your TiVo Series 1 and have installed a network card in it as described in Chapter 3 in the section "Networking Series 1 TiVos," you do not have to follow the procedure described in this section. The **nic_install** script provided with today's TurboNet and Airnet cards for the TiVo Series 1 automatically adds entries that start the FTP and telnet daemons to the **/etc/rc.d/rc.sysinit** script, along with its other modifications.

If you are hacking your TiVo Series 1 and have somehow installed a network card without also using the nic_install program, you can install Series 1 versions of the telnet (**tnlited**) and FTP (**tivoftpd**) daemons by installing the directories of TiVo software included in the hack_dir directory on the BATBD CD), explained in Chapter 10, in the section "Installing Software on Your TiVo." You then can add them to your TiVo's startup procedure by adding the following lines to the **/etc/rc.d/rc.sysinit** file on your TiVo:

```
/var/hack/bin/tivoftpd &
/var/hack/bin/tnlited 23 /bin/bash -login &
```

If you are hacking your Series 2 machine running a version of the TiVo OS earlier than 3.2, you should therefore have installed the Series 2 software from the BATBD CD as explained in "Getting a Command Prompt on a TiVo Series 2," earlier in this chapter. In that case, the following startup commands are already present in the **/var/hack/hackinit** file that was installed for you:

```
/sbin/tnlited 23 /bin/bash -login &
/var/hack/bin/tivoftpd &
```

If you are hacking your Series 2 using the Two Kernel Monte method and are running a TiVo software version later than 3.1 that **monte** boots for you, you also should install the Series 2 software from the BATBD CD, as explained in "Two Kernel Monte for the TiVo Series 2 ," earlier in this chapter. In that case, you must remount the TiVo's root filesystem so that it is writable before you can append to this file. To remount the root filesystem from a running TiVo in read-write mode, execute the following command:

```
mount -o rw,remount /
```

You then can add the following two commands to the end of the **/etc/rc.d/rc.sysinit** file in the root partition that is actively being used by the TiVo to which monte has been applied:

```
/sbin/tnlited 23 /bin/bash -login &
/var/hack/bin/tivoftpd &
```

You then should remount the root filesystem in read-only mode, as it should be, using the following command:

```
mount -o ro,remount /
```

The next time you start your TiVo, these daemons will automatically start.

OPENING YOUR 4.0 TIVO FOR NETWORKING

Aside from the inherent pain in hacking a Series 2 machine running Version 4.0 of the TiVo OS (and the related satisfaction when you succeed), Version 4.0 of the TiVo OS is more modern in other aspects; for example, it's paranoia about network connections. Version 4.0 of the TiVo OS uses a Linux application called "iptables" to set up a firewall on your TiVo that it uses to block most types of network connections. In order to telnet or FTP to your 4.0 TiVo, even after you have used monte, you will need to enable the ports used by those services. The easiest way to do this is to turn off the firewall, but my membership in the International Brotherhood of Unix Sysadmins and Circus Geeks would be revoked if I did not point out that this is a BIG security hole. (No more so than running an earlier version of the TiVo OS, but I'm not sure that's a good argument.)

To disable the firewall on your hacked 4.0 TiVo system so that you can telnet in and FTP files to and from the TiVo, execute the following command on your TiVo:

```
/sbin/iptables -F
```

This flushes (i.e., removes from memory) all of the rules used by the firewall, making it completely open to all network communications. If your TiVo has an IP address that makes it visible on the Internet, this means that school kids in China can now log in to your TiVo, create and destroy files, and configure it so that they can suck your recorded pornography down to their home systems. Don't do this unless your machine is isolated on your home network, or you don't care if someone hacks into it and turns it into an electronic paperweight or hacking zombie. If you're comfortable with not running a firewall, you may want to add this command to your 4.0 root filesystem **/etc/rc.d/rc.sysinit** file when you append the commands that start the telnet and FTO servers.

More subtle approaches to the firewall problem are preferable, but would take too long to explain here in all their glory. For more details about using **iptables**, especially in a more graceful mode than the sledgehammer proposed in this TIP, see the project's home page at http://www.netfilter.org.

Integrating Your TiVo with AOL Instant Messenger

If you're a fan of AOL's Instant Messenger and are using a hacked TiVo Series 1 on your home network, you may want to be notified when a buddy arrives or when someone sends you an instant message ("IMs you," to use the vernacular). In this case, you'll be happy to know that software is available for your TiVo that enables any networked TiVo to display onscreen messages—and, of course, it's free software.

Displaying instant messages and buddy notifications on your TiVo requires that you use an instant messaging client known as GAIM (GTK AOL Instant Messenger). GAIM is an Open Source project with a home page located at http://gaim.sourceforge.net. GAIM is completely compatible with the most popular instant messaging protocols, including AOL, MSN, Yahoo, Jabber, IRC, Gadu-Gadu(GG), Napster, and Zephyr, and it provides a central instant messaging console for anyone using any of those services.

Both the Windows and Linux versions of GAIM are freely available from the GAIM project's download page at http://gaim.sourceforge.net/downloads.php. The latest version for Linux, at the time of this book's writing, is provided in the connectivity directory on the BATBD CD that accompanies this book. The latest version for Windows, at the time of this book's writing, is provided in the Windows directory on the BATBD CD that accompanies this book. See Chapter 10 for information about accessing the software on the BATBD CD. Figure 7.1 presents the initial login or sign-on screen in the Linux version of GAIM. Figure 7.2 shows GAIM after signing on, which should be remarkably familiar to AOL Instant Messenger users.

FIGURE 7.1 *GAIM's Login screen on a Linux system*

FIGURE 7.2 *GAIM's Main screen on a Linux system*

After you install GAIM on your Linux or Windows system, you will have to install two additional components: An application that you must run on your TiVo to enable displaying instant message notifications, and a plugin to GAIM itself that can talk to the TiVo software. Both of these pieces of software were written by the TiVo hacker hermanator (who also ported GAIM to Windows). A zip file named gaim2tivo-0.2.zip contains this software and is available in the connectivity directory on the BATBD CD included with this book. This zip file also can be downloaded directly from the DealDatabase Forum thread on this subject, located at http://www.dealdatabase.com/forum/showthread.php?s=&threadid=14453. At the time this book was written, the latest version was Version 0.2.

To integrate GAIM with your TiVo, unpack the zip file and transfer the file "tivo_messenger" to your TiVo. Make sure that it's executable on your TiVo (**chmod 755 tivo_messenger**), and execute it in the background (**./tivo_messenger &**). You may eventually want to integrate it with the **/etc/rc.d/rc.sysinit** startup file that you use to start your favorite TiVo hacks. The gaim2tivo-0.2.zip archive file on the BATBD CD includes the source code for the TiVo messenger application, so you should recompile it yourself for the TiVo Series 2, though there seemed to be some problems with the onscreen display module.

Once you have the tivo_messenger application running on your TiVo, you must install the appropriate plugin on your Windows or Linux system.

To install the gaim2tivo plugin on a Linux system, do the following:

1. Copy the file gaim2tivo.so from the directory where you extracted the gaim2tivo archive to the directory used for GAIM plugins. This is usually the lib directory corresponding to the binary directory where the "gaim" program is installed on your Linux system. For example, if the gaim binary is located in **/usr/bin** on your Linux system, GAIM plugins probably are stored in the directory **/usr/lib/gaim**.

2. After starting GAIM, select the Tools menu's Plugins command. Click the Load button in the dialog box that displays, browse to the directory where you copied the GAIM plugin in the previous step, select the plugin, and click OK. The dialog box shown in Figure 7.3 will display.

3. Click Configure. The dialog shown in Figure 7.4 will display. Enter the IP address or hostname for your TiVo. Don't change the specified port number. Click Close to close the configuration dialog box.

FIGURE 7.3 *GAIM's Plugin screen on a Linux system*

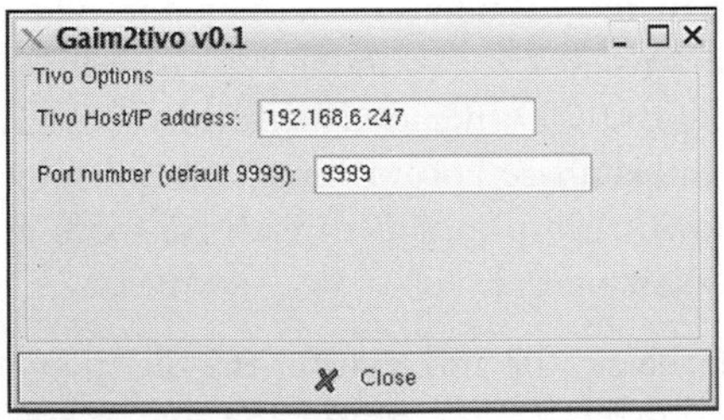

FIGURE 7.4 *GAIM's Plugin configuration screen on a Linux system*

To install the gaim2tivo plugin on a Windows system, do the following:

1. Copy the file gaim2tivo.dll from the directory where you extracted the gaim2tivo archive to the directory used for GAIM plugins. This is usually the directory C:\Program Files\Gaim\Plugins.

2. After starting GAIM, select the Tools menu's Plugins command. Click the Load button in the dialog box that displays, browse to the directory where you copied the GAIM plugin in the previous step, select the plugin, and click OK.

3. Click Configure and enter the IP address or hostname for your TiVo. Don't change the specified port number. Click Close to close the Configuration dialog box.

At this point, you can test GAIM by sending yourself an Instant Message. Your screen will display a message like the one shown in Figure 7.5. If you are connected to your TiVo through a serial connection, you will also see text like the following:

```
192.168.6.32:32879 connected
RECEIVED: Billvonhagen: You there?
```

The next time you or any of your GAIM buddies sign on, a sign-on message will display on your TiVo screen, as shown in Figure 7.5. This is a great way to watch TV while not missing any of those "important" messages from any of your friends or co-workers.

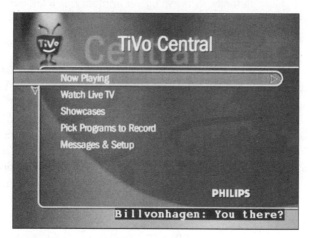

FIGURE 7.5 *GAIM's Plugin screen on a Linux system*

Caller ID and Your TiVo

Today, Caller ID is almost a fact of life—regardless of how many don't-call lists that state and local governments set up. Even if you are actually interested in talking to someone, Caller ID gives you some advance warning as to who's calling, long before you pick up the phone. This is all well and good if your Caller ID box is glued to a wall where you can always see it, or if you're willing to run over to it each time the phone rings. But what if you're doing something else, like watching your TiVo, and don't feel like moving unless absolutely necessary?

If you have a spare modem card lying around and your personal computer runs Windows, YAC, which stands for "Yet Another Caller ID Program," just may be the answer.

 NOTE

Unix and Linux have a long tradition of "Yet Another..." programs, the best known of which is YACC, which stands for "Yet Another Compiler Compiler." Since the fundamental design philosophy of Unix (and thus Linux) is to have many small, specialized utilities that work together to do more complex tasks, it's only natural that different people have different ideas about how those small utilities should work. Consequently, there was often one application to do a task, followed by another application that did the same task slightly differently, followed by yet another application that did the same task differently... I think you get the idea.

Jensen Harris's YAC program is a client/server Caller ID program that is available from http://www.sunflowerhead.com/software/yac. The server component runs on a Windows 2000 or later system and requires that an internal modem be present in order to monitor incoming calls and retrieve Caller ID information. Once an incoming call is received, the YAC server broadcasts the Caller ID information to any YAC client (known as a "listener" running on the local network). Each listener receiving the broadcast formats the information and displays it on the device where it is running—in our case, a TiVo Series 1. The current version of the TiVo's YAC Client is only supported on the TiVo Series 1. Maybe if we ask really nicely....

The YAC server software for Windows is provided in the file yac-0.16-win32.zip in the Windows directory on the BATBD CD. The TiVo listener software is provided in the file yac-0.15-tivo.tar.gz in the connectivity directory on the BATBD CD. If newer versions of this software are available, you should be able to download them from the Web site listed in the previous paragraph.

After you install and configure the YAC software on your TiVo, your TiVo will display messages like the one shown in Figure 7.6 when an incoming call is received.

FIGURE 7.6 *A Caller-ID notification from YAC on a TiVo screen*

News, Sports, Weather, and Your TiVo

After you've networked your TiVo, extracting information from a variety of online services is just a LMOP (Large Matter of Programming). TiVo hacker Zirak has a TiVo Control Station application, available at http://www.zirakzigil.net/tivo/TCS.html, which enables you to connect to, extract data from, and display summary information from a variety of online sources. Written in TCL, it displays up-to-date sports, stock quotes, and eBay and weather information on your TiVo. The application is easy to install and easily expandable by writing additional TCL modules. TCS currently works only on Series 1 machines. Figure 7.7 shows a sample screen from TCS, displaying a local weather map.

FIGURE 7.7 *A weather map displayed by the TiVo Control Station*

A copy of an archive file of the TiVo Control Station software is located in the file TCS_1.0.0.tar.gz in the connectivity directory on the BATBD CD. You can also download this file from its Web site (listed in the previous paragraph). To execute this program on your TiVo, transfer the file and unpack it in a directory such as **/var/hack**. This will create the directory **/var/hack/tcs**. To start TCS, simply **cd** to this directory and execute the file "starttcs," which starts TCS in the background.

 NOTE

TCS depends on other applications that may not be located on your TiVo. These programs are **jpegwriter** (for displaying weather maps), **newtext2osd** (for most onscreen displays), and a non-busy-box version of the **ps** command. Archive files containing all of these are located in the connectivity directory on the BATBD CD.

The TiVo Control Station enables you to execute the following special TCS command from your remote:

- *(clear)(0)(clear)* Lists running hacks on the screen
- *(clear)(7)(clear)* Displays stock quotes (requires an Internet connection)
- *(clear)(8)(clear)* Displays local weather (requires an Internet connection)
- *(6)(0)(clear)* Displays the available sports commands
- *(6)(1)(clear)* Major League Baseball scores, schedule and standings
- *(6)(2)(clear)* National Football League scores, schedule and standings
- *(6)(3)(clear)* NCAA college football, scores, schedule and AP/ESPN, *USAToday* polls
- *(6)(4)(clear)* National Hockey League scores, schedule and standings
- *(7)(1)(clear)* Various interest rates
- *(8)(1)(clear)* Changes the weather zip code from using the remote (valid until you restart your TiVo)
- *(8)(2)(clear)* Displays local (600 mile) weather radar.
- *(8)(3)(clear)* Displays national weather radar.
- *(9)(0)(clear)* Shows all TCS remote and network commands.
- *(9)(6)(clear)* Displays any updates available from the TCS Web site
- *(9)(7)(clear)* Displays all background processes/timers
- *(9)(8)(clear)* Resets all background timers—update everything NOW.
- *(9)(9)(clear)* Quits TCS
- *(mute)(mute)(clear)* Toggles the execution of greedy processes (NICE/MEAN)

As you can see from this list, TCS enhances your TiVo experience in a big way, providing access to a tremendous amount of extra information, all from your TiVo. As another example, Figure 7.8 shows stock quotes as displayed by TCS on a TiVo screen—uh-oh, time to sell!

FIGURE 7.8 *Stock quotes displayed by the TiVo Control Station*

TCS also provides commands that enable you to control other hacks that may be running on your TiVo. Since controlling these commands is somewhat specific to how they're installed and started on your TiVo, these command aren't discussed here. See Zirak's Web site for details.

Using TiVo's Home Media Option

TiVo's Home Media Option (HMO), introduced in early April, 2003, extends the basic capabilities and network awareness of Series 2 machines. TiVo's Home Media Option requires that your Series 2 is running Version 4.0 of the TiVo OS, and provides the following basic capabilities:

◆ The ability to share recordings between networked, HMO-enabled TiVos, known in TiVo terms as *multi-room viewing*. You can record a show on one of your TiVos and easily watch it on another by transferring it over your home network. You can also browse the Now Playing lists of other HMO-enabled TiVos to more easily select shows from the lists.

◆ The ability to schedule recordings over the Internet by connecting to tivo.com to schedule recordings up to 30 minutes before the actual broadcast—if your HMO-enabled TiVo is on a home network with an always-on, broadband connection to the Internet.

◆ The ability to access online music and digital photographs from any HMO-enabled TiVo. This is especially attractive to TiVo owners whose TiVo is part of a high-quality, home theater setup (though it works for me, too).

◆ The ability to export collections of MP3 files and playlists from Windows and Macintosh systems using platform-specific software called the TiVo Desktop. You can play online audio files in MP3 format, and can use playlists in the ASX, M3U, and PLS formats used by most online audio players.

◆ The ability to export collections of digital photographs from Windows and Macintosh systems by using platform-specific software called the TiVo Desktop. You can view digital photographs saved in the BMP, DIB, GIF, JPG, and PNG file formats.

If you have multiple Series 2 machines, the Home Media Option is activated on a per-TiVo basis. Current pricing of the Home Media Option is $99 for the first Series 2 machine in your home, and $49 for each additional TiVo Series 2 that you want to enable.

TiVo's Home Media Option requires that you have a USB (Universal Serial Bus) network adaptor for your Series 2 machine. A list of suggested USB adaptors for the Series 2 is discussed in Chapter 3, in the section "Networking the TiVo Series 2." If you want to take advantage of remote scheduling over the Web or want to play online audio or browse digital photographs stored on other people's TiVos, you must have an always-on, broadband connection to the Internet.

If it isn't clear already, TiVo's Home Media Option is only available for stand-alone Series 2 machines, and then only for Series 2 running Version 4.0 or better of the TiVo operating system. Although online petitions are being circulated to request that TiVo make the Home Media Option available for Series 1 and Series 2 DirecTiVos, I don't see much chance of this happening. The last revision of the TiVo OS for Series 1 machines was 3.2, and porting 4.0 to a TiVo Series 1 is a large effort. More importantly, the Series 1 systems are also somewhat underpowered by today's standards, and only have networking support through third-party products that are not officially endorsed by TiVo. (See Chapter 3, the section entitled "Networking Series 1 TiVos" for more information about Series 1 networking products.) While the performance issue could be addressed by clever programming, the core networking requirements of the Home Media Option make it unlikely that we'll ever seeing the Home Media Option on a Series 1. I'd be ecstatic to be proved wrong, however!

TiVo's Home Media Option is well worth the price of admission, IMHO (In My Honest Opinion). Your mileage may vary, but I doubt it. The next few sections explain how to take advantage of the specific capabilities of TiVo's Home Media Option.

Playing Music or Displaying Photos Using Your TiVo

Playing MP3 files stored on an online service or on a networked personal computer in your home is easy. TiVo provides software for Macintosh and Windows systems that makes it easy for you to export your online audio files so that they can be browsed and played from HMO-enabled TiVos. Known as the TiVo Desktop, this software is free, and can be downloaded from the TiVo Web site. Downloading and using the TiVo Desktop software for Windows systems was explained in Chapter 8, in "Installing and Using the Windows TiVo Desktop

Software." Downloading and using the TiVo Desktop software for Macintosh systems was explained in Chapter 8 in "Integrating Macintosh Systems with TiVo's Home Media Option."

If your online audio files are stored on a Linux system or on a Windows system in a format other than MP3, don't despair. While not officially supported by TiVo, Inc., it is possible to integrate Linux systems with HMO-enabled TiVos and play other audio formats from a Windows system. Integrating Linux systems with the Home Media Option is accomplished through a freely-available, open-source application known as the "Portable Open TiVo Home Media Option," and is explained in Chapter 9 in the section "Working with TiVo's Home Media Option from Linux." The folks at TiVo are certainly Open Source advocates and one of the best success stories ever for the power of Linux and the Open Source movement in general, so they released documentation and a sample plug-in for the Apache Web server written in the Perl language that showed how the Home Media Option software worked. (This is available from the page at http://www.tivo.com/developer.) This source code is the conceptual parent of the Portable Open TiVo Home Media Option project.

If your online audio files are stored in a format other than MP3 and are stored on a Windows system (or a system that you can mount from your Windows system over your home network), you can use J. River's Media Center software to export these audio collections so that they can be accessed from your TiVo. For more information about this, see Chapter 8, the section entitled "Playing Windows Audio Formats Other than MP3."

After you've exported your audio collection from your personal computer using one of the techniques discussed previously, you can browse the list from the "Music & Photos" menu on your TiVo (TiVo Central -> Music & Photos). Selecting this menu displays the screen shown in Figure 7.9.

This screen displays the name of each system exporting music and photos in a format compatible with the Home Media Option. The audio and photo collections on each system are listed separately, organized by the name of the system.

FIGURE 7.9 *Browsing for available music and photograph collections*

To play audio files or display photographs from any of these systems, select the name of the audio or photo collection that you want to browse. The TiVo displays a list of all files in the specified format available on that system, as shown in Figure 7.10.

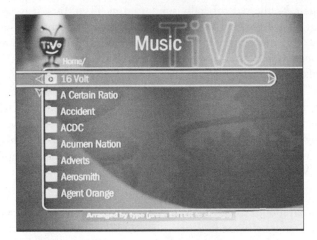

FIGURE 7.10 *Browsing an online music collection*

When a collection displays, select the folder containing the music that you want to play or which contains the photos that you want to display. Photo collections in a selected folder display immediately, while audio files are listed and can be played by selecting specific files or playlists.

That's all there is to it. The Home Media Option's ability to access online music collections from any TiVo/TV combination in one's home is incredibly handy at parties or when you simply want to listen to online music without sitting at your personal computer.

Scheduling Recordings on Your TiVo over the Internet

Hearing about an interesting upcoming show that you'd love to record is traditionally frustrating if you're not near your VCR. I've certainly seen things mentioned in the morning paper that I wanted to record. And what if you're held up at work, out of town, or simply forget to schedule a recording. You could always call your significant other or a friend, but that's somewhat embarrassing. The best solution for solving the problem of remote scheduling is scheduling its recording over the Internet. Network-capable DVRs, such as the TiVo, make this easy to do through an official, TiVo-supported solution for the TiVo Series 2 owners who have purchased TiVo's Home Media Option, or through an excellent TiVo application written by TiVo hackers.

For Series 1 and hacked Series 2 machines that cannot run TiVo's Home Media Option software, you already have an excellent tool for scheduling recordings over a network in the TiVo Web Project software, known more familiarly as TiVoWeb. The latest version of TiVoWeb available (as of this book's writing) is Version (1.94), which is included on the BATBD CD that accompanies this book. Installing and using this software is explained in Chapter 10 in the section "An Alternative UI in the TiVo Web Project." As explained there, using TiVoWeb from machines on the Internet requires some special configuration of your TiVo or home gateway so that the TiVo is visible from the outside world.

If you are using a Series 2 machine and have purchased TiVo's Home Media Option (HMO) for that TiVo, life is much easier. Purchasers of the HMO service can connect to TiVo Inc.'s primary Web site, browse the shows that the TiVo will receive, and schedule recordings from anywhere on the Web. This capability, officially known as the Remote Scheduling option, was rolled into the HMO package as part of the enhanced network-awareness of Version 4.0 of the TiVo software.

Once you've remotely scheduled a recording, the request to create that recording is then pushed to your TiVo during a specially scheduled call. This makes remotely scheduling recordings quite convenient because you can access the TiVo Web site from any machine that is connected to the Internet, and TiVo then handles getting the data down to your machine.

To schedule a recording over the Web using the Home Media Option:

1. Connect to the TiVo Web site and select the "I Have TiVo!" entry in the left-hand menu. Click the "TiVo Central Online" entry that displays in the left-hand menu. The screen shown in Figure 7.11 then displays. A shortcut to this screen is http://www.tivo.com/tco, but there is no guarantee that this URL will stick around forever.

2. Enter the email address and password that you used when you created your tivo.com account, and click "Sign In." The screen shown in Figure 7.12 then displays.

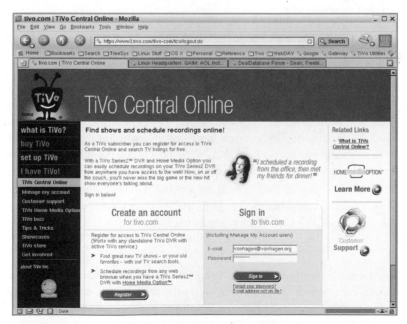

FIGURE 7.11 *The TiVo Central Online sign-on screen*

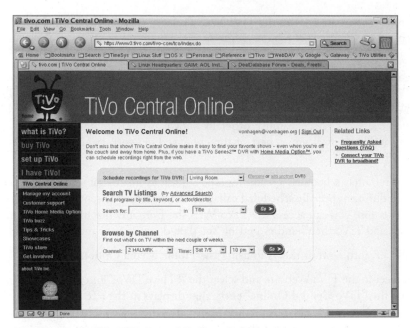

FIGURE 7.12 *The TiVo Central Online scheduling screen*

TIP

If you do not already have an account at tivo.com, you can click "Register" and create one by starting from this screen.

3. Click the "Schedule Recordings for TiVo DVR" drop-down box and select the TiVo on which you want to schedule this recording. All DVRs that you have registered with your TiVo account will be listed in this drop-down box, but you only have the ability to schedule recordings for HMO-enabled DVRs. All others will be shown with two leading asterisks in the list, indicating that they cannot be remotely programmed.

4. To search TV Listings in your area, enter a string that you want to search for, select where you want to search for that field (Title, Title or Description, or Actor/Director, for example), and click Go. After a few moments, a screen like the one shown in Figure 7.13 displays, which displays the results for my search for "Rockford Files" in the title.

5. Browse the list of results and click on the title of anything that you want to record. A screen like the one in Figure 7.14 displays, providing more detailed information about the show, its cast and crew (when available), and a list of the times that this show will be broadcast in the near future.

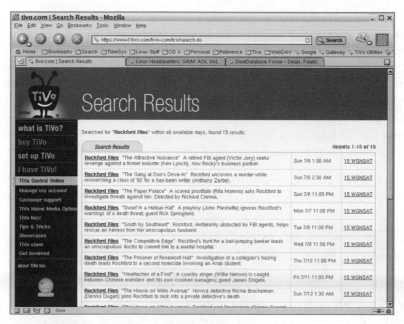

FIGURE 7.13 *The results of a TiVo Central Online search*

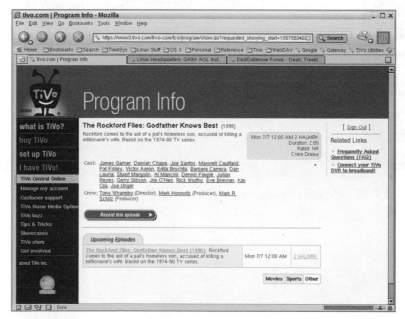

FIGURE 7.14 *A selected recording from a TiVo Central Online search*

6. To record this show, click "Record this episode," which displays a screen like the one shown in Figure 7.15. This screen shows your recording options for the selected episode, and enables you to change the TiVo on which you want to record this show, set recording options such as quality and priority, and lets you select a checkbox that results in tivo.com sending you e-mail about the status of scheduling this recording (not the status of the recording itself).

7. After selecting appropriate options, click "Schedule It!" to schedule the recording. A screen like the one shown in Figure 7.16 displays, confirming that the recording will be scheduled the next time the specified DVR connects to the TiVo service.

That's all there is to it! Barring communication failure or other acts of God, the selected recording will be scheduled on your DVR, and should be waiting for you one of these evenings.

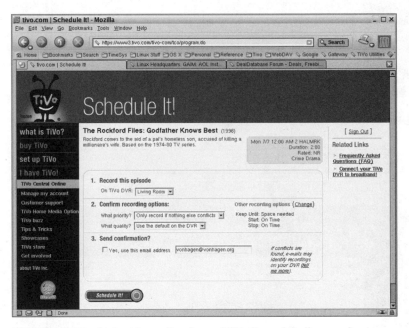

FIGURE 7.15 *A selected recording from a TiVo Central Online search*

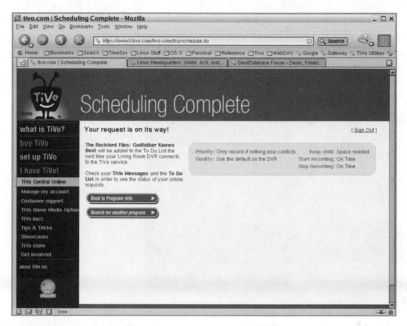

FIGURE 7.16 *Confirmation of a scheduled recording at TiVo Central Online*

Multi-Room Viewing on Your TiVo

TiVo's Home Media Option provides built-in support for multi-room viewing, which is the ability to browse and view stored recordings on other networked, HMO-enabled TiVos in your home. When you have multiple HMO-enabled TiVos in your home, each machine shows up on the Now Playings lists of the other TiVos by name. You set the name of your TiVo when you sign up for the Home Media Option from TiVo's Web site, or subsequently from TiVo's Web site using the "Manage My Account" portion of the site. These TiVo names are really only a convenience, and have nothing to do with the networked host name of your TiVo. I tend to give my machines descriptive names such as "Bedroom," "Living Room," and "Bathroom," which reflect the location where each TiVo is located.

Viewing a recording stored on a remote TiVo actually transfers that recording to your TiVo over your home network. You can watch the show as it is being transferred or simply transfer it and watch it later at your convenience. Depending on the speed of your home network (and especially on slower wireless networks), watching a show while it is being transferred can result in delays while you "catch up" with the portion of the show that has been transferred, and then have to wait while enough of the show transfers so that you can continue viewing. Even on wired networks, I prefer to transfer the shows and watch something else until the transfer has completed.

To view a recording stored on one networked, HMO-enabled TiVo from another, simply browse to the Now Playing list (TiVo Central -> Now Playing on TiVo) and browse to the bottom of the list. Any other HMO-enabled TiVo on your home network displays, as shown in Figure 7.17.

FIGURE 7.17 *Browsing other TiVos on your home network*

Selecting the name of another HMO-enabled TiVo displays the list of recordings stored on that DVR, as shown in Figure 7.18.

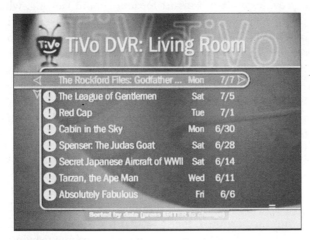

FIGURE 7.18 *Browsing the Now Playing list on a remote TiVo*

After you have identified a recording that you want to view on the TiVo you're currently using, selecting its name displays the screen shown in Figure 7.19.

FIGURE 7.19 *Selecting a recording stored on a remote TiVo*

At this point, you can select "Watch on this TV" to transfer the recording to the TiVo that you are currently using, or select "Don't Do Anything," which returns you to the list of shows available on the remote TiVo that you are currently browsing. If you select "Watch on this TV," a "Please wait..." message displays as the transfer begins. Once the recording begins transferring, the screen shown in Figure 7.20 displays.

FIGURE 7.20 *Options when transferring a show from a remote DVR*

At this point, you can either select "Start playing" to begin watching the recording on the TiVo that you are using as it is being transferred, or you can select "Continue browsing <tivo-name>" to continue browsing the list of recordings stored on the remote TiVo.

As shows are transferred from one TiVo to another, they show up in the Now Playing list of the TiVo to which they are being transferred with a red dot next to the filenames, just as if that TiVo was actively recording them. Recordings are transferred from one TiVo to another sequentially. If you select multiple shows from a remote TiVo, they are transferred in the order that they were selected. You can only view subsequently selected shows once the first has finished transferring.

HACKING THE TiVo

Chapter 8

Working with Your TiVo from Windows and Macintosh Systems

Although the TiVo is a Linux system, most of today's home computers are not. The ABATBD TiVo tool disk included with this book provides all of the tools you need for TiVo hacking on a standard desktop personal computer, but it works by booting Linux on that PC. All of the TiVo tools discussed in the other chapters of this book require the Linux operating system. So what can you do for a TiVo from a personal computer while actually running an operating system like Microsoft Windows? Luckily, you can do quite a bit.

If you are interested in investigating any of the other TiVo tools disks that are available on the Internet, you'll need to use your personal computer to burn copies of the CDs from the ISO images that you download. If you have hacked your TiVo to enable a bash prompt over a serial connection, you'll need to connect to the serial port to do anything interesting. If you've put your TiVo on your home network, you'll need to run an application on your personal computer to connect it to the network. If you want to export music or digital photographs stored on your personal computer so that your TiVo can play or display them using TiVo's new Home Media Option, you'll need to install the TiVo desktop software on your personal computer to export that music. All of these TiVo-related tasks require software that runs on your personal computer under its existing operating system. Whether you're using Mac OS X, older versions of the Mac OS, or some version of Microsoft Windows, you can do a lot for your TiVo from your existing desktop.

In addition to the native software discussed in the previous section, there are also a fair number of "hacker-oriented" tools available for Microsoft Windows and Mac OS X. The open source foundation of Linux makes it quite easy to port Linux (and therefore TiVo) software to other platforms, but differences in the graphical user interfaces for Linux and the PC/Mac software often makes it tough to port graphical tools. However, one area of Linux where this doesn't apply is supporting low-level components such as the **ext2** filesystem. Although there are some restrictions on what (and how) you can work with the TiVo's **ext2** filesystems, support for these filesystems is available for both Windows and Mac OS X, and you can easily use this to preview and explore TiVo filesystems, even when you're not directly connected to your TiVo.

 NOTE

This chapter uses the colloquial term "Windows" to refer to any version of Microsoft Windows. I realize that Microsoft believes that it owns the copyright to the term Windows, but I wanted this chapter to be readable and also didn't want it to look like I'd blasted the book with a shotgun loaded with copyright and trademark symbols. If you're a Microsoft Windows user, you know what I'm talking about when I say Windows. If you're not, you probably don't care. Similarly, this chapter uses the term "Mac OS" to refer to versions of the Macintosh operating system prior to any version of Mac OS X. Because Mac OS X is very different than previous versions of the Mac OS, it is explicitly identified where necessary.

Communicating with Your TiVo from Windows

After you have a command prompt running on your TiVo (described in Chapter 7, "Connecting the Universe to Your TiVo,") or have your TiVo on your home network (described in Chapter 3, "Exploring Your TiVo Hardware"), you're ready to start talking to your TiVo from your personal computer. This section explains how to use and configure Windows software to communicate with your TiVo, discussing software packages that come with Windows or are freely available on the Internet.

TiVo   **DIFFERENCES BETWEEN SERIAL & NETWORK LOGINS**

Serial and network connections to your TiVo are different in one important respect—whether or not you should log out when you're finished using them. The command-line prompt on your TiVo is a bash shell that is started by an entry in the **/etc/rc.d/rc.sysinit** startup file on your TiVo. It is a single process that is started once. Therefore, you do not want to terminate it before closing down your serial connection to the TiVo. If you do terminate it (by using the **exit** command or pressing Control-D, depending on how you've configured bash on your TiVo), it will not restart. You will have to reboot your TiVo in order to get another command-line prompt (unless you manually start another one using a network connection, which would be somewhat backward but functional).

Network connections to your TiVo work differently because each network connection starts individually by the telnet and FTP servers that you started on your TiVo. Terminating a network connection doesn't terminate the server. It only terminates one particular connection. The next time you connect to your TiVo over the network, the appropriate server (telnet or FTP) creates a new connection for you and starts the appropriate processes to communicate with it.

Serial Communications from Windows Systems

After you've attached a serial cable to your TiVo (as described in Chapter 3, in the section entitled "Attaching a Terminal Emulator or Serial Console") and have received a command prompt on your TiVo (described in Chapter 7), you can connect the serial cable from the TiVo to your Windows system's serial port and begin exploring your TiVo from your Windows system. While there are a number of different serial communication software packages available for Windows, this section focuses on the default terminal emulator provided with Windows systems.

All versions of Microsoft Windows come with a simple but functional terminal emulator called *HyperTerminal*, which is available from the Programs -> Accessories -> Communications menu. (If you can't find HyperTerminal on your Windows system for some reason, you can download it from http://www.hilgraeve.com/htpe/download.html.) After starting HyperTerminal by selecting it from the menu, the HyperTerminal application displays the screen shown in Figure 8.1, which prompts you to give the new serial connection that you are defining a name. Each HyperTerminal connection contains its own configuration settings, so you'll want to enter a name that will help you remember what this connection is for—perhaps "TiVo Serial Connection," as shown in Figure 8.1. Click OK to continue.

 NOTE

HyperTerminal is primarily designed for communicating with remote computer systems over a modem. If this is the first time that you are running the HyperTerminal program, it will display an initial dialog box that prompts you for some basic modem configuration information, such as your area code and any numbers that you have to dial to get an outside line. Although irrelevant in this case, you still have to supply your area code. Enter it and click OK to continue.

FIGURE 8.1 *Creating an initial HyperTerminal connection*

Next, HyperTerminal displays a "Connect to" dialog box where you supply information about the connection that you are establishing, as shown in Figure 8.2. If you have connected the TiVo's serial cable to your Windows system's first serial port, select COM1 in the "Connect using" drop-down list, and click OK to continue.

Next, HyperTerminal displays a screen in which you can specify the communications settings used for this connection, as shown in Figure 8.3. Specify 9600 baud as the "Bits per second" rate, and select "None" as the type of flow control to use. The other settings (8 data bits and no parity) are already correct. Click "OK" to continue.

FIGURE 8.2 *Specifying your communications port*

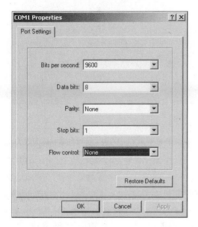

FIGURE 8.3 *Specifying your communication settings*

At this point, HyperTerminal closes its Configuration dialog boxes and displays its standard communication window. Press Control-l followed by the Return (Enter) key on your keyboard once or twice, and you should see a prompt from the TiVo's command-line interpreter, as shown in Figure 8.4.

Congratulations. You're connected! To ensure that HyperTerminal saves your configuration information, select the File menu's Save command. Your HyperTerminal configurations are saved on a special HyperTerminal menu that is added to the Programs -> Accessories -> Communications menu. In the future, you can start HyperTerminal using the settings you just created by selecting these settings by name from this menu.

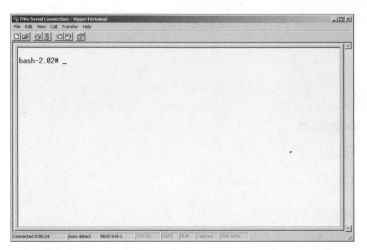

FIGURE 8.4 *A command-line prompt from your TiVo in HyperTerminal*

TIP

If you're not excited by the performance or appearance of HyperTerminal, an excellent alternative is Tera Term, which can be found at http://hp.vector.co.jp/authors/VA002416/teraterm.html. You can download a version of Tera Term for Windows 95/NT from http://hp.vector.co.jp/authors/VA002416/ttermp23.zip. This version worked fine on my Windows 2000 system, and IMHO (In My Honest Opinion) is visually and functionally superior to HyperTerminal for standard serial communications. Figure 8.5 shows a sample Tera Term screen after establishing a connection to your TiVo.

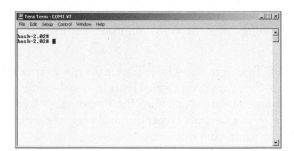

FIGURE 8.5 *A command-line prompt from your TiVo in Tera Term*

Transferring Files over a Serial Connection from Windows

If you're using a serial connection to your TiVo because you don't have a network card for your Series 1 machine or a USB network adapter for your Series 2 system, you may wonder how you can ever get some of those cool hacks from the BATBD CD (or ones that you've downloaded yourself) to your TiVo. Don't despair. You can still transfer files to your TiVo using tried and true serial protocols for file transfer. Unless you've been using computers for quite a while, you may never have transferred files in this way, but this was the default file transfer mechanism used by millions of home computer users long before graphical interfaces and networks were just gleams in Xerox PARC's eye. No worries, it's really quite easy. Most serial communication programs, including HyperTerminal and Tera Term, provide built-in support for serial file transfers. Your TiVo also comes with built-in applications for sending and receiving files over serial connections.

Serial file transfer protocols include xmodem, ymodem, and zmodem. The first of these was xmodem, which was invented in the late 1970s by Ward Christensen. All of these protocols automatically perform error-checking as they transfer data back and forth. The latest generation of serial communications protocols (from the early 1980s) is Chuck Forsenberg's zmodem, which includes support for restarting serial file transfers if a connection is interrupted for one reason or another, and also supports more sophisticated recovery from transfer errors (a problem on phone lines in the 1980s). TiVos provide the **rz** (Receive Zmodem) and **sz** (Send Zmodem) commands in all versions of the TiVo software.

To transfer a file to your TiVo using HyperTerminal (perhaps one of the archives of precompiled TiVo applications provided in the **hacks_dir** directory on the BATBD CD?), do the following:

1. After connecting to your TiVo as described in the previous section, start the **rz** program on your TiVo by typing **rz** at the bash prompt and pressing Return. Hyper-Terminal will display something like the screen shown in Figure 8.6.

FIGURE 8.6 *Starting a serial file transfer on your TiVo*

2. In HyperTerminal, pull down the Transfer menu and select the Send File command. The dialog box displayed in Figure 8.7 displays.

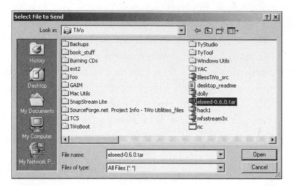

FIGURE 8.7 *Selecting the file to transfer in HyperTerminal*

3. Click Browse, navigate to the directory containing the file that you want to transfer, select that file, and click OK to close the Browse dialog box.

4. In the Protocol field at the bottom of HyperTerminal's Send File dialog box, select either the "Zmodem with Crash Recovery" or "Zmodem" entries. Different versions of HyperTerminal (and Windows) provide different serial transfer protocols. "Zmodem with Crash Recovery" is preferred, but "Zmodem" will do just fine.

5. Click Send to begin the file transfer. The dialog box shown in Figure 8.8 displays. The different fields in this dialog box provide status information about the file transfer as it proceeds, including a histogram that graphically displays the percentage of the file that has been transferred.

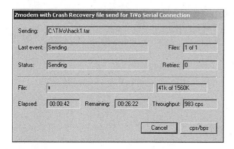

FIGURE 8.8 *Transferring a file in HyperTerminal*

6. Remember that this is a serial file transfer, and will therefore take a while, depending on the size of the file that you are transferring. The dialog box shown in Figure 8.8 closes automatically when the file transfer completes, and automatically terminates

the **rz** command running on your TiVo. (You may need to press Return once or twice to see the bash prompt again.)

Once the serial transfer completes, you can install the software you just uploaded to your TiVo using one of the mechanisms described in Chapter 10, "Getting and Installing New Software for Your TiVo."

Sending files from your TiVo to your PC works in much the same way as transferring them the other way. On the TiVo, you execute the **sz** command, followed by the name of the file that you want to send back to your PC. Once you press Return, HyperTerminal should automatically start the receiving end of the transfer, as shown in Figure 8.9. HyperTerminal will store the files that it receives at the top level of your Windows boot drive. If the version of HyperTerminal that you are using doesn't automatically start the receiving end of the file transfer, you can start it manually by selecting the Receive File command from HyperTerminal's Transfer menu, specifying "Zmodem with Crash Recovery" or "Zmodem" as the protocol, and then manually selecting the directory where you want to store the files you receive.

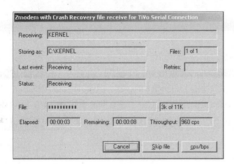

FIGURE 8.9 *Receiving a file in HyperTerminal*

Networked Communications from Windows

If you have added a network card to your Series 1 machine or a USB network adapter to your Series 2 TiVo, you will certainly want to connect to it over the network. The command-line prompt access discussed in the previous section is always useful, but serial file transfers are slow and clunky, though elegant in their simplicity. This section describes how to use standard Windows software to log in and transfer files to and from your TiVo over a network. The instructions in this and the next few sections assume that you installed (and started) the versions of the FTP and telnet daemons that are provided in the archives of TiVo hacks provided on the BATBD CD, or that were installed and started for you as part of installing the Turbonet or AirNet card in your TiVo. For information on installing the software from the BATBD CD on your TiVo, see Chapter 10, "Getting and Installing New Software for Your TiVo." For information on installing a TurboNet or AirNet card on your PC, see Chapter 3, in the section entitled "Networking Your TiVo."

TIP

If you're new to networking, see the general information about networking provided in Chapter 3, in the section entitled "Networking 101." Everybody must start somewhere—and what better motivation than your TiVo!

Using HyperTerminal for Network Communications

As discussed earlier in the section on serial communications using Windows systems, all versions of Microsoft Windows come with a simple but functional terminal emulator called HyperTerminal, which is available from the Programs -> Accessories -> Communications menu. The instructions for configuring a network connection in HyperTerminal are much the same as the instructions for configuring a serial connection.

TIP

If you already have configured a serial connection to your TiVo, don't select that connection from the HyperTerminal menu when configuring a network connection. Instead, select the standard HyperTerminal command from the Programs -> Accessories -> Communications menu. This enables you to define a new connection without accidentally overwriting your serial communication settings.

After starting HyperTerminal by selecting it from the menu, the HyperTerminal application displays the screen shown in Figure 8.10, which prompts you to name the new serial connection that you are defining. Each HyperTerminal connection contains its own configuration settings, so you'll want to enter a name that will help you remember what this connection is for (try "TiVo Network Connection," which I've used in this case, as shown in Figure 8.10. Click "OK" to continue.

NOTE

HyperTerminal is primarily designed for communicating with remote computer systems over a modem. If this is the first time that you are running the HyperTerminal program, it will display an initial dialog box that prompts you for some basic modem configuration information, such as your area code and any numbers that you have to dial to get an outside line. Though irrelevant in this case, you still have to supply your area code. Enter it and click OK to continue.

FIGURE 8.10 *Creating an initial HyperTerminal connection*

Next, HyperTerminal displays a "Connect to" dialog box that enables you to supply information about the connection that you are establishing, as shown in Figure 8.10 above. Select "TCP/IP (Winsock)" from the "Connect using" drop-down list, which displays the dialog box shown in Figure 8-11.

FIGURE 8.11 *Specifying a network connection in HyperTerminal*

Enter your TiVo's IP address in the dialog box shown in Figure 8.11 and click OK to continue. At this point, HyperTerminal closes its configuration dialog boxes and displays its standard communication window. Press the Return (Enter) key on your keyboard once or twice, where you should see a prompt from the TiVo's command-line interpreter, as shown in Figure 8.12.

Congratulations—you're connected! To be sure that HyperTerminal saves your configuration information, select the Save command in the File menu. Your HyperTerminal configurations are saved on a special HyperTerminal menu that is added to the Programs -> Accessories -> Communications menu. In the future, you can start HyperTerminal using the settings you just created by selecting these settings by name from this menu.

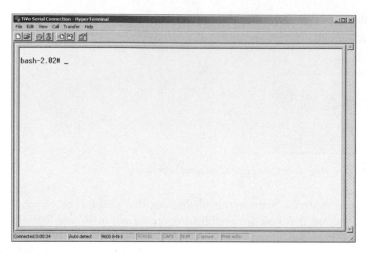

FIGURE 8.12 *A network connection to your TiVo in HyperTerminal*

 TIP

If you don't know your TiVo's IP address (which may be the case if it is allocated dynamically, using DHCP), you can determine what it is by executing the **/sbin/ifconfig -a** command from a serial connection to your TiVo. This command displays information about all of the Ethernet interfaces that are active on your TiVo in the following format:

```
lo      Link encap:Local Loopback
        inet addr:127.0.0.1  Bcast:127.255.255.255  Mask:255.0.0.0
        UP BROADCAST LOOPBACK RUNNING  MTU:3584  Metric:1
        RX packets:0 errors:0 dropped:0 overruns:0 frame:0
        TX packets:0 errors:0 dropped:0 overruns:0 carrier:0 coll:0
eth0    Link encap:Ethernet  HWaddr 00:40:36:01:B0:11
        inet addr:192.168.6.246  Bcast:192.168.6.255  Mask:255.255.255.0
        UP BROADCAST RUNNING MULTICAST  MTU:1500  Metric:1
        RX packets:0 errors:0 dropped:0 overruns:0 frame:0
        TX packets:0 errors:0 dropped:0 overruns:0 carrier:0 coll:0
Interrupt:29
```

You will want to enter the IP address shown in the eth0 (for "Ethernet Connection Zero") section. Your TiVo's IP address may change if you reboot your TiVo after using other network devices that dynamically allocate IP addresses, but you can always use a serial connection to your TiVo and the **/sbin/ifconfig -a** command to find out your TiVo's current IP address.

TIP

There are several shareware and freeware clients that enable Microsoft Windows systems to access other systems using network protocols such as telnet and secure shell (SSH). If you plan on using your Windows system to connect to Linux (or Unix) systems other than the TiVo, you will want to use a network communications client that supports SSH, which is a new, more secure replacement for telnet. The Tera Term program, mentioned earlier, is one of the most popular free applications for standard telnet connections, but requires an add-on module to support SSH (available at http://www.zip.com.au/~roca/ttssh.html). This may not work correctly with newer versions of SSH. One of the most commonly used and freely available clients with up-to-date SSH support is PuTTY, which you can download from http://www.chiark.greenend.org.uk/~sgtatham/putty/. The easiest way to download PuTTY and related utilities for Windows systems from this site is as a single Zip file. Once you have downloaded the Zip file, you can install PuTTY and its companion applications by creating a directory and extracting the contents of the Zip file into it. You can then start PuTTY like any other Windows application, by clicking on its icon.

Using FTP from Windows

FTP (File Transfer Protocol) is both the protocol for simple networked file transfers and the application that you execute to perform those sorts of transfers on most systems (including Windows). In terms of Microsoft's graphical standards, Windows provides a truly tragic version of FTP as part of all network-capable versions of Windows. However, it works, so it's hard to argue with that. And it should be immediately familiar to anyone who is familiar with using command-line FTP clients on other types of computer systems. Figure 8.13 shows the FTP client provided with Windows, in all its glory.

```
C:\WINNT\System32\ftp.exe                                    _|□|×|
ftp> open 192.168.6.246
Connected to 192.168.6.246.
220 You are in TiVo Mode.
220 Login isn't necessary.
220 Please hit ENTER at the login/password prompts.

User (192.168.6.246:(none)):
331 No Auth required for TiVo Mode.
Password:
230 Running in TiVo Mode.
ftp>
```

FIGURE 8.13 *The default Windows FTP client*

To transfer a file to or from your Windows system using the standard Windows FTP client, do the following:

1. Select the Start menu's Run command and enter "ftp" in the Open text entry box. The Windows FTP client displays, as shown in Figure 8.13.

2. Type the command "open <IP-Address>" in the FTP client window, where <IP-Address> is your TiVo's IP address. The FTP client displays a connection message, and eventually prompts you for the name of the user whom you want to connect to the TiVo. Since TiVos don't have user logins, press Return to continue.

3. The FTP client prompts you for the password of the user you are connecting as. Since TiVo's don't have user logins, press Return to continue.

4. The FTP client displays the standard "ftp>" prompt. At this point, you can use the commands shown in the following table to navigate to and transfer any file to or from your TiVo:

Common FTP Commands

FTP Command	Meaning	Action
bin	binary mode	Puts the FTP client into the mode necessary to transfer binary files.
cd <directory>	change directory	Changes to the specified <directory> on the TiVo.
get <file>	get file	Retrieves the specified <file> from the TiVo to your Windows system.
hash	display hashes	Causes the FTP client to display a hash mark ('#') for each 1K sent to or retrieved from the TiVo.
lcd <directory>	local change directory	Changes to the specified <directory> on your Windows system.
put <file>	put file	Sends the specified <file> to the TiVo from your Windows system.
quit	quit FTP client	Terminates the FTP session and the Windows FTP client.

That's all there is to it. As an example, a transcript of the commands that you would type in the FTP client to transfer the file **C:\sample.tar** to your TiVo's **/var** directory and exit the FTP client would be the following:

```
ftp> lcd c:\
Local directory now C:\.
ftp> cd /var
250 Directory change successful.
ftp> hash
Hash mark printing On  ftp: (2048 bytes/hash mark) .
ftp> bin
200 Type set to I.
ftp> put sample.tar
200 PORT command successful.
150 Opening BINARY mode data connection for KERNEL.
####
226 File transfer complete.
ftp: 11047 bytes sent in 0.00Seconds 11047000.00Kbytes/sec.
ftp> quit
```

TIP

If you're not excited by the performance or appearance of Windows' command-line FTP client, an excellent alternative is SmartFTP, which you can find at http://www.smartftp.com. You can download a version of SmartFTP for any flavor of Windows from http://www.smartftp.com/get/SFTPFull.exe. SmartFTP is free for personal, non-commercial use, although it turns into nag-ware after 30 days. If you're going to be using FTP in the future and need to talk to FTP servers directly, buying a copy of SmartFTP is a good investment. Figure 8.14 shows a sample SmartFTP screen after establishing an FTP connection to your TiVo. It's hard to argue that this isn't superior to the standard Windows FTP client shown in Figure 8.13.

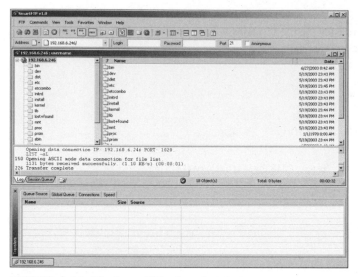

FIGURE 8.14 *The SmartFTP client for Windows*

Creating TiVo Tools Disks Under Windows

This book comes with the BATBD CD, a bootable TiVo tools disk that enables you to run Linux on your PC in order to perform the TiVo tasks and hacks discussed in this book. Though I believe that this contains a good selection of software for all Series 1 or Series 2 machines, any CD is just a software moment frozen in time. As new software or new versions of existing software becomes available, you're probably going to want to download and run it on your PC or TiVo. That isn't a problem for software designed to run on the TiVo, since you can download archive files to your PC, transfer them to your TiVo, and run the applications after unpacking the archives. If the software you're interested in runs under Windows, you have no problem at all and can install and execute it like any other Windows software. Even if the application you're interested in requires a Linux system, you can usually install and run it from a FAT-32 Windows partition, as explained in Chapter 10, "Getting and Installing New Software for Your TiVo," the section entitled "Running TiVo Software from Your PC."

However, if the TiVo software that you're interested in, for example, a new version of the BATBD CD, is only available as a CD-ROM image file, you may have a problem. CD-ROM images are usually referred to as ISO images because they contain images of a CD-ROM filesystem that is compliant with the International Standards Organization 9660 filesystem standard. Even if you have a CD/RW drive, Windows does not come with software that enables you to burn CDs from ISO images. Newer versions of Windows Media Player (8.x and greater) provide the ability to create CD playlists and burn audio CDs, but do not support burning CDs from ISO images.

Your CD/RW drive should have come with software to enable you to burn CDs from ISOs; if not, there are several excellent software packages on the Internet for doing this under

Windows. There are commercial software packages that provide a demonstration mode that you can use to burn CDs in emergencies or until you decide to purchase the software. Since the companies that wrote and supported these packages were cool enough to provide usable demonstration versions, you should be cool enough to actually pay for them after using them—but that's a philosophical issue. The two packages that I recommend for burning CDs under Windows are the following:

◆ Ahead Software's "Nero-Burning ROM" package. Ahead Software's Web site is http://www.nero.com/en, and you can download a demonstration copy of Nero from http://www.nero.com/en/content/download.html. The latest version at the time this book was written was Version 5.5. Aside from having one of the funniest and coolest names of any burning software that I've ever used, Nero is a great, usable package with a nice GUI that makes it easy to burn a CD from an ISO, or create lists of files that you want to burn to audio or data CDs. Figure 8.15 shows the "Nero-Burning ROM" software in action. You can purchase a license for this software for $49 if you download the software over the net rather than a physical CD. (You can always burn one using the software. ;-))

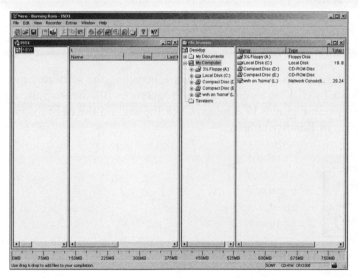

FIGURE 8.15 *The Nero-Burning ROM CD-burning software for Windows*

◆ VSO Software's Blindwrite Suite. VSO Software's Web site is http://www.vso-software.fr, and you can download a demonstration copy of Blindwrite Suite from the URL, http://www.vso-software.fr/download.htm. Blindwrite Suite is a simple, easy-to-use package that makes it almost trivial to burn a CD from an ISO, although it also supports creating audio and data CDs from lists of files that you assemble. Figure 8.16 shows the Blindwrite Suite software in action. You can purchase a license for this software for $29 if you download the software over the net.

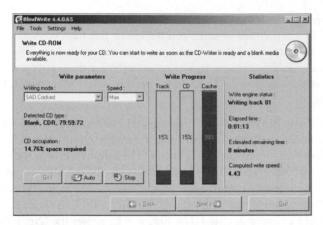

FIGURE 8.16 *The Blindwrite Suite CD-burning software for Windows*

There are plenty of other packages available to do this sort of thing—these are just my favorites. Of the two, I find Blindwrite Suite simpler for burning CDs from ISOs. Your mileage may vary.

After downloading and installing Blindwrite Suite, the procedure for using it to burn a CD from an ISO is as follows:

1. Double-click the desktop shortcut created when installing the software or execute Blindwrite Suite by clicking its entry in the Programs -> Blindwrite Suite menu. The dialog box shown in Figure 8.17 displays. Click the icon on the right to start the CD burning portion of Blindwrite Suite.

FIGURE 8.17 *Starting the Blindwrite Suite application*

2. If you're using the demonstration version of the software, the dialog box shown in Figure 8.18 displays. Click Test to continue (or enter the license that you received when you purchased the software, and then click Unlock). Accept the license that displays in the next dialog box (not shown—we've all seen licenses before).

3. The primary Blindwrite Suite dialog box displays, as shown in Figure 8.19. Make sure that the "Start CD writing wizard" entry is selected and click Next.

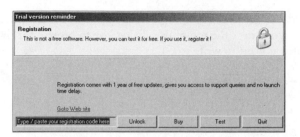

FIGURE 8.18 *Blindwrite Suite's register or demonstration dialog box*

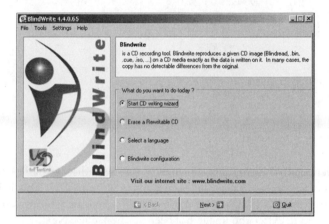

FIGURE 8.19 *Blindwrite Suite's Primary Tasks dialog box*

4. The "Select a CD-Writer" dialog box displays, as shown in Figure 8.20. If your CD writer is not already selected, click the drop-down arrow at the right of the dialog box and select the CD writer that you want to use from the drop-down list. After you've selected your CD writer, click Next.

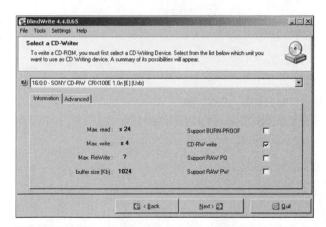

FIGURE 8.20 *Blindwrite Suite's Select CD Writer dialog box*

5. The "Select a CD-ROM Image" dialog box displays, as shown in Figure 8.21. Click the leftmost of the three icons near the top of this dialog box to browse for the location of the ISO file that you want to write to CD.

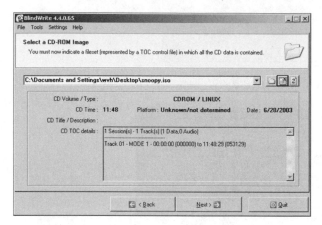

FIGURE 8.21 *Blindwrite Suite's Select CD Image dialog box*

6. The "CD Image verification" dialog box shown in Figure 8.22 displays. Click Start to verify the consistency of the ISO image that you want to write to CD. This is handy to verify that no errors were introduced when downloading and to avoid wasting a CD by burning crap to it. After the image has been verified, click Next.

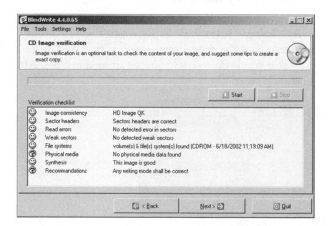

FIGURE 8.22 *Blindwrite Suite's CD Image Verification dialog box*

7. The "Write CD-ROM" dialog box shown in Figure 8.23 displays. Click Go! to begin burning the CD. The dialog box displays the progress of the write process.

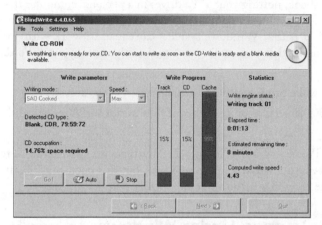

FIGURE 8.23 *Blindwrite Suite's Write CD-ROM dialog box*

8. After the CD has been written successfully, the summary "CD writing complete" dialog box shown in Figure 8.24 displays. Click Quit to exit Blindwrite Suite. You can now eject the CD you just burned by pressing the Eject button on the drive or by right-clicking on its entry in the "My Computer" dialog box and selecting the Eject command from the context-sensitive menu.

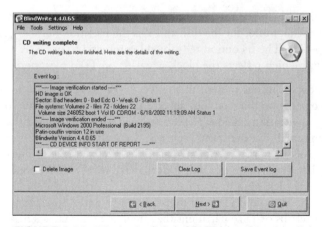

FIGURE 8.24 *Blindwrite Suite's CD Writing Complete dialog box*

After ejecting the CD, you can reinsert it in your CD drive to verify its readability, or simply shut down Windows and boot from the CD to try the one true test. As you can see from this process, burning a CD from an ISO under Windows is quite easy, and probably takes less time than downloading the ISO itself.

TiVo Disks and Windows Systems

As discussed earlier in this book, putting your TiVo drives in a personal computer that you can boot using the BATBD CD is a critical step in doing most TiVo hacking. The reason that you boot from the BATBD CD is that Windows systems can't read or work with TiVo disks. There are two primary reasons that you would want to directly access your TiVo disks from Windows:

◆ To use Windows while browsing the contents of your TiVo filesystems.

◆ To simplify copying large files or a number of files from your Windows disk to your TiVo disk.

Even if you can't access TiVo disks from Windows directly, there are easy solutions to both of these problems. There may be a few warts in the solutions, but this book is all about hacking, right? Perhaps you'll come up with a better solution—if so, please let me know!

Exploring ext2 Disk Images Under Windows

As discussed in Chapter 5 in the section entitled "Creating Image Backups Using **dd**," after booting your personal computer using the BATBD CD and selecting a boot option that provides access to TiVo partitions, you can use the **dd** command to create an image backup of a specific partition from your TiVo disk. You can create this image backup by using a command like the following:

```
dd if=<partition> of=<backup-file> bs=32k
```

This command tells the **dd** command to read from the disk specified as <disk> (probably one of **/dev/hdXY**, where **X** is the identifier for the disk and **Y** is the partition number), and write to the output file <backup-file>. The **bs** option tells the **dd** command to use 32K as both the input and output block sizes, which reflects the block size used on TiVo filesystems.

Some interesting hacking opportunities present themselves to Windows users once you have an image backup of a TiVo partition that contains an **ext2** filesystem. Specifically, you can use a freely available Windows application called *explore2fs* to browse the contents of the partition image as though it were an actual disk partition. Figure 8.25 shows the explore2fs application examining an image backup of one of my TiVo's **ext2** partitions. Pretty amazing! The explore2fs utility can't be used to update the disk images, but it does make it easy to use your Windows system to browse a TiVo's **ext2** filesystem to your heart's content, learning the location of files, viewing the contents of bash, TCL, and iTCL command scripts, and so on. Remember that this only works for image backups of TiVo partitions that are in **ext2** format, such as partitions 4 (your root or backup root filesystem), 7 (your root or backup root filesystem), and 9 (the **/var** partition) of any primary TiVo disk.

Versions of the explore2fs application for Windows 95 and NT are available in the Windows directory of the CD included with this book or from its Web site at http://uranus.it.swin.edu.au/ ~jn/linux/explore2fs.htm. This application worked fine on my Windows 2000 system, so I would

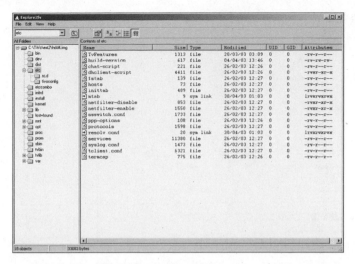

FIGURE 8.25 *Exploring an ext2 filesystem image under Windows*

assume that it will work on versions of Windows such as 98, ME, and XP. You can download the application itself from http://uranus.it.swin.edu.au/~jn/explore2fs/explore2fs-1.00pre6.zip. This is a prerelease, but it's free and worked great for me.

Once you've downloaded the explore2fs archive, extract its contents into a directory in your system and copy an image backup of one of your TiVo's **ext2** partitions to that same directory. Open explore2fs, select the File menu's Open File command, navigate to the disk image, and click Open. The explore2fs application displays a collapsed version of the **ext2** filesystem in the All Folders pane at the left. Click the plus sign to expand the image, and voila! All of the directories in the filesystem image display in the All Folders pane, while any files or symbolic links in a selected directory are listed in the pane at the right of the explore2fs application. You can then use standard Windows techniques to navigate through the filesystem. If you find a file that you actually want to examine, right-click on the filename in the right pane and select View from the context-sensitive menu. The explore2fs application invokes your default viewer, and you can explore the file to your heart's content. Figure 8.26 shows the file **/etc/rc.d/rc.sysinit** displayed in WordPad.

Admittedly, exploring an **ext2** filesystem image is only an interesting hack. Not having the ability to change the files is something of a drag, and it would (of course) be nicer if Windows could simply understand TiVo partition maps as well as **ext2** filesystems. There are some useful applications for Windows that understand **ext2** filesystems, the most promising of which is the Paragon Software Group's MountEverything software (http://www.mount-every-thing.com). Available for $39.95 from their Web site, this software enables you to mount **ext2** and **ext3** partitions from Windows 95, 98, ME, XP, NT, and 2000 systems, as well as access NTFS partitions from Windows 95, 98, and ME. Maybe if we all ask them really nicely... I know I have!

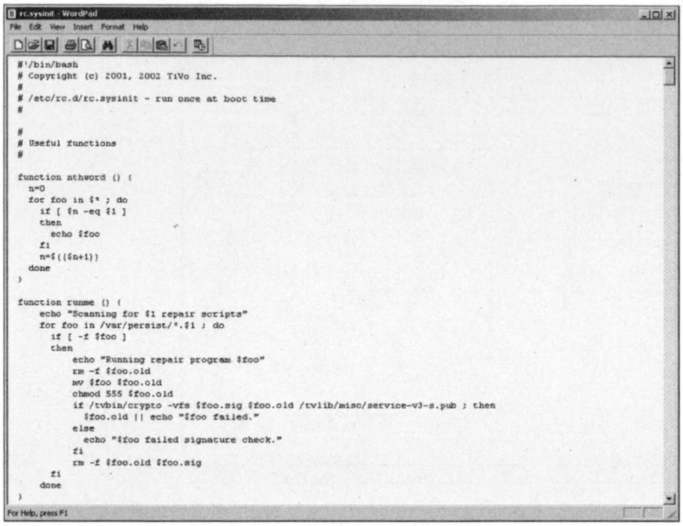

FIGURE 8.26 *Viewing a file from an **ext2** filesystem image under Windows*

Accessing Windows Disks from Your TiVo

The corollary of accessing TiVo disks from Windows systems is accessing Windows disks from TiVo systems. If you've put your TiVo on your network, you can take advantage of the power of Linux to mount any shared Windows disk on your TiVo. File copying doesn't get much easier than that.

The keys to mounting shared Windows disks on your TiVo are a loadable kernel module (**smbfs.o**) that knows how to access Windows shares via the SMB (Server Message Block) protocol, and a companion application (**smbmount**) that knows how to mount SMB filesystems on a Linux directory. These are both located in the BATCD's **hack_dirs/smb** directory. To use these to mount a Windows share on your TiVo, do the following:

1. After transferring **smbfs.o** and **smbmount** to your TiVo, load the **smbfs.o** module into the kernel using the following command:

   ```
   insmod -f -s smbfs.o
   ```

   This command inserts the module into the running TiVo kernel, forcing the kernel to ignore version differences and redirecting any error messages from the module to the system log (**/var/log/messages**).

2. Remount the TiVo's root filesystem so that the system can update the file containing the list of mounted filesystems (**/etc/mtab**). To remount the root filesystem in read/write mode, execute the following command:

   ```
   mount -o rw,remount /
   ```

3. Use the **smbmount** command to mount a share from your Windows system using a command like the following:

```
./smbmount //<system>/<share> <mountpoint> -U <user> -P <password> -I <IP-address>
```

When executing this command, <system> is the Windows name of your Windows system; <share> is the name of the Windows share that you are mounting; <mountpoint> is the name of the directory on your TiVo where you want to mount the Window share; <user> is your username on the Windows system; <password> is your password; and <IP-address> is the IP address of the Windows system. Using an IP address rather than a host name is necessary because your TiVo does not run DNS or the Windows equivalent (WINS), and therefore can't map the host name of your Windows system to its IP address without your help.

A sample command to mount a share named TiVo from the Windows host named win2k on the mountpoint **/var/mnt/win** using the username wvh, password guessme, and where the IP address of the host win2k is 192.168.6.244 would be the following:

```
./smbmount //win2k/TiVo /var/mnt/win -U wvh -P guessme -I 192.168.6.244
```

After executing this command, your Windows disk would be available through the TiVo's **/var/mnt/win** directory, and you would have the same privileges there as the user whose name and password you specified.

 NFS, ANYONE?

As discussed in Chapter 9, "Linux and the TiVo," in the section entitled "NFS," the TiVo supports the NFS (Network File System) distributed filesystem protocol, just like any other Linux system. There are a number of NFS utilities available for Windows systems, the least expensive of which is LabTam's ProNFS (http://pronfs.com, $40). While a demonstration version of this software is available, it times out too quickly to be useful to your TiVo in demonstration mode. Another alternative is installing Cygwin (http://www.cygwin.com), which is a complete GNU/Linux environment for Windows systems. As a complete GNU/Linux system, Cygwin provides built-in support for NFS and works just like NFS under standard, desktop Linux. Unfortunately, Cygwin is far outside the scope of this book—it deserves its own.

Integrating Windows Systems with TiVo's Home Media Option

Shortly after the release of Version 4.0 of the TiVo software, TiVo unveiled its long-awaited Home Media Option (HMO). Available only for Series 2 models and priced at $99 for your first TiVo (and $49 for each additional TiVo), the Home Media Option provides some exciting extensions to the functionality of your TiVo. The most impressive of these are as follows:

◆ You have the ability to share recordings between networked, HMO-enabled TiVos, known in TiVo terms as *multi-room viewing*. You can record a show on one of your TiVos and easily watch it on another by transferring it there over your home network. You can also browse the Now Playing lists of other HMO-enabled TiVos to more easily select shows from them.

◆ You have the ability to schedule recordings over the Internet. You can connect to tivo.com to schedule recordings up to 30 minutes before an actual broadcast if your HMO-enabled TiVo is on a home network with an always-on, broadband connection to the Internet.

◆ You have the ability to access online music and digital photographs from any HMO-enabled TiVo. This is especially attractive to TiVo owners whose TiVo is part of a high-quality, home theater setup (although it works for me, too).

◆ You have the ability to export collections of MP3 files and playlists from Windows and Macintosh systems using platform-specific software called the *TiVo Desktop*. You can play online audio files in MP3 format, and can use playlists in the ASX, M3U, and PLS formats used by most online audio players.

◆ Your have the ability to export collections of digital photographs from Windows and Macintosh systems using platform-specific software called the *TiVo Desktop*. You can view digital photographs saved in the BMP, DIB, GIF, JPG, and PNG file formats.

Most of these features are well documented on the TiVo Web site. The next section focuses on exploring some of the in and outs of exporting MP3 files from Windows systems using the TiVo Desktop, providing a few tips and tricks along the way.

Installing and Using the Windows TiVo Desktop

You can download the Windows version of the TiVo Desktop from the TiVo Web page at http://www.tivo.com/4.9.4.1.asp. After you download and install it, export your MP3 collections (known as *publishing* in TiVo Desktop terms), so that you can access them from any HMO-enabled TiVo. To do so, perform the following steps:

1. Select the TiVo Publisher command from the Start -> Programs -> TiVo Desktop menu on your PC. The TiVo Desktop displays, as shown in Figure 8.27.

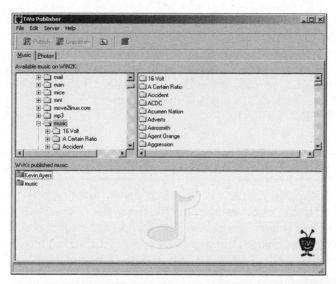

FIGURE 8.27 *TiVo Publisher for Windows via the TiVo Desktop menu*

2. To export a directory containing MP3 files, use the directory tree in the upper left corner of the TiVo Publisher to navigate to the directory that you want to export. Once you've found a directory that you want to publish, click the Publish button on the TiVo Publisher toolbar. Figure 8.28 shows the TiVo Publisher after navigating to and exporting a directory of music by The Cynics.

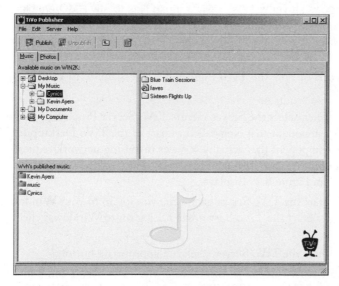

FIGURE 8.28 *Publishing a directory of MP3 files in the TiVo Publisher*

That's all there is to it——the TiVo Desktop is as easy to use as you would hope that a Windows program should be. Any directories of MP3 files and playlists that you publish from the TiVo Publisher will be visible on your TiVo under the TiVo Central -> Music & Photos menu. The name of a TiVo Server on a Windows system is created by combining your login name on your PC and the Windows name of that PC. For example, my Windows box is named "win2k" and my login there is "wvh", so my published collections show up on my TiVo as "Wvh's Music from WIN2K."

TiVo   SHARING FILES FROM LINUX SYSTEMS USING SAMBA

Samba is an application that you can run on a Linux system to export selected Linux directories so that they can be accessed from Windows systems, exactly as if they were standard Windows shares. Samba also includes applications that enable you to access standard Windows shares from your Linux systems. Explaining how to install and configure Samba on your Linux system is outside the scope of this book—there are already books dedicated to that topic.

If you are storing your MP3 audio files on a Linux system, you can make these files available to HMO-enabled TiVos by running the Personal TiVo Home Media Option software on your Linux system, as explained in Chapter 9, "Linux and the TiVo," in the section entitled "Working With TiVo's Home Media Option from Linux." If you don't want to use that option, another option is to share the directory containing your Linux music archive using Samba, permanently mount it on your PC like any other network drive, and then publish that directory using the TiVo Publisher. The TiVo server running on your Windows server will then deliver those files to any HMO-enabled TiVo DVR, just as if they were stored directly on your Windows system.

To configure some aspects of how the TiVo Publisher delivers music to your TiVo, take the following steps:

1. In the TiVo Publisher, select the Server menu's TiVo Server Properties command. The TiVo Server is a component that is installed as part of the TiVo Desktop for Windows, and is the component that actually services incoming network requests for access to publisher music, and then delivers them from your PC to your TiVo. The dialog box shown in Figure 8.29 displays.

2. To automatically start the TiVo Server each time you log in to your Windows system, make sure that the "Start the TiVo Server when I log on to Windows" checkbox is selected.

3. To pause or terminate the TiVo Server, click the appropriate button.

4. To configure some aspects of the performance of the TiVo Server component, click the Performance tab at the top of the TiVo Server Properties dialog box. The dialog box shown in Figure 8.30 then displays.

FIGURE 8.29 *The TiVo Publisher's TiVo Server Properties dialog box*

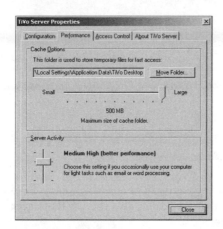

FIGURE 8.30 *The TiVo Server Properties Performance tab*

5. To change the size of the cache used when delivering audio files to a TiVo, drag the Cache Options slider to the right (to increase the size of the cache) or to the left (to decrease the cache size). When the TiVo requests a file, it is copied to the cache directory. Playing that song again will be faster if the song is already located in the cache. Changing the cache size determines the number of songs that can be cached. If the cache fills up, the oldest entries in the cache will be deleted to make room. Files are deleted from the cache, not from your music collection, of course!

6. To modify the amount of CPU time that your system dedicates to the TiVo Server process, drag the Server Activity slider up and down. The top setting, "High (best performance)," dedicates the majority of your PC's resources to the TiVo Server process, and should therefore be used only while your PC is essentially dedicated to exporting audio files and digital photographs. The lowest setting, "Low (moderate

performance)," should be used if you are actively executing processor-intensive tasks like audio/video editing, creating or editing large graphics files, or playing games. The two intermediate settings, "Medium (good performance)" and "Medium High (better performance)," can be selected to provide better trade-offs between local computing power and serving MP3 files and digital photographs.

7. To manage the Tivo DVRs that can access the collections of online audio and digital photographs that you publish using the TiVo Server, select the Access Control tab at the top of the TiVo Server Properties dialog box. The dialog box shown in Figure 8.31 then displays.

FIGURE 8.31 *The TiVo Server Properties Access Control tab*

8. To make your audio and digital photograph collections available to any TiVo that can access your home network, make sure that the "Allow all TiVo DVRs to access published media files" radio button is selected.

9. To limit the TiVo DVRs that can access your audio and digital photograph collections, select the "Only allow the selected TiVo DVRs to access media files" radio button, and then click the checkboxes next to the TiVo DVRs that you want to access your published files.

   Once you execute the TiVo Publisher, an icon for the TiVo Server displays in the system tray at the right or bottom of the Windows task bar. This icon indicates that the TiVo Server is running, and can be used to access the TiVo Server properties dialog boxes discussed previously, or you can shut down the TiVo Server. If you selected the "Start the TiVo Server when I log on to Windows" checkbox in the TiVo Server Properties dialog box, this icon also displays any time you reboot and login.

The TiVo Desktop is a great application if all of your online audio files are stored in MP3 format. What if they aren't? Luckily, third-party software exists that enables you to export collections of audio files in other formats to your HMO-enabled TiVos, as discussed in the next section.

Playing Windows Audio Formats Other than MP3

TiVo's Home Media Option uses open APIs that make it easy for software vendors to integrate it into their software. This is no surprise coming from a Linux and Open Source advocate like TiVo. TiVo sells TiVos, its service, and the Home Media Option that enables TiVos to play published collections of online audio files and digital photographs. Software vendors of digital audio and image software can integrate support for HMO into their software, enabling it to publish audio and image files in other formats. The end result of these sorts of partnerships is that life is better for everyone because users have more options, especially where non-MP3 audio files are concerned.

An excellent example of this is J. River's Media Center. Media Center software is easily integrated with your HMO-enabled TiVo and supports audio and video files in a zillion different formats, including a ton that I've never heard of. Most critical to Linux and Open Source fans is the Media Center's support for audio files encoded in the popular, Open Source OGG audio format. Windows fans should be delighted in the Media Center's support for audio formats such as ASX, ASF, WM, WAV, WAX, WMA, and RealMedia formats. Fans of classic audio file formats such as AIF, AIFC, AIFF, AU, and SND files will also be happy to know that J. River's Media Center enables them to publish audio in these formats so that they can be played through your TiVo. When used with the TiVo Home Media Option, my guess is that the Media Center converts files in all of these formats into MP3 on-the-fly and delivers the MP3 streams to your TiVo, but who cares—it works, and all my OGG files play fine through my HMO-enabled TiVos!

TIP

If your music is stored in OGG format, you're probably encoding and storing it on a Linux system (unless you're a very up-to-date Windows or Mac user who is clued in to the powerful, excellent, and Open Source OGG format). If you're storing your music on a Linux system and want to publish it to your HMO-enabled TiVo directly, check out the Personal TiVo Home Media Option software discussed in Chapters 9 and 10. This Open Source software enables you to publish music from your Linux box directly, without using Samba or any Windows-based software.

J. River's home page is http://www.musicex.com/mediacenter/index.html. You can download a 30-day demonstration version of the Media Center from http://www.musicex.com/mediacenter/download.html. After that, it's $39.95, which is a cheap price to pay for the power and flexibility it gives you.

NOTE

Even if you plan to use J. River's Media Center to publish your audio and digital image files to your HMO-equipped TiVo, you still will want to download and install the TiVo Desktop software as described in the previous section. The Media Center makes use of one of the components of the TiVo Desktop, the TivoBeacon, which advertises the presence of systems that are publishing music and digital images for use by HMO-enabled TiVos. The TiVo Server and J. River's Media Center can even run simultaneously on a single PC, though the rationale for doing so is unclear, and is straight from the Department of Redundancy Department.

After downloading and installing the Media Center software, the first time you execute the Media Center, it offers to search your disk for audio and digital image files in compatible formats, as shown in Figure 8.32.

FIGURE 8.32 *The Media Center's Import Media Files dialog box*

You can restrict this search to specific types of files by clicking Advanced and checking or unchecking various file formats. For more information about doing this, see the Media Center documentation. Now let's worry about interacting with your TiVo.

Once the Media Center has located files to publish, you can take the following steps to configure J. River's Media Center to serve files to any HMO-enabled TiVo DVR:

1. Within the Media Center application, enable its Media Server by selecting the Media Server command from the Tools menu's More Tools submenu. The dialog box shown in Figure 8.33 displays.

2. Select the Settings menu's Options command. The dialog box shown in Figure 8.34 then displays.

3. Click the Network icon at the left, and make sure that "Automatic port selection (recommended)" is selected, as shown in Figure 8.35.

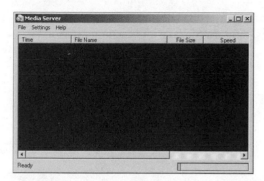

FIGURE 8.33 *The Media Center's Media Server dialog box*

FIGURE 8.34 *The Media Server's Options dialog box*

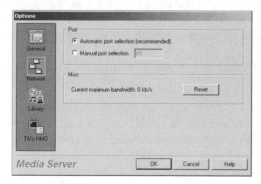

FIGURE 8.35 *The Network Panel in the Options dialog box*

4. Click the TiVo HMO icon at the left. The dialog box shown in Figure 8.36 displays. Click the "Support TiVo HMO on Port 8079 (with beacon on port 2190)" radio button, and make sure that the "Support all audio formats" checkbox is selected. Click OK.

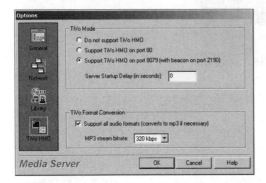

FIGURE 8.36 *The TiVo HMO Panel in the Options Dialog box*

5. If the Media Server is already running, a dialog box appears, displaying the message "Media Server is connected. Do you want to reconnect?" Click "Yes." If this dialog box does not appear, select the File menu's Share command to start the J. River Media Center's Media Server.

That's all there is to it. You can now go to any networked, HMO-enabled TiVo DVR, and browse and play music or display digital images exported by the Media Center. Any directories of audio files and playlists that are published by the Media Center will be visible on your TiVo under the TiVo Central -> Music & Photos menu. Much like the TiVo Server, the name of the Media Center on a given Windows system is created by combining your login name on your PC and the Windows name of that PC. For example, my Windows box is named "win2k" and my login there is "wvh", so my published collections show up on my TiVo as "wvh's Media Center Music on WIN2K".

As you might suspect, J River's Media Center is much more than an alternative to the TiVo Publisher, but discussing its other bells and whistles is outside the scope of this book. For more information about J. River's Media Center and other configuration options, see its documentation. And, buy a copy of the software.

TiVos and Mac OS X

Today's Macintosh computer and its operating system are truly works of art. Macs have always been the sexiest computers around, both in terms of appearance and usability. The Macintosh pioneered the graphical user interfaces in the home computer market, even though they got the idea for the GUI from Xerox PARC like everybody else. The Macintosh operating system, now simply known as Mac OS, has always been incredibly usable and eminently user-friendly.

The latest version of the Mac OS, known as Mac OS X, is better than ever before, largely because Apple used the NeXT Computer's NeXTStep and its underlying Mach operating system as the underpinnings of Mac OS X. As a Unix sysadmin for over 20 years, I never thought that I would see any version of Unix on the shelf at my local CompUSA, even in my wildest, nerdiest dreams. First, there was Linux, and now there's the Mac OS X—Unix-like systems with actual usable GUIs. Was that a pig that just flew overhead? What is next? Are the Cubs going to win the World Series?

As a popular personal computer operating system and as a system with its conceptual roots in Unix, Mac OS X is a natural for developing applications for and interacting with your TiVo. The fact that Mac OS X runs a Unix-like operating system makes it easy to port various TiVo software to Mac OS X, such as the BlessTiVo software discussed later in this chapter.

The remainder of this chapter discusses how to interact with your TiVo from your Mac OS X system, how to burn copies of TiVo Tools disks on Mac OS X from ISO images that you download, some cool hacks for exploring TiVo filesystem images on your Mac OS X box, and how to configure your Mac to export MP3 files to any networked, Home Media Option-enabled TiVo Series 2 DVR.

TiVo Disks and Mac OS X Systems

As discussed earlier in this book, putting your TiVo drives into a personal computer that you can boot using the BATBD CD is a critical step in doing most TiVo hacking. Unfortunately, booting from this CD requires a Pentium personal computer. Fortunately, there are a few things that you can do from your Mac OS X system without running Linux or having an x86-style PC—thanks largely to the fact that Mac OS X is based on Unix, which makes it much easier for Linux software to be recompiled for use under Mac OS X:

◆ Mount **ext2** partition images so that you can browse their contents from your Mac OS X system. This can be useful if you're familiar with using the Mac OS X Finder and want to use it to explore a TiVo filesystem while learning the bash, TCL, or iTCL command languages.

◆ Bless new TiVo disks from Mac OS X. While you can't interact with existing TiVo disks from Mac OS X, you can easily use the Mac OS X version of the BlessTiVo program (called OSXv4Blesser) to prepare a second disk that you can then add to your TiVo, expanding the space that it has available for storing recordings.

Even if you can't access TiVo disks from Mac OS X directly, there's still a fair amount that you can do for your TiVo from OS X. This book is all about hacking, right?

Exploring ext2 Disk Images Under Mac OS X

As discussed in Chapter 5 in the section entitled "Creating Image Backups Using **dd**," you can use the **dd** command on a Pentium-class system to create an image backup of a specific partition from your TiVo disk.

Some interesting hacking opportunities present themselves to Mac OS X users after you have an image backup of a TiVo partition that contains an ext2 filesystem (which you must have created on a Pentium system—sorry, but you can't read TiVo hard drives directly under Mac OS X). Specifically, you can install ext2 filesystem support on your Mac OS X system, transfer the filesystem image to your Mac, and then use the standard OS X disk image manipulation commands to mount and access and explore the filesystem image.

An alpha version of an ext2 filesystem for Mac OS X is available from SourceForge's Mac OS X Ext2 Filesystem project, located at http://sourceforge.net/projects/ext2fsx. The current version, at the time of this book's writing, is 1.0a3, which you can download as a mountable Mac OS X disk image from http://prdownloads.sourceforge.net/ext2fsx/Ext2FS_1.0a3.dmg? download.

After you've downloaded the disk image to your Mac OS X system, double-click it to mount the disk image on your desktop, and then double-click the file Ext2FS.pkg to begin the installation process. Ext2 support is provided through a Mac OS X kernel extension, so you'll be prompted for the administrative password for your system during the installation process; otherwise, installing ext2 support is exactly like installing application software on your OS X system.

After the ext2 kernel extension is installed, you will need to restart your system so that the kernel extension is correctly registered. At this point, the real fun begins! Transfer the ext2 filesystem image from the other system on which it is located, start the Mac OS X terminal application, and perform the following steps to mount the ext2 image on your Mac OS X system:

1. At the shell prompt, use the **sudo** command to execute the Mac OS X **hdid** command to map the filesystem image to a device on your Mac OS X system, using the following command:

    ```
    sudo hdid <image-file>
    ```

2. Replace <image-file> with the name of your ext2 filesystem image. The **sudo** command will prompt you for your system's administrative password. Enter that password and press the Return key.

    The **hdid** command will automatically load the ext2 filesystem driver and will mount the image file as UNTITLED. An icon for the filesystem image will appear on your Desktop, as shown in Figure 8.37.

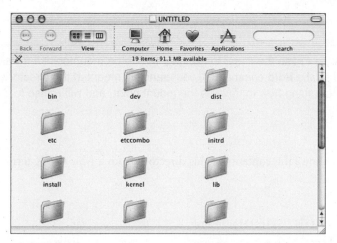

FIGURE 8.37 *Viewing a mounted TiVo filesystem image in the Finder*

Alternatively, you can mount the filesystem manually by performing the following steps:

1. At the shell prompt, use the **sudo** command to execute the Mac OS X **hdid** command to map the filesystem image to a device on your Mac OS X system, using the following command:

```
sudo hdid -nmount <image-file>
```

The **-nomount** option tells the **hdid** command not to mount the image, but just to map it to a device node. Replace <image-file> with the name of your ext2 filesystem image. The **sudo** command will prompt you for your system's administrative password. Enter that password and press the Return key.

The **hdid** command will return something like **/dev/disk1**, which is your new handle for the <image-file> that you want to mount.

2. Use the **sudo** command and the standard Mac OS X Mount command to mount the image on a directory on your Mac OS X system, using a command like the following:

```
sudo mount -t ext2 <handle> <mountpoint>
```

In this command, replace <handle> with the value returned from the **hdid** command (something like **/dev/disk1**), and replace <mountpoint> with the name of the directory on which you want to mount the TiVo ext2 filesystem image (something like **/mnt**, or the name of any other directory on your system).

That's all there is to it. At this point, you can use the terminal window or the Mac OS X Finder to navigate through the virtual TiVo filesystem that you've mounted.

NOTE

You will only be able to use the finder to navigate through a mountpoint if it was automatically created by the **hdid** command. If you manually mounted the directory, the Finder will not understand how to traverse the mount point, and will refuse to display its contents.

The following example shows the contents of this directory from a Mac OS X terminal window:

```
# ls /Volumes/UNTITLED
bin         etc         install     lost+found  proc        tmp         var
dev         etccombo    kernel      mnt         prom        tvbin
dist        initrd      lib         opt         sbin        tvlib
```

 TIP

As a good sysadmin, you should unmount the filesystem image before shutting down your Mac. You can do this using a command like the following:

```
sudo umount <mountpoint>
```

Where <mountpoint> is the directory on which you mounted the ext2 filesystem image.

Blessing a Disk Under Mac OS X

A TiVo devotee named Eric Wagner was kind enough to port the BlessTiVo utility to Mac OS X. While his old home page at mac.com is long gone, the Mac OS X version of BlessTiVo lives on thanks to the folks at Weaknees.com. You can download the Mac OS X version of BlessTiVo from http://www.weaknees.com/mactivo.php. The downloadable version of a StuffIt archive file containing a binhex version of the Mac OS X BlessTiVo application is located at http://www.weaknees.com/downloads/OSXv4Blesser.sit.hqx.

Most modern Macintosh towers contain one IDE drive and have a spare connection to which you can attach another. Open up your tower, jumper the IDE drive to be a slave, and connect it to the spare IDE connector on your system's primary IDE cable. You can usually place the second drive in the tray on top of the existing one (in the bottom of your Mac) while you're working with it.

Next, use StuffIt Expander to unpack the archive that you downloaded. This will produce a version of the BlessTiVo application that you can execute from the Mac OS X command-line inside a terminal window. The syntax of the command is as follows:

```
./OSXv4Blesser <device> <devicesize> <extratype> <extrasize>
```

The last two arguments are optional, and enable you to create additional partitions of types such as "swap" or "ext2." In this example, let's assume that you simply want to devote the entire drive to storage that your TiVo can use for recordings.

Figure 8.38 shows the OSXv4Blesser command's Help message when the command is executed with no arguments inside the Mac OS X Terminal application.

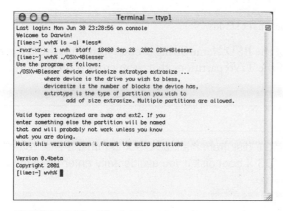

FIGURE 8.38 *The OSXv4Blesser's Help message in a terminal window*

The tricky parts of the OSXv4Blesser command are identifying the disk drive you've added to your Mac, and then determining how many blocks it has. To paraphrase Eric's original instructions:

> *"Now for the hard part, you need to determine how many blocks the drive has and under what /dev file its located. The best way I've found for this is IORegistryExplorer program provided by Apple as part of their development package/CD. The program presents a hierarchy that you traverse in the following layers:*
>
> *Root -> Computer -> PCI -> Bus -> Harddrive"*

After you traverse this tree to the level where you can actually see your drive (for example, something like "MAXTOR 4k080H4 Media"), you will see two properties: the BSD Name String, and the Size field. They will look something like the following:

```
BSD Name String disk0
Size Number 80026361344
```

When you have this information, you can determine the actual block count by dividing the specified number by 512. You then can run the OSXv4Blesser command, as in the following example:

```
sudo ./OSXv4Blesser /dev/<BSDname> <blockcount>
```

Where <BSDname> is the value of the BSD Name String property, and blockcount is the Size Number property divided by 512. The **sudo** command will prompt you for your system's administrative password, and then format the disk for use by the TiVo. The disk should then be ready to be added to your TiVo!

To verify that the blessing process worked correctly, re-execute the OSXv4Blesser command, as in the following example:

```
sudo ./OSXv4Blesser /dev/<BSDname> partitions
```

Where <BSDname> is the value of the BSD Name String property, and "partitions" is the word "partitions." This displays a list of the TiVo partitions that were created on the disk.

WARNING

Be very careful when blessing a disk from the Mac OS X command-line. You can easily destroy your current Mac OS X boot disk if you accidentally enter the wrong name. Enter a value and check it twice.

Creating TiVo Tools Disks Under Mac OS X

Unlike Windows, Mac OS X comes with an application that is capable of burning CDs from CD images that you have downloaded from the Internet. CD ROM images are usually referred to as ISO images because they contain images of a CD ROM filesystem that is compliant with the International Standards Organization 9660 filesystem standard. Even though you will not be able to run the majority of these on your Mac OS X system (or boot the system from any CDs that you create), you still may want to burn them on your Mac OS X system if your Mac is the only machine in your home with a CD burner.

The Disk Copy application provided with Mac OS X does an excellent job of burning CDs. This application is located in your Application folder's Utilities submenu. To create a CD from an ISO image using the Disk Copy Utility, take the following steps:

1. Start the Disk Copy application and select the File menu's Burn Image command. The Burn Image dialog box displays, as shown in Figure 8.39.

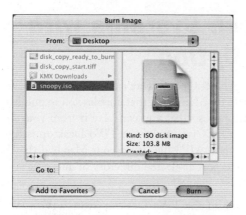

FIGURE 8.39 *Selecting an ISO Image in the Disk Copy utility*

2. Select the image that you want to burn to a CD and click the Burn button. After a bit of processing, the dialog box shown in Figure 8.40 displays. Click Burn to continue.

FIGURE 8.40 *Preparing to burn a CD using the Disk Copy utility*

3. The Disk Copy utility displays a progress bar as it burns the CD. When the CD is complete, the primary Disk Copy dialog box displays a success message, as shown in Figure 8.41.

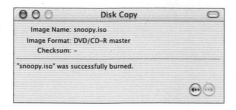

FIGURE 8.41 *A status message indicating successful CD creation*

After the status message displays, you can remove the CD from your CD burner and exit the Disk Copy utility.

Integrating Macintosh Systems with TiVo's Home Media Option

The general characteristics of the Home Media Option were explained earlier. TiVo provides a free version of the TiVo Desktop software for Mac OS X that enables you to publish all music or selected playlists from your iTunes Library so that you can play it from your networked, HMO-enabled TiVo. Unfortunately, the OS X version of the TiVo Desktop is tightly integrated with iTunes—so the only way to export MP3 files from your Mac is if they have been integrated into iTunes. You cannot simply export a selected directory of music, as you can with the Windows version discussed earlier in this chapter.

You can download the Mac OS X version of the TiVo Desktop from TiVo's Web page at http://www.tivo.com/4.9.4.1.asp. Once you download and install it, exporting your iTunes Library is almost trivial. To do so, take the following steps:

1. Start your OS X system's System Preferences application. This application is located in your Applications folder's Utilities folder.

2. Select the TiVo Desktop icon from the Other section at the bottom of the System Preferences dialog box. The Mac OS X TiVo Desktop displays, as shown in Figure 8.42.

3. To publish your entire iTunes Library, make sure that the "Publish my entire iTunes Library" radio button is selected. To publish only selected playlists, select the "Publish only these playlists" radio button and check the playlists that you want to publish.

4. If the TiVo Server is not already running on your Mac OS X system, click the Start button at the left of the TiVo Desktop dialog box. If a button labeled Stop displays at the left side of this dialog box, then your TiVo server is already running.

That's all there is to it! The name at the bottom of the TiVo Desktop dialog box shows the name under which you can find the music from your Mac in your TiVo's Music & Photos screen (TiVo Central -> Music & Photos).

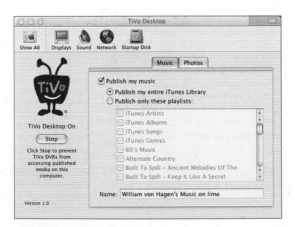

FIGURE 8.42 *The TiVo Desktop application on Mac OS X*

HACKING THE TiVo

Chapter 9

Linux and the TiVo

Linux is a freely available operating system that is gaining in popularity in the desktop, server, and embedded computing markets. The conceptual parent of Linux is the Unix operating system, written at Bell Labs in the 1970s. Many different versions of Unix have appeared since then, and Unix-like operating systems are the most popular operating systems used in server environments today.

One of the most attractive aspects of Linux as a Unix-like operating system is its source code that is downloaded easily from hundreds of sites on the Internet, which runs on a variety of hardware platforms and architectures including x86, MIPS, PPC, Super-Hitachi, SPARC, ARM, and XScale.

This chapter provides a basic introduction to Linux, its organization and operating model, the enhancements that TiVo, Inc. has made to Linux, and how to perform basic TiVo-related tasks under Linux.

Introduction to Linux and Open Source Software

Development of Linux began in 1991 when a Finnish college student named Linus Torvalds announced that he had begun work on a new operating system that was similar to MINIX. MINIX was a popular Unix-like operating system written by Professor Andrew Tanenbaum. It was widely used in academic circles because its complete source code was available in Tanenbaum's *Operating Systems* book. Written in the C programming language with some assembly language, MINIX was designed for 8086 systems, but provided a basic Unix-like environment and command set. Unfortunately, there were licensing requirements associated with doing extensive work or commercial deployments of MINIX, which made it unsuitable for wide deployment. In addition, MINIX was written as an academic tool rather than as an industrial-strength operating system.

Development of the Linux MINIX-like operating system was facilitated by the Open Software Foundation's GNU Project (http://www.gnu.org). Its goal was to develop a complete, free, Unix-like operating system and all the associated utilities. Founded by a legendary MIT hacker named Richard Stallman, the GNU Project popularized the concept of free software, which means that the source code for all GNU software is freely available and that the source code for subsequent enhancements made to GNU software also be made available. As the GNU Web site states, "Free software is a matter of liberty, not price." This principle of freely available program source code is known as *Open Source*, a term coined by Eric Raymond and popularized by the high quality and ideals of the GNU Project.

An operating system is just that—it operates your hardware, communicating with devices, scheduling and executing tasks, managing system-level resources such as memory, and so forth. However, without programs for users to execute, it isn't very exciting. The software being developed by the GNU Project was a perfect fit for a newly developed operating system. One of the earliest software packages developed by the GNU Project was GCC, the GNU C Compiler, an Open Source compiler for programs written in the C programming language.

GCC was designed to be easily portable to multiple operating systems, and comprised a complete development environment, which is tightly integrated with the GNU C Library that provides the function libraries that C programs require to run. The fact that most of the software from the GNU Project forms the core set of utilities that all Linux users depend on is the reason why Linux is often referred to as GNU/Linux.

Given a free C compiler and other applications, such as a command-line interpreter (bash) for actually running commands, Linux was born. In 1991, Linux sent a second, now famous e-mail message to subscribers of the comp.os.minix newsgroup, an Internet newsgroup dedicated to MINIX support and development. This message announced the wider availability of the Linux source code. GNU utilities such as bash, gcc, the GNU-make program, and others were successfully running on Linux. This was Linux 0.02. Since then, Linux has been ported to various platforms, extended by thousands of free utilities including a graphical user environment (GUI) based on MIT's X Window System, text editors, word processors, games, and just about everything else. And all of it is still free. While it is possible to buy CDs containing GNU Project and Linux software from a variety of companies, the charge for these CDs is for their packaging, production, and support—not for the GNU and core Linux software itself, which is and will always be free.

NOTE

The vendors of other operating systems, which are therefore competitors to Linux, like to confuse people by claiming that Open Source software is viral in nature, infecting any commercial products that it touches and spelling the end of commercial software products. This could not be further from the truth. GNU software conforms to licenses (GNU General Public License– (GPL), and Lesser GNU Public License –(LGPL)). The licenses guarantee that it will remain free, and they also explicitly state that no software that interacts with GNU software is affected by its Open Source nature unless it specifically incorporates code from Linux. These licenses also explicitly state that software compiled with Open Source libraries is not affected by their Open Source nature. So much for Fear, Uncertainty, and Doubt from companies such as Microsoft! The Open Source licenses used by Linux and the GNU Project are available at http://www.gnu.org/licenses/licenses.html. TCL and iTCL use the slightly different BSD License (for more information, see the section of this chapter that discusses TCL and iTCL).

Overview of the Linux Boot Process

The process of starting an operating system on a computer is known as *booting* the system, which refers to the old expression "pulling up one's self by your bootstraps." The heart of the Linux operating system is known as the *kernel*, which is compiled specifically for the different hardware architectures. When you boot a Linux system, the hardware loads a relatively small program known as a *boot-loader* from a special location on the disk, and then executes this bootloader. Next the boot-loader loads the kernel into memory and transfers control of the system to the kernel. The kernel probes the hardware and gathers information about its characteristics and the devices that are attached to the system, and then loads any device drivers that are required to communicate with that hardware.

Device drivers are small programs that are loaded by an operating system, and contain the specific sets of instructions necessary for the operating system to communicate with those devices (drives). In Linux, device drivers can be either compiled into the kernel or loaded separately. Each method has its advantages. Some device drivers are required for the kernel to communicate with a computer system's screen, disk drives, and other critical pieces of hardware, and are therefore compiled into the kernel. It would be impossible for the kernel to load a device driver from disk if it didn't understand how to obtain information from the drive at the hardware level. Similarly, the kernel must understand how information on that disk is organized so that it can find the specific data that it requires.

 NOTE

Device drivers that load separately are examples of what are known as *loadable kernel modules*. Device drivers that can load as modules are those that are for devices that aren't directly required by the boot process. As the name suggests, loadable kernel modules are complete sections of code that the kernel can load and they follow well-known conventions for integrating with it. Common examples of device drivers that are loaded as modules are drivers for network devices, sound cards, mice, special-purpose hardware such as USB or PCMCIA hardware, and so forth. All loadable kernel modules are not necessarily associated with specific physical devices. They also can be associated with logical devices and higher-level protocols, such as those used by network-based filesystems, kernel processes such as firewalling, and so forth.

Once the kernel loads into memory and completes its probe of the hardware, it sets a logical or physical device as its primary storage device (known as *mounting a filesystem*) and begins to execute programs from there.

Linux Filesystems and Initial RAM Disks

To access information on a storage device such as a hard disk, floppy disk drive, or CD ROM, the information on that device must be organized in a way that the computer can uniquely locate specific pieces of information. A *filesystem* is the term used for the organization of files and directories on a physical storage device such as a disk drive. Files are discrete sets of related information that the computer can locate and use. Directories provide a hierarchical way of organizing files, much like the drawers in a filing cabinet provide for the files that it contains.

As an example, a standard directory found in the initial filesystems used by most Linux system is a directory containing administrative and configuration information, **/etc**. The slash (/) at the beginning of the name of this directory indicates that it is available under the very top level of the Linux filesystem, which is known as the *root* of the filesystem. The directory /**etc** contains files such as those that provide information about users on the Linux system, which is stored in a file named /etc/passwd, and commands that the system should execute when it starts (stored in the directory /etc/rc.d, which stands for "Run Command Default"), and so on. Using a filesystem compromised of files and directories, known as a *hierarchical filesystem*, makes it easy for programs and users to locate files by name, as well as explore the contents of the filesystem by simply traversing the directory structure of the disk.

Linux supports many different types of filesystems, each with its own advantages and disadvantages. The types of standard Linux filesystems that are relevant to the TiVo are filesystems located on a Linux disk in a format known as EXT2 (Extended Filesystem 2), and in-memory filesystems known as initial RAM disks (also commonly referred to as an "initrd"). As we'll see later in this chapter in the section "TiVo Disk Information," TiVo also provides its own type of filesystem, known as MFS, which is a cross between a database and a filesystem that is specially designed to fulfill the performance and allocation requirements of recording and storing digital video in real-time.

Linux kernels can be set to use an in-memory filesystem known as an initial RAM disk as their initial root filesystem. These initial RAM disks are separate filesystems that are bundled into a Linux kernel when it is compiled, and provide certain advantages to a Linux system. In embedded systems that may not have disk drives attached, an initial RAM disk enables the system to boot without a disk, CD ROM, or floppy drive. Similarly, if the kernel requires that special device drivers load into the kernel, but you don't want to compile them into the kernel, they can be stored in an initial RAM disk and loaded from there.

TIP

RAM disks can be created in a number of formats, although those that are typically bundled into a kernel are either EXT2 or ROMFS filesystems stored in a compressed format known as *gzip* (GNU zip). By examining a kernel for the special sequence of bytes that identifies the beginning of a gzip file, you can extract an initial RAM disk from a compiled kernel. The extract_gzip.c file provided in the **src** directory of the CD that accompanies this book enables you to do just that. After uncompressing the extracted file (using the Linux command **gunzip FILENAME**), you can then mount this filesystem using a Linux command such as **mount -o loop FILENAME /mnt**. When mounted, it can be explored just like any other Linux filesystem.

When a Linux kernel that has been configured to use an initial RAM disk boots, it does the following:

◆ Formats a special portion of system memory to look like a disk drive.
◆ Loads the initial RAM disk into that portion of memory.

◆ Sets that RAM disk as its root filesystem.

◆ Executes any prespecified commands from that root filesystem, including loading any specified loadable kernel modules.

As the last stages of executing the startup commands specified in the initial RAM disk, the system typically mounts a standard Linux device as its "real" root filesystem, changes the / directory of its filesystem to that new device (known as "pivoting" to the new root filesystem), and begins executing commands from that filesystem.

Obtaining the Source Code for TiVo's Linux

As mentioned previously, Linux is and must remain Open Source, as are many of the utilities used by the version of Linux running on your TiVo. This means that TiVo must provide the source code for its version of Linux and any other Open Source utilities included in the software that ships with the TiVo. You can download these from the TiVo Web site at http://www.tivo.com/linux/index.html.

The downloadable files from TiVo for the current version of the TiVo OS (Version 4.0) are organized into several component files, organized into modules (loadable kernel modules), commands (GNU and other open source commands), libraries (GNU and other open source libraries for things such as MPEG encoding, display, and so on), Linux (the source for TiVo's kernel), and development (tools and libraries required for successful compilation and linking). Version 4.0 of the TiVo software is for only Series 2 machines, which use MIPS processors. The source code for earlier versions of TiVo's Linux kernel provides both PPC and MIPS versions.

 NOTE

It is important to differentiate between TiVo's use of Linux and TiVo's development and use of proprietary software. Your TiVo runs Linux as its operating system, but the user interface and many associated programs are all a proprietary product of TiVo, Inc. TiVo provides the code for the Open Source modules that help make your TiVo the great machine that it is. You will find the source code for the Open Source Linux utilities and libraries used by your TiVo on the TiVo Web site. You won't find the source for their proprietary tivoapp, myworld, or any similar programs there. We all want TiVo to survive, right? It's hard to do that if you give away your intellectual property.

Linux is completely supported on the MIPS platform, and many TiVo users actually use the **monte** approach discussed in Chapter 7, "Connecting the Universe to Your TiVo," to boot versions of Linux such as Debian-MIPS on their TiVos. Explaining how to integrate a standard version of Linux with the TiVo kernel, libraries, and command modifications is somewhat outside the scope of this book, but you can find lots of useful information on this topic on the TiVo forums discussed in Chapter 11, "Other TiVo Hacking Resources."

Overview of the TiVo Application Environment

Your TiVo is different from almost any other Linux system. For one thing, it's running in your living room. More seriously, your TiVo differs from a generic Linux system in a variety of user-level and system-level ways. This was necessary both to protect TiVo, Inc.'s intellectual property and to provide the performance and application environment required for a heavy-duty digital video recording appliance. Of course, this book is about hacking the TiVo, so I've already explained many of the ways that you can customize its startup sequence, configuration, and so on.

If you're already familiar with Linux, this section will help you identify aspects of the TiVo that are unique to its software and Linux configuration. If your TiVo is your first introduction to Linux, the topics in this section provide a convenient reference for things that you wouldn't expect to read about in generic Linux text.

The TiVo Startup Process

Like many computers, your TiVo boots from a Programmable Read-Only Memory chip (PROM). This PROM uses configuration information stored in permanent but rewritable memory (known as *flash memory*) to determine where to boot from, how to boot, and so on.

When you boot your TiVo, it first reads information about the location of your TiVo's root filesystem from the bootpage of your primary hard drive (which is stored in the first sector of the hard drive), and then checks the kernel partition associated with that root filesystem to verify that the kernel is correctly signed—in other words, that a value in the kernel header matches a calculated checksum for the kernel that it plans to boot. The kernel partition associated with a root filesystem is always one less than the partition identifier of the root filesystem. For example, if your root filesystem is set to **/dev/hda4**, the TiVo will first try to boot the kernel stored in the partition **/dev/hda3**. If this signature check fails, the TiVo attempts to boot from the other kernel/root filesystem pair on your disk. This initial check by the PROM against the contents of the kernel that you are trying to boot is the reason that you must boot a valid TiVo kernel/initrd combination as the first step in hacking a Series 2 machine, as explained in Chapter 7, "Connecting the Universe to Your TiVo."

Assuming that the TiVo has found a valid, bootable kernel and an initial RAM disk, it boots that kernel using the initial RAM disk as its primary root filesystem. The initial command executed from a TiVo's initial RAM disk is the file **/linuxrc** (Linux Run Commands). After temporarily mounting the system's actual root filesystem, this program performs a variety of system consistency checks, including checking the boot parameters with which you booted against hashed values stored in **/linuxrc** itself to verify that you haven't modified them. (Hence no more BASH_ENV hacks when your TiVo uses recent PROMs.) The most clever (or irritating) of which is to calculate SHA1 hash signatures of the majority of the files on the TiVo's actual root filesystem, and then compare them against values stored in a file called **/signatures** that is stored on the initial RAM disk. Files that do not match the precalculated signatures in the signatures file are simply deleted, with the exception of three files that are replaced with standard, unmodified TiVo versions if they don't pass the signature check. These files are as follows:

- ◆ */etc/rc.d/rc.arch* Command script containing architecture-specific startup commands
- ◆ */etc/rc.d/rc.sysinit* Command script containing diagnostic and startup commands
- ◆ */etc/inittab* Table of commands to run at various points during system initialization

The virgin copies of these three files are located in the **/fixes** directory in the initial RAM disk.

TIP

If you are hacking your TiVo, as described in Chapter 7, and receive the message "Can't find init" in your boot messages, you probably used a kernel/initrd combination with a signature file that didn't match the contents of your root partition. Your TiVo probably purged the root filesystem of files that didn't match. First, try to boot using your other root partition. If that fails, you will have to restore your root filesystem from an unstructured backup (best case), or completely restore your TiVo from a structured backup. It can happen to you—I have to confess that it has certainly happened to me.

If all of the previous tests have succeeded, your TiVo will execute the **/sbin/init** process, which will then execute the command script **/etc/rc.d/rc.sysinit**. This unmounts the initial RAM disk, performs various system consistency checks and diagnostics, checks for updates from TiVo, and then starts all of your favorite TiVo applications, such as the primary TiVo application or the myworld program.

TCL and iTCL

Though most GNU projects and Linux itself are primarily written in the C programming language, a wide variety of free programming languages are available for Linux systems. A very popular language, and the primary language used for most application development on TiVo systems, is the Tool Command Language (TCL). TCL is an interpreted language and associated interpreter for that language, and was written in 1988 by John Ousterhout.

iTCL, more formally known as "[incr TCL]," is a set of object-oriented extensions to TCL, designed to simplify the structure of complex TCL applications. iTCL adds support for objects to TCL, which can then be used as building blocks in iTCL/TCL applications. Objects consists of data structures and associated procedures (known as *methods*) that create, delete, and manipulate those objects. To further simplify things, objects are organized into classes that can inherit methods from others, or can override existing methods with methods more appropriate to a given class.

Both TCL and iTCL are Open Source projects hosted at http://www.sourceforge.net. The home page for TCL is located at http://sourceforge.net/projects/tcl. The home page for [incr TCL] is located at http://incrtcl.sourceforge.net/itcl.

Providing an in-depth guide to writing and debugging TCL and iTCL applications is outside the scope of this book; however, a variety of books on TCL are already available. Good online sources of information are the *TCL Reference Manual* at http://tmml.sourceforge.net/doc/tcl, and the [incr TCL] online reference information is located at http://www.tcl.tk/man/itcl3.1. A Web search for TCL, iTCL, or projects using them could keep you busy for days.

Many people initially find it odd that TiVo would select an interpreted language for initial GUI and user application development. Actually, given that TiVo began to develop and debug its software while the hardware that supported it was under development, using an interpreted language makes a lot of sense. Interpreted languages are often easier to debug than applications written in compiled languages, and they are inherently portable across different operating systems, Linux versions, and even different Linux platforms. I would assume that much of the early TiVo development was initially done on more common Linux platforms, such as x86 systems. At this point, little of the TiVo interface is written in TCL for performance reasons.

NOTE

If you've downloaded the updated Open Source code from TiVo's Web site, you will notice that it does not contain the source code for any modifications to TCL made by TiVo. TCL and, therefore, iTCL are released under a slightly different license than the GPL or LGPL license, known as the BSD license, which does not require this level of redistribution. For more information, see the general information about the BSD license at http://www.opensource.org/licenses/bsd-license.html .

TiVo's TiVoSH (tivosh) Application

Command scripts written for interpreted languages other than standard Linux shell commands typically identify the command interpreter that they are supposed to run under as the first line in the script. For example, Perl scripts typically begin with a line, such as the following, to tell the Linux command interpreter to execute these commands using the Perl interpreter:

```
#!/usr/bin/perl -w
```

TCL and iTCl scripts on the TiVo begin with the similar line:

```
#!/tvbin/tivosh
```

The previous section prepared you for finding lots of command scripts on your TiVo with extensions such as .tcl and .itcl, the extensions used by TCL and iTCL applications respectively. It may, therefore, be somewhat confusing that the most common command scripts found for the TiVo, even those posted on the Forums or Web sites discussed in Chapter 11, all invoke another application as their command interpreter, namely /tvbin/tivosh. The tivosh application is TiVo's enhanced version of TCL, and contains a large number of commands designed to make it easier to manipulate values and resources stored in the TiVo's MFS filesystem or by sending events to the primary TiVo applications. Tivosh is designed to use as a command-line application, so it has no direct control over the TiVo interface other than by manipulating the data that is used by the myworld application, the primary TiVo application.

NOTE

Like TiVo applications, such as myworld, the switcher, and many more, the actual **tivosh** command is actually a symbolic link to TiVo's monolithic "one app does all" application called *tivoapp*. These all were originally stand-alone applications, but began to be merged together in TiVo software release 2.0. Like the Linux **busybox** command (discussed later in this chapter), nowadays tivoapp does different things, depending on how it is called. For this reason, tivoapp clocks in at an impressive 16 MB in size.

Tivosh is based on TCL Version 8.0p2, using the TCLsh interpreter that it includes. Tivosh incorporates iTCL Version 3.0a1 and also adds a number of TiVo-specific commands to transactionally manipulate the MFS filesystem or to manage events on the TiVo. Given that most of the truly fun tivosh applications explore and manipulate the TiVo's MFS filesystem, see the sections later in this chapter entitled "MFS—TiVo's Media File System" and "Exploring MFS" for more detailed information (and examples) of using **tivosh**.

WARNING

Never type Control-c to exit from the tivosh application once you have executed any command there that accesses the TiVo's MFS filesystem—this will cause your TiVo to reboot instantly. Instead, use the **exit** command.

TiVo Disk Information

Because the TiVo Series 1 used a Power-PC processor, these TiVos inherited much of their disk formatting and layout information from applications originally developed for various versions of PowerPC Linux for Macintosh computer systems. Because PowerPC Linux had to understand the disk formats and disk partition layout used by Macintosh systems, the Series 1 machines based their disk layout and organization on the Macintosh partition format. The final partition table used in the TiVos is very close to the Macintosh partition format, but is slightly different at the kernel-level. By the time that the MIPS-based Series 2 models were released, information about this partition format was too deeply ingrained into the TiVo software to remove. Consequently, today's MIPS-based TiVo still uses the Apple partition format, even though the data itself is now byte-swapped compared to the TiVo Series 1.

The following sections discuss the organization of Apple Macintosh disks, explain the different types of partitions used on each, and then provide a detailed discussion of TiVo's own MFS filesystem, specially designed to support the requirements of real-time video recording and playback.

TiVo Disk and Partition Map

If you've ever installed a computer system or disk drive from scratch, you'll remember that one of the first steps in the process is partitioning and formatting the drive. Partitioning a drive divides it into discrete sections that are formatted separately and therefore can be separately addressed by your operating system.

NOTE

A slight extension of the partitioning concept is extended partitions, which is a special type of partition that contains other logical partitions. These extended partitions are largely an artifact of the disk drive sizes that grew faster than the ability of some operating systems to make use of the huge amounts of the additional space.

If you have hacked into your TiVo and want to look at the organization of your disk, you may be tempted to use the **df** command, which shows the disk usage for all mounted filesystems. This command returns something like the following, which isn't exactly what we wanted:

```
# df
Filesystem          1K-blocks     Used Available Use% Mounted on
/dev/hda7           10080488    988948   8579472  11% /
/dev/hda1             101089     29810     66060  32% /boot
/dev/hda8           30668576  23059468   6051208  80% /home
none                  515532         0    515532   0% /dev/shm
/dev/hda2            2016044      2276   1911356   1% /tmp
/dev/hda5           20161172   4249740  14887292  23% /usr
/dev/hda6           15116836   2918980  11429952  21% /usr/local
/dev/hdd1          196015808  76972756 109085968  42% /opt2
```

The numbers in the device names at left show the organization of each mounted partition on each disk. On a standard Linux system, what we actually need is the output of the **fdisk** command, which presents something like the following:

```
# fdisk -l /dev/hda
 Disk /dev/hda: 255 heads, 63 sectors, 10011 cylinders
Units = cylinders of 16065 * 512 bytes

    Device Boot    Start      End     Blocks    Id  System
/dev/hda1    *        1       13     104391    83  Linux
/dev/hda2            14      268    2048287+   83  Linux
/dev/hda3           269      395    1020127+   82  Linux swap
/dev/hda4           396    10011   77240520     f  Win95 Ext'd (LBA)
/dev/hda5           396     2945   20482843+   83  Linux
/dev/hda6          2946     4857   15358108+   83  Linux
/dev/hda7          4858     6132   10241406    83  Linux
/dev/hda8          6133    10011   31158036    83  Linux
```

The **fdisk** command is used on standard Linux systems. To examine the partition map on a Macintosh-format drive, you must use the **pdisk** command, which was discussed in detail in Chapter 4, "The Hacker's Tool Chest of TiVo Tools."

TIP

To view disks formatted on Macintosh systems from a standard Linux system, your kernel must support the Macintosh partition map format, which is located on the Partition Types menu in the File Systems section of your Linux kernel configuration menus. You also must have a version of the **pdisk** program on your system to interpret the filesystem map.

Sample output from the **pdisk** command is as follows:

```
# pdisk -l /dev/hdd
 Partition map (with 512 byte blocks) on '/dev/hdd'
 #:                type name              length   base    ( size )
 1: Apple_partition_map Apple                 63 @ 1
 2:              Image Bootstrap 1          4096 @ 64      ( 2.0M)
 3:              Image Kernel 1             4096 @ 4160    ( 2.0M)
 4:               Ext2 Root 1             262144 @ 8256    (128.0M)
 5:              Image Bootstrap 2          4096 @ 270400  ( 2.0M)
 6:              Image Kernel 2             4096 @ 274496  ( 2.0M)
```

7:	Ext2 Root 2	262144 @ 278592	(128.0M)
8:	Swap Linux swap	260096 @ 540736	(127.0M)
9:	Ext2 /var	262144 @ 800832	(128.0M)
10:	MFS MFS application region	1048576 @ 1062976	(512.0M)
11:	MFS MFS media region	24777728 @ 2111552	(11.8G)
12:	MFS New MFS Application	1024 @ 26889280	
13:	MFS New MFS Media	17104896 @ 26890304	(8.2G)
14:	Apple_Free Extra	4000 @ 43995200	(2.0M)

The first block of an Apple format disk drive contains the disk's partition map and boot information. As shown in the above list, partitions 2, 3, 5, and 6 contain raw data that is not in any recognizable filesystem format. Partitions 2 and 5 contain the TiVo's bootstrap code, loaded by the TiVo's PROM. Partitions 3 and 6 contain the TiVo's Linux kernel—one is a primary, and the second is used as a failsafe. (If you've hacked a Series 2 machine running TiVo's Version 4.0 software as explained in Chapter 7, one contains your original TiVo kernel, and the other one contains your hacked kernel image.)

Partition 8 is used as swap space by Linux, which is a specially formatted partition that Linux can use to store sections of programs from memory when they are not actually running, such as when they are waiting for user input or other events. This enables a Linux system to appear to have more memory than it physically contains. Inactive applications or code pages can be written to disk; the physical memory associated with them can be reused, and the programs can be loaded again from swap space when they are ready to run. This is known as *virtual memory*.

Partitions 4, 7, and 9 are standard Linux partitions in the standard Linux ext2 partition format. Partitions 4 and 7 are the root filesystems associated with the kernels in partitions 3 and 6, respectively. (Only one of partitions 4 and 7 is used at any given time—you can really only have one root partition at a time.) Partition 9 is the ext2 partition that is mounted as **/var** on a running TiVo, and is used to hold variable data.

The most interesting and unique aspects of a TiVo disk are partitions 10, 11, 12, and 13, which are TiVo Media File System (MFS) partitions. Discussed in more detail in the next section, MFS partitions are not mounted as are ext2 partitions, but are addressed directly through a library of MFS access functions provided on your TiVo.

The last partition of the sample TiVo disk drive is Partition 14, which is free space that cannot be allocated to any partition. If you've hacked your Series 2 system as explained in Chapter 7, you'll remember that all of the Series 2 hacks take advantage of this free space—if not, you have something to look forward to.

TIP

Disks using an Apple-style partition map can have a maximum of 16 partitions.

MFS—TiVo's Media File System

MFS stands for the Media File System, and is a hybrid of a filesystem and database that was created by TiVo. Unlike most classic filesystems, MFS partitions are not mounted to use, but accessed through a user-space library. For this reason, you will not find TiVo's MFS filesystem listed in the kernel configuration options in the TiVo kernel source.

Each MFS filesystem actually consists of a pair of allocated partitions. Each has an MFS Application Region that holds administrative and internal information, and an MFS Media Region where data is actually stored. There currently can be no more than 6 MFS partition pairs present on all of the disk drives in a TiVo system.

For the most part, MFS is a simple database populated by four types of elements:

- ◆ Directories (tyDir)
- ◆ Files (tyFile)
- ◆ Objects (tyDb)
- ◆ Streams (tyStream)

In MFS, each directory, file, and stream is indexed by a unique number called a filesystem ID (fsid). Many different Objects can be associated with a single Filesystem ID, leading to the subobjects mentioned earlier. Filesystem IDs are allocated incrementally for each new element that is created in an MFS filesystem, and provide a mechanism for objects to reference other elements within MFS, much as inodes do in a traditional Unix and Linux filesystems. Unlike standard Linux filesystems, where inode numbers are specific to a given filesystem, filesystem IDs are allocated sequentially across all MFS filesystems in a TiVo.

Exploring MFS

As explained in the previous section, MFS stores four basic types of information in different types of elements. The following sections provide more details about certain aspects of MFS and explain how to access them. These sections provide some examples that will help you get started exploring MFS on your own. Maybe TiVo will even document it at some point....

TIP

As with most hacking in general, much of the information about the contents and organization of MFS filesystems has been found by exploring and reverse-engineering the filesystem. The tivosh application is your friend!

Exploring Directories in TiVo's Media File System

One of the tivosh application's most useful commands is **mls**, which enables you to list an MFS directory. The **mls** command is equivalent to the **ls** command in Linux or the DIR command in DOS and Windows, and it provides a directory listing relative to some point in the MFS filesystem. The tivosh environment does not have the notion of a current directory, and so always requires an argument that begins at the root of the MFS filesystem. The **mls** command also only lists the first 50 commands in the specified directory—you must specify a prefix to use when listing subsequent entries.

A sample listing of the root of your MFS directories produced by **mls** looks like the following:

```
bash-2.02# tivosh
% mls /
Directory of / starting at ''
```

Name	Type	FsId	Date	Time	Size
----	----	----	----	----	----
Anchor	tyDir	79392	07/10/03	08:30	2496
AreaCode	tyDir	3078	04/19/03	14:59	16
Avalanche	tyDir	79395	06/03/02	08:23	20
AvalanchePP	tyDir	219041	04/29/03	16:59	4
CaptureRequest	tyDir	75720	07/06/03	15:42	92
Clips	tyDir	79387	06/03/02	08:32	44
Component	tyDir	190	01/07/02	23:25	40
CorrelationIndexPart	tyDir	75717	06/02/02	11:43	16
DataSet	tyDir	24	07/11/03	09:45	692
DataSetVersion	tyDir	220684	07/12/03	12:29	804
Database	tyDir	1891	07/13/03	05:01	444
DiskUsed	tyDir	220662	07/13/03	19:59	3016
Genre	tyDir	40	04/19/03	15:48	2856
GuideIndex	tyDir	3126	06/02/02	12:19	4
GuideIndex.temp	tyDir	2741	06/01/02	20:18	4
GuideIndexV2	tyDir	75493	07/13/03	05:07	372

This isn't a complete list, which would waste paper and would discourage you from looking yourself.

Like most filesystems, different directories in MFS store different types of information. Table 9.1 shows some of the more interesting directories on your TiVo and summarizes the types of information they can contain.

TIP

The **mls** command will only list a maximum of 50 entries at a time. If you are exploring directories with more than this number of entries, you can see the next set by supplying the name of the last result in the previous listing as an argument to the **mls** command.

Table 9.1 Interesting MFS Directories and Their Contents

Avalanche	Stores the downloaded data from "Advanced Paid Programming," showings that TiVo broadcasts
Clips	Video clips broadcast during the "Teleworld Paid Programming" programming
Component	The definitions of the IR codes for the IR blaster and the programmable remote
Famous	A list of famous actors and directors
Genre	The genre definitions for a stand-alone TiVo
GuideIndexV2	The indexes used to sort shows by title, keyword, actor, directory, and so forth. These indexes are used for finding the listings of when a program or series airs, as well as for a few internal purposes.
Headend	A listing of headends, which is the TiVo term for the groups of channels on cable, satellite, and over-the-air transmissions that you might receive.
MenuItem	The definition of the extra menu item in TiVo Central
MessageItem	Any mail items or messages that you receive from TiVo
Package	Information used to build the TiVo Central Showcases menus
Person	The definitions of actors, directors and writers used in the preferences engine when building lists of your personal preferences
Preference	All of the primary ThumbsUp or ThumbsDown data that any user of your TiVo has entered
Recording	Organized listings of all of the recordings requested by any user of your TiVo, including recordings that were automatically recorded by the TiVo
Resource	All of the fonts, images, sounds, and backgrounds used in the main TiVo interface
Schedule	The listings for all of the guide data by station and day

SeasonPass	All of the user's Season Passes, plus some behind-the-scenes capture requests from TiVo
Server	A link to every object in the database with a ServerId attribute set. (Objects and attributes are explained in the next section.) ServerIds are allocated by TiVo and used when making series, program, station, day, and broadcast selections.
Setup	TiVo's original configuration data, now deprecated and only used for a few things. (See the State directory.)
State	The new configuration data, split into a number of subdirectories,
SwModule	The software upgrade packages for your current TiVo software release
SwSystem	The resource group data for your current TiVo software release. The first database object in this directory contains the version number information for your current TiVo software release.
Theme	Information about your WishLists

Each directory can, of course, contain other directories. All file and directory names in the MFS filesystem are case sensitive. As a continuing example for use in the next section, the following example shows the contents of the TiVo's /Setup directory as listed from the **mls** command in tivosh:

```
bash-2.02# tivosh
% mls /Setup
Directory of / starting at 'Setup'
```

Name	Type	FsId	Date	Time	Size
----	----	----	----	----	----
Setup	tyDb	2697	07/06/03	16:35	3392
Showcase	tyDir	32165	07/12/03	12:29	508
ShowcaseIndex	tyDir	78865	07/13/03	04:59	216
ShowcaseIndex.temp	tyDir	78844	07/13/03	04:59	4
Star	tyDir	2474	01/07/02	23:36	36
State	tyDir	2701	05/01/03	03:42	248
StationTms	tyDir	92842	07/07/03	10:01	5468
SwModule	tyDir	5	05/02/03	21:09	164
SwSystem	tyDir	2469	05/01/03	21:59	40
Table	tyDir	21	01/07/02	23:23	52
Theme	tyDir	62475	07/07/03	23:32	56

```
   TuikRes                 tyDir     219587   04/29/03 17:03      44
   Uri                     tyDir      92843   06/10/02 13:19      20
   User                    tyDir       2703   04/30/03 06:07       4
   Uuid                    tyDir      32110   07/07/03 10:00    4284
   tmp                     tyDir      75524   07/13/03 21:59       4
```

Exploring Objects in TiVo's Media File System

An object holds a number of values in predefined fields called *attributes*. Continuing with the previous example, let's look at the /Setup object using the **dumpobj** command in tivosh:

```
bash-2.02# tivosh
% dumpobj /Setup
   Setup 75622/10 {
      IndexPath    = /Setup
      Source       = 75622/2108 75622/2459
      Version      = 2637
   }
```

The first line of the **dumpobj** command contains the string "Setup 75622/10". In the output from the **dumpobj** command, "Setup" refers to the type of the object and "75622/10" is the filesystem ID (fsid) and Sub-Object ID (subobjid) of the object. When multiple objects are stored under a single fsid, a subobjid is used to identify those sub-objects. All objects can be referenced by their fsid/subobjid; objects that can only be referenced by their fsid are known as *primary objects*. Primary objects are the only objects that can be referenced by the file system. Generally, any object that is only referenced from another object and not the filesystem will be the sub-object of that primary object. All primary objects should have an IndexPath or IndexUsedBy attribute set, which identifies their location in the filesystem.

"IndexPath", "Source" and "Version" are all attributes of this particular object. The types of objects that can be created in MFS and the attributes they can hold is dictated by a hardcoded list of valid MFS combinations known as a *schema*. At last, it's time to write our first tivosh script to extract the schemas from the MFS filesystem. Let's create the following script to dump all attribute/schema information from MFS:

```
#!/tvbin/tivosh
# 2002, embeem
#
set db [dbopen]
transaction {
  set types [db $db schema types]
  set i 1
```

```
foreach type $types {
  set attrs [db $db schema attrs $type]
  set j 1
  foreach attr $attrs {
    set ai [db $db schema attrinfo $type $attr]
    puts "$i $type $j $attr $ai"
    set j [expr $j+1]
    #13-15 never seem to be used -- embeem
    if { $j == 13 } { set j 16 }
  }
  set i [expr $i+1]
}
}
```

After creating a file named "queryschema.tcl" with the previous code example as its contents on the TiVo and making it executable, you could simply run it by typing **./queryschema.tcl**. However, since it dumps the schema for every object in the TiVo's MFS filesystem, you can pipe its output to the Linux **grep** command (installed in /var/hack/bin when you hacked your TiVo), using the following command:

```
./queryschema.tcl | grep Setup
```

The first few lines of schema information for the Setup object look something like the following:

```
43 Setup 1 Version int optional {} base
43 Setup 2 Expiration int optional {} base
43 Setup 3 Path string optional {} base
43 Setup 4 IndexPath string multi {} derived
43 Setup 5 IndexUsed object multi {} derived
43 Setup 6 IndexUsedBy object multi {} derived
43 Setup 7 IndexAttr object multi {} derived
43 Setup 8 ServerId string optional {} base
43 Setup 9 ServerVersion int optional {} base
43 Setup 10 Uuid string optional {} base
43 Setup 11 Unsatisfied string multi {} base
43 Setup 12 Bits int multi {} base
 ...
43 Setup 70 FrontIRBlasterOBSOLETE int optional {} base
43 Setup 71 AlternateBitratesOBSOLETE int optional {} base
43 Setup 72 TunerCountOBSOLETE int optional {} base
```

NOTE

I've eliminated 60 or so lines, so this book doesn't turn into a telephone book. There's a lot of data in there. Also note that the format of this output is the result of the formatting commands in the **queryschema.tcl** script, not of any inherent format in the data itself.

The first 12 attributes in this listing are common to all objects, while any others are unique to a specified type of object—the /Setup object, in this case.

The first and third fields of each line, both numbers, aren't important when you are manipulating objects in tivosh. The second field is the name of the object type, and the fourth field shows you an attribute of that type of object. The fifth field is the type of value that particular attribute can contain, and the sixth field specifies how many entries can or must be present for that attribute. The last item is either "base" or "derived," indicating if this is a value that is set externally or is derived from other data in the object.

The main commands for manipulating database objects in MFS are the **db** and **dbobj** commands. All **db** and **dbobj** commands need a database handle and also must be open inside a transaction. To get a database handle, you simply execute the command **set db [dbopen]** and wrap the transaction within a transaction statement. The outline of a simple tivosh query script would look something like the following;

```
#!/tvbin/tivosh
#
set db [dbopen]
transaction {
 CODE GOES HERE
}
```

If you are executing a transaction inside a tivosh script that requires a resource that may be busy, the basic skeleton of your script would look like the following:

```
#!/tvbin/tivosh
#
EnableTransactionHoldoff true
 set db [dbopen]
RetryTransaction {
  CODE GOES HERE
}
```

In a tivosh script that may need to retry a transaction, the EnableTransactionHoldoff variable takes a Boolean value that tells tivosh that it can wait until the specified transaction completes—in other words, until the database is available.

A bit of activity goes on behind the scenes when you manipulate an object. If you are dealing with a primary object, the database automatically increments the Version attribute, rebuilds the IndexPath and other derived types, and then relinks the object into the directory where it was located.

Exploring Resources and Resource Groups in TiVo's Media File System

Resource groups are an interesting part of MFS and provide a variety of information that you can examine and hopefully determine how to change in a useful way. A *resource* is an external definition of a string that the main program loads at runtime. This allows TiVo developers to customize applications in various ways without touching the executable, by essentially passing parameters. (Needless to say, it enables us to do the same thing!)

The current resource groups available on your TiVo are stored in the MFS database object /SwSystem/ACTIVE. Once you open this object, the ResourceGroup attribute for each entry in the list of the resource groups contains a list of items. These entries contain all of the text in the user interface, constants that control the bit rate of your mpeg encoder, the backdoor password, all kinds of default values, and a variety of other things that have not been identified yet.

The following script can be used to dump all the strings from the MFS resource groups, and uses the same numbers as the TivoWeb resource editor module discussed in Chapter 10. If you find something interesting, you can put it in a TiVoWeb resource (.res) file as explained in Chapter 10, and easily edit it from TivoWeb.

```
#!/tvbin/tivosh
#
# 2002, embeem
 EnableTransactionHoldoff true
 set db [dbopen]
transaction {
   set swsysa [db $db open "/SwSystem/ACTIVE"]
   set resgrp [dbobj $swsysa get ResourceGroup]
   set groupn 0
   foreach group $resgrp {
      set items [dbobj $group get Item]
      set itemn 0
```

```
foreach item $items {
  puts "$groupn $itemn [dbobj $item get "String"]"
  incr itemn
}
incr groupn   }
}
```

These sections are obviously an introduction to tivosh and the MFS filesystem—the complete story isn't currently known and may never be known unless TiVo decides to share additional information with the TiVo hacking community. As mentioned earlier, none of this is documented, so exploring is the only way to figure it out, determine what different MFS objects do, and see what you can do with the information you've obtained. If you're serious about TiVo hacking, share your scripts and the information that you obtain on the various TiVo forums, for the benefit of the entire TiVo community!

Using Serial Communications Under Linux

Like most other tasks under Linux, there are a variety of ways to do serial communications. This section explains how to use minicom, a popular serial communication utility for Linux that works fine from a terminal or a GUI command window such as an xterm. The minicom application is typically installed by default as part of most Linux distributions.

NOTE

If the minicom application is not installed on your system and you are running a Linux distribution that uses RPM packages, you can obtain a binary version for most Linux distributions from the central Linux resource at http://www.rpmfind.net. You can also download the source for minicom from the main minicom site at http://www.pp.clinet.fi/~walker/minicom.html, and then build and install it yourself.

Using minicom for Serial Communications

The first time you run minicom on your system, you must execute the command as the root user on your Linux system, as well as specify the **-s** command-line option to cause minicom to create its initial configuration file, /etc/minirc.dfl.

TIP

In general, when you first configure minicom, you should run through the instructions in this section as the root user on your Linux system to correctly configure minicom for communication with your TiVo. You can then use the Save setup as **dfl** command on the main minicom menu to save these settings as your system's default settings. This will enable you to subsequently run minicom using a standard Linux account.

The basic serial communications settings necessary for communicating with your TiVo are the following:

◆ The name of the serial port on your Linux system that you've attached the serial cable to that connects to your TiVo. On your Linux host, this is /dev/ttyS0 for the first serial port and /dev/ttyS1 for the second.

◆ Set the appropriate communication speed. The serial ports on a Series 1 machine run at 9600 baud. The serial ports on a Series 2 model run at 115,200 baud.

◆ 8N1 communications settings (8-bit communications, no parity, 1 stop bit)

◆ No software or hardware flow control

To configure minicom with these settings, do the following:

1. Start minicom from the command line. Most Linux distributions install minicom as /usr/bin/minicom.

2. Type the key sequence **Control-a z** to display the minicom command summary. (To type this key sequence, hold down the Control key while pressing the letter **a**; then release the control key and press the letter **z**.)

3. Type the letter **w** to enable line wrapping in minicom. You should see the message "Linewrap ON" display on your screen. If the message "Linewrap OFF" displays on your screen, press the letter **w** again to enable line wrapping. Some of the output that you may want to see in your serial console can be rather long. By enabling line wrapping, you can read everything that you are typing.

4. Type the key sequence **Control-a z** to redisplay the minicom command summary.

5. Type the letter **o** to display the Configure Minicom dialog box.

6. A menu of generic configuration options displays. Use the down-arrow key to scroll down and select the Serial Port Setup option, and press the Return key to display a configuration dialog box.

7. The current configuration settings for the serial port display—first, verifying that serial port that you have connected to your TiVo's serial cable is the same one listed in

the minicom Serial Port Setup dialog box. Type the letter **a** to enter the name of the correct device, if necessary. The name of the default serial port on most Linux systems is /dev/ttyS0.

8. Next, make sure that both Hardware flow control and Software flow control are set to "No." If Hardware flow control is currently set to "Yes," press the **F** key to change the setting to "No." If Software flow control is currently set to "Yes," press the **G** key to change the setting to "No."

9. The current communications settings are displayed next to the Bps/Par/Bits entry dialog box. If these are not 9600 8N1 or 115200 8N1 (depending on the model of TiVo that you want to communicate with), type the letter **e** to display the Communication Options dialog box. Once this dialog box displays, type the letter **q** followed by the letter **e** (for 9600 baud) or **i** (for 115200 baud) to configure minicom with these settings. Next, press the Return key to close the Communications Parameters dialog box and return to the Configure minicom dialog box.

10. Use the down-arrow key to scroll down to the **Exit** command, and press the Return key to close the dialog box.

At this point, press **Control-1** followed by the Return key to see if you are successfully connected to the TiVo board. If you see a "bash-2.02#" prompt each time you press the Return key, you are successfully connected to your TiVo. If you don't get a response, check your cables, settings, and (of course) make sure that you have enabled a command-line prompt on your TiVo using one of the mechanisms described in Chapter 7.

TIP

If you are experiencing intermittent problems or lost characters when communicating with the TiVo over a serial connection, you should check your Linux system to ensure that no other process is running on the serial port to which you have connected your TiVo. The most common processes you may see already running on this port are the Linux **agetty**, **mingetty**, or **mgetty** commands, which support various types of logins on serial ports. For more information on these commands, see the Linux online manual.

TIP

If you are using your TiVo's serial port to control your cable box or dish, you shouldn't try be running a bash shell on your serial port.

Transferring Files Using minicom

Once you have established a connection to your TiVo from the minicom application, the next thing that you will want to do (unless your TiVo is on a network) is to transfer some files there. The minicom application provides built-in support for popular serial file transfer protocols include xmodem, ymodem, and zmodem, kermit, and even pure ASCII file transfers. TiVos provide the **rz** (Receive Zmodem) and **sz** (Send Zmodem) commands in all versions of the TiVo software, so let's use that protocol.

To transfer a file to your TiVo using minicom (perhaps one of the archives of precompiled TiVo applications provided in the hacks_dir directory on the BATBD CD), do the following:

1. After connecting to your TiVo as described in the previous section, start the rz program on your TiVo by typing **rz** at the bash prompt and pressing the Return key. (Make sure that you're in a directory where you can create files, such as /var.)

2. In minicom, press **Control-a** followed by the **s** key. A menu of file transfer protocols displays, with the zmodem entry highlighted. Press the Return key. A screen, like the one shown in Figure 9.1, displays.

FIGURE 9.1 *Selecting the file to transfer in minicom*

3. Click Browse, navigate to the directory containing the file that you want to transfer, press the spacebar to highlight the file, and press the Return key.

4. A screen, like the one shown in Figure 9.2, displays. The different fields of this dialog box provide status information about the file transfer as it proceeds, including a histogram that provides a graphical display of the file transfer percentage.

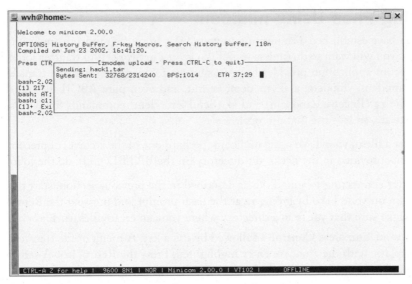

FIGURE 9.2 *Transferring a file in minicom*

5. Remember that this is a serial file transfer and will take a while, depending on the size of the file transferring. The dialog box shown in Figure 9.2 closes automatically when the file transfer completes, and automatically terminates the **rz** command running on your TiVo. (You may have to press the Return key once or twice to see the bash prompt again.)

When the serial transfer completes, you can install the software you just uploaded to your TiVo using one of the mechanisms described in Chapter 10.

Sending files from your TiVo to your Linux system works in much the same way as reverse transferring them. On the TiVo, you execute the **sz** command, followed by the name of the file that you want to send back to your PC. After you press Return, minicom should automatically start the receiving end of the transfer, and will store the files that it receives in the directory where you started minicom.

Using a Linux Shell

A *Linux shell* is the name given to a Linux command interpreter. When you log in to a Linux system, the login process typically starts a command interpreter in each terminal or console that you are running. As with most Linux applications, a variety of shells are available. The most common and popular of these is bash, which stands for "Bourne-Again Shell," and is a pun on the name of the author of the original Unix shell, Stephen Bourne. The remainder of this section applies specifically to the bash shell, although the basic concepts are the same in Unix and Linux shells, such as the C-Shell (/bin/csh), the Korn Shell (/usr/bin/ksh), and the others that you commonly find on modern Linux systems.

A shell displays a series of characters known as a *prompt* to let you know that it is ready to receive input. The standard bash prompt is the word "bash," followed by the version number of bash that you are running, followed by a hash mark if you are logged in as the root user. This bash prompt for Version 2.02 of bash (the version commonly found on a TiVo) would look like the following:

```
bash-2.02#
```

A shell reads the characters you type at a console or terminal window. Once you press Return, the shell first checks if the command that you typed is built into the shell. If it is, the shell executes the command immediately and redisplays its prompt to inform you that it is ready for another command. If the command is not built into the shell, the shell searches an internal variable known as an environment variable to find the command that you requested. The environment variable used by bash to locate commands is the PATH environment variable. The PATH environment variable is set to a colon-separated list of directories in which you want the shell to search for commands, in order. You can examine the current value of your PATH environment variable in bash in the following way:

```
bash-2.02# echo $PATH
/var/hack/bin:/bin:/sbin:/tvbin:/devbin
```

In this case, you tell the shell to echo the current value of the PATH environment variable, identifying it as an environment variable by preceding its name with a dollar sign ($). If you install new commands or simply want to search an additional directory for commands, you can use the bash **export** command to add a directory to the PATH environment variable, as in the following example:

```
bash-2.02# export PATH=/var/wvh/bin:$PATH
bash-2.02# echo $PATH
/var/wvh/bin:/var/hack/bin:/bin:/sbin:/tvbin:/devbin
```

In this example, the first mention of the PATH environment variable uses only its name (no dollar sign) because you are setting the value of the environment variable. The second mention of PATH, preceded by a dollar sign, ensures that the current contents of your PATH are included in the new value that you are setting.

A number of other environment variables are used in bash, but the PATH variable is the most critical one for finding and executing programs on your TiVo (or any Linux system, for that matter). A number of excellent books and online tutorials are available on bash. One of my personal favorites is the "Beginner's Bash" at http://linux.org.mt/article/terminal.

Job Control in the Bash Shell

Job Control is a feature of many Unix and Linux shells that enables a user to manage multiple processes within a particular shell. Job control enables you to suspend commands that are currently running, to interrupt running commands, restart suspended commands, and much more.

NOTE

The information in this section is generic to all Linux command interpreters and, therefore, also applies to the Unix command interpreters that they were modeled after. Since the TiVo runs Linux, I'm just going to say "Linux" from now on, but you may want to remember that this information also applies to all Unix or Unix-like systems, just in case you see one that isn't running Linux at some point.

Each time you type a command at a prompt on a Linux system and press Return or Enter, the shell runs that command for you, accepting any further input required by the command, and then sending the output of the command to the shell from where you started it. Normally, you can't execute another command until the first one has finished. This is usually a good thing, because you generally want the commands that you run to complete. However, Linux also enables you to run commands in ways that don't tie up your current shell. You can do this by running a command in the background or by suspending a command that is currently running. You can always run a command in the background from a Linux shell because this is a standard bash process control feature, but you can't suspend, interrupt, or restart them unless Job Control is available.

The next sections explain how to run commands in the background, how to redirect the output of your commands to files, and how to suspend, restart, interrupt, and manage commands from a bash shell.

Running Commands in the Background

Running a command in the background means that the shell executes the command for you, but doesn't tie up the shell—it runs the command in parallel with the shell, while enabling you to type and run other commands from the shell prompt. All the examples of getting a command prompt on your TiVo are done by running a copy of the bash shell in the background, usually started from the /etc/rc.d/rc.sysinit file on your TiVo's root partition.

To start a command in the background on a Linux system, you simply put an ampersand (&) at the end of the command. When running commands that display output in the background, you typically use Linux redirection commands to send the output of the command to a file so that it doesn't display on the same screen where you're currently using the command interpreter. Redirecting the output of a command to a file is accomplished by using the (>) symbol on the command-line. For example, to run the **ls** command in the background and redirect its output to the file "ls.out," you would type the following command at a shell prompt:

```
ls > ls.out &
```

The shell would display a message like the following after you pressed Return or Enter:

20903

This means that, in this case, the shell is running the **ls** command as its first job (often referred to as a *subprocess*), and that the process ID of this process is 20903. The process ID you see will always be different, because the ID number assigned to a given process depends on the number of other processes that are running or have been run on your system.

While a command runs in the background, you can check on its status by using the Bash shell's built-in **jobs** command, which lists all background tasks running under the current shell and displays their status. Executing the **jobs** command while our sample **ls** command runs in the background would produce output something like the following:

```
+  Running              ls >ls.out
```

This shows the same job number shown before, displays a plus sign (+) to show that the command actually is running, and displays the name of the command and the first 20 or so characters of any arguments supplied to the command on the command-line. When the command finishes, you will see a message like the following displayed by the bash shell:

```
+  Done                 ls >ls.out
```

This means that the command completed successfully.

Managing Commands in the Bash Shell

As mentioned earlier, you can always run a command in the background from a Linux shell, but you can't suspend, interrupt, or restart it unless job control is available. Job control is only available if the shell that you are running is associated with a specific device on your Linux system. Starting a command in the background and redirecting its input and output to a device is not the same thing as you did to start the bash prompt on your TiVo, as explained in Chapter 7. This is because the TiVo startup process that executed the command-prompt started the process in the background and then exited. Once the parent of any process exists, that process is no longer associated with a specific device, even though it can still send and receive input from any devices specified on the command line. A process that is not associated with a specific device is known as a *detached process* in Linux-speak.

When a command is running in the background and it isn't attached to a specific physical or network device, it can't receive the special commands that enable it to manage background or suspended processes. These special commands are **Control-z** (hold down the Ctrl key and press the letter "z"), which suspends a command, and Control-c (hold down the Ctrl key and press the letter "c"), which interrupts and terminates a command.

When job control is available, an alternative to running a command in the background is to run a command, suspend its execution for some period of time, and then restart it. This is a more advanced feature of job control, but it can be quite useful if you're executing some command that takes a long time to run and you suddenly remember that you want to execute some other, relatively quick command without restarting the first one. To suspend a command, you can type Control-z while the command is running, and you will see a message like the following displayed in your shell:

```
+  Stopped              /bin/ls>ls.out
```

If job control is available and you can suspend a running command, you can restart this command in the background by typing the bash shell's **bg** (background) command, which would display output like the following:

```
+ /bin/ls>ls.out &
```

You can also use job control to bring a background task into the foreground by specifying its job number and using bash's "**fg**" command. For example, to bring whatever job is running as job number 1 into the foreground, you could type the command "**fg %1**". The percent sign identifies the number as a job identifier. Similarly, to terminate a job that is running in the background, you could use the shell's built-in "**kill**" command. For example, to terminate whatever job is running as job number 1 in the foreground, you could type the command "**kill %1**".

If you are running a command in the foreground that you want to terminate, you can simply terminate the task if job control is active by typing Control-c. This tells the shell to terminate the command regardless of whether it's finished or not.

Like most aspects of Linux, there are a zillion more nuances to the concept of job control and the larger aspect of process management in Linux. Explaining all of these would be fun, but is somewhat outside the scope of this book. Many Web sites provide a good discussion of job control and process management on Linux systems, such as the about.com information on process management at http://unix.about.com/library/weekly/aa062501a.htm, and the information

TiVo GETTING A COMMAND PROMPT WITH JOB CONTROL

As mentioned earlier, you can only get complete job control in processes that are actually associated with a specific device. If your only goal is getting job control in your TiVo command prompt, you can do this by not running the bash command in the background. The downside of this is that this must be the last command in your **/etc/rc.d/rc.sysinit** command file, because it never exits, no commands after that line will be executed from the **/etc/rc.d/rc.sysinit** command file. To get a serial prompt with job control enabled on a TiVo Series 1, remove any other command that starts a bash shell in your **/etc/rc.d/rc.sysinit** command file, and put one of the following commands as the last line of the file:

```
exec </dev/ttyS3 &> /dev/ttyS3; /bin/bash
```

To do the same thing on a hacked TiVo Series 2, modify the file /var/hack/hackinit, remove the existing bash **startup** command, and add the following command as the last line of the file:

```
exec </dev/ttyS2 &> /dev/ttyS2; /bin/bash
```

You now can start, stop, suspend, and manage other processes from within the bash shell running on your TiVo's serial port.

about job control available at http://unix.about.com/library/weekly/aa072301a.htm. Most Linux books with reasonably large coverage of bash also will explain job control and process management in great, gory detail.

Popular Linux Software for the TiVo

Since the TiVo runs Linux, a large amount of freely available software is available for your TiVo. In many cases, this software is provided in archive files located in the hack_dirs directory on the CD that accompanies this book. This directory contains a complete set of my favorite Linux utilities for both Series 1 and Series 2 machines. Instructions for installing these on your TiVo are presented in Chapter 10, and also in the sections of Chapter 7 on getting a command-line prompt on your model of TiVo under most common versions of the TiVo operating system.

In other cases, you'll have to compile certain software packages for your TiVo yourself— perhaps using one of the cross-compilers provided in the xcompilers directory on the same CD. Cross-compilers are compilers that run on one type of computer system, but which provide output for another. The popular GNU compiler, GCC, is a great example of a freely-available, Open Source compiler that is easy to configure and use as a cross-compiler. Versions that produce executables for both the TiVo Series 1 and Series 2 machines are provided on the BATBD CD.

The next few sections discuss applications that you will probably want to use on your TiVo after you get a command-line prompt there.

Busybox

BusyBox is a truly impressive software package primarily designed for use in embedded Linux systems. Billing itself as "the Swiss Army Knife of Embedded Linux," BusyBox is a single executable that behaves differently based on how it was invoked. For example, if you create a symbolic link named "ls" to the busybox executable, and then type **ls**, BusyBox produces the same output as the standard Linux **ls** command. You can get the same result by executing busybox directly and specifying the name of the command that you want it to work like as the first argument on the command line. For example, executing the command **busybox ls** would have the same effect as executing the symbolic link to BusyBox described in this paragraph.

The version of BusyBox included in the hack_dir archives on the BATBD CD is a slightly older version, but it does everything I've asked of it. The version on the BATBD CD (for both Series 1 and Series 2 systems) displays the following message when executed with no arguments:

```
BusyBox v0.48 (2000.12.22-03:36+0000) multi-call binary -- GPL2
 Usage: busybox [function] [arguments]...
   or: [function] [arguments]...
          BusyBox is a multi-call binary that combines many common Unix
```

```
utilities into a single executable.  Most people will create a
link to busybox for each function they wish to use, and BusyBox
will act like whatever it was invoked as.
Currently defined functions:
    [, ar, basename, busybox, cat, chgrp, chmod, chown, chroot, clear,
    cmp, cp, cut, date, dc, dd, df, dirname, dmesg, dos2unix, du,
    dutmp, echo, expr, false, find, free, freeramdisk, fsck.minix,
    getopt, grep, gunzip, gzip, halt, head, id, init, kill, killall,
    length, linuxrc, ln, logger, logname, ls, lsmod, makedevs, md5sum,
    mkdir, mkfifo, mkfs.minix, mknod, mkswap, mktemp, more, mount,
    mv, poweroff, printf, ps, pwd, readlink, reboot, renice, reset,
    rm, rmdir, rmmod, rpmunpack, sed, sh, sleep, sort, swapoff, swapon,
    sync, tail, tar, tee, test, touch, tr, true, tty, umount, uname,
    uniq, unix2dos, update, uptime, usleep, uudecode, uuencode, wc,
    which, whoami, xargs, yes, zcat
```

That's one impressive list! Needless to say, BusyBox doesn't support all of the 10 zillion options available to some of the commands that it emulates, such as **ls** and **ps**, but it supports enough commands to help get the basic information you expect from certain commands.

The primary reason that you might want to have a single binary that does the same thing as so many others is to save space on systems with small amounts of available storage. BusyBox was originally written for the Debian Linux boot floppies by Bruce Perens, but was substantially rewritten and enhanced for general use in any small-footprint system by Erik Anderson. The size of each statically linked, stand-alone executable on a TiVo system generally ranges from 40K to 400K. BusyBox itself is only 248K in size, and each symbolic link to the busybox binary requires 7 characters (the number of characters in the word "busybox").

Not only does having a multicall binary (the name for an application that can be called in many different ways) save space, it also saves time. Building (and supporting) one binary and invoking it in 50 different ways is much faster than building 50 applications.

BusyBox has several homes, the most open of these is http://www.busybox.net. The source code for the current version of BusyBox is available from http://www.busybox.net/downloads.

Emacs

The choice of a text editor is a religious issue. However, I have been using versions of Emacs since 1983, and my fingers think in terms of Emacs' keystrokes. Hence, I highly recommend a version of Emacs for use on your TiVo, and have included one in the archives of popular TiVo applications provided on the CD that accompanies this book.

Emacs stands for "Editor Macros," and was originally compiled as a set of macros for a long-gone, but little-lamented, text editor that was known as TECO (Text Editor and Corrector).

Ironically, the Emacs macros were originally compiled and maintained by none other than Richard Stallman, founder and guru of the GNU Project. Because these ran on top of (and therefore required TECO), a version of Emacs was written for Unix systems in the early 1980s by James Gosling, who later went on to create Java. This version of Emacs, colloquially known as *gosmacs*, was eventually superceded by a free version of Emacs from the GNU project (big surprise) known as *GNU Emacs*.

Over the years, there have been many suggestions for alternate expansions of the Emacs' acronym. One of my favorites has always been "Eight Megabytes and Constantly Swapping," which was a problem in the 1980s, but is somewhat outdated since my home Linux box has a gigabyte of memory. Regardless, Emacs is big, requires a relatively large amount of memory by any standards, and also requires a fair amount of auxiliary disk space for hundreds of configuration files.

For this reason, many smaller re-implementations or versions of Emacs are freely available. The one included on the BATBD CD is NanoEmacs, which (as its name suggests) is designed to be small with relatively low memory requirements. It does not support configuration files, but does require that your terminal type (TERM environment variable) be set to something like "linux" or "xterm" because it uses a minimal version of the TERMINFO, terminal information database.

TIP

I'm sure that lovers of quaint modal text editors have already started composing nasty grams about my love for Emacs on a TiVo. For you guys, an Open Source version of vi, known as "vim" (Vi iMproved) is also provided for the Series 1 and Series 2 machines on the BATBD CD.

FTP

FTP is the classic networked file transfer application. Its name stands for File Transfer Protocol, which is the protocol that the FTP command implements. Both an FTP client and server are commonly found on Linux systems, but only the FTP daemon is included in the application archives on the BATBD CD. This enables you to use standard Linux to initiate a file transfer to or from a TiVo that is running the FTP daemon.

To start the FTP daemon on a hacked, networked Series 1 or Series 2 system, execute the following command:

```
/var/hack/bin/tivoftpd &
```

This starts the TiVo FTP daemon in the background, where it accepts standard FTP commands, such as those shown in the following table.

Popular FTP Commands

FTP Command	Meaning	Action
bin	binary mode	Puts the FTP client into the mode necessary to transfer binary files.
cd <directory>	change directory	Changes to the specified <directory> on the TiVo.
get <file>	get file	Retrieves the specified <file> from the TiVo to the system from where you connected.
hash	display hashes	Causes the FTP client to display a hash mark (#) for each 1K sent to or retrieved from the TiVo.
lcd <directory>	local change directory	Changes to the specified <directory> on the system from where you are connected.
put <file>	put file	Sends the specified <file> to the TiVo from the system from where you connected.
quit	quit FTP client	Terminates the FTP connection to the TiVo and closes your local FTP client.

 NOTE

Originally, TiVos were not intended to be logged in to, so they do not support authentication. When you connect to a TiVo running the FTP daemon, it will respond with a series of messages like the following:

```
Connected to 192.168.6.247.
220 You are in TiVo Mode.
220 Login isn't necessary.
220 Please hit ENTER at the login/password prompts.
Name (192.168.6.247:wvh):
331 No Auth required for TiVo Mode.
Password:
230 Running in TiVo Mode.
Remote system type is UNIX.
ftp>
```

You must press Return or Enter at both of the authentication prompts. At that point, you will be connected to the TiVo and can move around the filesystem to send or receive files, using standard FTP commands such as those shown in the table above.

GCC

As discussed earlier in this chapter, one of the earliest software packages developed by the GNU Project was GCC, the GNU C Compiler. GCC is an open source compiler for programs written in the C programming language. GCC was designed to be easily portable to multiple operating systems, and forms the core of a complete development environment for Linux systems. GCC is an excellent cross-compiler, which means that it is capable of producing binaries on one system that are formatted and designed to run on another type of system.

Cross-compilers that run on x86 desktop Linux systems and produce output for both the Series 1 (PPC) and Series 2 (MIPS) TiVos are found in the appropriate subdirectories of the xcompilers directory on the BATBD CD included with this book. For information on installing and executing them on your desktop Linux system, see Chapter 10, the section entitled "Installing Cross-Compilers for TiVo Development."

NFS

The Network File System, NFS, is a relatively easy way to move or share large numbers of files among networked computer systems. NFS, originally developed by Sun Microsystems, was one of the earliest network-oriented filesystems. Sun released the protocol specification for NFS early on in its history, and versions of NFS quickly became available for every Unix machine on the planet. NFS is supported on all Linux distributions, and is generally installed on any Linux machine as part of a Complete or Server installation.

NFS support for both Series 1 and Series 2 systems is provided as a loadable kernel module in the hack_dirs/kernel_modules directory on the BATBD CD. Different versions are available for different kernel versions for both types of systems. You can insert a loadable kernel module into the TiVo kernel using a command like the following:

```
insmod -f -s nfs.o
```

The **insmod** command's -f switch forces the **insmod** command to suppress errors about different kernel versions, while the -s option causes any error or logging messages to be directed to the system-error log.

Once the NFS kernel module is loaded into the TiVo kernel, you must make sure that your Linux system is running an NFS server that is exporting the filesystem that you want to mount on your TiVo. The filesystems exported from a NFS server are defined in the file /etc/exports. A sample entry to export the /home/wvh directory to any IP address on the 192.168.6 network, enabling read-write access and ignoring authentication issues when a remote NFS client tries to connect as root is the following:

```
/home/wvh   192.168.6.*(no_root_squash,rw)
```

WARNING

Be very careful when exporting NFS filesystems to systems that do not support authentication. Typically, NFS systems use an authentication package to validate that users have sufficient privileges to access, read, and write remote directories using NFS. Since the TiVo does not support authentication, your NFS server must enable connections from the TiVo that are interpreted as being equivalent to requests from the root user on your system. This gives anyone logged in on your TiVo complete access to any exported directory. You should restrict NFS connections so that they come from only trusted hosts (such as hosts on a private network), or only provide access to directories that you can afford to restore from backups should someone accidentally delete them. Exporting the root directory of a Linux system via NFS to an unauthenticated host is almost never a good idea.

Once you have created the /etc/exports entry for the directory that you want to export via NFS, you can start the NFS server on your Linux system by issuing the following commands as the root user:

```
/etc/rc.d/init.d/nfslock start
/etc/rc.d/init.d/nfs start
```

NOTE

Different Linux distributions use different types of NFS servers (kernel or userspace) and start them differently. These examples are from a Red Hat Linux system. You can often simply start the appropriate NFS components on your system by simply executing the command **exportfs –a** as the root user.

You should then be able to use the **exportfs** command on your Linux system to verify that the directory that you want to export via NFS is successfully exported. Using the /etc/exports entry cited previously, this command and its output would look like the following:

```
# exportfs
/home/wvh          192.168.6.*
```

After a filesystem exports from your Linux host, return to the TiVo and create the directory on which you want to mount the remote filesystem in a local directory that you have write access to (I typically use /var, and create the directory /var/nfs). You can then mount the remote directory on your TiVo using a command like the following:

```
mount -t nfs 192.168.6.32:/home/wvh /var/nfs
```

After mounting this directory, the output from the **df** command on your TiVo should show something like the following:

```
Filesystem              1k-blocks       Used Available Use% Mounted on
/dev/root                  126911      15695    104663  13% /
/dev/hda9                  126911      36307     84051  30% /var
192.168.6.32:/home/wvh   30668576   23093232   6017444  79% /var/nfs
```

You now can read and write files from your TiVo in the /var/nfs directory, and quickly and easily copy files to and from your TiVo using this directory.

For more information about using NFS on Linux systems, see the NFS FAQ at http://nfs.sourceforge.net. Keep in mind that not all of the discussion about authentication will be relevant, so you must be even more careful to only export a limited number of directories, and then only to trusted hosts. However, NFS can save an incredible amount of time in large file transfers, in either direction.

Telnet

Telnet is the original application for network-oriented access to remote systems via virtual terminals. Like the FTP command, the telnet application features both clients (running on your local system) and servers (that wait for incoming connections on a remote system). Like the FTP daemon, only the telnet daemon is provided on a TiVo system—however, this daemon (/sbin/tnlited, a "lite" version of the standard Linux telnet daemon) is already provided as a part of all standard TiVo software distributions, and does not have to be separately installed.

To start the telnet daemon on your TiVo, execute a command like the following:

```
/sbin/tnlited 23 /bin/bash -login &
```

This tells the telnet dameon to run on port number 23 (the standard telnet port on Unix and Linux systems), and to execute /bin/bash in login mode in response to any incoming connections. Because the TiVo does not support authentication, any incoming connection will be logged in instantly as the root user on your TiVo. This is unquestionably a security hole, so do not put your TiVo on a public network where randoms may be able to initiate telnet connections—unless you don't care if the entire machine is deleted.

You may want to add this command to the end of your hacked TiVo's /etc/rc.d/rc.sysinit file so that the telnet daemon is automatically started each time your TiVo boots.

TIP

If you don't know your TiVo's IP address (which may be the case if it is allocated dynamically, using DHCP), you can execute the **/sbin/ifconfig** -a command from a serial connection to your TiVo. This command displays information about all of the Ethernet interfaces that are active on your TiVo in the following format:

```
lo         Link encap:Local Loopback
           inet addr:127.0.0.1  Bcast:127.255.255.255  Mask:255.0.0.0
           UP BROADCAST LOOPBACK RUNNING  MTU:3584  Metric:1
           RX packets:0 errors:0 dropped:0 overruns:0 frame:0
           TX packets:0 errors:0 dropped:0 overruns:0 carrier:0 coll:0

eth0       Link encap:Ethernet  HWaddr 00:40:36:01:B0:11
           inet addr:192.168.6.246  Bcast:192.168.6.255
Mask:255.255.255.0
           UP BROADCAST RUNNING MULTICAST  MTU:1500  Metric:1
           RX packets:0 errors:0 dropped:0 overruns:0 frame:0
           TX packets:0 errors:0 dropped:0 overruns:0 carrier:0 coll:0
           Interrupt:29
```

You will want to enter the IP address shown in the eth0 (for "Ethernet Connection Zero") section for the name of the host that you want to telnet to from your Linux system. Your TiVo's IP address may change if you reboot your TiVo after using other network devices that dynamically allocate IP addresses, but you can always use a serial connection to your TiVo and the **/sbin/ifconfig -a** command to find out your TiVo's current IP address.

Burning CDs on Linux Systems

This section explains how to burn CD images from existing ISO images using a Linux system. Creating ISO images on Linux systems is accomplished using the robust and complex Linux **mkisofs** command. For more information about mkisofs, see the online manual page or download the latest version of the Linux package that contains it, CDRTools, from http://www.fokus.gmd.de/research/cc/glone/employees/joerg.schilling/private/mkisofs.html.

You can create CDs from ISO images using a number of Linux applications. The CD creation application most commonly found on Linux systems is cdrecord, and it is most commonly found in the directory /usr/bin.

The cdrecord application requires a SCSI CD drive, or that your CD drive has been designated as using the IDE-SCSI emulation mode provided by the Linux kernel. If you are using an

IDE CD drive, you can usually enable this mode by updating the configuration file used by the Linux boot loader that your system uses. The LILO bootloader uses the configuration file /etc/lilo.conf, while the GRUB bootloader uses the configuration file /etc/grub.conf. Regardless of which boot loader you are using, you can enable IDE-SCSI mode by appending an appropriate boot parameter to the kernel command line. For example, to enable IDE-SCSI mode on /dev/hdc, which is the CD drive in my primary Linux system, I would append the following:

```
hdc=ide-scsi
```

After rebooting and selecting the updated kernel entry, your CD drive should be listed in the output from the **cdrecord** command's **-scanbus** command-line option. Executing the **cdrecord** **-scanbus** command causes the cdrecord application to probe all actual or emulated SCSI interfaces in your system, and to list any CD drives that it finds, as shown in the following sample output:

```
# cdrecord -scanbus
Cdrecord 1.10 (i686-pc-linux-gnu) Copyright (C) 1995-2001 Jorg Schilling
Linux sg driver version: 3.1.24
Using libscg version 'schily-0.5'
scsibus1:
        1,0,0    100) 'TOSHIBA ' 'DVD-ROM SD-R1202' '1026' Removable CD-ROM
        1,1,0    101) *
        1,2,0    102) *
        1,3,0    103) *
        1,4,0    104) *
        1,5,0    105) *
        1,6,0    106) *
        1,7,0    107) *
scsibus2:
        2,0,0    200) 'SanDisk ' 'ImageMate II    ' '1.30' Removable Disk
        2,1,0    201) *
        2,2,0    202) *
        2,3,0    203) *
        2,4,0    204) *
        2,5,0    205) *
        2,6,0    206) *
        2,7,0    207) *
```

In my case, my system's CD drive was found as device 1,0,0 on the system's first SCSI bus (hence the leading "1").

To write an existing ISO image to CD, you simply specify the device that the **cdrecord** command should write to, the speed at which it should write, and the name of the ISO file to write to the specified CD drive. The following command would write the file "sample.iso" to the device reported as device 1,0,0, at speed 16x:

```
cdrecord dev=1,0,0 speed=16 sample.iso
```

If you're interested in seeing the intermediate progress of this command, you can specify the **-v** command-line option, which puts the **cdrecord** command in verbose mode, and displays numeric messages about the percentage of the disk that it has burned.

Working with TiVo's Home Media Option from Linux

In April 2003, TiVo released its Home Media Option, which was discussed in terms of Windows and Macintosh connectivity in Chapter 8, "Working with Your TiVo from Windows and Macintosh Systems." The Home Media Option's ability to play MP3 files is facilitated by software for Windows and Macintosh systems that enables those systems to export MP3 collections and iTunes libraries, respectively. Finally, the documentation from the TiVo Web site, where the TiVo Desktop software is available, (http://www.tivo.com/4.9.4.1.asp) states that no desktop software for Linux is available at the present time.

A fair amount of information on the internals of the Home Media Option is available from TiVo's Developer Web site at http://www.tivo.com/developer. After you accept their license agreement, you can download documentation and a sample Apache plug-in written in Perl that enables an Apache Web server to export collections of MP3 files and digital photographs to a TiVo running the Home Media Option.

 TIP

Make sure that you read the license before you actually accept it.

In frustration, I asked about this issue on the TiVoCommunity Forum, and received replies from members of SourceForge's Personal TiVo Home Media Option project (http://sourceforge.net/projects/ptivohmo). From there, you can freely download various files which, when installed, built, and configured on a desktop Linux system, enable you to export both MP3 and OGG-format audio files from your desktop Linux system to any TiVo running the Home Media Option. A tar file of this project is also located in the connectivity subdirectory of the CD that accompanies this book.

To install, configure, and start this software on your desktop Linux system, follow the steps below:

1. Extract the contents of the archive file from the CD that accompanies this book to a writable directory on your Linux system. Assuming that the BATBD CD was mounted at /mnt/cdrom, you could do this with the following command:

```
tar zxvf /mnt/cdrom/connectivity/TiVoServer-0.16.tar.gz
```

This creates the directory TiVoServer-0.16 in your working directory.

2. Change the directory to the TiVoServer-0.16 directory and execute the following commands as the root user on your system:

```
perl Makefile.PL
make
make install
```

3. Make sure that the file tivoserver.pl has been copied to your /usr/bin directory, (copy it there if not), making sure that it is executable by using the command:

```
chmod 755 /usr/bin/tivoserver.pl
```

 NOTE

The TiVoServer software requires that Perl and various Perl libraries be installed on your system. If any required libraries are missing, the **perl** command listed previously will list them and explain how to retrieve and install them. You should do this as the root user on your Linux system.

4. Copy the sample configuration file, tivoserver.conf, to the /etc directory in your Linux system and edit its contents. Specifically, you must correctly set the following entries, and all of the directories that they specify must exist:

   ◆ Create the directories specified by the tivo_cache_dir and tivo_image_cache_dir entries.

   ◆ Set the tivo_mp3_path variable to the name of the directory that contains the MP3 and OGG files that you want to export from your Linux system to your TiVo.

   ◆ Set the tivo_photo_path variable to the name of a directory containing any digital photographs that you want to export from your Linux system to your TiVo.

   You can change other options, but these must be in the correct order for the server to start.

5. Start the TiVoServer using the following command:

```
/usr/bin/tivoserver.pl --conf_file=/etc/tivoserver.conf
```

That's all there is to it! You can check the log file (/tmp/tivo.log unless you changed it in the configuration file) for the status of your Linux TiVoServer; or you can simply go to your Home Media Option-enabled TiVo Series 2, select Music & Photos from the TiVo Central menu, and start enjoying the music that you have stored on your Linux system from the comfort of your home theater.

 NOTE

You may eventually want to create a Linux startup file for this command. I created the file /etc/rc.d/init.d/tivoserver with the following contents:

```bash
#! /bin/bash
#
# tivoserver          Start/Stop the tivo HMO server.
#
# Source function library.
. /etc/init.d/functions
RETVAL=0
# See how we were called.    prog="tivoserver"
 start() {
   echo -n $"Starting $prog: "
   /usr/bin/tivoserver.pl --conf_file=/etc/tivoserver.conf
   RETVAL=$?
   echo
   return $RETVAL
}
 stop() {
   echo -n $"Stopping $prog: "
   killall /usr/bin/perl
   RETVAL=$?
   echo
   return $RETVAL
}
 restart() {
     stop
   start
}
 case "$1" in
   start)
     start
   ;;
   stop)
```

```
      stop
   ;;
  restart)
      restart
   ;;
  *)
    echo $"Usage: $0 {start|stop|status|reload|restart}"
    exit 1
esac
exit $?
```

Depending on the run level at which you start your Linux system, you can then link this file into the standard directories of startup scripts in /etc/rc3.d or /etc/rc5.d.

HACKING THE TiVo

Chapter 10

Getting and Installing New Software for Your TiVo

One of the best aspects of hacking your TiVo is that with a hacked TiVo it is possible to install a variety of interesting software on the machine, beyond the great software that your TiVo already runs out of the box. As explained in Chapter 7, "Connecting the Universe to Your TiVo," a lot of free software for your TiVo is already available on the Internet (or on the CD that accompanies this book). This software is all ready-to-run once you install and execute it on a hacked TiVo. Beyond the software on the CD, Chapter 11, "Other TiVo Hacking Resources," provides a variety of sources of free software that wouldn't fit on the CD or that I didn't have much experience with personally.

Unfortunately, just because software is available doesn't always make it easy to understand or install and use. Throughout this book, I've explained how to install and use a good number of interesting software packages, but you're bound to find something that sounds intriguing that isn't covered here. New packages are coming out every day, especially now that hackers and books such as this one have explained how to get into the TiVo Series 2 machines. Many of the most popular TiVo hacks were written in the early days of the TiVo revolution, when folks like Tridge, embeem, and others hacked into their Series 1 machines. Opening up the Series 2 machines, which are obviously faster and more powerful, extends that same hackability to the Series 2. Who knows what cool new software for your TiVo may appear tomorrow?

This chapter explains how to unpack and install software in the most common archiving and compression formats used in TiVo and Linux development, how to install the compilers provided on the BATBD CD so that you can compile your own software for your TiVo, and discusses some of the more interesting TiVo development projects going on at various spots on the Internet.

Installing Software on Your TiVo

Once you've found an interesting package that is supposedly already compiled for your TiVo, making sure that it's for your model of TiVo and figuring out how to extract software from the various archive file formats can be quite challenging.

Identifying Binary File Formats

After you've located some interesting TiVo software, you need to figure out whether it's for the TiVo model that you actually have. This is hard to do when just looking at a file. Ones and zeroes that are designed to run on a PPC-based TiVo Series 1 looks much like the ones and zeroes that are designed to run on a MIPS-based Series 2 machine.

If you're using a Linux system as your personal computer, you can easily get information about the platform any binary application was compiled for by using the **file** command. The **file** command has a number of options, but is usually used with a single argument, which is the name of the file in which you're interested. For example, using the **file** command to examine a file called "tnlited" from a TiVo Series 1 would look like the following:

```
# file tnlited
tnlited: ELF 32-bit MSB executable, PowerPC or cisco 4500,
        version 1 (SYSV), dynamically linked (uses shared libs),
            stripped
```

> **NOTE**
>
> The output of the **file** command typically displays on a single line—these examples are broken across multiple lines for readability.

While this is all very interesting, the most important part of the **file** command's output is the fact that this executable is compiled for use on a PowerPC system (such as the TiVo Series 1).

Similarly, using the **file** command to examine a version of the "tnlited" file from a TiVo Series 2 would look like the following:

```
# file tnlited
tnlited: ELF 32-bit MSB MIPS-I executable, MIPS, version 1 (SYSV),
         for GNU/Linux 2.2.15, dynamically linked (uses shared libs),
             stripped
```

In this case, the file is an executable compiled for a MIPS system, such as a TiVo Series 2.

Uncompressing ZIP and GZ Files

Most applications for systems like those for the TiVos are distributed in single files that have been compressed in special formats. This reduces the amount of space they consume and therefore reduces the time that it takes to transfer the file from one system to another. Two of the most common formats for compressing files for Linux systems (such as the TiVo) are the zip format and gzip formats. (Windows and DOS users should be quite familiar with Zip files.)

> **TIP**
>
> Binaries of the unzip utility for both Series 1 and Series 2 machines are found in the hack archives provided in the BATBD CD's hack_dirs directory. The gzip utility (which can both compress and decompress archives) is provided as part of the Series 2 software from TiVo. A version of the gunzip utility (which decompresses) is provided courtesy of BusyBox in the archives on the BATBD CD.

Files compressed using the zip utility generally have the file extension ".zip" at the end of their names. Zip archives can contain one or more files, but generally contain a number of files. These files may be included as standard files, or may be contained within a directory that is also archived in the zip file.

The **unzip** command decompresses archive files with a .zip extension, as in the following example:

```
$ unzip tivovbi-1.03.zip
Archive:  tivovbi-1.03.zip
  creating: tivovbi/
 inflating: tivovbi/tivovbi
 inflating: tivovbi/README
 inflating: tivovbi/LICENSE
 inflating: tivovbi/CHANGES
  creating: tivovbi/src/
 inflating: tivovbi/src/osd.c
 inflating: tivovbi/src/makefile
 inflating: tivovbi/src/osd.h
 inflating: tivovbi/src/font.h
 inflating: tivovbi/src/tivocc.c
```

In this case, the zip archive contains a directory—when the contents of the archive file are extracted, the directory is created first, and then all of the extracted files are created inside the directory.

TIP

If you aren't sure if an archive file contains a directory or whether it simply will dump files in your working directory, you can use the **unzip** command's -t (test) option to see what the archive contains without actually extracting files, as in the following example:

```
$ unzip -t tivovbi-1.03.zip
Archive:  tivovbi-1.03.zip
    testing: tivovbi/               OK
    testing: tivovbi/tivovbi        OK
    testing: tivovbi/README         OK
    testing: tivovbi/LICENSE        OK
    testing: tivovbi/CHANGES        OK
    testing: tivovbi/src/           OK
    testing: tivovbi/src/osd.c      OK
    testing: tivovbi/src/makefile   OK
    testing: tivovbi/src/osd.h      OK
    testing: tivovbi/src/font.h     OK
    testing: tivovbi/src/tivocc.c   OK
No errors detected in compressed data of tivovbi-1.03.zip.
```

The gunzip utility extracts the contents of archived files compressed using gzip. The gzip utility itself provides a -d option to enable it to perform decompression. (The gzip and gunzip binaries are often the same file on standard Linux systems.) Compressed files with the .gz extension are usually either single files or archives of some other type, which then must be extracted. On Linux systems, these archived files are usually tar format files, as discussed in the next section.

Both gzip and gunzip work silently, unless told to be verbose using other command-line options. To use gunzip to extract the contents of an archived file, simply issue the **gunzip** command followed by the name of the archived file that you want to decompress, as in the following example:

```
$ gunzip newtext2osd-1.4.tar.gz
```

This command would create the file newtext2osd-1.4.tar in the current directory, which then could be extracted using the **tar** command, as explained in the next section.

To use the **gzip** command to extract the contents of an archived file, simply issue the **gzip** command with its -d (decompress) option, followed by the name of the archived file that you want to decompress, as in the following example:

```
$ gzip -d newtext2osd-1.4.tar.gz
```

As in the previous example, this command would create the file newtext2osd-1.4.tar in the current directory, which could then be extracted using the **tar** command, as explained in the next section.

Extracting Files from TAR and TGZ Archives

The **tar** command, which stands for "tape archiver," is one of the oldest Unix commands, and it's not surprising that the format of the outputted files it produces (known as *tar files*) is probably the most common way in which directories are archived on Unix and Linux systems.

 TIP

Binaries of the tar utility for both Series 1 and Series 2 machines are provided in the hack archives found in the BATBD CD's hack_dirs directory. The **tar** command for a Series 1 system is provided courtesy of BusyBox. The **tar** command for a Series 2 machine is a stand-alone command.

To extract the contents of a tar file, you use the **tar** command's x (extract) and f (file) options. The f option must be followed by the name of the tar file that contains the contents you want to extract, as in the following example:

```
$ tar xf newtext2osd-1.4.tar
```

This would extract whatever was in the specified tar file to the current directory. Since most people usually like to see what they're getting from an archive, it is common to include the v (verbose) option, as in the following example:

```
$ tar xvf newtext2osd-1.4.tar
newtext2osd-1.4/
newtext2osd-1.4/README
newtext2osd-1.4/LICENSE
newtext2osd-1.4/CHANGES
newtext2osd-1.4/src/
newtext2osd-1.4/src/osd.c
newtext2osd-1.4/src/makefile
newtext2osd-1.4/src/osd.h
newtext2osd-1.4/src/font.h
newtext2osd-1.4/src/osd.o
newtext2osd-1.4/src/newtext2osd.o
newtext2osd-1.4/src/testgrid
newtext2osd-1.4/src/newtext2osd.c
newtext2osd-1.4/newtext2osd
```

You may also encounter archived files with the extension .tgz. These are tar files that also have been compressed using gzip, typically in a single operation. To extract the tar file contents on a TiVo, you can use a Linux pipe to tell the **gzip** command to decompress a file, write the uncompressed output, and then pipe that to a **tar** command that actually extracts the contents of the stream of data that it is receiving from the **gzip** command, as in the following example:

```
$ gzip -cd newtext2osd-1.4.tar.gz | tar xvf -
newtext2osd-1.4/
newtext2osd-1.4/README
newtext2osd-1.4/LICENSE
newtext2osd-1.4/CHANGES
newtext2osd-1.4/src/
newtext2osd-1.4/src/osd.c
newtext2osd-1.4/src/makefile
newtext2osd-1.4/src/osd.h
newtext2osd-1.4/src/font.h
newtext2osd-1.4/src/osd.o
newtext2osd-1.4/src/newtext2osd.o
newtext2osd-1.4/src/testgrid
newtext2osd-1.4/src/newtext2osd.c
newtext2osd-1.4/newtext2osd
```

📺 EXTRACTING TAR FILES WITHOUT THE TAR COMMAND

Extracting the contents of the first tar file you have on a TiVo can be challenging. The **tar** command is provided in the tar files provided on the BATBD CD. If you extract the contents of the tar file while your TiVo drive is in your PC and you've booted from the BATBD CD, it's no problem—the BATBD CD comes with a built-in version of the **tar** command. However, what if you forget, or need to transfer the file to a networked TiVo manually?

All TiVo software distributions include another early Unix archiving utility, cpio (which stands for Copy Input To Output). The version of this command provided on the TiVos can extract the contents of a tar file (specified as TARFILE in this example), using the following syntax:

```
cpio -iduvH tar < TARFILE
```

The **cpio** command options have the following meanings:

◆ I Extract files from its input

◆ d Create directories as needed

◆ u Unconditionally creates files, even if they already exist

◆ v Be verbose about what's going on

◆ H Use the specified archive format (tar, in this case)

An example of using this command on a TiVo is as follows:

```
# cpio -iduv -H tar < newtext2osd-1.4.tar
newtext2osd-1.4
newtext2osd-1.4/README
newtext2osd-1.4/LICENSE
newtext2osd-1.4/CHANGES
newtext2osd-1.4/src
newtext2osd-1.4/src/osd.c
newtext2osd-1.4/src/makefile
newtext2osd-1.4/src/osd.h
newtext2osd-1.4/src/font.h
newtext2osd-1.4/src/osd.o
newtext2osd-1.4/src/newtext2osd.o
newtext2osd-1.4/src/testgrid
newtext2osd-1.4/src/newtext2osd.c
newtext2osd-1.4/newtext2osd
388 blocks
```

This is just another example of the power and flexibility of Linux. The version of tar provided on many desktop Linux systems has built-in support for gzip compression and decompression. You usually can do all of this with a single **tar** command, such as the following:

```
$ tar zxvf newtext2osd-1.4.tar.gz
newtext2osd-1.4/
newtext2osd-1.4/README
newtext2osd-1.4/LICENSE
newtext2osd-1.4/CHANGES
newtext2osd-1.4/src/
newtext2osd-1.4/src/osd.c
newtext2osd-1.4/src/makefile
newtext2osd-1.4/src/osd.h
newtext2osd-1.4/src/font.h
newtext2osd-1.4/src/osd.o
newtext2osd-1.4/src/newtext2osd.o
newtext2osd-1.4/src/testgrid
newtext2osd-1.4/src/newtext2osd.c
newtext2osd-1.4/newtext2osd
```

Safe Locations for Storing Your TiVo Hacks

As mentioned earlier in this book, most TiVos perform a number of file and general sanity checks on the contents of their root partitions. TiVo's software update process can overwrite any of the default partitions on your TiVo, which may cause you to lose your hard-won TiVo hacks, if they're stored in the filesystems mounted at / or /var. Also, newer versions of the TiVo software are more and more paranoid about verifying the integrity and source of every piece of software in standard TiVo partitions. Versions of the TiVo software newer than Version 2.5 will delete modified versions of standard TiVo command files, programs, and libraries, replacing them with "stock" versions of the same files from the original TiVo software distributions. In some cases, directory hierarchies that are not present in the partitions provided with original TiVo software distributions will be automatically deleted.

As you amass a collection of your favorite TiVo hacks, you may want to consider creating a special partition on your TiVo disk in which to store these, and mounting this partition elsewhere on your TiVo to access your favorite tweaks. As a special partition, it will not be affected by TiVo software updates—its mount point may be deleted, but nothing else.

Manually creating a partition on your disk and formatting it with the right type of filesystem is complex, but it can be done as part of a disk upgrade if you create a new swap partition, leaving the old one (usually 64 MB in size) available for re-use, For some suggestions and troubleshooting pointers, see the TiVo Forums discussed in Chapter 11.

Installing Cross-Compilers for TiVo Development

As a Linux system, an exponentially larger amount of free software is available in source form that you may want to run on your TiVo. However, figuring out how to build software on a desktop system that is compiled to run on your TiVo can be perplexing, unless you're already familiar with software such as GCC and the concept of cross-compiling applications on one machine so that they will run on another.

The BATBD CD included with this book includes cross-compilers for both Series 1 and Series 2 machines. As discussed in Chapter 9, cross-compilers run on one type of system but produce binary output targeted for another type of system. In the case of the cross-compilers included with this book, they run on an x86 Linux system and produce output targeted for the TiVo Series 1 or the TiVo Series 2.

The BATBD CD includes the following cross-compilers for your TiVo:

- *xcompilers/Series1/usr.local.powerpc-tivo.tgz* An early cross-compiler for the TiVo Series 1 that requires relatively little disk space.
- *xcompilers/Series1/tivodev-2.5_linux-x86_dtype1.tgz* Version 1 of an extensive cross-compilation environment for the TiVo Series 1
- *xcompilers/Series1/tivodev-2.5_linux-x86_dtype2.tgz* Version 2 of the same extensive cross-compilation environment for the TiVo Series 1. It is somewhat larger, but much improved and enriched.
- *xcompilers/Series2/usr.local.tivo-mips_bu211.tgz* A cross-compiler for the TiVo Series 2 that includes Version 2.11 of the binutils package. (The binutils package contains compilation-related software like the GNU assembler, archiver, linker, loader, and so forth.)
- *xcompilers/Series2/usr.local.tivo-mips_bu213.tgz* A cross-compiler for the TiVo Series 2 that includes Version 2.13 of the binutils package.

Selecting and Installing a Cross-Compiler for the TiVo Series 1

If you are using a Series 1 machine, the usr.local.powerpc-tivo.tgz cross-compiler is a good starting point for your cross-compilation experiments. It is easier and smaller to install, although much less powerful. To install it, **cd** to the root of your computer and extract its contents, as in the following example:

```
# cd /
# tar zxvf PATH-TO-CD/xcompilers/Series1/usr.local.powerpc-tivo.tgz
```

After a hundred yards or so of output, the installation will complete. Your Series 1 cross-compiler then is installed in the appropriate subdirectories of /usr/local/tivo. To begin cross-compiling, all you have to do is add the directory /usr/local/tivo/bin to your PATH, as in the following example:

```
$ export PATH=/usr/local/tivo/bin:${PATH}
```

You should be ready to compile applications for your Series 1 machine using the standard **gcc** command.

WARNING

When using cross-compilers that have the same names as your desktop Linux system's compiler, make sure that you add this directory only to your PATH environment variable when you want to build applications for your Series 1 machine. If you arbitrarily add the directory /usr/local/tivo/bin to the front of your PATH, the cross-compiling GCC will be the first C compiler in your PATH at all times, and everything you compile will execute only on your TiVo—probably not what you had in mind.

For a much more complete TiVo development environment, install the xcompilers/Series1/tivodev-2.5_linux-x86_dtype2.tgz cross-compiler and general all-around development environment. This is Version 2 of a complete Series 1 development environment used by well-known TiVo hackers to build their favorite TiVo software. To do so, make sure your working directory is /home and extract the contents of xcompilers/Series1/tivodev-2.5_linux-x86_dtype2.tgz, as in the following example:

```
# cd /home
# tar zxvf /PATH-TO-CD/xcompilers/Series1/tivodev-2.5_linux-x86_dtype2.tgz
```

After extracting the contents of the archive, **cd** to the directory /home/tivodev and read the README file for complete instructions about taking advantage of this impressively complete and robust development environment. It contains much more than the us.local.powerpc cross-compiler, but it also requires substantially more disk space.

NOTE

Version 1 of the same development environment is provided in the file xcompilers/Series1/tivodev-2.5_linux-x86_dtype1.tgz on the BATBD CD, primarily for comparative purposes, but also in case you encounter problems with Version 2.

Selecting and Installing the Cross-Compiler for the TiVo Series 2

The decision as to which cross-compiler to install on your Series 2 machine is much simpler. Two are provided. The only difference is based on the version of the GNU binutils package that they include. The binutils package contains compilation-related software like the GNU assembler, archiver, linker, loader, and so on. I would definitely suggest that you first try the version based on binutils 2.1.3 (usr.local.tivo-mips_bu213.tgz), by changing the directory to the root directory of your Linux system and extracting its contents, as in the following example:

```
# cd /
# tar zxvf /PATH_TO_CD/xcompilers/Series2/usr.local.tivo-mips_bu213.tgz
```

After a huge amount of output listing the files that are installing, the installation will complete. Your Series 2 cross-compiler will be installed in the appropriate subdirectories of /usr/local/tivo-mips. To begin cross-compiling, all you have to do is add the directory /usr/local/tivo-mips/bin to your PATH, as in the following example:

```
$ export PATH=/usr/local/tivo-mips/bin:${PATH}
```

You now should be ready to compile applications for your Series 2 system using the standard **gcc** command.

WARNING

When using cross-compilers that have the same names as your desktop Linux system's compiler, make sure that you add this directory only to your PATH environment variable when you want to build applications for your Series 2 machine. If you arbitrarily add the /usr/local/tivo-mips/bin directory to the front of your PATH, the cross-compiling GCC will be the first C compiler in your PATH at all times and everything you compiled will only execute on your TiVo—probably not what you had in mind.

If you subsequently have problems using this cross-compiler, you can try falling back to the other version by deleting your current version and installing the older one in its place, as in the following example:

```
# cd /
# rm -rf /usr/local/tivo-mips
# tar zxvf /PATH_TO_CD/xcompilers/Series2/usr.local.tivo-mips_bu211.tgz
```

If you continue to have problems with the cross-compiler, the TiVo forums are your friends. Many people are actively using forums, so the problems that you are experiencing are likely configuration issues or slight cases of "pilot error."

Stand-alone TiVo Tools and Development Projects

This section highlights some of the more active TiVo development projects and tools that are available on the Web today.

An Alternate UI in the TiVo Web Project

The TiVo Web Project, aka TiVoWeb, is one of the more impressive bits of TiVo software I've ever seen. The TiVoWeb was created by a TiVo hacker, lightn (along with other contributors such as embeem), who deserves every kudos he's ever received for this truly amazing piece of software. The home page of the TiVo Web is at http://tivo.lightn.org. The ability of the TiVoWeb to schedule recordings from any Web browser is only a tiny subset of the bells and whistles that it provides. TiVoWeb enables you to control your TiVo remotely, get information about its status, view its log files, request updates from TiVo, and so forth. Most impressively, TiVoWeb provides access to the internals of TiVo's MFS filesystem and includes an easily expanded resource editor that lets you use TiVoWeb to peek and poke resource values. All this in a free application that "just works." It's absolutely incredible!

Using TiVoWeb on your home network is easy, since all of the machines on your home network can presumably access your networked TiVo. Accessing TiVoWeb from the Internet requires that you have an accessible TiVo from outside your home network. There are two ways to do this: through a proxy if you are running your own Apache Web server or a similar application, or through port forwarding on a home gateway, if that's what you're running to connect your home network to the Internet.

If your home network is connected to the Internet through a home gateway, the easiest way to make your TiVo available from the outside world is to set up port forwarding on the gateway. This means that when requests are received on a specific port of the IP address that corresponds to your home gateway, the gateway automatically forwards those requests to your TiVo. Needless to say, the TiVo also handles outgoing communication from your TiVo for any connections that have been established using port forwarding. Figure 10.1 shows the port-forwarding panel of the LinkSys gateway that I use at home. The TiVoWeb entry shows that any requests received on port 99 of my home gateway's external IP address will automatically forward to port 80 on my TiVo, which has the internal IP address 192.168.6.247.

 NOTE

Using port forwarding on your TiVo can be a serious security hole if your gateway does not require authentication before forwarding a connection.

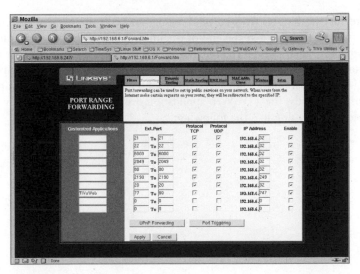

FIGURE 10.1 *Setting up port forwarding on a LinkSys home gateway*

To install TiVoWeb on your TiVo, you already must have a shell prompt or network service enabled—TiVoWeb isn't all that useful without the latter anyway. Once your TiVo is on your home network, do the following:

1. Mount the BATBD CD on your PC and change the directory to the top level of the CD.

2. Open an FTP connection to the TiVo and send the file tivoweb-tcl-1.9.4.tar to your TiVo using the following commands:

   ◆ *bin* Puts the transfer in binary mode.

   ◆ *hash* Turns on hashing to see packet transfers.

   ◆ *cd /var* Changes directory to a writable directory on your TiVo.

   ◆ *put tivoweb-tcl-1.9.4.tar* Transfers the file.

3. After the file has transferred, quit the ftp connection and open a telnet connection to your TiVo.

4. When you're connected, change directory to the directory where you put the ftp file, tivoweb-tcl-1.9.4.tar (/var if you followed the previous examples).

5. Extract the contents of the tar file using the following command:

```
tar xvf tivoweb-tcl-1.9.4.tar
```

   This creates the directory /var/tivoweb-tcl and populates it with the files required by TiVoWeb.

6. Change directory to the new tivoweb-tcl directory and edit the file tivoweb.cfg. Put a username after the equal sign at the end of the line beginning with UserName; put a password after the equal sign on the line beginning with Password. This isn't the most elegant security, since anyone on your home network can telnet to the machine and examine this configuration file. However, it is useful to set a password if you plan to expose your TiVo or just the TiVoWeb application over the Internet. Your tivoweb.cfg file should look something like the following:

```
UserName = wvh
Password = mypassword
Port = 80
Prefix =
Theme = daynight
DescriptionHover = 1
MultiDelete = 1
```

 NOTE

A version of the TiVoWeb application that is fully compatible with TiVo software Version 4.0 is under active development. I'm sure that when it's available, it will be just as impressive as the current version. It offers many of the features of TiVo's current remote scheduling mechanism today, with the exception of the fact that you can schedule directly on your TiVo over the Web, rather than going through TiVo's Web site.

7. If you are running a Series 1 or a Series 2 system that you have hacked using the Two Kernel Monte approach, execute the following command so that you can modify your TiVo's /etc/rc.d/rc.sysinit file:

```
mount -o rw,remount /
```

Next, use a text editor to add the following line to the end of the /etc/rc.d/rc.sysinit file so that the TiVoWeb application will automatically start each time you reboot your TiVo:

```
/var/tivoweb-tcl/tivoweb &
```

Now, execute the following command to make sure your root partition is read-only again, for security reasons:

```
mount -o ro,remount /
```

8. If you are running on a TiVo Series 2 and are not using the Two Kernel Monte approach, use a text editor to modify the file /var/hack/hackinit, adding the following command to the end of the file so that the TiVoWeb application will automatically start each time you reboot your TiVo:

```
/var/tivoweb-tcl/tivoweb &
```

9. You can now start TiVoWeb manually by executing the following command at the telnet prompt:

```
/var/tivoweb-tcl/tivoweb &
```

After you have TiVoWeb running on your TiVo, you can connect to it using any Web browser. Because you set a username and password when installing TiVoWeb , your browser will prompt you for the username and password before you can log in. After you enter the correct username and password, your browser displays TiVoWeb's main menu as shown in Figure 10.2.

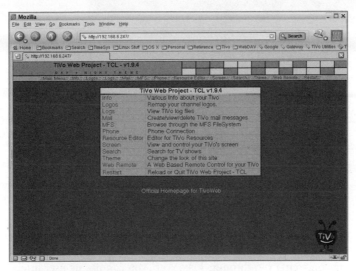

FIGURE 10.2 *TiVoWeb's main screen*

One of TiVoWeb's most interesting features is its Web Remote screen, shown in Figure 10.3. This screen provides a graphical image of a TiVo remote control on which you can click buttons to control your TiVo, just as if you were standing in front of it.

To change channels on your TiVo remotely, select the Web Remote command from the TiVoWeb menu. Next, click the Live TV button, enter the channel number(s) you want to switch to on the Web Remote screen, and click Select just as you would on your actual remote at home.

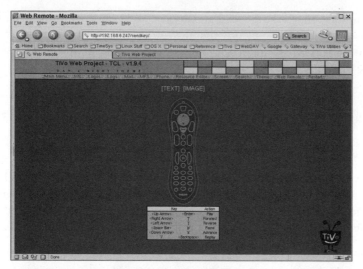

FIGURE 10.3 *TiVoWeb's Web Remote screen*

TIP

If you don't happen to recall the number of the channel where you want to tune your TiVo, TiVoWeb provides a convenient summary of all the channels that your TiVo receives. This is available by clicking on the Logos command in the TiVoWeb screen. A screen displays like the one shown in Figure 10.4, but customized for the list of channels that you receive. This screen enables you to associate graphical logos with various channels, and automatically displays logos for any stations associated with known networks or broadcasting systems.

To schedule recordings on your TiVo through TiVoWeb, you can use its user interface module (available on the main menu), which provides a Web-based approximation of the onscreen TiVo user interface—but in your favorite browser!

One of TiVoWeb's most interesting aspects is its ability to display and edit MFS Resources. (For more information about MFS, see Chapter 9, the section "The TiVo Filesystem.") To see the list of editable resources provided with TiVoWeb, click its Resource Editor menu entry, and a screen like the one shown in Figure 10.5 displays.

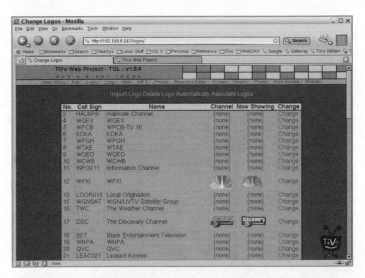

FIGURE 10.4 *TiVoWeb's channel listing with logos*

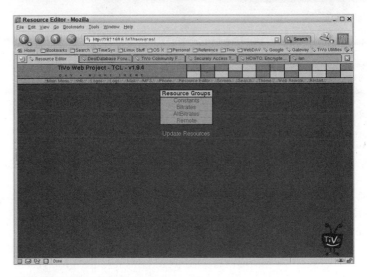

FIGURE 10.5 *TiVoWeb's Resource Groups screen*

Clicking one of the resource groups listed in this menu displays a list of edited MFS resources associated with that group, as shown in Figure 10.6. These resource groups are user-defined lists of MFS resource groups and item numbers. To change the value of a resource, enter the new values in the appropriate field and press Return or Enter on your keyboard. *Be very careful* when changing resources. Don't change them unless you're absolutely sure that you know what they do—or at least write down the old values before changing anything. After you change the value of a resource, you must click on the Resource Editor menu again and click the Update Resources link. This saves the updated resources and discards any cached values. You should also reboot your TiVo after changing resources, to ensure that your TiVo picks up the new values.

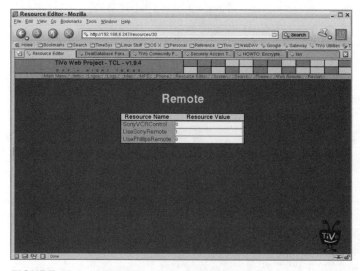

FIGURE 10.6 *A TiVoWeb Resource Editor screen*

Note that the remote resource group and the screen shown in Figure 10.6 are not available in the version of TiVoWeb that you installed from the BATBD CD. This is a resource group that I added to enable me to use a Sony remote control with my Phillips Series 1 machine. You can easily add resource groups by creating files with the extension .res in the module's subdirectory of your TiVoWeb installation. The file that I created to add this resource group is tvhack-30.res, and contains the following entries:

```
3.0

Remote SonyVCRControl     30   2

Remote UseSonyRemote      30   3

Remote UsePhillipsRemote  30   4
```

The first line identifies the version of the TiVo software for which this set of resource entries is valid. Each subsequent line identifies the resource group on which this entry should appear, the name that I assigned to this resource, and (most importantly) the MFS resource group and item number. The values in the sample file are specific to a TiVo Series 1 running Version 3.0 of the TiVo software. Note that the name of the resource group and the resource itself are user-defined—the only things that matter to MFS (and thus to TiVoWeb Project) are the two numbers representing the MFS resource group and item number.

You can easily expand TiVoWeb to edit other resources, as long as you know what they are. You can certainly have some fun by changing resource string values that occasionally display onscreen, but remember that your changes will be lost if a new version of the TiVo software is installed on your TiVo. The resource groups will almost certainly be different in different versions of the TiVo software—hence TiVoWeb's support for version numbers in resource definition files.

The TiVo Enhancement Development Team

The TiVo Enhancement Development Team is the current home of many of the original TiVo hacks, instructions, and development efforts. Hosted at SourceForge at http://tivohack.sourceforge.net, it is a useful repository. If you're looking for older TiVo Series 1 tips, tricks, or Linux add-ons, this Web site is a great place to look.

The Personal TiVo Home Media Option

As discussed in Chapters 8 and 9, TiVo's Home Media Option for the TiVo Series 2 machine running Version 4.0 of the TiVo software is an impressive extension to the power and usability of your TiVo. Playing online audio files and displaying digital photographs stored on Windows and Macintosh systems makes your TiVo an even more powerful part of your home theater system. However, the lack of similar software from TiVo for those of us who store our audio files on Linux systems (and in Linux-based formats such as OGG) was irritating to many people.

In frustration, I asked about this issue on the TiVoCommunity Forum, and received replies from members of SourceForge's Personal TiVo Home Media Option Project (http://sourceforge.net/projects/ptivohmo). This project provides a free, Linux-based server for digital audio and photographs to which your TiVo can instantly connect. Installing and configuring this software was explained in Chapter 9 in "Working With TiVo's Home Media Option from Linux." A tar file of this project is also located in the connectivity subdirectory of the CD that accompanies this book.

This is simply a great project. If you store your music on a Linux system, you need this software. It works well for me, but I'm sure that they'd be happy to have more contributors if you spot a missing feature or would like to exercise your Perl-hacking skills and contribute something to the TiVo Community.

Closed Captioning Support Using TiVoVBI

An early TiVo hack that led to many of the onscreen display routines used by almost every project that displays text on a TiVo screen, TiVoVBI is still a great piece of software. TiVoVBI enables the TiVo to decode and display closed caption and XDS data to the television screen, file, or console.

TIP

TiVoVBI is especially useful because even the TiVo's rewind command doesn't always enable you to catch what's being said, regardless of how many times you listen to it. To solve this problem, install TiVoVBI on your TiVo, activate closed captioning, rewind, and there you go! The missing phrases are displayed on your TiVo screen.

You can download a copy of the current version (1.03) from http://tivo.samba.org/download/mbm/tivovbi-1.03.zip. The software is also available in the connectivity directory on the BATBD CD.

NOTE

Installing this software on a TiVo running Version 3.0 or greater of the TiVo software also requires that you download the tvbi-test.o module from http://tivo.samba.org/download/mbm/bin (or get it from the connectivity directory on the BATBD CD), transfer it to your TiVo, and use the **insmod** command to insert it into your running kernel by using the following command:

```
insmod -f tvbi-test.o
```

If you will be running TiVoVBI in the future, you may want to permanently add this statement to your **rc.sysinit** or other system startup files.

TiVo Utilities Home Page

The TiVo Utilities Home is yet another fine repository of good TiVo software. The TiVo Utilities Home Page is hosted by SourceForge at http://tivoutils.sourceforge.net. This is a great place to look for Series 1 and Series 2 system software. Unlike many other TiVo sites, they've made a noble attempt at posting as much of whatever documentation is available for various TiVo hardware, and there is also a link to TiVo's own developer documentation and resources.

HACKING THE TiVo

Chapter 11

Other TiVo Hacking Resources

As Carl Sagan might have said, "There are billions and billions of Web sites on the Internet devoted to the TiVo." That might be a slight exaggeration, but the fact remains that there are a huge number of sites that mention the TiVo, provide reviews of TiVo hardware and the TiVo software, compare and contrast TiVos with other DVR hardware and software, and (best of all) provide tips and tricks for getting the most out of your TiVo.

Articles about the TiVo frequently note that the TiVo is unique among DVRs and perhaps in general in terms of the fanatical devotion of its owners. The TiVo has been discussed on the Oprah Winfrey and David Letterman shows, has been mentioned in a variety of situation comedies, and has been a central "character" in an episode of *Sex and the City*. It has become a verb (as in "I tivo'd that last night"), and it was even the favorite Christmas gift of FCC Chairman, Michael Powell, who referred to the TiVo as "God's Machine" in an interview at a recent consumer electronics show. I can't think of anything since the original Volkswagen Bug that has the same sort of fanatical army of devotees as TiVo—and it took the Bug a decade or so to achieve cult status.

One aspect of the TiVo's overwhelming online presence and vocal advocate groups is the fact that TiVos run Linux, which provides a lot of cross-over between TiVo groupies and Linux fanatics, the latter of whom are well-known for their missionary zeal. Given that the TiVo is one of the stellar successes of Linux in a commercial setting and that it displays none of the command-line awkwardness that people often associate with Linux—you've got a winning combination for every Linux advocate in the known world to say, "See, I told you so!" (The author included.) Add in the fact that the TiVo is eminently hackable, and you've got a winning combination that just begs to be discussed on Web sites, newsgroups, blogs, and discussions on SlashDot.

Another fun aspect of the TiVo's popularity on the Internet is the frequency with which industry observers and related pundits delight in predicting its imminent demise. This seems to come largely from a bunch of "late to the .com crash" critics with a last-shark-at-the-shipwreck mentality, wanting to make sure that they get a piece too. "Let's see, who's still around that might go down and make me look like Nostradamus?" To be fair, many aspects of the TiVo reek of the dot.com days, but even the most jaded among us have to admit that the cute TiVo guy is a lot more pleasant than a sock puppet. Among TiVo detractors are a huge number of bitter ReplayTV and UltimateTV fans out there, endlessly griping about how much better their now-deceased platforms were. You can't blame people for being sad when their pets have been put to sleep. I was a Berkeley Unix/SunOS fanatic for years—but sorry, it's over. (Though there's always Mac OS X—but I digress!)

This book wouldn't have been possible without the hundreds of Web sites, posts, questions, and discussions of TiVo tips, tricks, gotchas, and everything else. I want to give credit where credit is due by highlighting some of the most extensive and useful TiVo sites that are available on the Internet. In the discussion of each site, you will find out the type of TiVo the site is relevant to and, where necessary, any information that may be invalid or superceded.

NOTE

None of the sites discussed in this chapter are unilaterally endorsed by TiVo, Inc., including the TiVo Community Forum, which is partly sponsored by TiVo. That doesn't mean that they like everything they see there. Some employees of TiVo, Inc. may occasionally post messages or tips on various forums, but this does not mean that TiVo, Inc. endorses or even sanctions those posts.

To the best of my knowledge, none of the sites discussed in this chapter provide illegal software or instructions that describe illegal techniques. If it turns out that they do, I'm sorry. I do not maintain any of these sites, although I've certainly benefited from many of them. If you have a general problem, seek medical attention. If you have a problem with any of the sites or Web pages discussed in this chapter, take it up with their owners or maintainers.

Don't play with matches. Don't run with scissors. Don't look at things that offend you. Don't ruin things for other people.

A Byte of Fun—TiVo Advocacy Articles

TiVo advocacy is somewhat in decline, largely because the TiVo is a fact of life nowadays. Like Linux itself, the time and the need to proselytize is largely past—it's time to put the technology to work. However, if you just happened to stumble upon the TiVo or heard about it from someone who wasn't a rabid TiVo fanatic, you might enjoy reading a few articles and bits of commentary about TiVo and the TiVo phenomenon. If you're having a hard time convincing your siblings, parents, coworkers, or even a complete stranger that the TiVo is a great thing, perhaps a photocopy of this page could save you a lot of talking.

Here are some of my favorites from the past two years (organized alphabetically by author):

◆ Christine Chen's "My Life with TiVo" in *Fortune Magazine* online (http://www.fortune.com/fortune/technology/articles/0,15114,366870,00.html) is a fun article from May of 2001.

◆ Marjorie Dorfman's "What Is This Thing Called TiVo?," available at the URL http://www.bytebackonline.com/Articles_p/tivo_p.html is a humorous look, from 2003, at the TiVo phenomenon and some of the advantages of the TiVo.

◆ Brendan Koerner's doom and gloom article at http://slate.msn.com/id/2072037, entitled "TiVo, We Hardly Knew Ye," is my favorite entry in the "Funny, but Wrong" sweepstakes. Published in October, 2002, it would seem that rumors of the demise of the TiVo have been much exaggerated. It is somewhat surprising that a humor publication from MSN (the MicroSoft Network) would criticize the TiVo when its own Ultimate TV was the Ultimate Tur-Key.

◆ Heather Newman's posts for the *Detroit Free Press* are a great source of information for TiVo fans and advocates. A representative article from April, 2003, entitled "This Is a Recording: TiVo Is a Must for the Viewer," is available at the URL http://www.freep.com/money/tech/newman24_20030424.htm.

◆ David Pogue, writer of the "Circuits" column for *The New York Times*, the "Missing Manual" series of computer books, and a zillion other computer books over the years, is a well-known and vocal TiVo fan. Links to abstracts of his "Circuits" columns are available from http://www.davidpogue.com/TimesArchives.html, but you have to pay money to see them (unless you subscribe and wait for the next one). One of them (from January, 2003) has been preserved on the TiVo site itself, and is available in PDF at http://www.tivo.com/pdfs/productreviews/ny_times_0103_pogue.pdf.

◆ Ernest Svenson (aka Ernie the Attorney) has a fun "TiVo Changed My Life" blog at http://radio.weblogs.com/0104634/stories/2002/12/14/tivoChangedMyLife.html (2003). This is an entertaining site that also features links to other TiVo advocacy sites and information.

Online Forums for TiVo Information and Discussion

The best sites on the Web for discussing and sharing TiVo information are known as *discussion forums* or simply "forums." These sites enable people to read and participate in online discussions of TiVo-related topics. These online discussion topics are organized into different categories that reflect specific subjects or levels of expertise with the subject matter. Within each category and forum, each set of posts and replies on a single topic is organized into a sequence of messages known as a *thread*, which makes it easy to follow a specific online discussion. Organizing topics and discussions hierarchically makes it easier to find information on a specific subject or know where to post a specific question.

Forums work much like Web logs (*blogs*) or bulletin board systems (depending on what is familiar to you). After you've selected the forum that you want to view, your browser displays the first page of the threads that are available in that forum. Once you click on a thread, the first page of messages in that thread displays. You can scroll through various posts in that thread, reply to the thread, or reply to the specific individual who posted a given message.

Many of the forums discussed in this section use a software package called vBulletin (http://www.vbulletin.com) from Jelsoft Enterprises Limited to manage the forum and its threads (the TiVo Community Forum, http://www.tivocommunity.com, is a notable exception—it started out using UltimateBB). The vBulletin software is powered by great open source software such as PHP (the Personal Hypertext Preprocessor: http://www.php.net) and MySQL (My Structured Query Language: http://www.mysql.com), but is itself a commercial product with reasonable licensing charges.

The vBulletin software is a great framework for a wide variety of online communities, providing not only the software to power the site, but the associated administrative utilities and infrastructure required to manage it. Most online forums enable anyone to view forums and threads, but require that you actually log into the forum site to post messages. In order to log in, you must register with the forum and create a user account there. Requiring user accounts to post messages helps eliminate the possibility that people would post SPAM or offensive messages there, since each thread and reply to a thread is tagged with the online identity of the person who posted it.

Unfortunately, simply tagging each message with the community identity of the person who posted it doesn't always stop people from posting offensive, off-topic, or inappropriate messages. Everyone's standard of offensive language or subject matter is different. Off-topic or inappropriate messages (such as advertisements for commercial services) are different—while not offensive, they waste people's time. In order to eliminate these types of offenses, online forums are moderated. This means that someone is responsible for managing and maintaining the threads within each forum, deleting offensive or inappropriate messages whenever necessary, and offering suggestions to people who have asked questions or posted information that isn't relevant to the topic being discussed in a particular thread. Most moderators have a good knowledge of the forum topic themselves, and are willing to invest some of their time in order to ensure that the forums are as useful and understandable as possible. When reading the messages in a thread on a forum that uses the vBulletin software, you'll see several icons displayed at the end of each message. These provide convenient shortcuts for replying to the message or editing it (if you posted it originally). Each message also provides a convenient link for reporting a specific message to the moderator if you find it offensive, feel that it is inappropriate, or feel that it is unrelated to the topic.

Because the same software powers all of the forums discussed in this section, they have a similar look and feel. However, different forum sites host different categories and forums, they have different notions of the topics that are valid to discuss in each forum, and they provide different levels of online support and service to the TiVo community as a whole. The forums discussed in this chapter are organized alphabetically—not in terms of usability, relevance, or general good times.

TIP

If you are new to the TiVo or new to the notion of online communities, the various TiVo forums discussed in this chapter can be somewhat overwhelming. To dip your toe in the water, I'd suggest trying the TiVo Community Forum and beginning your online community experience by reading one of the Newbie or general discussion groups. If you are interested in topics that cannot be discussed there, you should try the DealDatabase Forum. If you are generally interested in Audio-Visual issues, you may then want to check out the AVS Forum. I've found lots of great information at all of these sites.

The AVS Forum

The AVS (AV Science, or Audio-Visual Science) Forum (http://www.avsforum.com) is often confused with the TiVo Community forum. The TiVo Community forum is dedicated to TiVo-related topics and discussions, while the AVS Forum views the TiVo as a single instance of an audio-visual device. You will certainly find TiVo-specific information on the AVS Forum, but the site in general has a much wider focus. The AVS Forum is operated and managed by the AV Science Corporation of Rochester, NY, USA.

The AVS Forum is a great site for anyone interested in any type of audio-visual equipment, associated rumors, or AV industry trends. I'm historically more of a computer guy than an AV fan, but my first visit to the AVS Forum changed all that. After reading a few posts about High-Definition televisions, plasma screens, and whizzy devices that I hadn't even heard of before, I found myself picturing a much more hi-tech living room and lifestyle than I'd ever dreamed. Use caution when visiting this site ;-).

TiVo WOULD YOU LIKE TO SEE A MENU?

In addition to forums and threads, each page of the AVS Forum also provides pull-down menus (which will only display or work if your browser supports JavaScript) that provide easy access to a variety of information. These are available at the top of each page, and provide entries for the following information and hyperlinks:

◆ *Members Area* General forum information, including information about registering, changing your personal preferences, the FAQ (Frequently-Asked Questions) for the vBulletin software, and various search features.

◆ *Services* A site-specific list of special features available on the AVS Forum site, such as special events, classified ads, and information about registering for the site.

◆ *Forums* A quick-reference to registration information, special areas on the AVS Forum, and related forums available on other sites (including the TiVo Community forum).

◆ *Alliance Sponsors* A set of quick links to sponsors of the AVS Forum.

◆ *About AVS* Links to the AVS Forum's privacy policy, contact information, information about subscribing to or becoming a sponsor of the AVS Forum, and a link to the people who developed the hierarchical menu JavaScript used in these menus.

Figure 11.1 shows the home page of the AVS Forum in a Web browser. The page where you can see all of the forums available on the AVS Forum is located at http://www.avsforum.com/avs-vb.

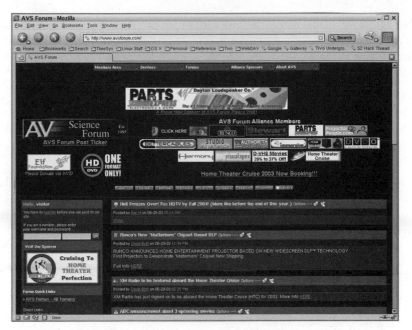

FIGURE 11.1 *The home page of the AVS Forum in a Web browser*

 TIP

If you're a regular visitor to the AVS Forum, an easy way to view a listing of the most recent posts on any of its forums is to click on the AVS Forum Post Ticker link, which is available at the top of each Web page on the AVS Forum. Clicking this link pops up a small dialog box that displays a scrolling list of the most recent posts made to any of the AVS forums. To view a specific post from this list, just click on its listing in the scrolling dialog box, and a new browser window opens on your screen, containing the selected post.

The AVS Forum is the largest and most extensive of any of the forums discussed in this chapter, largely because it is not just limited to DVRs, but discusses the entire spectrum of hi-tech home entertainment gear. The following list describes the AVS forums that I have found most useful in my DVR and TiVo education, along with a short description of each. These are listed alphabetically, rather than in the order that they appear on the AVS Forum Web pages. The

AVS forum was the original TiVo hacking forum, so it contains a seemingly endless archive of posts relating to hacking TiVo; some of the hacks date back to the earliest days of TiVo hacking. Eventually, the TiVo portion of AVS Forum branched off to its own site, `TiVo Community Forum`, where it remains today.

Remember that each of the categories and forums on the AVS Forum site contains its own threads, fanatics, and range of useful information. If you are interested in hi-tech audio/visual gear, you owe it to yourself to visit the site and search through all of its forums. The ones in the following list are simply my favorite AVS Forum areas—your mileage may vary:

◆ *AVS Forum Power Buys and Special Items* This forum area is for advertising special deals and purchases that are provided or authorized by the AVS Forum. Posting in this forum is restricted to AVS administrators and operators, and other authorized users. If you're looking for hi-tech audio/visual gear, you can find some great deals in this section.

◆ *Digital Recorders (PVR's) General* A forum for discussing any type of digital or personal video recorder. This forum is the place for general questions about cable boxes with built-in DVRs, as well as do-it-yourself hardware and software for putting one together on your own. The TiVo, ReplayTV, and Microsoft UltimateTV DVRs have their own forums, so discussion of these on this general forum will quickly be moved elsewhere. This forum prohibits any discussions of theft of service from any of the providers of DVRs. Posts on such topics will be squashed like a bug.

◆ *Dish Network & Dish PVRs* A forum for questions, answers, and general discussion of the DishNetwork and the DishPVR Digital Receiver/Recorder. Competing devices and systems such as the DirecTiVo should not be discussed here, only slandered. No discussion of hacking these systems is permitted.

◆ *Home Theater Computers* A forum that discusses the use of home computers as progressive-scan DVD players, video processors, HDTV tuners, music jukeboxes, home automation controllers, Internet/game machines, and just about anything else. This forum is primarily dedicated to discussion of the use of computers running the Linux and Microsoft Windows operating systems.

◆ *Microsoft UltimateTV PVR* A forum for questions, answers, and general discussion of the evolutionary dead-end also known as the UltimateTV.

◆ *Plasma and LCD Flat Panel Displays* Discussion, questions, and answers about Plasma and LCD (Liquid Crystal Display) Flat Panel Displays. This forum prohibits discussions of hacking these displays, which takes a lot of the fun out of it.

◆ *ReplayTV & Showstopper PVRs* A forum for questions, answers, and general discussion regarding the dearly departed RePlayTV and ShowStopper Digital Recorders.

◆ *Screens* Questions and answers about various types of display screens. This is a useful forum that has cleared up lots of newbie questions for me.

◆ *TiVo Community Forums* A hyperlink to the TiVo Community Forums, discussed later in this chapter.

◆ *Tweaks and Do-It-Yourself* Discussions of off-the-shelf and do-it-yourself items that can help improve the image, sound, or overall performance of your audio and home theater. This forum even discusses details like interconnects, speaker cables, power cords, and how to isolate one system from another. It's amazing how much of a difference a type of wire or connector can make in certainly circumstances.

◆ *Ultra Hi-End HT Gear ($20,000+)* This area hosts discussions, questions, and answers about any home theatre hardware with a manufacturer's suggested retail price of $20,000 (US dollars) or more. Would someone who reads and participates in this forum please send me a free DirecTiVo, since that's basically chump change for you?

The DealDatabase Forums

DealDatabase.com (see Figure 11.2) is a Web site that specializes in helping you find the best prices for a variety of online purchases. They do this by providing a number of categories in which one can post "deals" that are relevant to those categories. Standard categories include Auto(mobiles), Baby Stuff, Books & Magazines, Business & Office, Casinos, Clothing & Footwear, Computers, DVDs & VHS, Electronics, Rewards, Food, Freebies, Health & Beauty, Home & Garden, Jewelry, Music, Pets, Sporting Goods, Toys & Games, and a Miscellaneous category for anything that doesn't fit into any of the above categories. At any given time, you're likely to find special deals from online sites such as Amazon.com, Barnes&Noble.com, Best-Buy.com, Buy.com, Dell.com, DVDPlanet.com, JCrew.com, Staples.com, and many more.

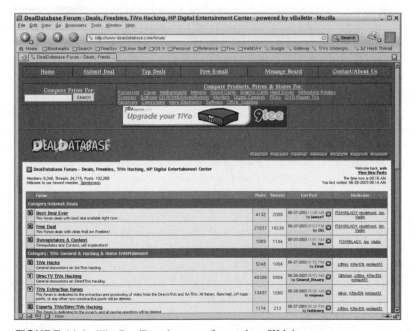

FIGURE 11.2 *The DealDatabase.com forums in a Web browser*

The aspects of DealDatabase.com are quite interesting if you're going online to shop, but not so much if your primary interest is TiVo hacking. To TiVo hackers, the most interesting aspect of the DealDatabase site is its Message Board section (http://www.dealdatabase.com/forum), which provides a forum for online discussions on a number of different topics—including TiVo hacking, of course!

Unlike the AVS and TiVo Community forums, the DealDatabase forum does not provide menus across the top, but rather provides a table of quick links to commonly-used features of the site, for example, getting to the home page, submitting a deal, a list of the top deals that are currently available, a free e-mail service, getting to its forums, and a page containing general and contact information for DealDatabase.com.

The DealDatabase forum provides a tremendous amount of useful information about TiVos and other types of DVRs. Since TiVo, Inc. is not one of its sponsors, topics such as video extraction and related software are fair game here, making the DealDatabase forum a great repository for this sort of information. The following list describes the DealDatabase forums that I have found most useful in my DVR and TiVo education, along with a short description of each. These are listed alphabetically, rather than in the order that they appear on the DealDatabase forum Web pages:

- ◆ *DirecTV TiVo Hacking* General discussions of hacking Series 1 and Series 2 DirecTiVos. This seems to be an incredibly useful, detailed forum, but as I've already confessed, I don't have one of these at the moment.

- ◆ *Experts TiVo/DirecTiVo Hacking* A high-end forum for TiVo wizards to share spells, cool software, and new ways of expanding TiVo hacking in general. People new to TiVo hacking should not post here. If you do post there and ask a silly or obvious question, you will be lucky if your post is quickly deleted before a flood of verbal and e-mail abuse descends upon you.

- ◆ *General TiVo Discussions* A general forum intended to host general questions, answers, and discussions about any TiVo-related subject.

- ◆ *HP Digital Entertainment Center* Hewlett-Packard's Digital Entertainment Center was a short-lived, Internet-aware home entertainment appliance for listening to Internet radio, online audio, and for recording CDs of the same. Wow! I can't believe that didn't catch on, especially since Linux, Mac OS X, and Windows can all do that using software without breaking a sweat.

- ◆ *NEWBIE TiVo/DirecTiVo Hacking* The description of this category on the DealDatabase forum describes it more amusingly than I can: "If you don't know anything at all and don't know how to read and don't know how to use the search and just have to ask that stupid question, ask it here."

- ◆ *TiVo Extraction Forum* At last! A forum dedicated to information and software for extracting and processing video from Series 1 and Series 2 stand-alone and DirecTiVo systems. This forum is not the place for philosophy, flames, trolling, or any other irrelevant activity. All Linux systems come with a special forum for discussing the latter topics, known as **/dev/null**.

◆ *TiVo Hacks* General discussions of hacking stand-alone Series 1 and Series 2 machines. This is a great forum, with a tremendous amount of useful information, discussion, and hardware and software tips and tricks.

◆ *TiVo Series 2 Hacking* A forum for questions, answers, and hacking discussions that is specific to the MIPS-based Series 2 TiVo. The latest versions of these machines are harder to hack than any other TiVo. If you own a TiVo Series 2, this forum is a great source of information, tips, and up-to-date hacks.

◆ *UltimateTV Hacking* A forum dedicated to questions, answers, and discussion of hacking Microsoft's UltimateTV systems. The traffic in this forum is dying down, as are the boxes themselves.

◆ *XBOX Hacking* A forum dedicated to questions, answers, and discussion of hacking Microsoft's XBOX home gaming systems. Now that they run Linux (although not without both hardware and software hacking), these appliances are probably worth a look. They're quite sexy as video game systems, but I'm prejudiced against supporting the evil empire unless necessary. The discussion of hacking them is quite cool, and it would be nice to have a box stamped "Microsoft" running Linux at home.

The TiVo Community Forums

Located at http://www.tivocommunity.com, the TiVo Community forums are probably the best-known sites for TiVo information, discussion, sharing TiVo hacks and software, and for any other TiVo-related topics. This site and its forums were one of the earliest TiVo community sites (if not the earliest), and were founded to provide TiVo users and fans with a place to discuss and exchange ideas, software, and TiVo tips. They provide a great deal of information about all types of TiVos, including sections dedicated to using TiVos in the United Kingdom (UK), a community of TiVo fans and hackers whose postings are unfortunately often overlooked or buried under the flood of postings from TiVo-maniacs in the United States.

As one of the earliest TiVo sites, the TiVo Community Forums have a much stricter set of rules on posting and participation than other TiVo-related forums discussed in this chapter. These rules are available at the URL http://www.avsforum.com/avs-vb/rules.html. Specifically, the AVS Forums reflect the paranoia about Video Extraction that is still rampant in much of the TiVo community. You can't blame them—the recording and motion picture industries have a long history of isolationism and secretism to maximize profit margins, rather than trying to innovate to give people what they want at an affordable price. At any rate, any talk of Video Extraction on the AVS Forums is verboten. If you post questions about video extraction or—gasp!—software to help people do it, your posts will be deleted, your medals and insignia will be torn from your uniform, your sword will be broken in half, and eighty pizzas will be delivered to your house, collect. Don't try it!

WOULD YOU LIKE TO SEE A MENU?

In addition to forums and threads, each page of the TiVo Community Forum also provides pull-down menus (which will only display or work if your browser supports JavaScript) that provide easy access to a variety of information. These are available at the top of each page, and provide entries for the following information and hyperlinks:

◆ *Members Area* General forum information, including information about registering, changing your personal preferences, the FAQ (Frequently-Asked Questions) for the vBulletin software, and various search features.

◆ *Services* A site-specific list of special features available on the TiVo Community Forum site, such as special events, classified ads, and information about registering for the site.

◆ *Forums* A quick-reference to registration information, special areas on the TiVo Community Forum, and related FAQs and forums that are available on other sites (many of which are discussed elsewhere in this chapter).

◆ *Top Sponsors* A set of quick links to sponsors of the TiVo Community Forum. One notable presence here is TiVo, Inc., which isn't surprising, but is certainly welcome! Support for and permissiveness towards the TiVo hacking community is one of the things that makes the TiVo a great box to own and hack—and has certainly fostered its adoption by hundreds of thousands of people!

◆ *About Forum* Links to the TiVo Community Forum's privacy policy, contact information, information about subscribing to or becoming a sponsor of the TiVo Community Forum, and a link to the people who developed the hierarchical menu JavaScript used in these menus.

Figure 11.3 shows the main screen that displays when you connect to the TiVo Community Forums in a Web browser.

 TIP

If you're a regular visitor to the TiVo Community Forum, an easy way to view a listing of the most recent posts on any of its forums is to click the TiVo Forum Post Ticker link, which is available near the top of each page within the TiVo Community site. Clicking this link pops up a small dialog box that displays a scrolling list of the most recent posts made to any of the TiVo Community forums. To view a specific post from this list, just click its listing in the scrolling dialog box, and a new browser window opens on your screen that contains the selected post.

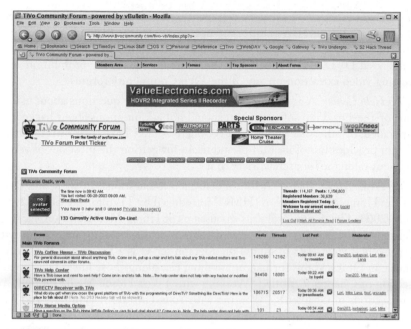

FIGURE 11.3 *The TiVo Community AVS Forums in a Web browser*

The TiVo Community Forum is all about TiVos, and therefore provides more information about TiVos and TiVo hacking than any other site. Folks from TiVo even participate in the forums and threads on this site, making it more authoritative than others. It's also a great place to pick up hot TiVo rumors. However, because TiVo, Inc. is one of its sponsors, topics such as video extraction and related software are forbidden, evil topics that are eliminated without mercy whenever they appear (and they do. Who reads the FAQ anyway?). The following list therefore contains almost all of the forums on the TiVo Community site, since most of them are relevant, along with a short description of each. They are listed alphabetically, rather than in the order that they appear on the TiVo Community Forum Web pages:

◆ *DIRECTV Receiver with TiVo* A forum dedicated to discussing DirecTiVo systems. This forum prohibits any discussions of hacking the Digital Subscriber Service required to use the DirecTiVo (and other TiVo models, though the DirecTiVos have many special requirements and associated hacks).

◆ *Season Pass Alerts* Like it or not, TiVo guide data is not always up-to-date, largely due to broadcast networks changing their schedules, mis-identifying something, and so on. This forum provides a place for TiVo fanatics to post "alerts" about Season Pass problems or other scheduling weirdness that might cause you to miss a show that you expected to TiVo. These alerts also include messages suggesting when you should pad various shows (i.e., increase the amount of time after the normal conclusion of the show to continue to record) due to interruptions, over-runs, and other random events. This is an incredibly useful forum if you keep up with it.

◆ *TiVo Coffee House, TiVo Discussion* A chatty, general-purpose forum for discussing TiVo news, TiVos, TiVo culture, and upcoming devices that will feature the TiVo software. If we're lucky, upcoming devices from Toshiba and Pioneer that feature integrated DVD recording support should finally squash the prohibition against discussing video extraction on any of the TiVo Community forums.

◆ *TiVo Help Center* A general-purpose forum for asking questions about using the out-of-the-box TiVo software. You should not ask questions about hacked, upgraded, or otherwise-modified TiVos here——they have their own forums. This forum provides lots of useful tips and tricks for getting the most out of your TiVo without taking a Torx screwdriver to it.

◆ *TiVo Home Media Option* A forum dedicated to questions, answers, and discussion of the Home Media Option (HMO) introduced by TiVo for the Series 2 systems in mid-2003. This forum prohibits discussions of Home Media Option hacking or related topics. See the HMO-related sections of this book for more information, especially if your MP3 or digital photograph server is a Linux box, you store your music in OGG/Vorbis format, or anything else along those lines. The Linux-specific section of Chapter 9 entitled "Working with TiVo's Home Media Option," or various sections of Chapter 8, "Working with Your TiVo from Windows and Macintosh Systems," might be useful to you.

◆ *TiVo Suggestion Avenue* This forum provides a place for posting suggestions that you'd like TiVo, Inc. to consider in upcoming software releases. The folks from TiVo read this forum, and some of the suggestions posted here have made it to subsequent releases of the TiVo software. Maybe you'll get lucky, too....

◆ *TiVo UK* A forum dedicated to questions, answers, and general discussion of using TiVos in the UK. Discussion of Skybox, the connectivity service in the UK, is also a valid topic here.

◆ *TiVo Underground* A forum dedicated to discussions of TiVo hacking. It's sometimes hard to differentiate general topics from topics specific to certain models of TiVos, but this is still a great forum. It is populated by smart, friendly wizards and is knee-deep in software, good instructions, and so on. Information specific to hacking the TiVo Series 2 is easily found on the DealDatabase forum. As always, any discussion of theft of service or video extraction is forbidden here, and will be terminated quickly. Long-time TiVo hackers remarked to me with some sadness that TiVo Underground has become little more than a glorified support section for topics forbidden in the TiVo help forum, such as hacked TiVos.

◆ *TiVo Upgrade Center* This forum is dedicated to discussions, questions, and answers about upgrading your TiVos. This forum provides reviews of various upgrade kits, dealers, and discusses potential problems and their solutions. Discussions of TiVo hacking, even if related to an upgrade, should be posted in the "TiVo Underground" forum in the same category of the TiVo Community site. As always, any discussion of theft of service or video extraction is forbidden here.

TiVo Hardware Web Sites

Relatively few sites on the Web actually discuss the TiVo hardware beyond discussing the types of hard drives and networking devices that you can use with your TiVo. Specific sites for obtaining TiVo upgrades, network hardware, or related tools and parts are discussed in Chapter 3 in the section, "TiVo Hardware Supplies on the Net." This section focuses on sites that provide general information about stock TiVo and related hardware. The following sites provide useful information about TiVos and related hardware:

◆ *Inside DirecTiVo* Part of the 9thTee.com Web site discussed elsewhere in this book (and this chapter), the page can be found at the URL http://www.9thtee.com/insidedirectv-tivo.htm, which provides lots of great photos of the internals of a Series 1 DirecTiVo, even providing information about the chips that it contains, the purpose of each, and (in many cases) links to reference information about those chips. Truly a labor of love.

◆ *Inside Series 1 TiVo* Part of the 9thTee.com Web site discussed elsewhere in this book (and this chapter), the page can be found at the URL http://www.9thtee.com/insidetivo.htm, which provides lots of great photos of the internals of a Series 1 TiVo, even providing information about the chips that it contains, the purpose of each, and (in many cases) links to reference information about those chips. This was the first site to provide this sort of detailed information about TiVo internals, and has been a great asset to the TiVo community for years (as has 9thTee.com itself).

◆ *Inside Series 2 TiVo* Part of the 9thTee.com Web site discussed elsewhere in this book, the page can be found at the URL http://www.9thtee.com/insideseries2tivo.htm, which provides some photographs of the internals of a Series 2 TiVo.

◆ *JTAG Support for Series 1 TiVos* This site, available at the URL http://penguinppc.org/embedded/tivo/hardware/jtag.shtml, discusses how to attach JTAG devices to the edge connectors found on Series 1 systems. JTAG (Joint Test Action Group) is a low-level hardware/software debugging interface used for hardware and operating system development. Since the edge connector discussed on this site is only available on the Series 1 machine and DirecTiVo motherboards, this site is of limited utility for anyone but the true hobbyist.

◆ *Linux/PPC for PowerPC 4xx* This site, available at the URL http://www.borg.umn.edu/~grant/Linux, provides hardware and software information about the IBM reference hardware on which the Series 1 systems were originally based. Largely only useful for historical purposes. (Any discussion of software here is not only outdated, but doesn't include any discussion of the TiVo-specific software that makes the TiVo what it is.)

◆ *PVR Comparisons* This site, available at the URL http://www.pvrcompare.com, provides comparisons of various TiVo, ReplayTV, and UltimateTV models. Although parts of it are outdated, this is a good site for getting some comparative information about the hardware and hardware capabilities of various types of PVRs.

◆ *Series 1 Edge Connector Information* This site, available at the URL http://
penguinppc.org/embedded/tivo/hardware/edgecon.shtml, provides detailed
information about the edge connector on the TiVo Series 1 motherboards.

◆ *SiliconDust.com* This site, available at the URL http://silicondust.com, is the home
page of the makers of the TiVoNet, TurboNet, and AirNet network adaptors for
Series 1 TiVos. As such, it deserves a special mention here. Networking your Series
1 systems would be impossible without the pioneering work done by Andrew
Tridgell and the subsequent amazing developments done by Nick Kelsey (a/k/a jafa)
at SiliconDust.

◆ *TiVo Hardware Questions* Part of the TiVo Forum FAQ discussed later in this section, this FAQ (available at the URL http://www.tivofaq.com/index.html?http://
www.tivofaq.com/Hardware.html, is a good source of useful information about
working with and using the TiVo hardware without taking a Torx screwdriver to it.
It explains what the lights mean on the front of the TiVo, how different remotes and
services work, and how to hook up your TiVo to almost everything but your toaster
or Jini network.

◆ *TiVo Rev 0 PPC 403 Oak Evaluation Kit* This site, available at the URL http://pen-
guinppc.org/embedded/tivo/hardware/oak.shtml, discusses the IBM reference board
that was the parent of the Series 1. Historically interesting, but it is largely irrelevant
these days.

Various TiVo FAQs and Help Sites

FAQs, which stands for "Frequently Asked Questions," are a common way of disseminating
commonly asked information on specific topics, making it available to a much wider audience
than paper documentation could ever hope to read (with the exception of this book, I hope).
FAQs are generally simple text or HTML files that provide a centralized source of information about a given topic. Like its companion acronym, RTFM (Read The F***ing Manual),
FAQs hope to reduce the number of times any given question is asked by writing it down
once, so that people who are inclined to read documentation can do so—as well as provide an
online source for information that is searchable on the Internet.

Much of the online documentation for Internet-related topics can be downloaded from
ftp://rtfm.mit.edu/pub, including many general FAQs (available in ftp://rtfm.mit.edu/pub
/faqs). Unfortunately, this does not include various FAQs about the TiVo and TiVo-related topics. The next few sections discuss the primary TiVo FAQs that I've found over the years, providing URLs where they can be found and an overview of contents and relevance today.

Hacking the TiVo FAQ

No relation to this book (except in spirit), the Hacking the TiVo FAQ was the original TiVo
FAQ, providing general and increasingly detailed information about hacking your TiVo. The
latest version of this FAQ is available at http://www.tivofaq.com/hack/faq.html in its entirety.

You can search for specific information through its Web-based wizard at http://www.tivo-faq.com/hack/faq.html.

Unfortunately, to quote this FAQ itself, "This FAQ is obsolete." It deals entirely with Series 1 topics, and even in that context discusses hacks and hacking techniques that were first-generation solutions. For example, it focuses on doing backups using Dylan's Boot Disk, which was the first TiVo tools floppy available. This aside, it focuses on doing backups using **dd** (explained in this book), but does not discuss using the newer, faster, and less disk-intensive MFS Tools utilities (also discussed in this book).

If you are a hard-core Microsoft Windows user, this FAQ does contain some information available nowhere else, such as how to back up the TiVo using some dedicated Windows utilities. However, these are superceded by improvements in tools disks, such as the one included on the CD with this book.

This is an interesting FAQ, but is basically no longer relevant except for historical purposes.

The Hinsdale FAQs

Bill "Hinsdale" Regnery's TiVo upgrade FAQs, available at http://www.newreleasesvideo.com/hinsdale-how-to, are the standard by which most TiVo upgrade information is judged. These FAQs are eminently usable discussions of the complete procedures necessary to add disk space to and generally upgrade your TiVo. These FAQs are constantly kept up-to-date, and contain a tremendous amount of information oriented towards Microsoft Windows users that explains caveats and additional information to think about when upgrading a TiVo using your Windows PC.

The URL referenced in the first paragraph actually contains pointers to two additional Hinsdale FAQs, as well as to the Hinsdale site where you can buy prepacked upgrade kits or even send your TiVo for repair or upgrading. (The URL for this section is http://www.newreleasesvideo.com/hinsdale-how-to/upgradeservice.html). The latest Hinsdale upgrade FAQ is at http://www.newreleasesvideo.com/hinsdale-how-to/index9.html, and uses Version 2.0 of the MFS Tools utilities as the core of the backup and upgrade procedure. An older version of the FAQ is also available at the URL http://www.newreleasesvideo.com/hinsdale-how-to/index2.html. The older version uses TiVoMad, BlessTiVo, and Version 1.1 of the MFS Tools utilities in its upgrade procedure. If you are upgrading a Series 1 system, the information in this older FAQ (all of which is also discussed in this book) may still be useful to you.

The TiVo community would be a much poorer place if not for the Hinsdale FAQs and the work that has gone into them.

Seth's TiVo FAQ

Seth's TiVo FAQ, available at http://www.sethb.com/TiVo, is a site that contains lots of good information, maintained by Seth Bokelman, a long-time TiVo evangelist. It provides a good deal of general TiVo information, as well as a good listing of USB network adaptors that work with various models of TiVos. It's generally a good read, and it is a good source of introductory TiVo information for people new to the TiVo. It also features a picture of the front cover of this book, so it must be good ;-).

TiVo Forum FAQ

This FAQ, available at http://www.tivofaq.com, is informative even though it uses frames. It is closely allied with the TiVo Community Forum. They explain their relationship to TiVo and provide lots of great background information about TiVo, its partners, how to use the forums, and various sections on using your TiVo. It explains what the lights mean on the front of the TiVo, how different remotes and services work, and how to hook up your TiVo to almost everything. This FAQ is oriented towards using your out-of-the-box TiVo, without opening it up or doing any sort of hacking. It touches upon TiVo hacking topics, but generally only provides hyperlinks to other FAQs or sources of information on those topics. It's a great "Getting Started" FAQ for your TiVo—and a great starting place for answers to your questions before posting them on the TiVo Community Forums.

TiVo Network Hack How-To Guide

Steve Jenkins is a long-time TiVo hacker and knows his stuff. His Network Hack FAQ, available at http://tivo.stevejenkins.com/network.html, is a great source of information about hacking and networking your TiVo. This FAQ focuses on networking TiVo rather than on upgrading their disks, which makes it a great central source of information not easily found elsewhere online. The FAQ is frequently updated and therefore almost always reflects the latest and greatest in TiVo networking techniques. Links that enable you to download any of the files referenced in the FAQ are provided at http://tivo.stevejenkins.com/downloads.

Steve's site at http://tivo.stevejenkins.com is also fun in general, with a good sense of humor. One especially cool thing that it provides is a downloadable graphic that represents a hacked TiVo. This is available at http://www.stevejenkins.com/tivo/downloads/sticker.zip. The idea is that you download it, print it off on transparent, adhesive paper, and then affix it to your TiVo. Voila! TiVo Hacks inside.

TiVoHelp.com

Though not a FAQ per se, this site contains a good deal of information about getting started with your TiVo, fixing various problems, as well as links to many other TiVo sites. This site is available at http://www.tivohelp.com, and is designed to perform some blog-like functions, enabling you to add to or update it. If you have problems with any aspect of the site, you can check out a static version of the site at http://www.tivohelp.com/archive/tivohelp. swiki.net/6.html.

One especially useful section of this site is its "Home/LAN Configuration" section, which goes into great detail about setting up a home network. Another useful section discussed

Microsoft Windows utilities for connecting to and interacting with your TiVo, including text editors that you can use on Windows systems without changing the end-of-line characters that Linux systems, such as the TiVo, require.

TiVoStuff.com

Though not a FAQ, this site contains links to a variety of TiVo How-To information (including some forbidden topics) and to most of your favorite TiVo software. Available at http://www.tivostuff.com, this is an attractive, nicely designed site that provides a good deal of useful information.

DirecTiVo Sites and Information

As mentioned in the introduction to this book, I don't own a DirecTiVo and therefore don't know much about the internals of these systems, or where they differ from standard Series 1 and Series 2 model TiVo—which is often necessary for hacking them. Large parts of community forums such as the AVS, DealDatabase, and TiVo Community forums (discussed earlier in this chapter) are devoted to DirecTiVo (aka DTiVo) hacking. One of these days I'll move beyond the four stand-alone TiVos that I currently own, and will branch out into DirecTiVo-land. Until then, one can only dream....

Luckily, the Internet steps in where some people can't afford to tread. Aside from the forums mentioned earlier, the following is a list of good sources of DirecTiVo-specific information and software:

◆ *DarkWing's (aka Wanker) DTiVo Links* Available at http://www.angelfire.com/darkside/wanker, this site is a tremendous central location for DirecTiVo tips, tricks, scripts, hacks, and general information.

◆ *DirecTiVo Hacking Information* Available at http://shelob.mordor.net/dgraft/directivo.html, this site is a tad spartan, but it is also a great central location for DirecTiVo and general TiVo information. There is too much stuff on this page to list it all——so check it out if you're looking for something special.

TiVo Software Download Sites

The CD that accompanies this book provides a good collection of the software that you will need to hack your TiVo, compile programs for it, or work with it from other systems. Unfortunately, a single CD can't hold everything—even a DVD would be hard-pressed to keep up with the flood of TiVo software, kernels, source code, and associated documentation that is available for TiVos on the Internet. This section attempts to fill in any gaps left unfilled by the CD that accompanies this book, providing links to my favorite online sources of TiVo-related software and general information.

The entire TiVo community benefits from the work and dedication of TiVo hackers everywhere. This includes those who collect available software and provide Web sites that make it easy for all of us to obtain the latest and greatest software, tips, and tricks. To the best of my knowledge, none of the sites listed in this section provides illegal software or instructions, or explains illegal techniques. In general, don't look at things that offend you, and don't use things that are illegal. That's just the "right thing to do."™

The following are my favorite sites for browsing and downloading the vast armada of TiVo-related software available on the Internet:

- *Craig Leres' TiVo Downloads* Available at http://www.xse.com/leres/tivo/downloads, this site provides older downloads for the Series 1 TiVo, but still can be useful if you're running an older TiVo.

- *DarkWing's (aka Wanker) DTiVo Links* Available at http://www.angelfire.com/darkside/wanker, this is a great software download site for all things DirecTiVo.

- *TiVoStuff.com* Available at http://www.tivostuff.com, this is a great site containing links to most of your favorite TiVo software. As discussed earlier, its "How-To" section also provides a great set of pointers to TiVo-related Web sites, including some that discuss forbidden topics.

- *TiVoWeb Project* The other sites in this section provide links to a variety of software. This one provides just one. While the site only contains the TiVoWeb software, "only" is a misnomer here. Long before TiVo introduced the Home Media Option, TiVoWeb enabled you to access and manage your TiVo over a network, from any Web browser. This is an amazing piece of work. Available at http://tivo.lightn.org, TiVoWeb is discussed in more detail in Chapter 10 entitled "An AlternateUI in the TiVo Web Project."

- *TiVo Hacking Links* Primarily a hard-core developer/download site, this site provides links to a variety of TiVo-related hacking and download sites and also maintains a TiVo hacking wiki and some traditional forums at http://alt.org/wiki/index.php/TiVoHackingLinks.

Index

1/8-inch male jack, 64
9thTee.com, 78, 87, 90, 102–104, 188, 233
10-Base2, 84
10-BaseT, 84
30-second Skip mode, 43, 51
100-BaseT, 84
1000-BaseT, 84

A

About Unix Web site, 328
Acrobat Reader, 181
actors, defining sets, 58–59
add-on services, identifying, 5
Adobe Acrobat Reader, 181
Adobe Web site, 181
Advanced Paid Programming entries, 46
Advanced WishLists, 59–60
advertising, 6, 10
agetty command, 322
AirNet cards, 87–88, 103, 140, 210
   DHCP (Dynamic Host Control Protocol) server, 93
   software required for installing, 90–94
   SSID value, 92
All Programs option, 30
allocation units, 121–122, 126
alternate boot partition, 118
Anderson, Erik, 330
AOL Instant Messenger, 238–241
Apache Web server, 247
appliation software, 108

application environment, 305–308
ar (archive file), 146
archive files, 137–138
Arpanet, 83
asterisk * wildcard character, 58
AT. command string, 80
AT&K0 (K zero) command, 80
AT&T Series 2 TiVos, 68, 73
attaching TiVo disk drives to PCs, 70–73
attributes, 316
AT&W0 command, 80
AT&W1 command, 80
audio files, 246–248
authentication, 332
auto-detection byte swapping, 125
automatically recording shows, 56
automating Backdoor mode, 50–53
AutoTest mode, 26, 48
Auto_test mode unlocked! message, 48
Avid One Media Composer, 6–7
Avid Technology, 6–7
AVS (Audio-Visual Science) forum, 50, 102, 368–371
AVS Forum Power Buys and Special Items forum, 370
AVS Forum Web site, 17

B

Backdoor mode, 26
   activating, 28–36
   automating, 50–53
   Channel Down key, 28

   earlier TiVos, 30–31
   later TiVo models, 32–36
   V 3.0, 30–31
   V 3.1, 32–36
backdoors
   commands, 182
   enabling, 28–36, 52–53
   known codes, 31
"Backdoors enabled!" message, 30
backing up
   advanced options, 161–163
   associated with specific recordings, 162
   changing operating system, 179–181
   disk drives, 33, 123–124
   excluding /var, 161
   incompatible, 165–166
   incremental, 148, 163
   limiting to certain-sized streams, 162
   MFS Tools, 155–163
   multiple-disk TiVo systems, 160–161
   overview, 145–147
   rc.sysinit file, 212
   restoring MFS Tools created, 168–178
   restoring to larger drive, 170–171
   restoring to two drives, 171–173
   selected information, 163–165
   storing, 148–151
   structured, 145–147
   TiVo, 143–144
   unstructured, 145, 147
   when to back up, 147–148

backup command, 163
backup files
    compressing, 158–159
    consistent, 217
    contents, 157
    disk images without interme-
        diate, 198–200
    restoring, 157
    Season Passes, 165
    size of, 157
    WishLists, 165
Bamboozled at the Revolution
    (Motavelli), 8
Barton, Jim, 7–8
"bash: no job control in this
    shell" message, 214
bash (Bourne-Again Shell) shell,
    259, 324
    bg (background) command,
        328
    commands, 325
    export command, 325
    fg command, 328
    job control, 325–329
    jobs command, 327
    kill command, 328
    managing commands,
        327–329
    PATH environment variable,
        325
    prompt, 325
    running commands in back-
        ground, 326–327
    searching for commands, 325
    serial ports, 322
    starting, 212
    startup command, 328
    terminal emulator, 209
    version number, 325
bash-2.02# prompt, 322
BASH_ENV environment vari-
    able, 210, 214, 220,
    222–223, 231, 234–235

BATBD CD (Bill's Accumulated
    TiVo Boot Disk), 33,
    136–139
boot option, 152
BusyBox, 329–330
byte-swapped kernel, 179
connectivity directory, 137
extract_gzip program, 222
floppy directory, 137
gaim2tivo-0.2.zip file,
    239–240
hack_dirs directory, 137, 345
hack_dirs/kernel_modules
    directory, 333
hexedit command, 132
HISTORY file, 138
img directory, 138
img_monte directory, 138
isolinux directory, 138
killinitrd directory, 138
Linux versions, 149
macintosh directory, 138
monte-mips directory, 138,
    223
mounting, 164, 229
NanoEmacs, 331
RAM (Random-Access
    Memory) disks, 137
s1swap boot option, 164, 176,
    177, 189, 192, 195, 198,
    202–203, 205, 211
s2 kernel, 177
Series 1 machines, 137
Series 2 machines, 137
settings-backup directory, 138,
    164
src file, 138
tar command, 349
TCS_1.0.0.tar.gz file, 244
text directory, 138
TiVoWeb, 248–249
tivoweb-tcl-1.9.4 tar archive
    file, 138
windows directory, 138
x86bin directory, 139

xcompilers directory, 139, 333
xcompilers/Series1/
    tivodev-2.5_linux-
    x86_dtype1.tgz
    cross-compiler, 351
xcompilers/Series1/
    tivodev-2.5_linux-
    x86_dtype2.tgz cross-
    compiler, 351
xcompilers/Series1/usr.local.
    powerpc-tivo.gz cross-
    compiler, 351
xcompilers/Series2/usr.local.
    tivo-mips_bu211.tgz
    cross-compiler, 351
xcompilers/Series2/usr.local.
    tivo-mips_bu213.tgz
    cross-compiler, 351
BATBD floppy disk, 110
Beginner's Bash Web site, 325
Big-Endian, 127
bin command, 355
binary files, identifying formats,
    344–345
/bin/bash command, 212
/bin/bash file, 221
binutils package, 351
BIOS (Basic Input Output
    System), examining disk
    drive configuration, 71–72
blessing disk drives, 114–117,
    294–296
BlessTiVo command, 114–117
BlessTiVo utility, 113–117,
    138–139, 206
    adding second drive, 204–206
    extra space on new drive, 197
    versions, 114
Blindwrite Suite, 273–274
block size, changing, 175–176
blown modems, 77–78
BNC (Bayonet Neill-Concelman,
    or Baby N Connector)
    cables, 84

Boat Anchor Mode, 39
boot disks, 133–134
    BATBD (Bill's Accumulated
        TiVo Boot Disk),
        136–139
    boot block, 135
    burning, 33
    as disk images, 135
    Dylan's Boot Floppy, 139
    Johnny Death's Boot CD,
        139–140
    Kazamyr's Boot CD, 140
    Linux partition, 33
boot drive, 72
boot information, reading and
    writing, 117–119
boot parameters, 118–119, 180,
    234
boot partition, 56, 117–118
boot process and swap space, 173
boot sector, 118
bootable kernel, cloning, 228
boot-loader, 301–302
bootpage, 118–119, 139
bootpage command, 118–119,
    177–178, 180, 211, 218,
    220, 226–228, 234–235
bootpage -p <drive> command,
    234
bootpage utility, 117–119
boot-param command, 56
bootparams command, 53
Bourne, Stephen, 324
bpage option, 117
broadcasts, showcasing
    upcoming, 10
BrookTree chips, 183
Browse By Channel button, 23,
    57
Browse By Time button, 24, 57
Browse dialog box, 264
browsing shows, 57
BSD license, 307
buddy notifications, 239–241
Burn Image dialog box, 296–297

burning CDs and Linux,
    336–338
business partners, 9–11
BusyBox, 139, 329–330
busybox command, 308
byte order, changing, 176
byte swapped kernel, 167
byte swapping and auto-
    detection, 125
ByteBack Online Web site, 365
byte-order, 127–128
ByteSex Web site, 183
byte-swapped boot configuration,
    33
byte-swapping, 150, 152, 176

C

cable box, 24
cables, 64
Caller ID, 52, 242
Caps Lock key, 34
capturing transcript of input and
    output, 133
Category 5 cabling, 84
CCEE (Clear-Clear-Enter-
    Enter) codes, 27, 36–37
cd command, 351
CD drive, Eject button, 36
CD Image verification dialog
    box, 276
CD writing complete dialog box,
    277
cdrecord application, 135, 336
cdrecord command, -scanbus
    command-line option, 337
CD-ROM image files, 272
CDRTools package, 336
CDs, byte-swapped boot config-
    uration, 33
cd/var command, 355
cd/var/settings-backup command,
    165
CEC (Clear-Enter-Clear) 6
    code, 60

CEC (Clear-Enter-Clear) codes,
    27, 37–40
Central menu, 13
chain-boot hacked kernel, 235
Change Dial Options menu,
    81, 99
change directory command, 213
changing channels, 24–25
Channel Change port, 54
Channel Down key, 28
channels
    changing, 24–25
    clearing list of selected, 37
    recording specific, 57
    remotely changing, 357–358
Channels You Watch screen, 37
chattr command, 234
checksums, 29
Chen, Christine, 365
Christensen, Ward, 263
Chryon, 7
Cinemax, 10
Cisco 802.11b cards, 88
clip files, hidden, 46
Clips On Disk screen, 46
clock, 43
cloning
    disks, 33
    root partition, 178
closed captioning support,
    361–362
CLSIP (Compressed SLIP), 83
Cntrl Out port, 63
codes, automating, 50–53
COM1, 54, 63
combined DVD/PVRs, 11
command files, default, 211
command interpreter, 63,
    324–329
command prompt, 208
    job control, 328
    monte, 224
    Series 1 machines, 209–214
    Series 2 machines, 214–221
command suite, 120

command-line interpreter, 261
commands
  checking on status, 327
  interrupting and terminating, 327
  killing, 328
  managing with bash shell, 327–329
  restarting in background, 328
  ROM monitors, 53–56
  running in background, 326–327
  secret, 24–53
  suspending, 327
commercials, skipping through, 43
Communication Options dialog box, 322
competition, 16–18
comp.os.minix newsgroup, 301
compressed backup and MFS Tools, 158–159
configuration, saving changes, 56
Configure Minicom dialog box, 321
connectivity directory, 137
connectors, 12
convergence, 2–3
copy command, 213
copying rc.sysinit.save file, 213
cpio (Copy Input To Output) utility, 146, 349
Craig Leres' TiVo Downloads Web site, 382
crashes, 147
Create New WishList command, 59
Create WishList screen, 59
creeping featurism, 3
cross-compilers, 139, 351–353
cryptographic chip, 5
C-Shell, 324
custom remote controls, 22–23
Cygwin, 281

D

&D0 command string, 80
d7o, 209
daemons, 140
DarkWing's DTiVo Links Web site, 381, 382
data
  putting on videotape, 181–182
  restoring, 165–166
  verification and hashing, 29
databases
  hashing algorithm, 28
  manipulating objects, 317
dates, 46
db command, 317
dbobj command, 317
dd command, 117, 121, 135, 199, 226, 228–229, 278
  conv=swab conversion option, 154
  entering wrong disk name, 197
  "forgiveness" options, 155
  kernels, 167
  progress indicator, 153
  sync option, 155
  unstructured backup of disk, 153
  unstructured backup of partition, 153
dd utility, 33, 145, 194–195
  conv=noerror,sync options, 196
  <filename> argument, 167
  image backups, 147, 152–153, 155
  noerror option, 196, 199
  restoring image backups, 166–167
  sync option, 196, 199
DealDatabase Forum thread, 239
DealDatabase forums, 371–373
default command files, 211
Delay: prompt, 42

delay values, 42
Delete Message command, 6
Denon and Marantz, 17
desktop video-editing device, 7
detached processes, 327
Detroit Free Press Web site, 366
/dev directory, 146
devbin-s2 directory, 139
development projects, 354–362
/dev/hda device, 115, 120
/dev/hda8 partition, 151
/dev/hda14, 113
/dev/hdb device, 115, 120
/dev/hdc device, 115, 120
/dev/hdd device, 115, 120
/dev/hdX9 partition, 164
device drivers, 187–188, 302
/dev/ttyS0 serial port, 63, 65
/dev/ttyS1 serial port, 65
/dev/ttyS2 serial port, 65
/dev/ttyS3 serial port, 65, 212
df command, 151, 309, 335
DHCP (Dynamic Host Control Protocol), 86, 101
DHCP Server, 100
diagnostic features, 36–37
Dial Prefix command, 81
Dial-in Configuration Code, 36
Digital Recorders (PVRs) General forum, 370
DIP switches, 79
DirecTiVo Hacking Information Web site, 381
DirecTiVo machines, 12, 15
  AirNet cards, 88
  disconnecting fan on drive bracket, 67
  Series 2, 138
  tuners, 12–13, 15
  Web sites, 381
directories, 302
  defining sets, 58–59
  identifying, 52
  Linux, 150

listing contents, 212
MFS (Media File System)
    filesystem, 313–316
ROM (Read-Only Memory)
    filesystem image,
    131–132
DirectTV systems, 3
DirectTV Receiver with TiVo
    forum, 375
DirecTV systems, 18
DirecTV TiVo Hacking forum,
    372
Discovery Channel(s), 10
discussion forums, 366–376
Dish Network & Dish PVRs
    forum, 370
DishPVR, 18
disk consistency check, 173
Disk Copy application, 296–297
Disk Copy dialog box, 297
disk drives, 66
    adding, 14, 73–75, 150
    amount of RAM to track
        usage, 121–122
    attaching to PCs, 70–73
    backing up, 33, 123–124,
        159–160
    backing up partition map, 110
    blessing, 114–117
    BlessTiVo utility, 204–206
    cloning, 33
    device drivers, 188
    different types of, 76
    direct write access, 111
    directly modifying, 132
    efficiency of storage, 121–122
    erasing first few sectors, 117
    examining configuration,
        71–72
    expanding set of MFS vol-
        umes, 121–123
    expanding volumes, 170
    expanding with disk images,
        194–200

IDE (Integrated Drive
    Electronics) cable, 67
image backup, 152–153, 155
incorrectly reporting size, 116
jumpers, 70–74
larger swap partition, 113
LBA (Logical Block
    Addressing), 116
manually identifying connec-
    tion, 72
marrying and unmarrying,
    110, 114, 201
master, 70
MFS Tools utilities, 201–204
power connector, 67
preparing second, 113–117
putting in PC, 33
read errors, 194
removing, 66–69
replacing, 186–187, 189–192
restoring, 123–127
second, 200–206
Series 1 machines, 68
slave drive, 70, 74, 115
spinning up, 76
structured backup, 194
suspected failure, 194
three partitions on, 117
TiVo 1 machines, 109–113
TiVo-capable partitions, 110
unstructured backup, 153
upgrading without backup
    files, 192–194
using together, 110
verifying restored with MFS
    Tools, 177
writing TiVo ID string to
    third partition, 117
writing valid bootpage, 117
disk images, 135
    expanding disk drives,
        194–200
    without intermediate backup
        files, 198–200

Disk Space Usage screen, 32
Display key, 4
displaying
    green screen, 236
    photos, 246–248
DLink, 86
D&M Holdings, 17
DMA (Directory Memory
    Access), 137–138, 140
DNS (Distributed Name Service)
    servers, 86
Dorfman, Marjorie, 365
double quotation marks ("), 58
double-headed IR emitters, 25
drive racks, 71
dsscon=true command, 232
DTR, disabling, 80
dual-LNB dish, 15
dumpobj command, 316
DVRs (Digital Video Recorders),
    2
Dylan's Boot Disk, 110–111
Dylan's Boot Disk Web site, 139
Dylan's Boot Floppy, 139
dynamic IP addresses, 85–86

E

earlier TiVos and Backdoor
    mode, 30–31
Easter eggs, 26
eBay, 71, 105–106
EchoStar Communications
    Corporation, 18
EE (Enter-Enter) codes, 27,
    41–43
elapsed time display, 43
ElectricLegs, 78
electronic devices, 3
Emacs, 234, 330–331
embeem, 209
Encore, 10
encryption and hashing, 29
Enter key, 4

EPROM (Erasable Programmable Read-Only Memory), 78
"Error-Unable to find complete string" message, 94
/etc directory, 302–303
/etc/grub.conf file, 337
/etc/inittab file, 221, 306
/etc/lilo.conf file, 337
/etc/minirc.dfl file, 320
/etc/passwd file, 303
/etc/rc.d directory, 211, 303
/etc/rc.d/init.d/tivoserver file, 340–341
/etc/rc.d/rc.arch command script, 306
/etc/rc.d/rc.arch file, 221
/etc/rc.d/rc.sysinit file, 53, 87, 221, 238, 259, 279, 306, 326, 328, 335, 356
    correct settings for external modem, 81
    "Error-Unable to find complete string" message, 94
    http_get application, 51
    incorrectly executing, 233–234
ethereal, 101
Ethernet, 83
Ethernet cable, 84, 99
exit command, 259
Exit (Ctrl-c) keyboard shortcut, 35
expansion brackets, 105
Experts TiVo/DirectTiVo Hacking forum, 372
explore2fs application, 222, 278–279
exportfs -a command, 334
exporting
    directory containing MP3 files, 283
    NFS (Network File System), 334

ext2 disk images
    Mac OS X, 292–294
    Windows, 278–279
ext2 filesystem, 146, 258, 303
EXT2 format, 70
ext2 partition, 70, 150–151, 168–169
    image backup, 278–279
    mounting, 216
ext2fs, 128
Ext2FS.pkg file, 292
EXT3 format, 70
ext3 partitions, 70, 216
external modems, 78–82
extract_gzip program, 222
extract_gzip.c file, 303
extracting
    files from TAR and TGZ archives, 347–350
    tar files, 355
    TAR files without tar command, 349
    video, 145
ExtractStream, 182

F

factory password, 54–55
FAQs (Frequently Asked Questions), 108, 378–381
fast-forward speed, 41–42
FAT Telnet, 63
FAT32 filesystem, 149, 151
FAT-32 (32-bit File Allocation Table) format, 70
FAT-32 partition, 70
fdisk command, 150, 310
features
    diagnostic, 36–37
    hidden, 25–53
    undocumented, 26
fees, 4
fg command, 328
File -> Burn Image command, 296

file command, 344–345
files, 302
    directly modifying, 132
    identifying for backup data, 125
    transferring over serial connection, 263–265
filesystems
    adding disks and partitions to, 150
    block size, 175–176
    byte order, 176
    disk usage for all mounted, 309
    Linux, 302–304
    listing, 150
    MFS, 303
    mounting, 151, 302
    mounting images, 154
    root, 303
Finder, navigating through mountpoint, 294
firewalls, 238
/fixes directory, 306
flash memory, 305
flat IR emitters, 25
Flix, 10
floppy directory, 137, 139
flow control, 80
fonts, changing onscreen, 47
FOOBAR Web site, 204
Forsenberg, Chuck, 263
Fortune Magazine online Web site, 365
forums, 366–376
Frankensteinian brackets, 14
free space, estimating, 32
fsck command, 154
FSN (Full Service Network), 7–8
FTP (File Transfer Protocol), 236–237, 269–271, 331–332
FTP client, 270
FTP daemon, 140, 236–237, 331

G

GAIM (GTK AOL Instant
    Messenger), 239
gaim2tivo plugin, 240–241
gateways, 85
GCC (GNU C Compiler),
    300–301, 333
gender bender, 62–63
gender changer, 62
General TiVo Discussions forum,
    372
genromfs command, 131–132
genromfs utility, 138–139
GG (Gadu-Gadu), 239
gigabit Ethernet, 84
GNU Emacs, 234, 331
GNU Project Web site, 300, 301
Goldmember, 10
gold-star advertising, 10
Gosling, James, 331
gosmacs, 331
GPL (GNU Public License),
    138, 140, 301
green screen, 236
grep command, 317
GRUB bootloader, 337
Guided Setup, 76–77
gunzip command, 347
gunzip FILENAME command,
    303
GZ files, uncompressing,
    345–347
gzip command, 348
gzip utility, 303, 347
gzipped ext2 filesystem images,
    222

H

&H0 command string, 80
hack_dirs directory, 137
Hacking the TiVo FAQ, 108,
    378–379
hackinit script, 219

hacks_dir directory, 263, 323
hardware, 3
    diagnostic log file, 5
    directly manufacturing, 9
    features, 12–14
    models, 12–14
    outsourcing, 9
    supplies on Internet, 103–105
    Web sites, 377–378
Harris, Jensen, 242
hash command, 355
hash keys, 28
hash values, 28
hashing, 28–29, 35, 174
Hayes command set, 80
Hayes Web site, 80
Hayes-compatible modems, 80
HBO, 10
hda device, 112
hdb device, 112
hdc device, 112
hdd device, 112
hdid command, 292–293
HDRs (Hard Disk Recorders), 2
Heartfield, Trevor, 109
Helvetica Italic, 47
Helvetica screen font, 47
Hendriks, Erik, 209
hermanator, 239
hexadecimal editor, 33
hexedit (hexadecimal editor)
    command, 35, 132
hexedit command home page,
    132
hexedit utility, 33–35, 139, 141
hidden clip files, 46
hidden features, 25–53
hidden recordings, 45
hierarchical filesystem, 303
high-performance video
    workstations, 7
Hilgrave Web site, 260
Hill, Mike, 113
Hinsdale, 103–104
Hinsdale FAQs, The, 379

HISTORY file, 138
HMO (Home Media Option),
    10–11, 209, 245
    displaying photos, 246–248
    Linux, 338–341
    Macintosh, 298
    multi-room viewing, 253–256
    "Music & Photos" menu, 247
    playing music, 246–248
    scheduling recordings over
        Internet, 248–252
    Series 2 machine, 86
    USB (Universal Serial Bus)
        network adaptor, 246
    Windows, 282–290
home cable boxes, interacting
    with, 24
home gateways, 85, 86, 354
Home Theater Computers
    forum, 370
home theater setup, 245
home video service, 7
How Stuff Works Web site, 85
HP Digital Entertainment
    forum, 372
http_get application, 51
http_get command, 52
hubs, 84–85, 100
HyperTerminal, 54, 62–63
    communication window, 261
    communications settings used
        for this connection, 260
    Connect to dialog box, 260,
        267
    network communications,
        266–267
    saving configuration, 261
    serial files transfers, 263–265

I

&I0 command string, 80
id option, 117

IDE (Integrated Drive Electronics) cables, 67, 70, 75
IDE interface, 149
identifying TiVo, 4–5
idetivo_bswap_data function, 128
ideturbo module, 128
IEDs (Intelligent Entertainment Devices), 2
ifconfig command, 100
$IFS environment variable, 220, 231
image backups, 147
   dd utility, 152–153, 155
   partitions, 154
   restoring, 165–167
image files, verifying integrity, 154
img directory, 138–139
IMG extension, 135
img_monte directory, 138
incompatible backups, 165–166
incremental backups, 148, 163
initial RAM disks, 222, 302–304
Inside DirecTiVo Web site, 377
Inside Series 1 TiVo Web site, 377
Inside Series 2 TiVo Web site, 377
insmod command, 362
installing software on TiVo, 344–350
instant messages, 239–241
int.disabled prompt, 42
integrators, 9–11
int.enabled prompt, 42
Inter: prompt
Intercil Prism2, 88
Internal Field Separator, 220, 231
internal serial number, 4
International Standards Organization 9660 file-system standard, 272

Internet, 83, 108
   always-on connectivity, 83
   broadband connection, 245
   dialup connections, 83
   hardware, 103–105
   scheduling recordings, 248–252, 282
   TiVo-related information, 108
interpreted languages, 307
Interrupt and Terminate Command (Control-c) keyboard shortcut, 327, 328
interstitials, 42
intital RAM disk, 305–306
   /fixes directory, 306
IP (Internet Protocol) addresses, 85–86, 268–269, 336
iptables application, 238
IR (infrared) amplifier, 102
IR Blaster, 24–25
IR emitters, 25
IR receiver, building small hood around, 25
IRC, 239
ISA network card, 87
ismod command, 333
ISO extension, 135
isolinux directory, 138
iTCL, 306–307
.itcl extension, 307
iTunes, 135

J

Jabber, 239
job control and bash shell, 327–329
Johnny Death's Boot CD, 139–140
jpegwriter, 244
JTAG Support for Series 1 TiVo Web site, 377
jumpers, 70–74

K

Kazamyr's Boot CD, 140
Keorner, Brendan, 365
kernel Configuration menu, 153
kernels, 187
   booting as part of boot process, 222
   chain-boot hacked, 235
   dd command, 167
   extracting, 226–227
   initial RAM disks, 303–304
   recompiling, 153
key presses, randomly generating, 48
keywords, defining sets, 58–59
kill command, 328
killinitrd command, 235
killinitrd directory, 138
Knoppix Linux, 132, 141
Knoppix Linux Web site, 141
known backdoor codes, 31
Korn shell, 324

L

Lang, Steven, 119
later TiVo models and backdoor mode, 32–36
LBA (Logical Block Addressing), 116
Lempel-Zev compression, 158
Levin, Gerald, 7
LGPL (Lesser GNU Public License), 301
lifetime service, 4, 78
lightn TiVo hacker, 354
LILO bootloader, 337
Linksys gateway, 83, 86
Linux, 16, 134, 310
   agetty command, 322
   boot process, 301–302
   boot-loader, 301–302
   burning CDs, 336–338
   BusyBox, 329–330

cdrecord, 135

change directory command, 213

command interpreter, 63, 212, 324–329

copy command, 213

cpio (Copy Input to Output), 146

dd command, 33, 121, 135, 195, 196, 199

detached processes, 327

device drivers, 187–188, 302

/dev/ttyS0, 54, 63

df command, 151

directories, 150

Dylan's Boot Disk, 111

Emacs, 330–331

exporting directories, 284

ext2 filesystems, 146

EXT2 format, 70

ext2 partitions, 128

EXT3 format, 70

extra space allocated, 32

fdisk command, 150

filesystems, 302–304

FTP (File Transfer Protocol), 331–332

GAIM (GTK AOL Instant Messenger), 239

GCC (GNU C Compiler), 333

grep command, 317

history of, 300–301

HMO (Home Media Option), 338–341

identifying binary file formats, 344–345

image backups of partitions, 154

initial RAM disks, 302–304

installing gaim2tivo plugin, 240

Internal Field Separator, 220, 231

iTCL, 306–307

kernel, 116, 187

Linux shell, 324–329

loopback filesystem, 154

ls command, 159, 161

mgetty command, 322

mingetty command, 322

minicom, 54, 62–63

MIPS platform, 304

modify data in raw Linux partitions, 33

monte program, 209

mount command, 150

mounting and unmounting filesystem, 167

netcat utility, 182

NFS (Network File System), 333–335

NFS servers, 334

OGG format, 287

partitions, 175, 311

prebuilt compilers, 139

RAR utility, 147

recompiling kernel, 153

root filesystems, 311

root partition, 174

running commands in background, 326–327

serial communications, 320–324

shutting down, 36

software for TiVo, 329–335

source code for TiVo's, 304

split command, 147

stty sane command, 209

swap space, 311

sync command, 217, 225

tail command, 212

tar format, 138, 146

TCL (Tool Command Language), 306–307

telnet, 335

tools, 131–133

/usr/bin/minicom file, 321

/var partition, 174

YACC (Yet Another Compiler Compiler), 242

zlib library, 158

Linux shell, 324–329

Linux/PPC for PowerPC 4xx Web site, 377

/linuxrc (Linux Run Commands) file, 305

linux-utils package, 133

Little-Endian, 127

LMOP (Large Matter of Programming), 243

log files, 40

logical or, 59

loopback address, 51

ls command, 157, 159, 161, 212, 326–327, 329

M

&M1 command, 80

Mac OS X

blessing disks, 291, 294–296

BlessTiVo, 114

Disk Copy application, 296–297

ext2 disk images, 292–294

hdid command, 292, 293

iTunes, 135

mounting ext2 partition images, 291

Roxio Toast, 135

System Preferences application, 298

TiVo Desktop, 298

TiVo disks, 291–296

TiVos, 290–291

tools disks, 296–297

unmounting filesystem image, 294

Mac OS X Ext2 Filesystem project, 292
Macintosh
communicating with TiVo, 63
exporting MP3 and digital photograph collections to TiVo, 11
HMO (Home Media Option), 298
Partition Support, 153
pdisk (Partition Disk) utility, 127, 129–131
serial ports, 63
macintosh directory, 138
Macintosh-format drive, 310–311
mad31 directory, 110
mad32 directory, 110
Main Street, 7
Make Test Call command, 43, 82
MakeDisk.bat script, 111
male DB9 connector, 64
master disk, 117–119
master drives, 70, 149
Media Center, 247, 287–290
Media Player, 272
Menu Item backdoor screen, 46
menus, accessing internal information, 38
Messages & Setup -> Recorder & Phone Setup -> Cable/Satellite Box -> Cable Box Setup menu, 25
Messages & Setup menu, 6, 16
Metcalf, Bob, 83
MFS Application partitions, 34
MFS filesystem, 119, 146, 162, 303
directories, 313–316
elements, 312–320
objects, 316–319
resource groups, 319–320
resources, 319–320

MFS (Media File System) partitions, 126, 174, 204, 311
MFS resources, 358–361
MFS Tools, 109, 119–127, 137, 146, 150, 194
adding partitions from second drive, 203–204
adding second drive, 201–204
backups, 155–163, 159–160
compressed backup, 158–159
extra space on new drive, 197
marrying and unmarrying disk drives, 110
mfstool utility, 120
preparing second drive, 114
README file, 119
restoring backups created using, 168–178
simple backup, 156–158
structured backup, 148
verifying disks restored using, 177
Version 1.0, 121, 128, 140
Version 2.0, 112, 121, 128, 140
MFS volumes
adding, 125
expanding, 121–122
extending set, 127
information about, 124
mfsadd_a utility, 110
mfsadd_ab utility, 110
MFS_HDA environment variable, 121
MFS_HDB environment variable, 121
mfs_stream utility, 182
mfstool add command, 121–123
mfstool backup command, 146, 151, 177, 192, 216–217, 225
-1 -9 option, 123
-1 <size> option, 162

-1N option, 124
-a option, 123, 159–160, 190, 193
capacity of drive backing up, 156
command-line options, 123–124, 155
compressing backup files, 158
connecting to mfstool restore command with pipe (|), 178–179
displaying output, 156
-f <fsid> option, 162
-fN option, 123
levels of compression, 158
-o option, 124, 157
-s option, 124, 161
-T option, 124
-t option, 124
-T <size> option, 163
-t <size> option, 163
-v option, 124, 161
mfstool info command, 124
mfstool mfsadd command, 197, 200–203
mfstool restore command, 123, 125–127, 150–151, 157, 191, 193, 217
-B option, 125, 176
-b option, 125, 176
command-line options, 125–127
connecting to mfstool backup command with pipe (|), 178–179
-i option, 125, 169, 171
-l option, 125
-p option, 125, 175
-q option, 126
-r scale option, 126
-r <value> option, 175
-s option, 126, 173
-v size option, 126, 174

-X drive option, 126
-x option, 127, 170–171
-z option, 127
mfstool utility, 33, 120
    add command, 121–123
    command-line arguments, 120
    default values for disk(s), 121
    environmental variables, 121
    mfstool backup command, 123
    mfstool info command, 124
    mfstool restore command, 123,
        125–127
mfstools.1 directory, 140
mfstools.2 directory, 140
mgetty command, 322
Microsoft Ultimate TV PVR
    forum, 370
mingetty command, 322
minicom, 54, 62–63, 320–324
minicom Web site, 320
MINIX, 300
MIPS platform and Linux, 304
MIPS processors, 128
MIPS-based Series 2 TiVo, 110
mkisofs command, 336–338
mkswap, 128
mls command, 313–315
/mnt directory, 150, 211
/mnt/cdrom/img directory, 218
/mnt/cdrom/img_monte directo-
    ry, 229
/mnt/hacks file, 220
/mnt/home directory, 151
/mnt/home/my_tivo.bak file, 156
/mnt/tivo/etc/rc.d/rc.sysinit file,
    231
/mnt/tivo/etc/rc.d/rc.sysinit.old
    file, 231
/mnt/var partition, 164
/mnt/windows directory, 150–151
mobile racks, 71
model numbers, 13–14
modems, 76
    blown, 77–78
    default speed, 79

dialing prefixes for different
    speeds, 82
external, 78–82
Hayes-compatible, 80
repairing, 78
TiVo Series 1, 78
modes, secret, 24–53
monte command, 235–236
monte command prompt, 224
monte Web site, 209
monte-mips directory, 138, 223
mount command, 150–151
mount -o loop FILENAME
    /mnt command, 303
MountEverything software, 279
mounting
    ext2 partitions, 216
    ext3 partitions, 216
    filesystem images, 154
    filesystems, 302
    partition images, 154
    partitions, 173
mountpoints, 150, 173
MP3 files, 246, 338–341
Mr. Deeds, 10
MSN Web site, 239, 365
multiple-disk TiVo systems,
    backing up, 160–161
multi-room viewing, 245,
    253–256, 282
MuscleNerd, 209
music
    OGG format, 287
    playing, 246–248
"Music & Photos" menu, 247
Music & Photos screen, 298
MusicEx Web site, 287
mwstate Insert file, 39–40
My Computer dialog box, 277
"My Life with TiVo," 365
MySQL, 366
myworld application, 39–40

N
NanoEmacs, 331
Napster, 239
NAT (Native Address
    Translation), 86
NBC, 10
Nero, 135
Nero-Burning ROM package,
    273
Nero.com Web site, 273
netcat utility, 182
NetFilter Web site, 238
network adapters, 99–100
network cards, 91
network packet-sniffing utility,
    101
networking
    basics, 83–86
    Series 1 models, 87–91
    Series 2 machines, 95–99
    TiVo, 10–11, 82–101
networks
    communications, 266–267
    connections, 259
    DHCP Server, 100
    Ethernet, 83–84
    gateways, 85
    hubs, 84–85, 100
    making daily calls, 99–101
    moving large numbers of files,
        333–335
    packets, 85
    partnering with, 9–10
    routers, 85
    switches, 84, 100
    verifying connectivity, 100
    Windows, 265–271
New York Times, The Web site,
    366
NEWBIE TiVo/DirecTiVo
    Hacking forum, 372
Newman, Heather, 366
news, 243–245
NewTek, 6–7

newtext2osd, 244

NFS (Network File System), 281, 333–335

NFS servers, 334

NIC (network interface card) installation command, 90

nic_install program, 87, 94–95, 210, 237

/nic_install/nic_install command, 90

"No device specified" message, 205

no picture or Welcome screen, 233

node 30, 60

Node Navigator, 38, 60

noinitrd command, 235

non-routable IP addresses, 85

Now Playing list, 45, 48–50, 254

Now Playing Options screen, 48–49

Now Playing screen, 46, 48, 170, 181

NTFS (NT File System) format, 70, 149, 151

null-modem adapter, 54

null-modem connector, 62–64

NVRAM (nonvolatile random access memory), 80

O

objects
    attributes, 316
    MFS (Media File System) filesystem, 316–319
    schema, 316–317

Offset: prompt, 43

offset values, 42

OGG format, 287

OmniRemote Pro, 102

one-time subscription charge, 4

online forums, 366–376

Open: prompt, 42

open <IP-Address> command, 270

Open Source movement, 134

Open Source software, 300–301

opening TiVo, 65–66

OpenSource WEb site, 307

Operating Systems, 300

operating systems
    changing during backup, 179–181
    Easter eggs, 26
    obtaining older versions, 214
    upgrades to, 143
    version 4.0, 238

optimizing partition layout, 174–175

OSXvBlesser command, 295

other directory, 140

Ouija screen, 27, 30, 41

Ousterhout, John, 306

overshoot correction, 38, 42–43

P

PACELink, 105

packaging system-level software, 133

packets, 85

paid programming, automatically downloading, 5

PalmOS 3.0, 102

partition images, mounting, 154

partition map, 34, 128, 309–311

partitions
    adding from second, 203–204
    adding to filesystem, 150
    allocation unit size, 122
    directly modifying, 132
    displaying, 226–227
    editing, 34
    identifying, 34
    image backup, 152–153, 278–279
    manual creation of, 127, 129–131, 174

MFS Application, 34
    mounting, 173
    optimizing layout, 125, 174–175
    organization of mounted, 310
    safe locations for storing TiVo hacks, 350–351
    scrolling, 34
    Series 1, 152
    unable to mount, 168
    unmounting, 213
    unstructured backup, 153
    viewing organization, 151
    zeroing out, 127

partnering with networks, 9–10

passwords, 54–55

PATH environment variable, 325, 352–353

PCMCIA 802.11b cards, 88–89

PCMCIA adapter, 88

PCs
    attaching TiVo disk drives to, 70–73
    BIOS Setup options, 195
    boot drive, 72
    drive racks, 71
    EXT2 partition, 70
    EXT3 partition, 70
    FAT-32 partition, 70
    IDE interfaces, 70
    single free IDE connector, 114
    terminal emulators, 54
    updating BIOS Setup options, 190

PDAs as remote control, 102

pdisk command, 129–131, 150, 169, 174, 177, 204, 217, 226–227, 310–311

pdisk utility, 34, 117, 127, 129–131

pdisk-p/dev/hdX command, 177, 203

PDRs (Personal Digital Recorders), 2

PDVs (personal desktop videos), 6

Perens, Bruce, 330

perl command, 339

Perl scripts, 307

Personal Television Service, 8

Personal TiVo Home Media Option Project, 338, 361

Phone Dialing Options screen, 81, 99–100

phone lines, 76–77

photos, displaying, 246–248

PHP (Personal Hypertext Preprocessor), 366

Pick Programs To Record screen, 32

pipe (|), 151, 178–179

PIP/Window button, 23

Plasma and LCD Flat Panel Displays forum, 370

Play bar, displaying and hiding, 44

playing music, 246–248

Pogue, David, 366

pop-up messages, 6

Portable Open TiVo Home Media Option project, 247

power connector, 67

power supplies, 66, 233

PowerTrip device, 76, 105

PPC processor, 128

PPP (Point-To-Point Protocol), 83

prebuilt compilers, 139

PriceWatch Web site, 71

primary IDE interface, 149

primary (IDE-1) interface, 70

primary objects, 316

Prism2.5 chipset, 88

privacy concerns, 6

/proc directory, 146

program listings, 5

programs
    Easter eggs, 26
    schedule information, 9

Programs -> Accessories -> Communications menu, 260–261, 266–267

Programs -> Blindwrite Suite menu, 274

PROM (Programmable Read-Only Memory), 56, 305

prompt, 325

ProNFS, 281

ps command, 244

PTCMs (Pre-TiVo-Central Messages), 6

PTVs (Personal Television Receivers), 2

PTVUpgrade.com, 104, 233

PTVupgrade.net, 102

publishing, 282

put command, 355

PuTTY, 269

PVR Comparisons Web site, 377

PVRs (Personal Video Recorders), 2, 18–19

PVRUpgrade.com, 188

Q

queryschema.tcl file, 317

R

&R1 command string, 80

RAM (initrd) disk, 222

RAM (Random-Access Memory) disks, 91, 137

Ramsay, Mike, 7–8

randomly generating key presses, 48

RAR utility, 147

Rate1: prompt, 42

Rate2: prompt, 42

RAWRITE.EXE utility, 137, 139

Raymond, Eric, 300

rc.arch file, 212

rc.net file, 212

rc.sysinit script, 51, 110, 212

rc.sysinit.save file, 213

ReadTheTruth Web site, 80

rebooting TiVo, 39

Record by Time or Channel menu, 57

Record LED, 41

Record Time/Channel button, 24

recording
    30-minute buffer of television, 57
    hidden, 45
    scheduling, 57–58
    specific channel, 57
    while watching shows, 13
    Wishlists, 58–59

recurring monthly charge, 4

reference platform, 9

remote controls, 22–25, 32, 102

remotely changing channels, 357–358

ReplayTV, 16–17

ReplayTV & Showstopper PVRs forum, 370

ReplayTV Advanced FAQ Web site, 17

ReplayTV and TiVo FAQ Web site, 17

ReplayTV devices, 10

ReplayTV FAQ Web site, 17

ReplayTV Revealed Web site, 17

ReplayTV vs. TiVo Comparison Web site, 17

.res (resource) file, 319

resource groups, 319–320

ResourceGroup attribute, 319

resources, 319–320

restore command, 163, 165

restoring
    advanced MFS Tool options, 173–177
    backup file, 157
    byte-swapping, 176
    changing block size, 175–176
    changing byte order, 176
    data, 165–166

disabling auto-detection, 176
disk drives, 123–127
image backups, 165–167
MFS Tools backup, 168–178
RFCs (Request for Comment), 85
ribbon cable, 67
River, J., 247, 287
RJ-45 connectors, 84
ROM (Read-Only Memory) filesystem for 3.x TiVos, 138
ROM (Read-Only Memory) filesystem image, 131–132, 218–219, 229
ROM monitors, 53–56
ROMFS filesystem image, 222
/romfs.img file, 218, 229
root filesystem, 117
    active, 218
    cloning, 228
    default, 218
    extracting, 226–227
    identifying active, 228
    kernel partition, 305
root partition, 174
    active, 211, 226
    cloning, 178
    files and directories, 211
    identifying, 177–178
root user, 108
routers, 85
Roxio Toast, 135
RPMFind Web site, 320
RTS, disabling, 80
runideturbo environment variable, 112–113
rz (Receive Zmodem) command, 263, 323

S

s1swap kernel, 177
s2 kernel, 177

safe locations for storing TiVo hacks, 350–351
Safety Web site, 85
Samba, 284
Samba Web site, 362
satellite box, 24
Save (Ctrl-x) keyboard shortcut, 35
Save setup as dfl command, 321
Save to VCR command, 181
/sbin/ifconfig -a command, 268, 336
/sbin/init file, 221, 235, 306
Schedule Suggestions, 37–38, 45–46
scheduling
    shows to be recorded, 57
    tips and tricks, 56–60
scheduling recordings, 57–58
    over Internet, 248–252
    from Web browsers, 354–361
schema, 316–317
screen display fonts, 47
Screens forum, 370
script command, 133
script utility, 139
Search By Title button, 23, 30
Search By Title screen, 30, 41
Search Prompt (Ctrl-s) keyboard shortcut, 34, 35
search string, 35
Search Using Wishlists button, 23
Season Pass Alerts forum, 375
Season Passes, 11, 16, 57
    backup files, 165
    displaying scheduled items from, 37
    restoring, 165
secondary IDE interface, 149
secondary (IDE-2) interface, 70
secret commands, 24–53
secret modes, 24–53
security, user-level, 108
seek time, 174

seeking, 174
Select a CD-ROM Image dialog box, 276
Select a CD-Writer dialog box, 275
selling viewing information, 5
Send File dialog box, 264
sendkey command, 51–52
serial cable, 64
Serial Cntrl Out connector, 81
serial communications
    basic settings, 321
    Linux, 320–324
    minicom, 320–322
serial connections, 259, 322
serial console, attaching, 62–65
serial file transfers, 263–265
serial number, 5
Serial Port dialog box, 322
serial ports, 62, 64–65
    bash shell, 322
    checking network configuration, 100–101
Series 1 Edge Connector Information Web site, 378
Series 1 machines, 12–14
    adding disk drives, 73
    adding second drive, 14
    AirNet cards, 88
    BATBD CD, 137
    Cisco 802.11b cards, 88
    coming apart easily, 65
    command prompt, 209–214
    command-line access, 101
    cross-compilers, 351–352
    disk drives, 68
    FTP and Telnet access, 99
    Macintosh partitioning and disk/data format conventions, 128
    modems, 78
    mounting bracket, 68
    multistrand IDE cable, 67
    networking, 87–91
    partitions, 152

power connector for second drive, 74
PPC processor, 128
remote control, 22
removing disk drive, 66
selecting correct model, 15
serial ports, 64–65
TiVoMad utilities, 109–113
TurboNet network card, 87
upgrading and expanding, 109–113
version 3.1 software, 210
Warranty void if this seal is broken sticker, 66
Series 2 60-MB AT&T TiVos, 75
Series 2 DirecTiVo, 9
Series 2 machines, 4, 12–14
adding disk drives, 73
adding second drive, 14
BATBD CD, 137
coming apart easily, 65
command prompt, 214–221
command-line access, 101
cross-compilers, 353
disconnecting fan on drive bracket, 67
expansion brackets, 105
Frankensteinian brackets, 14
FTP and Telnet access, 99
Home Media Option, 86
IDE cables, 75
MIPS processors, 128
MIPS-based, 110
networking, 95–99
power considerations, 75–76
remote control, 22
removing disk drive, 68–69
ribbon cable, 67
selecting correct model, 15
serial ports, 64–65
Series 1 software on, 108
software versions, 98
special brackets, 74, 75

static IP address, 86
Two Kernel Monte, 221–232
USB ports, 95
variations in, 68
wired USB Ethernet adapters, 96–97
wireless USB adapters, 97–98
Y-power cable, 75
Server -> TiVo Server Properties command, 284
service fees, 4
service number, 4–5
service providing television listings, 4
service-related messages, 6
Set Dial Prefix command, 81
setf MFS volume, 126
Seth's TiVo FAQ, 379–380
settime command, 43
settings-backup directory, 138, 164
/Setup object, 316–318
setup.sh script, 110, 112–113
SHA1 hash signatures, 305
SHA1 (Secure Hash Algorithm) Version 1.0, 29
shared libraries, 110
shell prompt, 208
shells, 325–327
shortcuts for remote controls, 23–24
showcases, 10, 46–47
Showcases screen, 46
shows, 4, 13, 56–59
ShowTime, 10
Shutdown Now command, 36
/signatures file, 305–306
Silicon Graphics, 7
SiliconDust.com, 87, 90, 95, 102–103, 378
skinnable, 102
Skip mode, 43
skipping through commercials, 43
slave drives, 70, 74, 149

SLIP (Serial Line Internet Protocol), 83
smart searches, 11
SmartFTP, 271
SmartHome Web site, 25
smbfs.o module, 280
smbmount application, 280
smbmount command, 281
software, 3–4, 9
application software, 108
diagnostic log file, 5
download Web sites, 381–382
identifying version, 15–16
installing on TiVo, 344–350
Linux software for TiVo, 329–335
protection against upgrades, 180
releases and hashes, 35
system software, 108
version, 111
SONICblue, 17
SONICblue Web site, 16
Sony Remote, 22–23
sorting Now Playing list V. 3.0 TiVos, 48–50
source code, 304
SourceForge Web site, 239, 292, 307, 338, 361
special characters in show titles, 58
special codes, 25–53
Special Mode: DEBUG option, 37
Speed1: prompt, 41
Speed2: prompt, 42
Speed3: prompt, 42
spinning up disk drives, 76
split command, 147
splitter, 75
sports, 243–245
SPS (Select-Play-Select) codes, 27, 43–44
src file, 138

SSH (secure shell), 269
Stallman, Richard, 300
stand-alone models, 15
stand-alone tools and development projects, 354–362
standard input and output, 151
star menu item, information about, 46–47
Start -> Programs -> TiVo Desktop menu, 282
startup process, 305–306
Starz, 10
static IP addresses, 85, 86
status message, 43–44
stealing service, 144–145
storage space
  increasing, 186
  recording capacity, 186
storing backups, 148–151
structured backups, 145–151
stty sane command, 209
su command, 141
subprocesses, 327
sudo /bin/bash command, 141
sudo command, 292, 293, 296
Suggestions screen, 38, 45
Sundance Channel, 10
SunFlowerHead Web site, 242
superuser, 108
Suspend Command (Control-z) keyboard shortcut, 327
Sutter operating system, 17
Svenson, Ernest, 366
swap partitions, 126, 128, 157
swap space, 127, 172–173, 311
switches, 84, 100
/SwSystem/ACTIVE database object, 319
sync command, 217
System Information screen, 16, 28, 30
  amount of storage available, 203
  CCEE (Clear-Clear-Enter-Enter) codes, 36–37

CEC (Clear-Enter-Clear) codes, 37–40
Special Mode: DEBUG option, 37
storage available, 206
TiVo software version, 111
verifying increased storage capacity, 117
viewing amount of storage, 191
system software, 108
system-level software, 133
sz (Send Zmodem) command, 263, 265, 323

T

Tab key, 34
tail command, 212
Tanenbaum, Andrew, 300
tar (tape archiver), 146
TAR and TGZ archives, extracting files from, 347–350
tar command, 347–348, 350
tar files, 355
tar format, 138
TCL (Tool Command Language), 7, 306–307
.tcl extension, 307
TCL Reference Manual, 307
TCL scripts, 307
tcpdump, 101
TCP/IP (Transmission Control Protocol/Internet Protocol), 83
TCP/IP Settings menu, 99
TCS (TiVo Control Station), 243–245
TCS_1.0.0.tar.gz file, 244
TECO (Text Editor and Corrector), 330
television
  30-minute buffer of, 57
  viewing habits, 5

TeleWorld, 8
Teleworld Paid Programming entries, 46
Telnet, 63, 236–237, 269, 335
Telnet daemon, 95, 236–237
Tera Term, 262, 269
TERM environment variable, 331
terminal emulators, 54, 62–65, 209
TERMINFO terminal information database, 331
testing dial options, 100
text directory, 138
Thumbs Up key, 32
time-shifting, 2
TiVo
  integrated with DirectTV systems, 3
TiVo, ReplayTV, and UltimateTV Feature Comparison Web site, 18
"TiVo, We Hardly Knew Ye," 365
TiVo Central, 16, 30, 32
TiVo Central -> Messages & Setup -> Recorder & Phone Setup -> Phone Connection -> Make Test Call command, 43
TiVo Central -> Messages & Setup -> Restart or Reset System -> Guided Setup command, 77
TiVo Central -> Pick Programs to Record -> Record by Time or Channel command, 57
TiVo Central -> Pick Programs To Record -> ToDo List command, 45
TiVo Central -> Pick Programs to Record command, 27

TiVo Central -> Programs to Record -> Search Using Wishlists page, 59

"TiVo Changed My Life" blog, 366

TiVo clock
setting, 43

TiVo Coffee House, TiVo Discussion forum, 376

TiVo Community Forum, 365, 366

TiVo Community Forums, 370, 373–376

TiVo Customer Care, 6

TiVo Customer Care telephone number, 6

TiVo customer support Web site, 104

TiVo Desktop, 246
installing and using, 282–286

TiVo Developer's Web site, 338

TiVo disks
information, 308–311
Mac OS X, 291–296
partition map, 309–311
Windows, 278–280

TiVo drive
displaying partition map, 34

TiVo DVRs, 286

TiVo Enhancement Development Team, 361

TiVo Extraction forum, 372–373

TiVo Forum FAQ, 380

TiVo FTP daemon, 95

TiVo Guy introductory animation button, 23

TiVo Hacking Links Web site, 382

TiVo hacks
safe locations for storing, 350–351

TiVo Hacks forum, 373

TiVo Hardware Questions Web site, 378

TiVo headquarters

initiating special call, 37

TiVo Help Center forum, 376

TiVo Home Media Option forum, 376

TiVo HQ Web site, 86

TiVo Inc.
depriving of service revenue, 144–145

"TiVo Installation and Viewer's Guide," 181

TiVo intersititials
duration of, 42
logging, 42

TiVo IP address, 336

TiVo King, 188

TiVo Messages, 6

TiVo models, 14–15
attaching terminal emulator or serial console, 62–65
networking, 10–11

TiVo Network Hack How-To Guide, 380

TiVo operating system, 3

TiVo publisher, 283–286

TiVo Publisher command, 282

TiVo Repair Kit Guide Web site, 78

TiVo Rev 0 PPC 403 Oak Evaluation Kit Web site, 378

TiVo Series 2 Hacking forum, 373

TiVo Server Properties dialog box, 284–286

TiVo service
daily calls to, 5
licensing different levels, 11
subscriptions to, 9

TiVo software, 48, 111

TiVo Software Index Web site, 135

TiVo store, 104

TiVo Suggestion Avenue forum, 376

TiVo Suggestions screen, 37

TiVo UK forum, 376

TiVo Underground forum, 376

TiVo Upgrade Center forum, 376

TiVo Utilities Home Page, 362

TiVo version 3.x, 99

TiVo version 4.x systems, 99–100

TiVo Viewer's Guide, 57

TiVo *vs.* UltimateTV Comparison Web site, 18

TiVo Web application, 138

TiVo Web page, 282, 298

TiVo Web Project (TiVoWeb)
displaying and editing MFS resources, 358–361
installing, 355–357
Web Remote screen, 357

TiVo Web site, 181, 249, 304, 338

tivoapp binary, 50

TivoBeacon, 288

tivoftpd-0.0.1 directory, 140

tivoftpd.ppc daemon, 237

TiVoHelp.com, 380–381

TiVo-like devices, 2

TiVolution showcase, 10

TiVoMad utilities, 109–113, 137

tivo_messenger application, 240

tivo_mp3_path variable, 339

TiVoNET cards, 87, 90–94, 103, 140

TiVoNET directory, 140

tivo_photo_path variable, 339

TiVos, 2
accessing Windows disks, 280–281
adding disk drives, 73–75
additional information about, 26
affecting behavior of, 37–40
amount of storage, 13
application environment, 305–308
authentication, 332
backing up, 143–144
basic concept, 8

business partners, 9–11
competition, 16–18
connectors, 12
convergence, 3
crashes, 147
default hostname, 118
default IP address, 118
default MAC address, 118
in direct sunlight, 25
extracting video, 145
fast-forward, 10
Guided Setup, 76–77
hardware, 3
history, 6–9
Home Media Option, 10–11
identifying, 4–5
integrators, 9–11
IP address, 268–269
lifetime service, 78
Linux, 3–4, 16
Mac OS X, 290–291
manufacturer, 13
networking, 82–101
obtaining IP addresses with
        DHCP, 86
opening, 65–66
Personal Television Service, 8
phone line, 76–77
power supplies, 66
rebooting, 39
receiving programming and
        guide updates over net-
        work, 99
receiving signals from any
        other IR sources, 25
reliability, 3
root filesystem, 117
running out of guide data, 39
serial number, 5
serial ports, 62, 64–65
Series 2, 4
service number, 4–5
software, 3–4
startup process, 305–306

unplugging before working on,
        66
updating configuration infor-
        mation, 77
user interface, 4, 16
TiVoServer-0.16 directory, 339
tivoserver.conf file, 339
tivoserver.pl file, 339
TiVoSH (tivosh) application,
        307–308, 313–314
TiVoStuff.com Web site,
        381–382
TiVoVBI, 361–362
TiVoWeb, 248–249
TiVoWeb Project Web site, 382
tivoweb.cfg file, 356
tiVoweb-tcl-1.9.4 tar file, 138
tivoweb-tcl-1.9.4.tar file, 355
TLC (The Learning Channel),
        10
TMC (The Movie Channel), 10
/tmp/mwstate file, 39
tnlited daemon, 237
ToDo List, 45–46
ToDo List screen, 37–38
"Too many command line
        options" message, 205
tools
    BlessTiVo, 113–117
    bootpage utility, 117–119
    Linux, 131–133
    MFS Tools, 119–127
    overview, 109–133
    pdisk (Partition Disk) utility,
        127, 129–131
    stand-alone, 354–362
    TiVoMad utilities, 109–113
tools disks
    Mac OS X, 296–297
    Windows, 272–277
Torvalds, Linus, 300
Torx screwdriver, 65
transaction code, identifying, 52
Transfer -> Send File command,
        264

transferring files, 331–332
    minicom, 323–324
    serial connection, 263–265
Tridgell, Andrew, 87
troubleshooting
    displaying green screen, 236
    no picture or Welcome screen,
        233
    stuck at second Welcome
        screen, 235–236
    stuck at Welcome screen,
        233–235
TTT (Thumb-Thumb-Thumb)
        codes, 27, 45–47
TurboNet cards, 87, 103, 140,
        210
    DHCP (Dynamic Host
        Control Protocol) serv-
        er, 93
    software required for
        installing, 90–94
TV tuner card, 182–183
/tvbin/mfsadd_new, 110
Tweaks and Do-It-Yourself
        forum, 371
Two Kernel Monte, 221–232
two-connector IDE cable, 75
TyStudio, 182

U

-U command-line argument, 52
UDP (Universal Data Packet), 83
Ultimate TV Hacking forum,
        373
UltimateTV, 18
UltimateTV Hacking Forum
        Web site, 18
Ultra High-End HT Gear
        forum, 371
UltraEdit, 234
umount command, 220
"Unable to connect to /dev/hdx"
        message, 205

uncompressing ZIP and GZ files, 345–347
undocumented features, 26
Unix
    cdrecord, 135
    dd command, 135
    split command, 147
    YACC (Yet Another Compiler Compiler), 242
unmounting partitions, 213
unmount/mnt/test command, 167, 177
unstructured backups, 145, 194
    large size of, 155
    space requirements, 148–151
    splitting into multiple files, 147
unzip command, 346
unzip utility, 345
upgrade kits, 189
upgrades
    considerations, 187–188
    disk without using backup files, 192–194
    items necessary for, 188–189
    software protection against, 180
uplink port, 85
Uranus Web site, 278
URLs, 52
USB (Universal Serial Bus) network adapters, 98, 246
USB ports, 95
used TiVos, 106
user interface, 4, 16
user-level security, 108
/usr/bin/minicom file, 321
/usr/lib/gaim directory, 240
/usr/local/tivo/bin directory, 352
/usr/local/tivo-mips/bin directory, 353

V

valid device names, 118
/var directory, 271
/var partition, 219, 230
    filling up, 37
    increasing size, 173–174
    specifying size, 126
/var/hack directory, 137, 219, 230
/var/hack/hackinit file, 218, 222, 237, 357
/var/hack/tcs directory, 244
/var/log/kernel file, 101
/var/log/Otclient call log, 82
/var/log/tvdebuglog file, 37
/var/log/tverr log file, 37
/var/log/tvlog file, 47
/var/mnt/win mountpoint, 281
/var/packages directory, 52
/var/partition, 218
/var/settings-backup directory, 165
/var/tivoweb-tcl directory, 355
VCRs compared with PVRs, 2
Vector Company Web site, 262
Verify password: prompt, 54
verifying disks restored using MFS Tools, 177
Version 3.0
    Backdoor mode, 30–31
    sorting Now Playing list, 48–50
Version 3.1, 32–36
vfat partition, 150
video editing, 7
video extraction, 143, 182–183
video on demand, 7
Video Toaster, 7
videotape, putting data on, 181–182
viewer-related events, 5
viewing habits, 5
vim (Vi iMproved), 331

virtual filesystem, 154–155
VSO Software Web site, 273
vsplit utility, 182

W

Wagner, Eric, 294
warranty, 61, 65
Warranty void if this seal is broken sticker, 66
Weaknees.com, 74, 76, 102, 105, 188, 233, 294
weather, 243–245
Web browsers, scheduling recordings from, 354–361
Web sites
    DirecTiVo, 381
    hardware, 377–378
    software loads, 381–382
Welcome screen, 233–236
Westerns, 10
"what is password?" prompt, 54
"What Is This Thing Called TiVo?," 365
Windows
    accessing disks from TiVo, 280
    audio formats other than MP3, 287–290
    bootable CD, 72
    COM1, 54, 63
    communicating with TiVo, 259–271
    Dylan's Boot Disk, 111
    editing TiVo or Linux text files, 234
    explore2fs, 222
    exporting MP3 and digital photograph collections, 11
    ext2 disk images, 278–279
    FAT32 filesystem, 151

FAT-32 (32-bit File Allocation Table) format, 70
filesystem used by, 149
FTP (File Transfer Protocol), 269–271
GAIM (GTK AOL Instant Messenger), 239
HMO (Home Media Option), 282–290
HyperTerminal, 54, 62–63, 260–261
intalling gaim2tivo plugin, 241
Nero, 135
networked communications, 265–271
NFS utilities, 281
NTFS filesystem, 151
NTFS (NT File System) format, 70
RAR utility, 147
reformatting or damaging TiVo drive, 72
serial communications, 259–261
SSH (secure shell), 269
telnet, 269
TiVo disks, 278–280
TiVo-related utilities, 138
tools disks, 272–277
transferring files over serial connection, 263–265
Windows directory, 138
Windows FTP client, 270

Windows TiVo Desktop, 282–286
wired USB Ethernet adapters, 96–97
wireless phone jacks, 77
Wireless Settings menu, 99
wireless USB adapters, 97–98
WishLists, 11, 16, 58–59
    backup files, 165
    displaying scheduled items from, 37
    restoring, 165
&Wn command string, 80
World Wide Web, 83
Write CD-ROM dialog box, 277
writing bootpage information, 119

X

'x' (extended) command, 55
x86bin directory, 139
XBOX Hacking forum, 373
xcompilers directory, 139
xcompilers/Series1/tivodev-2.5_linux-x86_dtype1.tgz cross-compiler, 351
xcompilers/Series1/tivodev-2.5_linux-x86_dtype2.tgz cross-compiler, 351
xcompilers/Series1/usr.local. powerpc-tivo.gz cross-compiler, 351

xcompilers/Series2/usr.local.tivo-mips_bu211.tgz cross-compiler, 351
xcompilers/Series2/usr.local. tivo-mips_bu213.tgz cross-compiler, 351
xmodem, 263

Y

YAC (Yet Another Caller ID Program), 242
Yahoo, 239
ymodem, 263
Y-power cable, 75

Z

Zephyr, 239
Zero key, 32
ZeroWing, 28
.zip file extension, 345
ZIP files, 345–347
Zirak, 243
zlib library, 158
zmodem, 263

About the CD

The CD included with this book is both bootable and mountable. You can boot Linux from the CD on any Pentium-class personal computer in order to work with TiVo disks and partitions. If you boot from the CD, you can subsequently mount the CD using the Linux mount command in order to access other software stored on the disc. You can also mount the CD on a Windows or Macintosh personal computer by inserting it into your CD drive in order to access the software that is stored on the CD. The contents of the CD are explained in the section of Chapter 4 entitled "BATBD—Bill's Accumulated TiVo Boot Disk."

License Agreement/Notice of Limited Warranty